PRAISE FOR
Jeff Pearlman's
Boys Will Be Boys

"A gritty, no-holds barred portrait."

—Barry Horn, *Dallas Morning News*

"Jeff Pearlman does a masterly job of exposing the '90s Cowboys as shameless frauds and adulterers, sex addicts, and drug fiends."

—John Gonzalez, *Philadelphia Inquirer*

"It's tempting to call *Boys Will Be Boys* the real-life sequel to *North Dallas Forty*. But in fact, it's more than that. With immaculate reporting, Jeff Pearlman has constructed a marvelous rise-and-fall narrative. Here's the truth about America's team delivered in a profane page-turner—entertaining, enlightening, and where you least expect it, inspiring. Put another way: This book rocks."

—Mark Kriegel, *New York Times* bestselling author of *Pistol and Namath*

"The Cowboys of the 1990s had everything: great players, great characters, great parties, great hair. Now, finally, they have the great writer to tell their story. Jeff Pearlman has written a rip-roaring book filled with terrific reporting and vibrant prose. To appreciate football's modern era in all its crazy glory, you've got to read *Boys Will Be Boys*. It's a flat-out winner."

—Jonathan Eig, *New York Times* bestselling author
of *Opening Day* and *Luckiest Man*

"Jeff Pearlman is an insider's insider. With vivid details that place you in the Dallas huddle—and in the team hotel rooms—Pearlman expertly peels the hedonistic layers off the unforgettable characters of the dynastic Cowboys, taking you on a raucous and reflective joyride behind the color, chaos and karma of America's team in the '90s."

—Selena Roberts, columnist, *Sports Illustrated*

"Just when I thought I knew all the inside info from the glory days of the '90s, along comes Jeff Pearlman with this look back. A truly great read."

—Randy Galloway, columnist, *Fort Worth Star-Telegram*

Catherine Pearlman

About the Author

JEFF PEARLMAN is a columnist for SI.com and a former *Sports Illustrated* senior writer. He is the author of the *New York Times* bestsellers *Boys Will Be Boys* and *The Bad Guys Won!* and the critically acclaimed *Love Me, Hate Me*. He lives with his wife and children in New York. Visit him at www.jeffpearlman.com.

BOYS WILL BE BOYS

The Glory Days

and Party Nights

of the

Dallas Cowboys

Dynasty

Jeff Pearlman

HARPER

NEW YORK · LONDON · TORONTO · SYDNEY

HARPER

A hardcover edition of this book was published in 2008 by HarperCollins Publishers.

HarperCollins books may be purchased for educational, business, or sales promotional use. For information, please e-mail the Special Markets Department at SPsales@-harpercollins.com.

FIRST HARPER PAPERBACK PUBLISHED 2009.

Designed by William Ruoto

Library of Congress Cataloging-in-Publication Data is available upon request.

ISBN 978-0-06-125681-3

17   18   OV/RRD   20 19 18

To Frank Zaccheo,
the Sunday-morning Austin Road quarterback . . .

After we won our first Super Bowl I was sitting at a bar and a guy offered to buy me a drink. I turned him down. Tony Dorsett tapped me on the shoulder and said, "Hey, young buck, you better take advantage of everything they're trying to give you. Because they'll forget about you one day." I was like, "C'mon, you're T.D.!" But now it's been a while. Now I know what he meant. Even Cowboys fade away.

CLAYTON HOLMES,
former **DALLAS COWBOYS** *cornerback*

MAY 12, 2007, FLORENCE, S.C.

★

CONTENTS

Chapter 1

SCISSORS TO THE NECK

You can do a lot of things in life. You can't stab a teammate with a pair of scissors.
—Kevin Smith, Cowboys cornerback

MICHAEL IRVIN KNEW he was screwed.

There, dangling in his right hand, was a pair of silver scissors, bits of shredded brown skin coating the tips. There, clutching his own throat, was Everett McIver, a 6-foot, 5-inch, 318-pound hulk of a man, blood oozing from the 2-inch gash in his neck. There, standing to the side, were teammates Erik Williams, Leon Lett, and Kevin Smith, slack-jawed at what they had just seen.

It was finally over. Everything was over. The Super Bowls. The Pro Bowls. The endorsements. The adulation. The dynasty.

Damn—*the dynasty.*

The greatest wide receiver in the history of the Dallas Cowboys—a man who had won three Super Bowls; who had appeared in five Pro Bowls; whose dazzling play and sparkling personality had earned him a devoted legion of followers—knew he would be going to prison for a long time. Two years if he was lucky. Twenty years, maximum.

Was this the first time Irvin had exercised mind-numbing judgment? Hardly. Throughout his life, the man known as The Playmaker had made a hobby of breaking the rules. As a freshman at the University of Miami fourteen years earlier, Irvin had popped a senior lineman in the head after he had stepped in front of him in a cafeteria line. In 1991, Irvin allegedly shattered the dental plate and split the lower lip of a referee whose call he disagreed with in a *charity* basketball game. Twice, in 1990 and '95, Irvin had been sued by women who insisted he had fathered their children out of wedlock. In May 1993, Irvin was confronted by police after launching into a tirade when a convenience store clerk refused to sell his eighteen-year-old brother, Derrick, a bottle of wine. When Gene Upshaw visited Dallas minicamp that same month to explain an unpopular contractual agreement, Irvin greeted the NFL union chief first by screaming obscenities, then by pulling down his pants and flashing his exposed derriere.

Most famously, there was the incident in a Dallas hotel room on March 4, 1996—one day before Irvin's thirtieth birthday—when police found The Playmaker and former teammate Alfredo Roberts with two strippers, 10.3 grams of cocaine, more than an ounce of marijuana, and assorted drug paraphernalia and sex toys. Irvin—who greeted one of the on-scene officers with, "Hey, can I tell you who I am?"—later pleaded no contest to a felony drug charge and received a five-game suspension, eight hundred hours of community service, and four years' probation.

But stabbing McIver in the neck, well, this was different. Through the litany of his boneheaded acts, Irvin had never—not once—deliberately hurt a teammate. Did he love snorting coke? Yes. Did he love lesbian sex shows? Yes. Did he love sleeping with two, three, four, five (yes, five) women at a time in precisely choreographed orgies? Yes. Did he love strip clubs and hookers and house calls from exotic dancers with names like Bambi and Cherry and Saucy? Yes, yes, yes.

Was he loyal to his football team? Undeniably.

Throughout the Cowboy reign of the 1990s, which started with a laughable 1–15 season in 1989 and resulted in three Super Bowl victories in four years, no one served as a better teammate—as a better *role model*—than Michael Irvin. He was first to the practice field in the morning, the last to leave at night. He wore weighted pads atop his shoulders to build muscle and refused to depart the complex before catching fifty straight passes without a drop. Twelve years after the fact, an undrafted free agent quarterback named Scott Semptimphelter still recalls Irvin begging him to throw slants following practice on a 100-degree day in 1995. "In the middle of the workout Mike literally threw up on himself as he ran a route," says Semptimphelter. "Most guys would put their hands on their knees, say screw this, and call it a day. Not Michael. He got back to the spot, ran *another* route, and caught the ball."

That was Irvin. Determined. Driven. A 100-mph car on a 50-mph track. Chunks of vomit dripping from his jersey.

Following the lead of their star wide receiver, Cowboy players and coaches outpracticed, outhustled, out-*everythinged* every other team in the National Football League. Sure, the Cowboys of the 1990s were bursting with talent—from quarterback Troy Aikman and running back Emmitt Smith to defensive backs Deion Sanders and Darren Woodson—but it was an unrivaled intensity that made Dallas special. During drills, Irvin would see a teammate slack off and angrily lecture, "Don't be a fuckin' pussy! Be a fuckin' soldier! Be *my* soldier!" He would challenge defensive backs to rise to the highest level. "Bitch, cover me!" he'd taunt Sanders or Kevin Smith. "C'mon, bitch! C'mon, bitch! C'mon!" When the play ended he'd offer a quick pat on the rear. "Nice job, brother. Now do it again." Irvin was the No. 1 reason the Cowboys won Super Bowls in 1992, '93, and '95, and everybody on the team knew it. "The man just never stopped," says Hubbard Alexander, the Dallas wide receivers coach. "He was only about winning."

And yet, there Michael Irvin stood on July 29, 1998, staring down at a new low. The scissors. The skin. The blood. The gagging teammate. That morning a Dallas-based barber named Vinny had made the two-and-a-half-hour drive to Midwestern State University in Wichita Falls, Texas, where the team held its training camp. He set up a chair inside a first-floor room in the Cowboys' dormitory, broke out the scissors and buzzers, and chopped away, one refrigerator-sized head after another.

After a defensive back named Charlie Williams finished receiving his cut, McIver jumped into the chair. It was his turn.

Although only the most die-hard of Dallas Cowboy fans had heard of him, Everett McIver was no rookie. Not in football, and certainly not in life.

Born and raised in Fayetteville, North Carolina, McIver played at Division II Elizabeth City State as a defensive lineman. He was the type of player NFL coaches and personnel experts find intriguing—huge, overlooked, bursting with untapped potential, and, most important, hungry.

As a twenty-one-year-old college junior, McIver and his girlfriend had a daughter, Morquisha. Fatherhood was a monumental lifestyle change for the football star. As teammates focused their attentions toward dorm bashes and cute coeds, McIver was rushing home after practices to change diapers and cuddle with his baby girl. In myriad ways, McIver was the most fulfilled he had ever been.

When Morquisha reached three months, however, doctors determined that she was suffering from an irregular heartbeat, and further tests revealed that the infant had two left ventricles and none on her right side. Shortly thereafter, Morquisha McIver died in surgery. "Ever since then, there's not too much that can deter me," McIver said. "Nothing can keep me out or hold me down."

In 1993 the San Diego Chargers signed McIver as a rookie free agent. He was cut several months later, signed by Dallas, and placed on the practice squad. From August through December, McIver was a Cowboy rookie scrub, forced to sing his fight song and pick up sandwiches from the local deli and call teammates "sir" and "mister" and whatever else they desired. "Being a rookie with the Cowboys could be tough," says Clayton Holmes, a defensive back. "You just had to suck it up and try to survive unscathed."

Many of the veterans, like Irvin, defensive end Charles Haley, and offensive lineman Nate Newton, dismissed McIver as a marginal, insignificant player. Unaware of the tragedy he had faced, they resented his quiet demeanor and low-key approach. McIver came off as lazy and laconic. He was an easy target.

Yet after a rough start, McIver's career picked up. He joined the New York Jets in 1994 and later spent two productive years in Miami as a Dolphin. With the Cowboys struggling behind an aging, oft-injured offensive line, team owner Jerry Jones tossed a five-year, $9.5 million contract McIver's way. The lineman had left Dallas as a joke and five years later was now returning as a potential cornerstone. "He's an example of how if you have skill, a good work ethic to develop it, and be persistent, you can play at a high level in the NFL," Jones said at the time. "We're thrilled to have him here."

Michael Irvin, however, wasn't thrilled. As far as he was concerned Everett McIver was simply the same nobody from earlier days. He was a Band-Aid for a franchise in need of a defibrillator. Indeed, in 1997 the once-mighty Cowboys had experienced one of their worst seasons, finishing 6–10 and missing the playoffs for the first time in seven years. The downfall could be attributed to any number of reasons. Whereas once the team was a high-flying collection of young, athletic studs, players were now creeping into their late twenties and early thirties. Dashers had gradually become plodders. Hard hitters had started to shy away from big licks.

Moreover, free agency had picked the roster apart. Though everyone who followed the NFL knew of Aikman, Smith, and Irvin, a team is only as good as its parts. With each Super Bowl triumph, more and more players were gobbled up by other franchises. Where was Alvin Harper? Mark Stepnoski? Kenny Gant? Jay Novacek? The players who emphatically put the D in Big D? For that matter, where were Jimmy Johnson and Barry Switzer, the two swagger-packed coaches who had led the team to three Super Bowl titles in a span of four years?

Most notably, the Cowboys—largely winners on the football field—had spiraled out of control off of it. Drinking. Drugs. Strippers.

Prostitutes. Orgies. Late nights out and hungover practices. Some, like Irvin, could immerse themselves in the lifestyle and still arrive at Texas Stadium 100 percent ready to play on Sundays. Many could not. The Cowboys were sloppy and lethargic and dull and clearly lacking . . . *something*.

For a hypercompetitor like Irvin, the losing was too much. The man who was all about devotion to the game had turned bitter. He was well aware that *these* Cowboys were not *his* Cowboys. So when Irvin walked into that room and saw McIver in the barber's chair, something inside snapped.

"Seniority!" Irvin barked.

McIver didn't budge.

"Seniority!" Irvin screamed again. "Seniority! Seniority! Punk, get the fuck out of my chair!"

"Man," said McIver, "I'm almost done. Just gimme another few minutes."

Was Everett McIver talking to Irvin? Was he *really* talking to Irvin? Like . . . *that?*

"Vinny, get this motherfucker out of the chair," Irvin ordered the barber. "Tell his sorry ass to wait his fuckin' turn. Either I get a cut right now, or nobody does."

Standing nearby was Erik Williams, McIver's fellow lineman. "Yo, E," he said to McIver, "don't you dare get out of that chair. You're no fuckin' rookie! He can't tell you what to do!"

Sensing trouble, the barber backed away from McIver's head. McIver stood and shoved Irvin in the chest. Irvin shoved back. McIver shoved even harder, then grabbed Irvin and tossed him toward a wall. "I'm the littlest guy in the room," says Kevin Smith, "so I just yell, 'Leon, do something!'" Lett, the enormous defensive linemen, tried separating the combatants. It was no use. "The whole scene was crazy," says Smith. "I couldn't believe what I was seeing. I mean, we were on the same team."

In a final blow to harmony, McIver cocked his right fist and popped Irvin in the mouth. "I just lost it," said Irvin. "I mean, my head,

I lost it." Irvin grabbed a pair of scissors, whipped back his right arm, and slashed McIver across the neck. The motion was neither smooth nor slick, but jagged, like a saw cutting felt. The tip of the scissors ripped into McIver's skin, just above his collarbone and inches from the carotid artery. McIver let loose a horrified scream.

"Blood immediately shoots all over the room," says Smith. "And we're all thinking the same thing—'Oh, shit.'"

For a moment—as brief as a sneeze—there was silence. Had Michael Irvin, soul of the Cowboys, stabbed a man—*his teammate*—in the neck? Was this what the once-mighty Dallas Cowboys had become? What the great Michael Irvin had sunk to?

Then—mayhem. The Cowboys' medical staffers stormed the room, past a dumbstruck Irvin, and immediately attended to McIver. As their bloodied teammate was whisked away, none of the lingering Cowboys knew the extent of the damage. Was McIver in critical condition? Would he live?

Either way, every single man in the room had to have understood that this was more than *just* a fight. The storied Dallas Cowboys of the 1990s—the organization of pride and honor and success; the organization whose players would never dare hurt one another; the organization that dominated professional football—was dead and buried.

How in the world had it come to this?

Chapter 2

SAVE YOUR GAS

*[Jerry Jones] looked, I imagined, like a collector for
a loan shark. I was certain he had the tact and sensitive
heart of a hit man. I even created a crime for him—moral
assault and battery on Tom Landry. I wondered if the immigra-
tion authorities could deport him.*
—Galyn Wilkins, columnist, *Fort Worth Star-Telegram*

CARDBOARD BOXES SURROUND the desk—listless reminders that
a lifetime of accomplishment can be carted away in the briefest of milliseconds.

Not that Tom Landry is thinking of it this way. The man who
coached the Dallas Cowboys for twenty-nine years has never been the
sentimental type. He is a person who prides himself on robotic mannerisms; who purposefully conceals his eyes beneath the brim of a fedora to
keep the outside world at arm's length. Emotions? Who needs emotions?

Yet while Landry refuses to open himself to displays of vulnera-
bility, his feelings are, on this Sunday afternoon in February 1989,
painfully clear. Just one day earlier, after completing eighteen holes at
the Hills of Lakeway Golf Course near Austin, Texas, Landry was
unceremoniously greeted by two men: Tex Schramm, the Cowboys'
longtime president, and Jerry Jones, the team's new owner. Their message was simple and brutal: You're fired.

Come again?

You're fired.

So now, sitting in his office in the Dallas Cowboys' famed Valley Ranch complex, packing up the assorted trinkets and mementos of his life, Landry says little but speaks volumes. Having paced the sideline in a gray or blue blazer for nearly three decades, it is shocking to see him so *human* in a flannel shirt and mismatched checkered dress slacks. He is no different from the canned CPA or insurance adjuster, mechanically placing this in that box, that in this box. Friends and coworkers pop their heads in, offer a supportive word, quickly duck out. It is too painful. "The shock on his face was still registering," says Dick Mansperger, the longtime Cowboys scout. "Tom was the type of person who didn't believe there were bad people out there plotting against him. He had been with the Cowboys since the first door was unlocked. It was like someone coming home and telling you it's not your child anymore."

It has often been said that Tom Landry was the face of the Dallas Cowboys, and while such sentiment holds true, it does not extend far enough. Tom Landry was *the* Dallas Cowboys. The face. The mind. The *soul*. Born and raised in the Rio Grande Valley town of Mission, Texas, Landry entered the world prepackaged to be a Cowboy. "As far back as I can remember," he once said, "everything I did revolved around football." Landry starred as a quarterback at Mission High before accepting a scholarship to the University of Texas. His time as a Longhorn was interrupted by World War II, during which he started building the eventual reputation as a heroic deity by serving as a bomber copilot over Germany. He crashed but once, following a bombing run over Czechoslovakia. "We came down between two trees that sheared our wings off," he recalled later. "But we had no gas so the plane didn't burn and we all walked out of it."

Landry returned to school following the war and played fullback and defensive back for the Longhorn squads that won the 1948 Sugar Bowl and, his senior year, the 1949 Orange Bowl. Upon graduating, he joined the New York football Yankees of the All-America Conference, and later went to the NFL's New York Giants. Landry spent eleven years in New York, first as a player, later as an innovative defensive coordinator who designed the now-famous 4-3 alignment.

Then, in January 1960, Landry caught a break. The twelve NFL owners voted Dallas an expansion franchise. It was, at best, a quixotic move, what with northeast Texas serving as the heart of the collegiate football Bible Belt. Who would pay hard-earned money to watch a bunch of professionals when the likes of the University of Texas, Southern Methodist, and Texas Christian were readily available?

Clint Williams Murchison, Jr., was willing to take the risk. The son of a high-powered Texas oil baron, Murchison was a whiskey-swilling multimillionaire intrigued by a good old-fashioned game of chance. He paid $500,000 for the rights to the Dallas Cowboys, and shortly thereafter hired Tex Schramm, the former assistant to the president for the Los Angeles Rams, to run the operation. Though just forty years old, Schramm was wise enough to insist that Murchison agree—in writing—to let him hire the team's first head coach.

Savvy, smart, and well versed in the ways of the league, Schramm interviewed two men for the job. The first was Sid Gillman, the former Rams head coach who would go on to innovate stretch-the-field offenses with the San Diego Chargers. The second was Landry—the oddest of fits. Whereas Schramm liked women, liquor, and never-ending stories, Landry was a born-again Christian who measured each word and preferred soft classical music to prolonged dialogues. "People want to know what makes Tom tick, and he's too smart to tell them," William "Rooster" Andrews, his longtime friend, once said. "He was born polished. He's such a gentleman it's almost spooky."

Schramm offered Landry a five-year contract paying $35,000 per season, then hired Gil Brandt to be head of player personnel. A relative baby at age twenty-seven, Brandt's hobby while majoring in physical education at the University of Wisconsin was studying college game films to determine what separated the great players from the good ones. He was an unrivaled football geek, content to spend his days and nights poring over scouting reports and game recaps as girls and beers floated past his dorm room unnoticed.

Together, Schramm, Landry, and Brandt conquered the game. But it would take time. "The NFL gave us the pleasure of selecting three of the worst football players off of each team in the league, refused to give us a draft, and then said, 'OK, boys, let's play,'" Landry once recalled of the initial season. "It wasn't easy."

In 1960, the mighty Cowboys went 0–11–1, losing their first ten games before salvaging a 31–31 tie against the Giants. Those Cowboys ran for a grand total of six touchdowns, kicked six field goals, and subjected starting quarterback Eddie LeBaron to a league-high twenty-six sacks. "LeBaron used to raise his hand for a fair catch before taking the snap from the center," Landry once uncharacteristically cracked. Worse than the on-field performance was the setting. The Cowboys practiced in Burnett Field, an abandoned minor league baseball stadium lacking heat and hot water for the showers. At night, toaster-sized rats would sneak through the locker room and gnaw on the players' shoes. On Sundays the team played in the fabled Cotton Bowl, where approximately 8,000 fans filed into an 80,000-seat stadium. "I remember trotting out onto the field before one game," Landry once wrote, "and wondering if we'd shown up on the wrong date."

Despite his posting losing records in his first five seasons, calls for Landry's dismissal were ignored. "There was a greatness about the man that eclipsed our record," says Joe Bailey, the team's business manager. "What effective leaders have in common is a vision of where they want to go and the ability to persuade and sell that vision internally and externally. They consider the position a privilege, not a right. And they're totally trustworthy. That was Tom Landry."

The Cowboys finally broke through in 1966, capturing the NFC East title with a 10–3–1 record—the first of twenty straight winning seasons. From 1966 through 1985, Landry's Cowboys won two Super Bowl titles, five NFC titles, and thirteen divisional titles. The coach once mocked for his icy demeanor (players anointed him Pope Landry I) was now being praised as insightful. His drafts (with an enormous nod to Brandt, the personnel king) were inspired, resulting in one All-Pro pick after another. There was Navy's Roger Staubach in the tenth round of 1964, Elizabeth City State's Jethro Pugh in the eleventh round of '65, Penn State offensive lineman Tom Rafferty in the fourth round of '76. The Cowboys used their two No. 1 selections in 1975 on Maryland's Randy White and Langston's Thomas "Hollywood" Henderson, then took Bob Breunig of Arizona State with their fourth pick. It was Dynasty Building 101, and no one could argue when, in 1979, Bob Ryan of NFL Films dubbed the Cowboys "America's Team."

Landry and Co. were innovators, leaders in the fields of marketing and self-promotion. Under Schramm, a gaggle of female high school students known as the CowBelles & Beaux morphed into the high-kicking, scantily dressed Dallas Cowboys Cheerleaders. When Texas Stadium opened in 1971, Schramm made certain to include 196 luxury suites—the NFL's first "business-class" seating.

By the late 1970s, the Cowboys were the envy of professional sports—the New York Yankees and Montreal Canadiens and Boston Celtics rolled into one. They played in five of the decade's ten Super Bowls, winning in 1971 against the Miami Dolpins and 1977 versus the Denver Broncos. "The America's Team concept had swept the country," said Henderson, a Cowboy outside linebacker from 1975 to 1979. "It was mostly because of Tom Landry and his Christianity that the masses identified with the organization. That was the catalyst. But then came Tex Schramm's genius of promoting America's Team so that every patriot from places like Butte, Montana, stationed around the world, would say, 'That's *my* team.'"

In other words, the Cowboys possessed football magic.

Football aura.

Football greatness.

Then, one day, it vanished.

The reasons are numerous. Other teams followed the Cowboys' lead by investing dollars and manpower into scouting collegiate players.

The Dallas drafts went from dazzling (first-round pick Tony Dorsett in 1977) to horrific (first-round pick Rod Hill in 1982). Cocaine infiltrated the locker room, sapping the team's on-field brilliance and supposed moral superiority. Rampant steroid use led to more and more injuries—pulled groins, torn hamstrings, ripped quads. In 1984 Murchison sold the franchise to Harvey "Bum" Bright, a Texas oilman who viewed the Cowboys as an investment, not a lifeblood. The player strike of 1987 irreparably split the roster, with stars like Dorsett, Danny White, and Randy White crossing the picket line and incurring the wrath of once-loyal teammates.

The head coach lost his way.

It happens to all of us. The miles add up, the brain gets a tad fuzzy. The Cowboys' descent kicked off on January 10, 1982, when they lost the NFC Championship Game in San Francisco on a since-immortalized 6-yard touchdown pass from Joe Montana to Dwight Clark. Dallas dropped the NFC title game the following season as well, and in 1984 finished 9–7 and missed the playoffs. By 1986 they'd sunk to an unnerving low, completing the year with a 7–9 mark, Landry's first losing season in more than two decades. "When I got to Dallas, I felt like the team I just played on at UCLA was athletically superior," says Mark Walen, a defensive tackle selected in the third round of the 1986 draft. "We had linebackers better than anyone the Cowboys put out there."

As he aged, Landry's mind began to wander. He'd forget the names of plays and players, make illogical calls and later explain things to the media with garbled thought patterns. "We were just getting our butts beat week after week," says Kevin Gogan, an offensive guard, "and Coach Landry would never get anybody's names right. I was always 'Grogan.'"

Landry's worst transgression was sticking with the antiquated Flex Defense, a 4–3 scheme he invented in the mid–1950s. Geared toward stopping the run, the Flex featured two offset linemen reading the various blocks, while other linemen attacked and clogged up the blocking patterns. As offensive linemen grew bigger by the year, the Flex suffered.

Teams like the Redskins, boasting a bevy of elephantine offensive linemen nicknamed "The Hogs," would blow the Cowboys off the line and dominate the trenches. "Tom was a great coach," says Garry Cobb, a Dallas linebacker in 1988 and '89, "but he was the last to see that his defense was out of date."

By 1988, Landry and the Cowboys had bottomed out. A season that began with the slogan "Blueprint for Victory" concluded with Dallas's finishing last in the NFC East with a 3–13 mark. Landry may have still been a god, but he was no longer a god with a team worth watching. In a telephone poll conducted by the *Dallas Times Herald*, 61 percent of respondents wanted Landry gone.

"The public perception was not good," says Bill Bates, a Cowboys safety. "The excitement at Texas Stadium didn't exist. Everyone came to the games and just sat on their hands. You'd score a touchdown and it'd be, 'Yeah—nice play.' No one screaming or jumping up and down. Something had to change."

For years, Bum Bright wanted Tom Landry fired.

The owner of the Dallas Cowboys *loathed* his head coach. He loathed his apparent coldness and his impassive sideline demeanor. Mostly, he loathed the arrogance. Where others saw steely and determined, Bright saw a holier-than-thou fraud who had somehow conned the good people of Texas into believing he was more than your run-of-the-mill football coach.

Bright had first met Landry in 1957, when Bear Bryant left Texas A&M to coach the University of Alabama. Asked to help find a replacement at his alma mater, Bright sat down with Landry for a lengthy one-on-one interview. "I was," he recalled years later, "singularly unimpressed."

Fast-forward to 1988, when Bright's holdings were in financial free fall. Four years earlier, following his acquisition of the Cowboys, he had spent $71 million to purchase Texas Federal Savings & Loan and merge it with Trinity Savings and Loan. When he added Dallas

Federal Savings and Loan for $107 million, Bright became the world's seventh-largest privately held mortgage broker.

Near decade's end, however, hundreds of American banks filed for bankruptcy. Bright's personal worth plummetted from $600 million to $300 million in less than a year. He had to sell the Cowboys. Lacking the emotional attachment of a true fan, Bright cared little whether a prospective owner would maintain the roster, trade everyone, change uniform colors, hire overweight cheerleaders, or switch the name from "Dallas Cowboys" to "Northeast Texas Mule Beaters." No, all he needed was the assurance that Landry would be fired. It was a strange condition, but a condition nonetheless. Bright simply never "got" Landry—never *got* the legion of followers who would have dived from a bridge for the man; never *got* the cultlike way opposing coaches bowed in his direction; never *got* the perpetual cold shoulder he gave the owner. As the franchise fell from dynasty to doormat, Bright's frustration morphed into a stinging resentment. Landry, in his eyes, was a failure who preyed upon the loyalties of others. He had to go.

Among those vying to take over America's Team were a band of Japanese businessman (the archconservative Bright would have sooner eaten his spleen than sell America's Team to a nationality of people he still detested over Pearl Harbor); a posse led by former Cowboy quarterback Roger Staubach and Denver billionaire Marvin Davis; Don Carter, owner of the NBA's Dallas Mavericks; Jerry Buss, owner of the NBA's Los Angeles Lakers; and hotelier Robert Tisch. "Bum would like to see the Cowboys carry on the tradition that has been built over three decades," John J. Veatch, Jr., the managing director of Salomon Brothers' Dallas office, told the *Wall Street Journal*—and it was pure garbage. What Bright wanted was someone to fork over $180 million for the team, the stadium, the new Valley Ranch headquarters, and the $34 million debt.

What he wanted was Jerral Wayne Jones.

An obscure Arkansas oil driller with a cache of loose women and loose business dealings, Jones was fishing in Cabo San Lucas, Mexico, on September 8 when he opened to page 10 of that day's *Wall Street*

Journal. A headline caught his eye: LIKE MANY OTHER TEXAS INSTITUTIONS, THE COWBOYS HAVEN'T FOUND A BUYER.

The Cowboys? The *Dallas* Cowboys?

Jones was euphoric. Ever since his boyhood in Little Rock, Arkansas, Jones had always possessed an indefatigable desire for big. He wanted big things. Huge things. He could talk any girl into a dance, any store owner into handing over a free gumball or two. In his first year at North Little Rock High School, Jones willed himself to become the freshman team's starting quarterback, even though he weighed a mere 120 pounds and played with a hairline fracture in his upper right arm. The beatings from opposing defenses were brutal—but Jones loved the glory and spotlight of the position. The quarterback did things; went places.

While his father, Pat, who first supported his family by selling chickens, rabbits, and eggs from the back of a truck, was building the thriving Modern Security Life Insurance Company from hard work and elbow grease, young Jerry was paying close attention. "I learned early on," says Jones, "that if you bust your ass and go after exactly what you want, you'll get it."

By the time he enrolled at the University of Arkansas in 1959, Jones was a junior executive in the family insurance business, earning $1,000 per month. At the same time he attended classes and played fullback for the Razorbacks, Jones was a full-fledged entrepreneur. He sold shoes from the trunk of his car, purchased the rights to a pizza parlor, and operated a taxi service that shuttled Razorback fans from the airport to the football stadium.

As teammates were solely focused on the next week's contest versus Tennessee, young Jerry was focused on the next decade's potential for economic expansion. His short-term postcollegiate goal: Make boatloads of money. His long-term goal: Own a football team.

The sport was in his blood, an ingrained love that germinated in his five years at Arkansas. When coach Frank Broyles recruited players, he assumed 80 percent would fail to survive his taskmaster ways.

Indeed, of the sixty freshman players who began with Jones, a mere eleven lasted. Limited as a fullback, Jones was gradually transitioned to offensive guard, and excelled. The scrappy 6-foot 200-pounder not only started for the 1964 national championship team, but earned an undergraduate degree in finance and a master's degree in speech and communication. "Jonesie had this unique way of verbalizing in very few sentences his very innermost feelings and convictions," said Jim Lindsey, a wingback with the Razorbacks. "I played four years of college football and seven more in the pros. But I was never around a more inspirational leader."

With no shot at a professional football career, Jones followed an unconventional path. Less than two years after leaving school to work for his father in life insurance, Jones attempted to purchase Barron Hilton's 80 percent share of the San Diego Chargers of the American Football League. "I was very excited," says Jones. "To be so young and have the chance to own a professional team—it was a dream." When Hilton offered a 120-day, $50,000 option on his $5.8 million stake in the Chargers, Jones turned to his father, who advised the twenty-four-year-old to walk away. The Chargers were later sold to a group headed by Eugene Klein and Sam Schulman for $10 million. Jones was disappointed, but he believed the opportunity would arise again.

With his football dreams on hold, Jones used much of the $500,000 he garnered from the 1970 sale of Modern Security Life to enter the mysterious world of oil and gas exploration (aka "wildcatting"). For Jones, a swashbuckling risk-taker with an unparalleled desire to strike it rich, the career choice was a natural. "Nobody," *Sports Illustrated*'s Ed Hinton once wrote, "plays hunches harder than a wildcatter looking for a lock, a hole card, a secret advantage in searching out oil deposits," and it was true. Adhering to the unorthodox practice of drilling for "close-in" reserves between the dry holes of previously abandoned leases, Jones hit it big. The first thirteen wells he sunk in 1971 and '72 struck oil. By 1981 Jones had made $10 million.

Over the ensuing decade, Jones and partner Mike McCoy (who would later become the Cowboys' vice president) formed the Arkoma Production Company to man the fertile, gas-rich Arkoma Basin in northwestern Alaska, then earned nearly $174.8 million from a corporate buyout in 1986. The obscure, up-from-the-sticks Jones was now one of America's wealthiest men.

Throughout his gas and oil career, the failed Chargers purchase haunted Jones. Sure, digging through Arkansas and Oklahoma for black liquid gold was lucrative, but the work lacked *purpose*. Jones wanted to mold something, wanted more than a big bank account and a luxurious Little Rock, Arkansas, home for his wife, Gene, and their three children. Hence, in 1988 Jones managed to spend four hours tagging along with coach Bill Walsh and general manager John McVay of the San Francisco 49ers—neither of whom had ever heard of this strange man with the Arkansas drawl. Jones certainly had the means, but he needed a crash course in NFL-ese. "I knew I wanted to own a franchise one day," Jones says. "And if you're gonna meet with someone, it might as well be the best."

So there he was, months later, floating on a bay in Mexico while reading in the *Wall Street Journal* of the sale of the Dallas Cowboys. With Arkansas lacking its own professional football entity, the state's 2.3 million residents either rooted for the (relatively) nearby Cowboys or ignored the professional ranks altogether. Jones was hardly the type of guy who studied every NFL roster, but he knew enough about America's Team to believe there'd be no better opportunity. He called Salomon Brothers, who patched him through to Bright. The introduction was simple and, in hindsight, historic: "Mr. Bright, my name is Jerry Jones. I'd like to buy your football team."

The forty-six-year-old immediately topped Bright's wish list. Armed with a thick wallet and a love of football, Jones's greatest attribute was that his stewardship would guarantee the demise of Tom Landry. Such was confirmed during one of the initial conversations between the two multimillionaires, when Jones volunteered his plan to hire

Jimmy Johnson, his former Arkansas teammate and the current head coach at the University of Miami.

In his seven years as a writer with the *Dallas Morning News*, Ivan Maisel could count on one hand the number of articles he had written about the Cowboys. Maisel's beat was college football, after all, and there was little need for his contributions to the coverage of the professional game.

On the night of February 24, 1989, however, Dave Smith, the *Morning News* executive sports editor, presented members of his staff with a code-red order: Find Jerry Jones and Jimmy Johnson. According to mounting rumor, the incoming owner and would-be future coach were in town and preparing officially to take control of the Cowboys. There were reported spottings here and there, and Smith desperately wanted to beat the rival *Dallas Times Herald* to the story.

Throughout the afternoon Maisel had tried at all costs to avoid Smith's glare, hiding in his tiny corner office with the door shut. It didn't work. "Ivan!" shouted Smith. "Jones and Johnson might be staying at the Mansion on Turtle Creek. Go sit in the lobby and wait 'em out!"

Maisel knew damn well there was no way two men trying to lay low would take residence at a famed five-star hotel (they were actually staying at an Embassy Suites), but orders were orders. "So I got there at four-thirty, trying to do my best to not get my ass thrown out," Maisel says. "I'm sitting in a chair, looking like I'm waiting for Elvis to walk through the lobby."

At 7:15 P.M. Maisel called Chris Worthington, the *Morning News*'s sports editor, to ask if he could leave. "Yeah," he told Maisel. "Go on home." Maisel immediately contacted his girlfriend, Meg, who was back in town after a lengthy business trip and had been craving Tex-Mex. "Let's go to Mia's," Maisel suggested. Located on Lemmon Avenue in Dallas's Uptown area, Mia's was *the* Tex-Mex restaurant for many of the city's biggest names in politics, sports, and entertainment (including a certain taco-loving coach named Landry). People literally drove across the state to indulge in Butch and Ana Enriquez's brisket tacos, which were stuffed with tender brisket, sautéed onions, and tangy poblano-chili strips.

At approximately 7:45 P.M., Ivan and Meg strolled into Mia's, placed their names on the waiting list, and patiently stood against a wall located to the left of the restaurant's main entranceway. Surrounded by an ocean of people, Ivan and Meg leaned in toward one another, speaking quietly and minding their own business. Then, without warning, the door opened. In walked Jerry Jones and Jimmy Johnson, accompanied by their wives.

"Ivan," said Meg, "you just turned white."

"Oh, shit," Maisel said, his mouth agape. Then, he turned back toward Meg. "I've gotta go do this," he said. "I'll be right back."

Maisel weaved his way through the restaurant, sliding along the L-shaped bar toward a space directly behind Johnson. Having covered the collegiate game for one of the nation's elite sports sections, Maisel knew Johnson well. He tapped him on the shoulder and watched as Johnson's jaw dropped. "Ivan," said Johnson, "what the hell are you doing here?"

"I live two blocks away," said Maisel. "What are *you* doing here?"

Johnson introduced Maisel to Jones and Jones's wife, Gene, and chatted for a couple of minutes. Maisel returned to Meg and waited for Johnson and Jones to be seated. As soon as they were placed at a table, Maisel snuck through the kitchen, out the back door, and straight to a phone to call Worthington. They had to get a shot of this.

Unfortunately for the *Morning News*, there were no available photographers. Well, there was one, but referring to Mark Kegans as a "photographer" was quite a stretch. A twenty-four-year-old intern from little-known Hardin-Simmons University, Kegans spent the majority of his time at the *Morning News* locked in a photo lab as a technician.

He knew how to work a camera, but so, for that matter, do most six-year-olds.

Robert Hart, one of the paper's photo editors, scribbled "MIA'S; 4322 LEMMON AVE" on a piece of scrap paper and handed it to Kegans. "If you don't get anything," he told the intern, "don't come back."

Kegans sped to Mia's, parked his red Datsun 240SX, and dashed through the front doorway. He nervously approached Jones and Johnson's table. "Guys, I'm sorry," he said. "I'm with the *Dallas Morning News* and I have to take your picture."

"Okay," said Jones. "Just make it quick."

Click.

Click.

Click.

Click.

Click.

Click.

"That's good," said Johnson. "It's enough."

With that, Kegans returned to the *Morning News* office, loaded his roll into the film processor, and prayed. In the twenty-five minutes it took for the six photographs to develop, Hart laid on the pressure. "There better be something here," he said, "This is your life as a photographer on the line."

The pictures emerged from the machine. They were non-artistic, non-dazzling, non-eye-catching—and absolutely, positively perfect. There, sitting across from one another and engaged in conversation, were Jones and Johnson. It was as good as official: The Cowboys were under new management.

On the morning of February 25, 1989, readers of the *Dallas Morning News* woke up to find one of the most breathtaking sports-related front pages in the city's 143-year history. Beneath the headline COWBOYS

SALE NEAR; LANDRY LIKELY OUT and alongside one of Kegans's photographs ran a piece from staff writer Bernie Miklasz, who cobbled together a story utilizing Maisel's encounter along with various other sources. It began:

> Arkansas millionaire Jerry Jones and Cowboys owner H. R. "Bum" Bright were locked in negotiations all day Friday, attempting to make final a purchase that would give Jones control of the Cowboys and Texas Stadium Corp. A source with knowledge of the negotiations said that Jones has offered Bright $130 million for the team and stadium leases.
>
> By all indications the purchase, which could become official Saturday, would abruptly terminate the 29-year regime of Tom Landry, the only head coach in the Cowboys' history. Jones, according to several sources close to him, plans to replace Landry with University of Miami coach Jimmy Johnson.

The article was jarring, the picture even more so. How could Jones and Johnson come to Dallas and strip Tom Landry of his job and then his dignity by celebrating at the legendary coach's favorite restaurant? Throughout the city the news was blasphemous. The local talk radio stations were bombarded with venomous calls—*Who was this Jones guy? How could he dump Coach Landry like that? The Cowboys were an institution, not merely another team. This was evil; nightmarish; pathetic; wrongheaded.* A handful of solitary voices begged the city for patience. The request was roundly ignored. Patience? *To hell with patience.* "My first impression was that this Jones guy had a chance to make it," says Norm Hitzges, the longtime Dallas radio personality. "Or that he had a chance of becoming the NFL's version of the Hindenburg."

When Jones initially learned of the franchise's availability, he told himself he would fork over whatever it took. After all, a dream was a dream. Yet the eventual deal was, in hindsight, a steal. Though Bright had wanted $180 million, he wound up settling for significantly less:

$90 million for the team, $50 million for the stadium, and $10 million to assume the mortgage on the team's headquarters. After four days of negotiating, Bright and Jones had one of their final battles on the morning of February 25 at the Bright Banc on Stemmons Freeway, when they disagreed over $300,000 in closing fees. Bright pulled a quarter from his pocket. "Let's flip for it," he said.

Jones called tails. The coin landed heads up.

"Oh well," said Jones with a chuckle. "You just made three hundred thousand dollars." (Bright later presented Jones with a quarter glued to a block, along with a note reading, "You'll never know if it was a two-headed coin.")

Midway through the meeting Tex Schramm arrived, looked at Johnson (who had attended at Jones's insistence), and roared, "You need to get your ass out of town! Your people have embarrassed Tom Landry enough already." Though Schramm himself had been trying to deftly, *sensitively* nudge Landry aside for the past few years, there were proper ways to go about it. Dinner at Mia's was not one of them.

Johnson heeded the advice and caught the next flight to Miami. Jones and Schramm, meanwhile, had their own flying to do. Bright assured Jones that he would have no problem firing Landry as his final act of ownership, but Jones refused. He believed that, as the new boss, it was his duty to confront Landry face-to-face. Bright wasn't one to argue the point—as long as Landry was a goner, he was content. "Bum Bright owed it to Tom to pick up the phone and give him a heads-up that the sale was going through," says Bob Ackles, the team's director of player personnel. "But Bum didn't like Landry and felt he owed him nothing."

With his time dwindling, Landry followed the course of action of many imperiled men before him . . . and *fled*. Schramm had asked the coach to remain in Dallas so that Jones might speak with him, but Landry had little interest in making his ousting an easy process. As most Dallas residents were learning of his imminent demise from the *Morning News,* Landry was piloting his Cessna 210 to Lakeway, Texas, where his family owned a weekend getaway house. As if the big news of the day were a 4-H bake sale (and not his dismissal), Landry headed out to the Hidden Hills golf course, where he played eighteen holes with his son, Tom Landry, Jr.

By the time Jones and Schramm reached Hidden Hills on the evening of February 25, the sky was darkening. Only two golfers—Landry and his son—remained at the facility; they were practicing their putting. With Schramm at his side, Jones approached the men and introduced himself. The four retreated to a sales office, where Jones and Landry sat face-to-face. "This is with absolutely no disrespect to you," Jones said. "But I'm here and so is Jimmy."

Having seen Landry on TV, oh, ten thousand times, Jones expected his reaction to be subdued and polite. "I'll always regret going there," says Jones. "I misread the situation. I wanted to do the right thing and tell him in person. I thought it would be honorable. But it didn't come off that way. I'll always be haunted by that."

"You could have saved your plane trip down here," Landry snapped. "As a matter of fact, you could have handled this whole thing a lot better. This whole thing is just a bunch of grandstand tactics. You had no obligation to do this. You could have saved your gas."

With that, the third-winningest coach in NFL history began to cry.

Later that evening, Jones and Schramm returned to Valley Ranch to announce the takeover of America's Team. With approximately twenty-five reporters waiting in an auditorium, Jones stepped into Schramm's private bathroom and shaved. Normally cool under pressure, Jones found himself sweating profusely.

Upon leaving the bathroom, Jones was approached by Doug Todd, the team's veteran media relations director. Todd had handled Super Bowls and drug scandals, surprising trades and shocking deaths. "You'll enter the room and there will be a dais on the right," Todd told Jones as he tightened the knot atop his tie. "And over here will be a row of chairs—"

"Hold on," snapped the new owner. "I can handle it. I can handle it."

But he couldn't. Jones was not merely an outsider purchasing a football team—he was an outsider purchasing the soul of Dallas in the midst of a citywide slump. The same financial crisis that had done in Bright was impacting hundreds of thousands of denizens. Within the past seven years not a single new business had relocated to downtown Dallas. The murder, rape, and aggravated assault rates were the highest in the city's history, and the public schools were being compared with those in Detroit and Houston. "Dallas was suffering from a self-confidence crisis," says Steve Bartlett, who served as mayor from 1991 to 1995. "If the sports team did well the people would start feeling better about themselves too. But at the time the Cowboys were terrible and people were angry. That's what Jerry was walking into."

The press conference was a disaster. In what would come to be known as the "Saturday Night Massacre," Jones took the podium (Johnson remained in Miami) and presented himself as a backwoods Arkansan bumpkin powered by a heart of coal. With dozens of team employees apprehensively looking on, Jones kicked things off by exclaiming, "This is like Christmas for me!" and followed with a meandering seven-minute, twenty-four-second monologue that detailed his euphoria and excitement.

"I had a little media experience when I played at Arkansas," says Jones. "But I had no idea what I was doing. Admittedly, it was terrible."

When he finally got around to the beloved Landry, Jones's words lacked depth and empathy. "This man is like Bear Bryant to me, like Vince Lombardi to me," he said, suppressing a giddy smirk. "If you love competitors, Tom Landry's an angel." Collectively, the assembled media groaned. Landry may well have deserved to be fired—*but by this yokel?* Jones would promptly be nicknamed "Jethro" after the doltish Jethro Bodine character from TV's *The Beverly Hillbillies*.

"Jerry was so obviously in over his head," says Jim Dent, the veteran Dallas writer. "In the media, we felt stabbed in the heart by the way he fired Landry. Jerry just dropped out of nowhere, and the opinion was, What the hell does this guy know? That press conference cemented the belief."

At his best, Jones came off as dumb. He called Johnson "the best coach in America" and said that, as the new owner, he would be involved with everything from "jocks to socks."

Standing beside his new boss, Schramm shrunk by the second. Though his relationship with Landry ran hot and cold, there was always respect. At one point a reporter asked of Schramm's status. "He's standing right next to me, isn't he?" Jones said. Told that Schramm was actually standing behind him, Jones said, "He's a little behind tonight. We've got an evolving thing. Tex and I just initially talked this morning at nine o'clock. We've got a lot of settling to do."

Like Landry, Schramm was a goner. The man who had constructed the Cowboys would soon take a job as president of the new World League of American Football. Gil Brandt, the personnel wizard, was eventually jettisoned too.

With a tilted grin, Jones assured the masses that he "needed" the holdover employees to show him the way. Then he went on a firing spree, unloading dozens upon dozens of longtime Cowboy workers. "On his first full day he had a bunch of us come into his office," says Carlton Stowers, the outgoing editor of *Cowboy Weekly,* the team's self-published tabloid. "He gave us the ol' I-don't-know-what-I'm-doing speech. The next day the ticket manager got a note saying she had to be out of the building by five o'clock. She'd been with the team for twenty years."

On Monday, February 27, Tom Landry—his boxes packed, his office empty—addressed his players one final time. The former head coach entered a room at Valley Ranch and, as always, removed his hat. Following a lengthy pause, he began to speak softly. "This will be our last . . . meeting together," he said, taking deep breaths. "We will . . . all go on. You'll . . . all find that in . . . adverse situations, strength . . . comes through. I believe that . . . through all of this . . . that we'll all learn.

But what . . . makes me sad is . . . that I . . . had a lot . . . of plans for . . . next season, and my . . . dreams have . . . been dashed. I love . . . you all, and . . ."

Landry paused. He dabbed his moist eyes with a sleeve, took a deep breath, wiped away more tears. The assembled Cowboys were shocked. "He kept trying to talk, basically about handing the command over to Jimmy, and he tried to talk a little more, and he cracked a little more," says Garry Cobb, the linebacker. "Then he just started crying. And crying. He never finished the speech. He collapsed on the floor and the other coaches came and tried to console him. And he was done. Everyone filed out."

For some players, Landry's departure was a gleeful case of what-goes-around-comes-around. A handful of Cowboys even celebrated with drinks at a nearby pub. How many athletes had Landry cut during his years leading the Cowboys? Now he was getting his. "Tom probably fired ten thousand football players without ceremony," says Crawford Ker, the longtime Cowboys offensive lineman. "Every dog has his day."

For most, however, Landry's demise proved heart-wrenching. Here was a decent man who embodied a life of rectitude. "He wanted you to be a great football player," says Jeff Rohrer, a Cowboys linebacker from 1982 to 1989. "But he really wanted you to be a great person.

"The way they did him at the end, it just wasn't right. You don't treat a legend that way. Jerry Jones and Jimmy Johnson had a lot to prove. Not to me and not to the players, but to all of Dallas."

Chapter 3

THE RIGHT MAN

*Jimmy didn't know any of the damn plays, but
you could break your arm and that dude would make
you believe it didn't hurt.*
—Kevin Gogan, Cowboys offensive guard

WHEN JOURNALISTS FIRST learned that Jerry Jones would be hiring Jimmy Johnson to coach the Dallas Cowboys, they all but attacked their keyboards in an effort to paint the portrait of a pair of lifelong best friends triumphantly taking the reins of America's Team.

The story line was irresistible—teammates and roommates at the University of Arkansas who had learned at the knee of legendary coach Frank Broyles and were now, nearly thirty years later, making good. Jones was the studious financial whiz who would go on to earn millions, Johnson the gridiron guru destined to pace the sidelines of the nation's elite football powerhouses. Wrote William Oscar Johnson in *Sports Illustrated:* "The Jones-Johnson friendship is a heartwarming thing, to be sure, going back a quarter of a century to their college days. They used to lie in bed at night talking about how much they wanted football always to be a part of their lives."

Indeed, Jones and Johnson were friendly at Arkansas, and—based on the alphabetical proximity of their surnames—roomed together on road trips. They may well have even discussed their futures once or twice. But the stereotypes were, at best, far-fetched. Boasting a 149 IQ and a degree in industrial psychology, Johnson stood out as Jones's intellectual superior. He was the forward thinker. The *deeper* thinker. The one who would likely go on to a successful career as an industrial psychologist. As for the kinship, Johnson found Jones to be an arrogant braggadocio. Jones considered Johnson aloof and dismissive. "We haven't done half a dozen things socially since we've known each other," Johnson once said. There was "like" between the two. Just not *strong* like.

Well schooled in Jones's Madonna-esque need for attention, Johnson—drawn by the prospect of an NFL dream job—went along for the ride. He'd drink beers with Jones, pose shoulder to shoulder, hug and laugh and guffaw. He would put up with Jones's antics because this was the Dallas Cowboys.

To Jones's credit, he was bringing in the ideal man to deal with the scrutiny of replacing a legend. Born on August 14, 1943, Johnson was raised in the Texas boomtown of Port Arthur, where blue-collar whites and blacks attended separate schools, used separate toilets, ate at separate restaurants, yet bonded over similarly arduous existences. As his peers were choosing to stick mostly within their racial boundaries, color rarely seemed to occur to young Jimmy. If you could play ball, you could play ball. "Jimmy never thought there was any difference between him and the blacks," his father, C. W. Johnson, said. "And he didn't like it when anybody said anything about it, either."

Perhaps that's because, economically, C. W. and Allene Johnson's family had more in common with blacks than whites. Jimmy grew up poor, the youngest son of a father who toiled for the Gulf Oil refinery and, later, the Townsend Dairy. While he didn't earn much, C. W. worked hard and expected the same from his two sons. It was this ethic that helped Jimmy emerge as a big man at Thomas Jefferson High, which he attended with a certain sloppily dressed, music-loving gal named Janis Joplin. (In a typical jock-meets-hippie clash, Johnson mockingly tagged Joplin "Beat Weeds.") With rare exception, Johnson was respected across social and economic lines as the school's top athlete (he earned all-state honors on the offensive and defensive lines) and as an accelerated student who, in the words of *Sports Illustrated*'s Ed Hinton, "could solve algebra problems at a glance and write term papers worthy of A's the night before they were due." He was nicknamed "Scar Head" by a childhood buddy named Jimmy Maxfield—an ode to both his eternally cut-up noggin (largely the product of wrestling matches between Jimmy and older brother Wayne) and the determination that inspired him to attack all challenges.

During his senior year at Thomas Jefferson in 1960–61, Johnson was heavily recruited by two dozen major colleges, including Alabama and its tenacious young coach, Paul "Bear" Bryant. Given that his parents were born and raised Arkansans, however, he signed with the Razorbacks. Johnson's freshman coach, a twenty-four-year-old novice named Barry Switzer, was immediately impressed by the noseguard's ferocity, and his varsity coach, the esteemed Broyles, looked upon Johnson as a team leader. As a senior against Nebraska in the 1965 Cotton Bowl, Johnson accumulated twelve tackles as the Razorbacks won 10–7 to capture their first national championship. "I got my first taste of the concept of winning it all," Johnson once wrote. "I thought, 'Now that's the way to end a playing career.'"

With the Razorbacks' success, collegiate programs from across the country came to Fayetteville to learn the vaunted "Arkansas Monster Slide Defense." Intelligent and articulate, the soon-to-graduate Johnson was asked to explain the intricacies of Broyles's system. One of the men to sit in on a Johnson lecture was Louisiana Tech head coach Joe Aillet, who was taken aback by the twenty-one-year-old's maturity. When Tech's defensive coordinator suffered a heart attack that would cause him to miss the '65 campaign, Aillet offered Johnson the job. At the time, Jimmy was spending the summer working as a shipyard welder, desperate to earn some extra money to support his new wife, Linda Kay (whom he had met as an undergrad and married the summer before), and their toddler son, Brent. "They said they'd pay me a thousand dollars a month for three months," Johnson wrote. "One thousand dollars a month, in 1965! I said, 'Hey, I'll be there.'"

In his three months at Louisiana Tech, Johnson shed his aspiring psychologist skin and transformed into an aspiring football coach. He loved the plotting and the strategy—taking a concept, writing it on a chalkboard, and watching it come to life. That Tech finished a mediocre 4–4 mattered little to Johnson. Through four years of college he was never quite sure where life would lead him. Now, he had an idea.

Johnson spent the spring of '66 as a graduate assistant at Arkansas, and that fall moved his family to Picayune, Mississippi, best known as the world's tung oil capital. As an assistant coach at Picayune High School, he helped a team that had gone 0–10 the year before . . . to go 0–10 again. "With all my expertise in coaching," he wrote, "we came *close* to winning a game." Though Johnson cherished tung and its mystical healing powers, he dreaded the nonstop losing. Salvation came in the form of a call from Switzer, who informed Johnson that Wichita State was searching for a young, inexpensive defensive assistant. Johnson left Picayune before the school year had ended and reported to Larry Lacewell, Switzer's friend and the Shockers' defensive coordinator. "Jimmy immediately struck me as extremely smart," says Lacewell, who later worked with Johnson in Dallas. "He's moody, he can be a horse's ass, and he enjoys the role of coming off as a complicated person. But I'll tell you something—that boy knew his football and how to reach players."

Johnson spent the two years after Wichita working as a defensive assistant under Johnny Majors at Iowa State, and in 1970 was hired as defensive line coach by the University of Oklahoma. Though 517 miles from Port Arthur, Norman felt like home, what with Switzer and Lacewell also serving as assistants to head coach Chuck Fairbanks. The three were inseparable, raising hell in the local bars and spending long nights downing beers and talking football. "Jimmy was probably the most fun guy on that staff," says Lacewell. "We all did some crazy, crazy stuff." There was a nude midnight streak across campus; setting Switzer's door on fire. "Tons of shit," says Lacewell. "Just great stuff. When you're an assistant there's a level of freedom you don't have when you're running the program."

Johnson left Oklahoma in 1973 to join Broyles as Arkansas' defensive coordinator. His big break was supposed to come three years later, when Broyles announced his retirement to devote full attention to his duties as the school's athletic director. At age thirty-three Johnson assumed he would be the successor. Instead, Broyles hired Lou Holtz, an outsider coming off a disastrous 3–10 season leading the New York Jets.

Johnson spent the next two years as an assistant at the University of Pittsburgh and then finally, in 1978, his moment arrived. Oklahoma State University was looking for a new head coach, and a member of the search committee happened to be Kevin Leonard, a close friend of Jerry Jones's. "I told him Jimmy Johnson would do wonders," says Jones. "Jimmy was still pretty young, but I always knew he could do magic at the head of a program." Before accepting the position at OSU, Johnson made a call to Switzer, then the head coach of the University of Oklahoma. "It's always better to be a head coach than an assistant," Switzer told him. "But I'm warning you now—I'm going to beat your ass every single year."

With Oklahoma State on probation for an array of NCAA violations, the program Johnson inherited was in shambles. In his first season in Stillwater, Johnson had only fifty-five scholarship players. (Most Big 8 rivals had ninety-five.) Outgunned and undermanned, Johnson invited any and all male Oklahoma State students to join the squad. His team finished with a shocking seven wins and led the nation with nearly two hundred names on its roster. There was Kay the marketing major, Boockvar the aspiring doctor, Platt the soon-to-be stockbroker. Lacking gear for so many "players," one equipment manager found a discount store selling soccer shoes for $3 a pair.

Although he never turned Oklahoma State into a national power,

Johnson gained recognition as one of the nation's top young coaches. "The job Jimmy did there," says Switzer, "was amazing." Like Switzer, Johnson differentiated himself from the other white men who monopolized America's sidelines. He could reach back into his Port Arthur roots and comprehend the pain of being a black male trying to make it, coming from nothing. "It goes beyond not being prejudiced," says Melvin Bratton, who later played for Johnson at the University of Miami. "Jimmy was white, but you don't think of him racially." In 1983 Oklahoma State turned the corner, going 8–4 and defeating Baylor, 24–14, in the Bluebonnet Bowl.

Unfortunately for Stillwater's football hard-core, Johnson wouldn't be around very long. As Oklahoma State was climbing its way up the Big 8 ladder, Sam Jankovich, the University of Miami's athletic director, was looking for someone to replace Howard Schnellenberger, the head coach who had departed for the upstart United States Football League after leading the Hurricanes to the '83 national championship. Midway through a convention of college coaches in the spring of 1984, Jankovich pulled Johnson aside and asked for recommendations. "You know," Johnson replied, "I wouldn't mind living on the beach."

Several weeks later Jankovich offered Johnson the job—with one catch. To come to Miami, he would have to inherit Schnellenberger's staff for at least a year; the athletic director felt it the honorable thing to do, given Schnellenberger's last-minute departure. Johnson sought out wisdom from dozens of peers, none of whom advised him to leave Oklahoma State. Finally, he asked Lacewell. "Jimmy, I'd go," he said. "You coached at Oklahoma one time; you know their firepower. You can't win a national championship at Oklahoma State. But you can win one at Miami." Lacewell's words rang true.

Upon arriving at Miami, however, Johnson found himself in a toxic environment. Three of Schnellenberger's assistants (defensive coordinator Tom Olivadotti, offensive coordinator Gary Stevens, and an administrative assistant named Bill Trout) had applied for the head coaching position. Johnson's first meeting with the staff was less than promising. He was greeted with a grim-faced silence. As Johnson began to speak, the bitter Olivadotti dropped his keys on the table, picked them up, dropped his keys on the table, picked them up. "I've seen your teams play," Olivadotti said, "and I really don't think our philosophies could coexist. Your teams don't play the way *we* want to play."

"I'm sure that we can work with each other," Johnson replied before leaving for his introductory press conference. Inside, he fumed.

To Johnson's delight, Olivadotti resigned. To his dismay, the other assistants remained. Though the defending national champions played well in Johnson's debut season, winning eight of their first ten games, much of Johnson's time was spent worrying whether his coaches were poisoning his milk.

In Miami's second-to-last game, Johnson's team blew a 31–0 halftime lead to Maryland, allowing Terrapins quarterback Frank Reich to pick the defense apart in a staggering 42–40 loss. The following week, the Hurricanes struggled against Boston College before staging a late drive to grab a 45–41 lead. On the last play of the game, 5-foot, 9-inch quarterback Doug Flutie scrambled away from the defense and threw a Hail Mary that was caught in the end zone by Gerard Phelan, giving BC the victory and college football one of its defining moments. Even before Flutie threw the ball, Trout had left his position in the press box. He was resigning from Johnson's staff, and felt no need to remain for the final play.

The season ended with a 39–37 Fiesta Bowl loss to UCLA, and as soon as the clock read 0:00 Johnson pledged he would never tolerate an experience akin to the 1984 season again. The morning after the game he held a press conference, announcing a restructured staff of Oklahoma State refugees committed to Johnson's way. To the new Miami way.

The Hurricanes of 1985 were brash, bold, and dominant. They went 9–1 through the first ten games and would complete the regular season with a November 30 home matchup against Notre Dame. Entering the game, the Fighting Irish were 5–5, a record that had the South Bend faithful desperate for redemption. If there was any hope of defeating the Hurricanes, it was that maybe, just maybe, the players would win one last game for the Gipper—er, Gerry Faust, their inept outgoing coach.

Instead, the Hurricanes humiliated their once-proud visitors, 58–7. The nationally televised game was a coming-out party for the "new" Hurricanes. Miami's players taunted and strutted, trash-talked, and end-zone danced. When safety Bennie Blades intercepted a second-quarter pass and returned it 61 yards for a touchdown, he slowed at the 2-yard line to high-five a teammate. When the 'Canes closed the third quarter with a 37–7 lead, Johnson demanded that his quarterbacks continue to throw the ball. With 71 seconds remaining, Miami ran a reverse. From his seat in the CBS booth, broadcaster Ara Parseghian—the former Notre Dame head coach—asked whether Miami had heard of this thing called decency. "It's time for Jimmy Johnson to show some compassion," said the man who, in his day, had led the Irish to a 69–13 win over Pittsburgh, a 48–0 win over Purdue, and a 44–0 win over, ahem, Miami. "This is not right."

From that day forward, the Miami Hurricanes were no longer another collegiate football team. They were thugs. Hoodlums. In an era when many universities still instructed their coaches to recruit black players *but not that many black players,* Johnson prowled the state of Florida seeking out great athletes, race be damned. "Jimmy got us," said Brett Perriman, an African-American and former Hurricane receiver. "He understood what it takes to win."

As long as his players attended classes, showed up on time to practices and games, and dominated the opposition, he could not care less how they carried themselves. At, say, Notre Dame or UCLA or Florida State, black players were asked to conform to a white society. At Miami, white society would conform to the players. "I really would have run through a wall for Coach Johnson," says Bernard Clark, an African-American and former Miami linebacker. "He took a chance on us, so we owed it to him."

In late September of 1986, top-ranked Oklahoma came to town to play the No. 2 Hurricanes at the Orange Bowl. Switzer's Sooners were led by linebacker Brian Bosworth, the brash *Sports Illustrated* cover boy with the multicolored flattop haircut. The night before kickoff, neither Miami tailback Melvin Bratton nor his roommate, fullback Alonzo Highsmith, could sleep. "It's five-thirty in the morning and I'm just lying there looking around," Bratton said. "Me and High are like kids at Christmas. We are so ready to get their ass. Oklahoma's been getting all the hype. It's Bosworth this and Bosworth that. I said, 'High, fuck the Boz and fuck that fade haircut of his. Let's call that sonofabitch and wake his ass up.'"

Bratton had heard the Sooners were staying at the Fontainebleau Hilton. He called the front desk and was patched through to Bosworth's room.

"Hello?"

"Is this Boz?" Bratton asked.

"Yeah . . ."

"Well, this is Melvin fuckin' Bratton and Alonzo Highsmith, and this is your fucking wake-up call, motherfucker! And at high noon we'll see your sorry ass in the Orange Bowl and we're gonna kick your fucking ass!"

As soon as Bosworth hung up, Bratton and Highsmith told Hurricane defensive lineman Jerome Brown of the "exchange." Brown summoned the entire defense to his dorm room, from which they called the hotel and asked to be connected to Sooners quarterback Jamelle Holieway. "*Ja-may-yal*, come out and *paaa-lay-yay*," Brown taunted. "Come on out, *Ja-may-yal*." When he later learned of the calls, Johnson nearly fell over laughing. And why not? His Hurricanes had won, 28–16.

Johnson was now known as a top-flight coach. But with mounting attention came trouble. While Johnson blamed his program's negative reputation to a media unwilling to credit inner-city black kids (for the record, Johnson graduated 75 percent of his players), the Hurricanes did tolerate a fair share of lawlessness. In the course of one season one player was arrested and charged with possession of cocaine and a handgun; another was arrested and charged with possession of steroids; Brown accidentally left a handgun in a shopping cart; defensive end

Daniel Stubbs was charged with a misdemeanor offense after he was caught siphoning gas from a nearby car; Highsmith accepted money from an agent; and rapper Luther "Luke" Campbell of 2 Live Crew allegedly paid players for good performances.

"Not really true," Campbell now says. "The football team had a lot of bad things going on around campus at the time—shooting guns, breaking into dorms. So I became something of a mentor. Kept the kids out of strip clubs and shit like that."

Wrote *Sports Illustrated*'s Rick Reilly: "Miami may be the only squad in America that has its team picture taken from the front and from the side."

Come season's end, the lone team standing between an undefeated season and the top-ranked Hurricanes was No. 2 Penn State. The two legendary programs would meet in the Fiesta Bowl in Arizona for the national championship. For the media, this was perfect. Penn State was professional, Miami thuggish. Penn State was Joe Paterno, the grandfatherly head coach who had just been named *Sports Illustrated*'s Sportsman of the Year. Miami was Johnson, advanced professor of hooliganism. Penn State won with dignity, Miami with lawlessness. In the lead-up to the game, the Fiesta Bowl hosted a steak fry for the two schools. With three thousand fans in attendance, Penn State's players arrived in suits and ties, while Miami's representatives were decked out in black sweat suits and, following a swift wardrobe change, army fatigues. Both teams were asked to perform a comedy sketch. Penn State went first, and all was fine until Nittany Lion punter John Bruno, Jr., cracked, "We even let the black guys eat with us at the training table once a week." When Bruno followed up by mocking Johnson's famously helmet-shaped hair, Miami's players had had enough. "We didn't sit down with the Japanese the night before Pearl Harbor," Brown announced, "and we're not going to get up here and act like a bunch of monkeys to entertain you people." With that, Brown and his teammates walked out.

Because the majority of media representatives didn't arrive in Tempe until the following afternoon, reports of the steak fry omitted vital details. Included in most stories were the fatigues and the "class-less" walkout. Excluded were the racist joke and the overtly hostile re-actions to Miami's players from the 99.9 percent white attendees. Once again, Johnson was pegged as the leader of a band of disrespectful an-archists. When Penn State shocked Miami 14–10, a nation smiled. Miami had received what it deserved.

Johnson coached two more years at Miami, leading the school to the 1987 national championship. Yet there was always that *image*. Johnson clashed with the school's president; recruited players with cocky demeanors and seedy backgrounds; turned a university that had worked hard to enhance its academic reputation into a place that seemed to invite bad apples.

When Jones came calling with an offer to leap to the NFL in 1989, Johnson was ready. "I like guys willing to walk the line," says Jones. "I brought Jimmy to Dallas because he's been through tough situations and he handled them better than anyone else could. He was the right man for a hard job."

Chapter 4

THE ASTHMA FIELD

I'm not saying we were naïve to the NFL. But I didn't know what division we played in.
—Dave Campo, Cowboys secondary coach

HE WAS A free-agent kicker.

That's the first thing people need to remember about Massimo Manca, the man who—by the dual powers of mythology and bluster—unintentionally started this whole dynasty thing.

Before there were the legends of Troy Aikman, Emmitt Smith, and Michael Irvin, there was a side practice field in Irving, Texas, on a weekend in March 1989. This is where the Dallas Cowboys veterans and free agents gathered for a standard three-day "voluntary" (translation: choose to attend or wind up slinging Slurpees at the nearest 7-Eleven) minicamp; the place where Jimmy Johnson would have an early opportunity to evaluate his players and set a tone.

Ah—tone. Wasn't that the key here? If Johnson was painfully aware of one thing, it was that the Dallas Cowboys—now *his* Dallas Cowboys—were woefully short on talent. Save for Michael Irvin, the prior season's first-round draft choice, and Herschel Walker, the veteran running back who had piled up 2,019 total yards in 1988, the roster was a collection of long-past-their-prime veterans (Ed "Too Tall" Jones, Tom Rafferty), doomed-to-be-mediocre pups (Danny Noonan,

Bob White, Jeff Zimmerman), and blah nobodies taking up space (Steve Folsom, Manny Hendrix). "I remember going into one of my early defensive meetings and there were five or six players older than I was," says Dave Wannstedt, then the Cowboys' new thirty-six-year-old defensive coordinator. "That's a bad sign."

Though the upcoming draft would yield, among others, UCLA quarterback Troy Aikman, Syracuse fullback Daryl Johnston, and Pittsburgh center Mark Stepnoski, Johnson knew that counting on rookies to win games was akin to depending on the federal government to deliver timely tax refunds.

It was March 18, 1989, and the Cowboys were already toast.

Minus talent, Johnson's strategy was to mold via torture. Viable or not, the new Cowboys headman believed he could take a wad of used bubble gum, pound it into the ground, and uncover a brick of gold. As an introduction to the Johnson Academy of Brutalization, on the first day of minicamp all Cowboy players were required to run sixteen 110-yard sprints under a certain time threshold before they could participate in general drills. "It was brutal," says Ron Burton, a third-year linebacker. "I don't think a lot of the guys were used to having to prove themselves *before* camp even started."

One man certainly unaccustomed to such a regimen was Manca. Born on the island of Sardinia, Manca attended high school in Reno, Nevada, then spent three seasons in the mid-1980s kicking for Penn State. Like many players of his ilk, Manca's postgraduate years were an NFL travelogue. He kicked three games as a strike player for the Cincinnati Bengals in 1987, and the following year attended training camp with the San Francisco 49ers. In the spring of 1989 Manca auditioned at a free-agent kicking combine in Reno and earned an invitation to the Cowboys' camp.

Through his trials, Manca had come to understand that the kicker was expected solely to hone his craft. At Penn State, the 5-foot, 10-inch, 211-pound Manca lifted weights and ran stairs about as often as he shaved six-legged alpacas. It was no different with the Bengals and 49ers. "So when I showed up with the Cowboys I was totally out of shape," says Manca. "As a kicker you know you won't be doing anything too strenuous."

On his first day with the Cowboys, Manca was standing along the perimeter of the practice field, watching his new teammates divide into sprint groups, when an assistant coach pointed his way. "Manca!" the coach yelled. "Jump in there with the linebackers and running backs!"

Gulp. Manca turned to his left, where he spotted a gaggle of sleek, muscular men with pumpkin-sized calves. He completed the first two or three runs without much trouble. The next two—a little harder. The next two—a *lot* harder. By the eighth sprint, Manca was walk-jogging, sweat pouring down his face. Johnson was not amused.

"Manca, get off the field!" Johnson yelled. "You're embarrassing yourself."

"I've got asthma," explained Manca, turning to the best half-truth he could muster. (On the one hand, Manca did indeed suffer from asthma as a young kid. On the other hand, Manca hadn't been a young kid in, oh, ten years.)

"Asthma, huh?" said Johnson. "Then go inside and talk to the doctor. But don't come back here until you're ready to compete."

That was it.

Or was it?

In the hours . . . days . . . weeks that passed, each retelling of the "Massimo Manca Incident" served to embroider Johnson's increasingly larger-than-life aura. What began as "Don't come back here until you're ready to compete" morphed into "You have no business being here"; which morphed into "Get the hell out of my face!"; which morphed into the the now-immortal "The asthma field is over there!" Manca beat-down.

"I remember it vividly," says Steve Folsom, a Cowboys tight end. "The guy was having an asthma attack on the field, and Jimmy just kicked him off."

"One kid was trying to breathe, and he just couldn't," says Willis Crockett, a Dallas linebacker. "I was right there. Jimmy points and says, 'The asthma field is over there.'"

"I was a witness," swears Ray Horton, the Cowboys' safety. "Jimmy was yelling at our trainer, 'You get him off my field right now! You cut his ass right now and get him off my field!'"

"It's a true story," says Jim Jeffcoat, the defensive lineman. "The guy's name was Luis Zendejas. Jimmy looked at him and said . . ."

Before long, Manca was no longer a free-agent kicker with little chance of making the squad, but a strong halfback. A beefy linebacker. An offensive lineman with a grizzly bear's might and Paul Bunyan's size. Manca was the greatest football player who had ever lived, and Johnson had banned him from the game for life. *Asthma? I'll show you asthma!*

"The whole thing grew to a ridiculous level," Manca says. "It wasn't that big of a deal."

No matter. Thanks to one disposable kicker, Johnson had taken the first step in molding the Cowboys into *his* Cowboys: He had scared the bejesus out of his players. *If Coach is willing to banish someone because of a life-threatening asthma attack, well, what the hell will he do to me?*

Nestled against the Santa Monica Mountains and surrounded by more than 14,800 acres of natural open space, Thousand Oaks is the sort of sleepy town one expects to find in South Dakota or Kansas, not in the action-packed state of California.

With the exception of the Conejo Valley Botanic Garden and an occasional celebrity sighting (Thousand Oaks's residents include Frankie Valli, Mariel Hemingway, and Belinda Carlisle), the main draw is the campus of Cal Lutheran University. Boasting majestic scenery and one of the state's better liberal arts programs, the school is both beautiful and respected.

It is here that the 1989 Dallas Cowboys began to take shape.

For the previous twenty-six years that the Cowboys called Thousand Oaks their home-away-from-home, training camp was an annual exercise in dullness. Under Tom Landry, workouts went as planned, assistant coaches understood what to expect, and returnees knew that—

unless they were inflicted with incurable blindness—their spots were mostly secure.

No more.

The Cowboys congregated for their first official training camp meeting on the morning of July 28, 1989, and if one thing became blatantly clear to holdovers from the Landry Era, it was that their new coach was an entirely different breed—and completely insufferable. For nearly forty-five minutes, Johnson blathered on about what could be accomplished with the power of teamwork; how effort and unity could move even the largest mountain; and *blah, blah, blah, blah.* "Listen," he said. "We're gonna play like champions, we're gonna act like champions, and we're gonna be champions."

He then presented players with a formula for success that *oozed* goofiness: PA + E = P.

Translation: Positive attitude plus effort equals performance.

"It wasn't a good start," says Todd Fowler, a running back who had played under Landry for four seasons. "Whereas Coach Landry treated you like a man, Jimmy stormed in there with this fire-and-brimstone approach, running all over the place like a high school kid."

Under Johnson, workouts lasted interminably. Weight work was mandatory and excessive. "I don't blame Jimmy for his approach, because we had a lot of young guys who needed molding," says Rafferty, who was then a thirty-five-year-old center. "But for me to go out and work three hours on Wednesday, three hours on Thursday, three hours on Friday, and then have fresh legs Sunday, well, I couldn't do it."

Instead of confronting players about their shortcomings or work habits, Johnson often dropped hints to reporters, hoping an uncomfortable headline might evoke an inspired performance. Instead of calmly advising or encouraging, Johnson would jump up and down on the field, screaming for the entire state of California to hear. Early in camp kicker Shaun Burdick missed an imaginary "game-winning" field goal from 63 yards. Johnson bolted toward the line of scrimmage and called lineman Dan Sileo—*who wasn't even on the field*—offside. He had Burdick take the kick again, this time from 58 yards. When he made it, Johnson exploded with glee. "Everything is a habit!" Johnson said. "The more you can reinforce winning, the more you get in the habit of winning!"

Rookies heard this and nodded.

Veterans heard this and rolled their eyes.

Making matters worse was Johnson's soft spot for former Hurricanes. Among the eighty-six players in camp, five had played for Johnson at Miami. Two seconds after cursing out a rookie from Syracuse or Pittsburgh, Johnson would yuk it up with Randy Shannon, a former Hurricane linebacker short on skills but long on pedigree. "Every day it seemed like Johnson was bringing in another one of his guys," says Charvez Foger, an eighth-round draft pick from Nevada-Reno. "It was a bad sign for someone like me."

Fearful of young players latching on to negativity, Johnson fired quickly. When linebacker Steve DeOssie screamed at one of the assistant coaches, he was immediately traded. When defensive tackle Kevin Brooks refused to report to minicamp, he was traded too. Fifth-round draft choice Keith Jennings reported to camp twenty pounds overweight and was deemed unwelcome. "He doesn't fit into our plans," Johnson said. Receiver Ray Alexander was called for delay of game after spiking the ball in an exhibition; "Ray," Johnson coolly informed the media afterward, "isn't with us anymore."

"Jimmy was a rah-rah guy and his coaches were idiots," says Jeff Rohrer, a veteran linebacker. "I was used to being coached by Hall of Famers who had played in the NFL. But Jimmy and his guys didn't know the game the way the guys who coached me before them did. And to compare them to [Landry assistant] Ernie Stautner? Are you kidding me? Are you friggin' kidding me? C'mon. There *was no comparison*."

Despite mounting hostility amongst veteran Cowboys and a roster long on ineptitude, Johnson—who added fourteen new players and pledged to rid himself of as many listless holdovers as humanly possible—was convinced his team would compete. "All he cared about was winning," says one Cowboy. "When I was with the Redskins [coach] Joe Gibbs would say, 'OK, fellas, don't mess with street drugs or steroids, because that's not how we do things here.' Jimmy, on the other hand, would say, 'Don't mess with street drugs or steroids, because the drug test is in a week and you don't wanna get caught.' It was obvious Jimmy lacked some character in his pursuit of greatness."

In April, after more than twenty years of marriage, Johnson came home from a jog around Valley Ranch, turned to Linda Kay, the wife who had dutifully followed him from one city to another, and said, "I want a divorce." Johnson was not so much shedding a spouse as gaining free time to focus on the Cowboys. Winning in the NFL required 100 percent dedication. That's why Linda Kay was gone, and why he would spend the coming years treating his two sons, Brent and Chad, like third cousins. "You knew one day Jimmy would look back at his kids and think, 'Was it really worth missing their lives?'" says Alonzo Highsmith, his fullback at Miami. "But when he was coaching it was football first, second, third, and fourth. Nothing came fifth."

Dallas opened its exhibition season in mid-August with road wins against San Diego and Oakland, then traveled to Denver to face a Broncos club that had played in two of the last three Super Bowls. Johnson knew his team was overmatched, and he also knew that Dan Reeves, the Denver coach and a longtime Cowboy player and assistant, had badly wanted to replace Landry and was irked by the snub.

In a physical contest that ignored the general let's-take-it-easy rules governing preseason football, Denver quarterback John Elway played the entire game, completing 26 of 50 passes for 355 yards. But this was far from a blowout. With one second remaining in regulation, Elway threw an 18-yard bullet to receiver Mark Jackson to force overtime. That the Cowboys lost on a David Treadwell field goal was, to the coaches along the Dallas sideline, insignificant.

"After that game, I think a lot of us were convinced that we had a pretty good team on our hands," says Dave Campo, the Cowboys secondary coach. "We had taken Elway's best punches without flinching, and we kept coming at him with a real intensity."

The Cowboys wrapped up the preseason by winning their final

game against Houston. Suddenly the negativity and doubt of just weeks earlier was replaced by a stirring optimism. Perhaps Johnson's initial evaluation was wrong. Perhaps the Cowboys were more talented and driven than first advertised. They stared down Elway. They beat a Houston team projected to be Super Bowl–ready. The Dallas Cowboys were good. Really good. A winning record was a possibility. Maybe even the playoffs. "We truly came to believe in ourselves," says Wannstedt. "We were set for the season to begin."

Now all the team needed was a quarterback.

When the Cowboys selected Troy Aikman with the first pick in the 1989 NFL Draft, everyone from opposing coaches and executives to fans and journalists knew the drill.

Though the savvy, strong-armed Aikman left UCLA as one of the best quarterbacks in school history, having led the Bruins to a 20–4 mark over two seasons, the NFL was a long way from the Pacific-10 Conference. Johnson would keep a veteran quarterback around to begin the season, absorb some blows, and help Aikman learn the intricacies of the league. Over time Aikman would assume increased responsibility. Maybe he'd mop up now and then, enter the second half of a blowout. Finally, perhaps in year two or three, Aikman would be named the starting quarterback of the Dallas Cowboys.

It was the tried-and-true way of professional quarterback development.

Jimmy Johnson was anything but tried and true.

During the 1988 season, the Cowboys were quarterbacked by Steve Pelluer, a fifth-year veteran out of the University of Washington who could throw a little, run a little, and do just enough to lose. Though Johnson was open to the idea of bringing Pelluer back, he refused to meet the quarterback's demand of a one-year contract in excess of $600,000. He also decided against re-signing veteran backup Danny White, who tersely told the media that Johnson and Co. had no remote idea what they were doing.

Perhaps he was right.

On July 7, barely three months after Jerry Jones had hailed Aikman as "the redeemer," the Cowboys used the first pick of the supplemental draft to select—of all things—another quarterback. And not just any quarterback.

Steve Walsh of the *University of Miami*.

The media didn't understand it. Cowboy players didn't understand it. Aikman, who had signed a six-year, $11.037 million contract, certainly didn't understand it. Even Steve Walsh didn't understand it. By using a first-round supplemental choice, the Cowboys were surrendering their first-round selection in the following year's regular draft. It was insane.

"My initial reaction was 'Huh?'" says Walsh, who'd led Johnson's Hurricanes to a 23–1 record and the 1987 national title. "I was very surprised. But Jimmy told me I was part of his strategy to build a championship team."

Guarded and somewhat reclusive by nature, Aikman learned of Walsh's addition (from TV reports, not his coach) and immediately contacted his agent, Leigh Steinberg, to come up with a plan. The options were nonexistent—he could neither demand a trade nor insist Johnson name him the starter. As soon as Walsh signed a four-year, $4.1 million contract, Johnson announced that the quarterback position was up for grabs. "This is not a formality," he told *Sports Illustrated*. "They know they'll get an equal chance."

Though Johnson loved the air of uncertainty that kept his rookie quarterbacks on edge, the move had a decidedly negative impact. As two of the nation's top college quarterbacks in 1988, Aikman and Walsh had met at a handful of preseason all-America events. Their relationship, OK to begin with, turned cool in Dallas. The two would talk on the sidelines, but only when necessary. They would compare notes, but only out of obligation. In the exhibition games, they split time. It was, for lack of a better word, awkward. "Troy felt threatened by me," says Walsh. "I understood it. Jimmy was my college coach, not his."

In the Dallas locker room, a line was drawn. There were Aikman guys. There were Walsh guys. Aikman's backers listened to country music and wore blue jeans and related to his country boy aura. Walsh's backers were the former Hurricanes in camp and other Florida-bred players who stayed true to one of their own. Jerry Rhome, the team's quarterback coach, buddied up to Aikman and shunned Walsh. Tension reigned. Frost filled the air when the two men were in the same room. Neither performed well enough nor poorly enough to determine a clear-cut front-runner. When Aikman excelled, Walsh seemed to play well. When Aikman struggled, so, it seemed, did Walsh.

Aikman?

Walsh?

Aikman?

Walsh?

Aikman?

Walsh?

"Having both of them was a terrible idea," says David Shula, the offensive coordinator. "It created tension that we really didn't need. Steve was very, very bright, a tremendous leader, and a great competitor. But Troy had these physical tools that jumped off the page, and he kept thinking, 'Wait a minute. You drafted me No. 1 and then you take another quarterback No. 1?' Steve would never have the arm strength of Troy. Not even close. But Steve had the smarts . . ."

And that was the dichotomy. Walsh was known as the skinny (6–foot–3, 195 pounds) intellectual, Aikman the burly (6-foot–3, 220 pounds) stud. They morphed into caricatures, slotted into neat little compartments. "Troy was not dumb by any means," says Walsh, "and I am a good athlete. But sometimes people get an idea and run with it."

Though he did his best to maintain an air of neutrality, Johnson was secretly pulling for Walsh. It wasn't simply a soft spot for all things Miami. No, Johnson loved the idea of flashing a middle finger toward conventional thinking. "I was always walking on eggshells," says Johnson. "I didn't want to buddy up to Troy because Steve would become upset. But Steve and I had this natural relationship, so I couldn't get too close to him, either."

Clearly, Walsh was the coach's guy. In a closed-door meeting, Johnson turned to Jones and said, "Troy might have more talent, but Steve can take us to a Super Bowl." Assistant coaches praised Aikman's poise, strength, and accuracy. Johnson saw him as stiff and mechanical. He questioned whether Aikman was smart enough to succeed in the NFL, and if he possessed the inner fire to own a huddle. In the days leading up to the Cowboys' exhibition finale, a 30–28 win over the Oilers at Texas Stadium, Johnson pulled Brad Sham, the team's radio announcer, into his office. "You know what I'm thinking of doing," Johnson told Sham. "I'm thinking of starting—"

Sham cut the coach off. "Jimmy," he said, "if you start Steve Walsh the fans will burn your house down. You have to give this Aikman kid a chance."

Shortly before the season began, Johnson followed convention—not his gut—and reluctantly tabbed Aikman as the man to lead the Cowboys.

He hoped the young signal caller was ready.

Chapter 5

HENRYETTA TROY

Day in and day out Troy Aikman developed into the perfect quarterback. Some players are good in practices and others are better in games. Troy was the same everywhere—absolutely awesome.
—Cliff Stoudt, Cowboys quarterback

TROY AIKMAN OFFICIALLY joined the Dallas Cowboys on April 20, 1989, a day as wild as any he had ever experienced. After waking up at four o'clock that morning, Aikman, along with agent Leigh Steinberg, drove to the team's Thousand Oaks facility, where he negotiated the finer points of a contract with Jerry Jones via satellite uplink. Upon agreeing to the six-year, $11.037 million deal, Aikman bolted for Los Angeles International Airport and boarded Jones's Texas-bound private jet. As soon as the quarterback arrived at Valley Ranch, he was introduced to twenty or so reporters, all eager to grill the newest face of the franchise. The media came away immediately impressed—Aikman was as poised and polite as any Dallas rookie in recent memory.

Once the press conference ended, Aikman headed out for an evening on the town with Jones—dinner, drinks, the works. It was a dazzling welcome to his new life, but when he finally called it a night, Aikman spent thirty fruitless minutes trying to hail a taxi. Frustrated, he strolled over to a parked limousine and begged the driver for a ride. *Surprise!* The stretch was occupied by ten attractive, giddy, alcohol-loaded Southern Methodist University coeds celebrating a twenty-first birthday.

Aikman jumped in, gladly accepting the lift.

Welcome to heaven.

Welcome to Dallas.

This is the stuff golden boy legend is made of. It's Joe Namath. It's Don Meredith. It starts with a blue-eyed, strawberry blond heartthrob and ends with a pair of panty hose draped over the bedpost.

It is not, by any means, Troy Aikman.

Though the new savior sauntered into town armed with classic Hollywood looks, good ol' boy charm, and an $11 million contract, he was, in fact, the anti-stereotype. Neither gregarious nor chummy, the twenty-two-year-old Aikman preferred a few cold Budweisers and a flick on the VCR to a night on the town. He dated, but was anything but a playboy. He partied, but only in the comfort of trusted friends. He was suspicious of motives and questioned why people craved his company. He talked freely to the media, but not *too* freely. Any comparisons to Namath or Meredith died immediately. Aikman was more Joe Montana. He didn't want to be the golden boy. "It takes a while for someone to gain my trust," he said. "Loyalty and trust are important to me."

While Aikman preferred outsiders (and, for that matter, teammates) to see him as the Dallas Cowboy quarterback and leave it at that, those who broke through the shell discovered a young man whose life story went well beyond pump ball–throw ball. "Troy is so much more than a football player," says Brad Sham, the Cowboys' radio announcer. "The game is a big part of his being. But it's not who he is."

Once upon a time, Aikman seemed as likely to guide the world's most famous football team as Mindy Cohn was to win an Oscar. Raised in the Southern California town of Cerritos, Troy was an ordinary baby until, at eight months, his parents struggled to slide shoes over his feet. Initially unalarmed, Ken and Charlyn Aikman began to fret when their son's legs bowed below his knees and his toes curled under his feet. The diagnosis was clubfoot.

For the succeeding five months Troy wore casts on his feet, until, shortly after his first birthday, they were replaced by special shoes—white high-tops with the toes jutting out at exaggerated angles. Troy kept the shoes on at all hours, and had his heels strapped together at night.

Though he overcame the condition to become one of the town's best schoolboy jocks, Troy was a sensitive kid who suffered through nightmares and depression. At age ten his grandfather died, and Troy started to obsess over death. The worries kept him up late into the night—a common fear for adults in their sixties and seventies, but unusual for a child tearing up Little League. Twelve-year-old Troy's unease was hardly helped when his father announced that, following his dream of operating a ranch, the family would be relocating to Henryetta, Oklahoma.

Home to 6,500 people, a nine-hole golf course, two lakes, and one of the state's better Labor Day carnivals, Henryetta was famous across the nation for, well, absolutely nothing. Not only was the Aikman clan (Troy, his parents, and his two older sisters) relocating to the middle of nowhere, but they would be living in a trailer until their house was constructed. The ranch the family resided on stretched over 172 acres. Everything smelled like manure. Troy's morning job was to feed the pigs.

Seriously. He fed the pigs.

"We ended up seven miles out of town on dirt roads that were too rough to ride your bike on," Aikman said. "It was tough. Even at that age I could see my athletic career falling apart."

Like countless boys growing up outside of Los Angeles, Troy had envisioned himself one day starting at shortstop for legendary University of Southern California baseball coach Rod Dedeaux.

How was he supposed to get to USC now, languishing in the troughs of far-off Henryetta?

We all have moments when life swerves. You choose to take the elevator and meet your future wife. You duck into a bathroom stall, look down, and find a wallet stuffed with $100 bills. You get hit by a bus crossing the street.

For Troy Aikman the moment came at age thirteen, when his father asked whether he was thinking of signing up for junior high school football.

"He was a tough old country boy who loved football," Aikman wrote of his father in his book, *Things Change*. "He liked the roughness of it. I knew what he wanted, so I signed up. If he hadn't asked, I might never have played. I never rebelled against my father. Never."

Back in California, Aikman's prodigious arm had made him an obvious peewee-league quarterback. Upon coming to Oklahoma, however, he decided to keep quiet and see if coaches would assign him to a less pivotal position. Young Troy cherished sports, but shied away from the attention accompanying them. Hence, Troy Aikman began his junior high gridiron career as a burly fullback–tight end who bruised easily and loathed excessive contact.

He returned to quarterbacking as a freshman at Henryetta High School, and as a sophomore won the starting job for the Fighting Hens. In his first varsity game, Aikman led a stirring come-from-behind win over archrival Checotah High. A star was in the making.

Yet in his three years as the varsity stud, Aikman never adopted the persona. He was a soft-spoken kid on a ranch who worked Saturdays in a store called Western Auto, drove around in his pickup truck, and liked a pinch of Skoal between his lower lip and his gum. If Aikman was driven by one thing, it was not football glory, but that ever-present ticking clock. When would he die? How would he die? Why did he have to die? *Tick . . . tick . . . tick.* "I remember when my father turned forty, he wouldn't open his gifts for two weeks," Aikman wrote. "He took it hard."

Those sorts of anxious moments stuck with Aikman. Though Troy was not raised in the church, he gave religion a try. As a high school senior he was rebaptized—fully soaked in a dunk tank as the spirit of Jesus Christ washed away his sins. The parishioners sang and cheered and embraced the new follower, but the fear didn't disappear. Death hung there. It still hangs there.

For some, the burden would be too great. An obsession with death can thrust one into an unyielding spiral of depression. With Aikman, it has had the opposite impact. When he played sports, he played passionately. People often mistake his sleepy eyes and casual facial expressions for boredom or indifference. Not so. More than most, Aikman wants to feel and experience and live.

From across the dining room table, Troy the high school jock watched his father leave early every morning and come back exhausted late at night. One could throw five hundred job descriptions into a hat and struggle to pick two that are more physically demanding than ranching and pipeline construction. Ken did both. Years later, Troy still recalls the day he spotted a bandage wrapped around his father's finger.

"Dad, let me see your finger," the son said.

"It's nothing," Ken answered.

When the gauze wrap was finally removed, Troy was nauseated. Ken had sliced off the tip of his finger, and the cut was so deep the bone was exposed.

"Don't worry," said Ken. "I'll be all right."

"Part of the reason I play the way that I play and don't fear getting hit . . . was wanting to prove to him that I was tough too," Aikman wrote. "I think that deep down, I always wanted to prove that I was as tough as he was and that I could take anything that he had to give. And I think that through football I was able to prove that to him."

In his three years at Henryetta's Cameron Field, Aikman established himself as an elite quarterback on a crummy team. Populated by gawky receivers and slow halfbacks, the Fighting Hens went 12–18 behind Aikman. "None of us matured as soon as Troy did," said Rick Gazalski, Aikman's 165-pound center. "Some of the teams we played were huge. We were doing what we had to do to make sure he didn't get hurt."

Fortunately for Aikman, high school wins and loses had no impact on his future. He possessed a big arm and a veteran's poise, and people took notice. The first important college coach to see Aikman for who he could be was a University of Oklahoma assistant named Merv Johnson. One day, while working Oklahoma's 1983 summer prep football camp, Johnson's eyes focused on the tall, handsome kid with the most breathtaking spiral this side of Steve Bartkowski. Johnson rushed into the office of Sooners head coach Barry Switzer. "I've got this kid from Henryetta who you have to see!" said Johnson. "He's kind of special."

How many times had Switzer heard that one before? There was always another "this fantastic passer" or "this one-of-a-kind halfback," and 99 percent of them wound up playing intramural flag football for their college fraternities. "So I went down to the practice field," recalls Switzer, "and I watched this young quarterback set up and drop back, and when he threw the ball, I could not believe a high school kid had the release, the prototype, the natural ability to hold the ball and his motion and the delivery, and have the ball jump out with the RPMs on it that his did. And I watched him and I walked over and told him, 'I want you to start thinking about becoming the Sooners quarterback, because I'm offering you a scholarship right now.'" Switzer's pitch was a strong one: *Come to Oklahoma—land of the famed wishbone offense—and we'll start passing the ball just for you.*

Indeed, Aikman was promised that, with the right quarterback, the Sooners would be more than willing to air it out. In Switzer's mind, Aikman would team up with star running back Marcus Dupree to comprise the greatest backfield in OU history.

How could the quarterback say no?

Though Aikman arrived at Oklahoma filled with dreams of guiding one of the nation's elite college football programs to new heights, fantasy never matched reality.

First, it took the new Sooner quarterback half a week to figure out that Switzer—a man known to speak with his gut, not his conscience—had promised a Mercedes SL65 and supplied a Dodge Dart. When Aikman signed with the Sooners, they were tooling around enough with the I-formation that Switzer could point to game tapes and bellow, "See, we're changing!" But the Sooners weren't changing, and never intended to. It was a snake-oil sale made by yet another snake-oil coach—and Aikman was furious. "Barry wanted to run the wishbone.

No bones about it," said Aikman of the run-oriented offensive system. "I mean, he told me they were going to stay in the I and the wishbone was obsolete when I was getting recruited, and four days after signing day they're back in the wishbone."

As his father would have done, Aikman grit his teeth. On October 27, 1984, an ankle injury to senior quarterback Danny Bradley forced the freshman to make his first collegiate start. Ranked No. 2 in the nation, the Sooners traveled to the University of Kansas to battle a 2–5 team that had not defeated Oklahoma in nine years. Even with a jittery freshman at the helm, it looked to be a cakewalk.

The first freshman quarterback to start for the Sooners in nearly forty years, Aikman was a disaster. Kansas blitzed at will, forcing him into a well-choreographed reenactment of *Jeff Komlo: The Detroit Lions Years.* He threw fourteen passes. He completed two. Three others were intercepted, one of which was returned for a touchdown. The Sooners lost, 28–11.

To Aikman's credit, he accepted the setback with remarkable stoicism. While transferring crossed his mind more than once, especially while he languished on the sideline for the rest of the year as Oklahoma reached the Orange Bowl, Aikman returned for his sophomore season determined to make the situation work for him.

Reinvigorated by a summer off, Aikman won the starting job, and Switzer briefly attempted to incorporate a few more passes than usual. The Sooners started the year 3–0, and with Miami coming to town for game number four Aikman was once again a star on the threshold. Although Oklahoma was the nation's top-ranked team, the Hurricanes brought with them to Norman's Owen Field a threatening cockiness that screamed, "We will pummel you!" With 9:18 remaining in the first half and the Hurricanes leading 14–7, Aikman was driving his club down the field when he faced a third-and-10 from the Miami 17. The quarterback dropped back, looked to pass, and was hammered into the turf by Miami defensive tackles John McVeigh and Jerome Brown. Aikman screamed while grasping for his left ankle, which had snapped in half. His season was over.

Standing on the sideline for the rest of the year, Aikman watched as freshman Jamelle Holieway—a swift wishbone maestro—led Oklahoma to an 11–1–0 record and the national title. Aikman was witness to the future of Oklahoma football, and it didn't involve him.

When the season ended Aikman told Switzer that he had decided to transfer. Though he assumed his coach would be angry, Switzer was emphatically supportive. "I hated it, but I looked at it more from a father's standpoint, trying to do what's right for the player," Switzer says. "He told me the schools he was interested in [UCLA, Arizona State, Iowa, and Miami], and I called the coaches as soon as I could." It wasn't an easy sell.

When Switzer spoke with UCLA coach Terry Donahue and detected the all-too-common reluctance to accept a transfer, he went on the offensive. "This kid is different," Switzer said. "He will be a first-round draft choice, and he needs to be in your offense."

Aikman wound up enrolling at UCLA, where he sat out the required year before emerging as one of the nation's most explosive quarterbacks. In his two seasons as a starter for the Bruins, Aikman compiled 41 touchdown passes and only 17 interceptions. Donahue insisted on short, precise, 10- to- 15-yard outs, and Aikman delivered. As a senior he won the Davey O'Brien Award as the nation's top quarterback, a first for UCLA. "His talent was otherworldly," says Jerry Rhome, an offensive assistant with the Cowboys. "Tom Landry, Gil Brandt, and I worked him out at UCLA, and it was the greatest workout I've ever seen. He was as smooth as glass, and as strong as a bear. It was just, 'Wow!'"

Chapter 6

WOULD THE MOTHER WHO LEFT HER 11 KIDS AT TEXAS STADIUM PLEASE COME AND GET THEM!

Grown men crying.

**—Jerry Fowler, Cowboys assistant equipment manager,
on his memory of the '89 season**

THE OPTIMISM WAS palpable.

The mood was euphoric.

The Dallas Cowboys were back.

Emphasize that—the Dallas Cowboys were BACK!

Back from 3–13. Back from a tumultuous offseason. Back from the hell of discarding Tom Landry.

Back.

For the first time in years, there was a genuine belief the Cowboys could compete in the National Football League. Their new coach brought with him an attitude; a swagger; a *need* for victory. Fourteen new players appeared on the roster. Bitter has-beens were shown the door. Aikman and Walsh arrived with stellar pedigrees. Herschel

Walker was one of the game's best runners. Dallas had gone 3–1 in the preseason, highlighting speed and power in one convincing display after another. "With each exhibition win we started to think we were pretty strong," says Walsh. "We'd defy expectations."

FOOTBALL IS REBORN IN BIG D! screamed the headline from Mike Rabun's United Press International story.

Pfft!

On September 10, 1989, the Cowboys trumpeted their rebirth by traveling to New Orleans and getting beaten. No, scratch that. Not beaten—stomped. Squashed. Humiliated in every sense of the word.

Saints 28. Cowboys 0.

"And," says Dave Campo, the Dallas assistant, "it should have been worse."

Much worse.

Before 66,977 fans, the Saints became the first of many teams to pummel Aikman, who threw for 180 yards while being sacked three times, intercepted twice, and pressured incessantly. "I taught Troy an important lesson," recalls Tom Rafferty, the Cowboys' veteran center. "When someone on your team yells, 'Look out!' you'd darn well better duck."

Just how horrific was Dallas? The Cowboys set a franchise record for fewest rushing yards in a game (20), and possessed the ball for less than fifteen total minutes. Trailing 7–0 early in the second quarter, Johnson blew his team's only real scoring opportunity by attempting a fake field goal on fourth-and-9 from New Orleans's 30-yard line. Holder Mike Saxon, who was supposed to pick up the ball and run for the yardage, was bottled up by the Saints' defenders. His 4-yard pass to kicker Roger Ruzek was both feeble and ugly. "It did not work," a humiliated Johnson said afterward. "Obviously."

When the game mercifully came to an end, a shell-shocked Johnson and his equally shell-shocked coaches retreated to the visitors' locker room and sat silently. Of the thirteen members of the staff, only four were holdovers from the Landry Era. Most of the others had come from the University of Miami, where ass-whuppings were administered, not received. "That might be when I first realized that I had been fooling myself during the preseason," says Johnson. "Truthfully, the teams I coached at Miami would have beaten my Cowboys." Inside the subdued quarters, Johnson snapped himself out of the malaise to remind his players that the season was a long one; that half the league's teams would lose their first game. But only the arrival of Jerry Jones lightened the mood. The new owner went locker to locker, shaking hands and offering reassurances. "We're building something special," he told defensive lineman Jim Jeffcoat. "It might take time, but it'll be worth the wait. Just be patient."

Here was a different side to the new Cowboys owner, who, after an awful introductory press conference, dug himself an even deeper hole by firing one holdover employee after another, then insisting that the team's vaunted cheerleaders dress more skimpily and behave more provocatively (following a near revolt by fourteen of the women, Jones backtracked). Beyond the blunders and buffoonery, however, was a disarming man who lavished first-class treatment upon his players. The Cowboys led the league in team-hosted shindigs, in golf outings, in lavish presents like golf clubs and expensive liquor. Jones placed suggestion boxes around Valley Ranch and rarely took criticism personally. "If you could get any of his detractors to spend five minutes with Jerry, he would have zero detractors," says Mike Fisher, who covered the team for the *Fort Worth Star-Telegram*. "Nobody talks about this stuff, but early on there was a Valley Ranch janitor who died while visiting Mexico. His family couldn't get his body back to the U.S., so Jerry contacted the Mexican government and worked it out. Who does that?

"Unfortunately," says Fisher, "back then generosity didn't guarantee wins."

Indeed.

The true bottoming-out for the Cowboys may have come in Week 3, when a capacity crowd of 63,200 fans packed Texas Stadium for the new regime's home debut. Traveling to Texas were the archrival

Washington Redskins, a once-mighty opponent which, like Dallas, was off to an 0–2 start (the Cowboys had fallen to Atlanta in Week 2). "Our rivalry is certainly as big as it ever was," Washington coach Joe Gibbs said before the game. "The only difference now is that we are both trying to get a win." In his ten years as a college head coach, Johnson had faced his fair share of humiliation. But nothing would *ever* compare with what came next.

To kick off the afternoon, Jones escorted actress Elizabeth Taylor to the center of the field and asked referee Pat Haggerty if the cinematic diva might call the coin toss. With a straight face, Haggerty announced, "Captains of Dallas meet the captains from Washington! Captains from Washington meet Liz Taylor and Jerry Jones!"

Dexter Manley, the Redskins' star lineman, glanced at the weathered thespian as if she were a piece of rotted ham. "I didn't want to shake their hands," he said later. "This is football, man, not Hollywood."

Jones's self-aggrandizing stunt infuriated Johnson. He watched with horror from the sideline, wondering aloud whether he was employed by a professional football team or a variety show. It was hardly the last time he would feel this way. Before long, the sideline would morph into a parade of celebrities and corporate bigwigs, ranging from Bill Cosby to Prince Bandar bin Sultan to Florida governor Lawton Chiles to country singer Charlie Pride to the Reverend Jesse Jackson.

If the coin toss was a comedy, the game was a horror film.

Washington 30, Dallas 7.

The Cowboys compiled a mere ten first downs and were outgained by 183 yards. Receiver Art Monk, a Redskin since 1980, pivoted toward a pack of reporters after the game and said dryly: "I was not covered four times out there today. That's pretty unbelievable in the NFL."

Aikman was terrible, but, once again, so was the offensive line, which allowed four sacks and unyielding pressure. Walsh was inserted to start the fourth quarter, and he too was pummeled. The team's only score came in the first quarter, when defensive end Jim Jeffcoat returned a fumble for a touchdown. "For the next three hours," wrote

David Casstevens in the *Morning News,* "Cowboys fans sat in unhappy, disapproving silence, like grandparents at a Sex Pistols concert." As spectators glumly filed out of the stadium, several found flyers beneath their windshield wipers that read: WOULD THE MOTHER WHO LEFT HER 11 KIDS AT TEXAS STADIUM PLEASE COME AND GET THEM!

There were two patterns the Cowboys fell into throughout the 1989 season, both as predictable as the city's 5 P.M. rush-hour gridlock:

A. Every Sunday, they would lose.
B. Every Monday there would be between five and twenty new faces auditioning for jobs.

With each defeat, Johnson and his staffers grew increasingly aware of the gaping talent holes tearing the season apart. The Cowboys were thin at nearly all positions. They lacked depth across the offensive line, speed in the secondary, and power at linebacker. Their receivers were slow and unathletic, their tight ends barely relevant. Hence, the team was on the lookout for anyone with a modicum of gridiron experience and an ounce of talent to fly to Valley Ranch for an audition.

"It was sick," says Dave Wannstedt, the defensive coordinator. "We'd sign a half-dozen players on a Monday, give them a playbook on Tuesday and have them play the following Sunday. You couldn't put in a junior high school playbook in three days, and we were asking these guys to execute an NFL offense and defense."

The Cowboys were last in the league in every measurable statistic, but first in *Who-the-hell-is-that-guys.* Among the men who suited up for Dallas in 1989 were immortals like:

★ Scott Ankrom, wide receiver, Tulsa. Ten games, no catches.
★ Onzy Elam, linebacker, Tennessee State. One game, no tackles.

★ Kevin Scott, running back, Stanford. Three games, two carries, -4 yards.

★ Curtis Stewart, running back, Auburn. Two games, zero carries.

"Everybody—absolutely everybody—was worried they were going to be cut," says Steve Henrickson, a linebacker who lasted one month. "It was uncomfortable, but I think Jimmy liked that. Even Troy Aikman seemed nervous. You just never knew when your time was up."

The most unusual sign-and-cut story of the season began on the Monday before the Redskins game, when the Cowboys agreed to terms with Kevin Lilly, an ornery defensive end who had recently been cut by San Francisco.

Upon arriving in Dallas, Lilly checked into his hotel. The following morning he walked to the parking lot and found the windows of his Nissan 300Z shattered and his T-top stolen. During his first practice, he learned to despise Johnson. "He was in Too Tall Jones's face, Tom Rafferty's face—yelling at these guys who were the epitome of pro ball," says Lilly. "He was running the show like a high school program."

Lilly signed his contract on a Tuesday.

Lilly practiced on Wednesday and Thursday.

Lilly posed for the *team picture* on Friday.

Lilly played against the Redskins on Sunday.

Lilly was released on Monday.

Despite auditioning every humanoid this side of David Whitehurst, John Oates, and Kitty Dukakis, the Cowboys failed to improve. They fell hard to the Giants in Week 4, losing both the game (by a 30–13 score) and Aikman, who suffered a broken index finger in his non-passing hand and would miss five weeks.

If Johnson had left camp believing his team might compete, he was now a realist. The Cowboys of Onzy Elam, Scott Ankrom, and an eclectic assortment of here-today-gone-tomorrow nobodies were not good enough for the NFL. They would win three games, perhaps four, and go down as the laughingstocks of an otherwise awesome NFC East.

So, the head coach decided—What the hell? Why not try something crazy?

In modern American history, few sports figures have possessed the mythological aura of young Herschel Walker. At Johnson County High School in Wrightsville, Georgia, in the late '70s, he was a 6-foot-1, 215-pound halfback with 4.2 speed and thighs the size of fire hydrants. While most boys were busy chasing girls, Walker spent his free time tying one end of a 15-foot steel cable to a mud-grip truck tire and the other end around his waist. He would proceed to run dozens of windsprints—20 yards, 40 yards, 60 yards. "He used to drag me over to the track on Sunday afternoon, our one day off, and we'd pull the tire until I couldn't pull it no more," said Milt Moorman, a boyhood friend. "But Herschel, he'd be pulling on it till it got slap dark."

There was nothing Walker couldn't do. He was a straight-A student who ranked first in a graduating class of 108. As a high school senior he rushed for 3,167 yards and 45 touchdowns. In track and field he won three individual events at the Class A state championships (the 100- and 220-meter dashes and the shot put) and anchored the mile relay team to victory. So enormous was young Herschel that his mother had to purchase extra swaths of fabric to make his three-piece suits fit. Walker's upper body, wrote *Sports Illustrated*'s Terry Todd, looked "rather like a dark brown, triangularly shaped nylon sack filled with just the right number of 16-pound shots."

After being recruited by more than a hundred colleges, Walker attended the University of Georgia, where his legend went national. In 1980 Walker set the NCAA freshman rushing record with 1,616 yards, leading the Bulldogs to an undefeated season and a national championship. "Herschel Walker!" wrote Jim Minter, editor of the *Atlanta Journal-Constitution*. "Thank God that magnificent young man is not cutting plywood in Johnson County. Thank God for [Chief Justice] Earl Warren."

Two years later Walker wrapped up his collegiate legacy, winning the Heisman Trophy as a junior and deciding—against the wishes of every football fan in the state of Georgia—to turn professional at age twenty. He joined the New Jersey Generals of the fledgling United States Football League, where a $1.5 million contract awaited. Walker spent three seasons as the league's dominant presence, rushing for 2,411 yards, a professional football record, in 1985. But it was here, in an oft-amateurish spring football venture that died after three years, that the first needles were thrust into the Walker balloon.

Yes, Herschel Walker was built like Lou Ferrigno, ran like The Flash, and put up huge numbers. But he wasn't really that, *ahem*, good.

"When it came to strength and power, Herschel was your man," says Mark Walen, a Cowboy defensive tackle. "But being a great athlete is about much more than strength and power. Herschel couldn't dribble a basketball. I mean, he literally couldn't bounce the ball twice in a row."

The USFL folded following its 1985 season, and Walker was assigned to the Cowboys, who had selected him on a whim in the fifth round of the most recent draft. He was immediately pitted against Tony Dorsett, the legendary tailback in his tenth season with the organization. Dorsett resented Walker from the get-go, especially when the Cowboys signed the newcomer to a five-year, $5 million deal. "You had two ball carriers," says Timmy Newsome, a longtime Dallas running back, "neither willing to block for the other." Dorsett, who had moaned about being underpaid for years, finally seemed justified in his complaint. Despite 10,832 career rushing yards and two Super Bowl appearances, he was making "only" $450,000. On the day after Walker's introductory press conference, Dorsett held his own to gripe about a lack of respect from the organization. "That's how pissed off Tony was," says Bob Ackles, the team's director of player personnel. "Tony's pride was bruised."

Though Walker played well for the Cowboys, gaining 3,142 rushing yards from 1986 through '88 and prompting Dorsett's trade to Denver in 1988, he never quite fit in. His long-term goal was not the Pro Football Hall of Fame, but becoming an FBI agent. His interests ranged from bobsledding to karate to ballet—Walker studied dance in college, and in 1988 performed with the Fort Worth Ballet's Maria Terezia Balogh.* Walker was strange. Quirky. A word search puzzle addict. "My problem is I have never let people get to know me," Walker said. "I have never said I was Superman. I don't brag. I just answer questions."

Todd Fowler, a Cowboys running back who played against Walker in the USFL and roomed with him for three training camps in Dallas, recalls a warm, soft-spoken man who "probably still has the first dollar bill he ever earned."

Says Fowler, "Herschel only ate one meal a day. At breakfast and lunch he'd drink juice and stuff. After we'd get out of meetings, he and I would go to Carl's Jr. He'd get a double burger and fries. That's all he'd eat the entire day. Plus, he only slept four hours per night. You'd get up to piss at two A.M. and Herschel would be in the living room reading his Bible or doing push-ups or sit-ups."

To Johnson, Walker was an overhyped enigma who, despite being just twenty-seven, was on the downside of his career. In the humiliating opening loss to the Saints, Johnson ran Walker a grand total of ten times for 13 yards. When the Pro Bowler complained aloud about the lack of opportunity, Johnson fired back to the press. "Last year Herschel rushed for over fifteen hundred yards," he said, "and Dallas won only three games." Though Walker's activity level increased the next few Sundays, neither side was happy.

"Truthfully, we weren't that excited about Herschel Walker," says Johnson. "I wanted a nifty back and he didn't have that."

---

* In April 2008 Walker revealed in his autobiography, *Breaking Free*, that he suffers from dissociative identity disorder, a multiple-personality disorder that caused Walker to live as an array of characters and lifestyles. Hence, his quirkiness wasn't mere quirkiness.

One morning during a meeting of offensive coaches at Valley Ranch, Johnson charged into the conference room and made an announcement. "I've got a solution for the problem!" he said.

"What problem?" asked Hubbard Alexander, the team's receivers coach.

"Our team," said Johnson. "We have to make a big trade, and I know who we're gonna put out there."

The coaches started throwing out names.

"Michael Irvin." Nope.

"Steve Walsh." Nope.

"Jim Jeffcoat." Nope.

"We're gonna put big ol' No. 34 on the board," said Johnson. "We're gonna trade Herschel Walker for picks and players, and we're gonna make a killing."

David Shula, the team's offensive coordinator, was aghast. "But Jimmy," he said, "he's the only thing we've got."

Johnson was unmoved. "Well," he said, "we're terrible with Herschel, we'll be terrible without Herschel."

Before long, Cleveland and Minnesota were battling one another for Walker's services. The first nibble came from Browns GM Ernie Accorsi, who called Johnson and offered a package of draft picks. "I told Jerry that we had a deal on the table, but let's see if we can do better," says Johnson. He telephoned Mike Lynn, the Vikings' GM, and informed him Walker was off the market—*almost.*

"We might have an interest," Lynn said, playing coy.

"You *might*?" Johnson snickered. "Well, here's the deal. We've got to respond to the offer we have by the end of the day. So if you're interested, you'll have to get back to us before then."

Within forty minutes, Lynn faxed Johnson a proposal. "It's good," Johnson said. "But you've gotta do better." When Lynn called back, he presented the Cowboys with a package that made Johnson's extremities go numb. In exchange for Walker, the Cowboys' third- and tenth-round draft picks in 1990, and their third-round draft pick in

1991, Minnesota would send Dallas its first- and second-round picks in 1990, '91, and '92, a third-round choice in 1992, and five players—running back Darrin Nelson, linebackers Jesse Solomon and David Howard, cornerback Issiac Holt, and defensive end Alex Stewart.

Bingo!

Before the trade was officially announced, Johnson approached Shula and said, "I've got good news and bad news."

"Well," said Shula, "what's the good news?"

"The good news," said Johnson, "is that we're gonna be awesome."

"What's the bad news?" Shula asked.

Johnson squealed like a sorority girl: "I just traded Herschel Walker to make us awesome!"

Shula immediately searched for the nearest ledge.

"Herschel was all we had," he says. "Everyone else was a bunch of nobodies."

Like Shula and the majority of Cowboy fans (who tied up the organization's phone lines for hours with blistering calls), the media was less than enamored. Wrote Mike Rabun of United Press International:

Let's go over this one more time to make sure we've got it right. He was the most gifted athlete in the franchise's 30-year history and other than Roger Staubach he was probably the most valuable. He was revered in the community, a popular link between the team and its fans during a time when most such links had already been severed. And yet the Dallas Cowboys paid Herschel Walker more than $1 million to pack his bags and leave town. They wanted him gone so bad they paid him to go away. And why on earth would they do that? The reason is cloaked in veils of fog and smoke—it is difficult to identify positively but enough teasing glimpses exist to cause the curious to seek the truth. Is Walker a Minnesota Viking simply because the Cowboys received so much for him they couldn't turn down the deal? It just doesn't wash.

Though Johnson (and, to a lesser extent, Jerry Jones) would eventually be hailed with pulling off the most lopsided trade in NFL history, 99 percent of the (dis)credit must go to Lynn, a nice man, a good dresser, and a lousy football executive. While the Cowboys viewed Walker as productive-yet-flawed, a wide-eyed Lynn envisioned the Herschel of Johnson County High barreling over hapless defenders. "Mike Lynn was a businessman, not a football guy," says Ackles. "He didn't talk to any of the Vikings' personnel guys before making the trade, he didn't consult [head coach] Jerry Burns. When those guys found out, they were livid."

Had he sought the input of Burns, Vikings personnel administrators Jerry Reichow and Frank Gilliam, or any of the team's players, Lynn would have been warned about selling the farm for a battered mule. "Herschel wasn't a thousand-yard guy," explains Lynn. "He was a fifteen-hundred-yard guy and he took magnificent care of himself. It just didn't work out."

Because of the uncommon complexity of the deal, media outlets initially reported that Dallas received five veterans and a couple of picks for Walker. In fact, each veteran player was assigned a draft value—Solomon a No. 1 in 1990; Howard a No. 1 in 1991; Nelson a No. 2 in 1991; Holt a No. 2 and 3 in 1992; Stewart a No. 2 in 1990. If any of the players were not on the Cowboys' roster as of February 1, 1990, Johnson and Co. would receive the assigned conditional picks. Lynn, being—*what's the kind way to say this?*—unwise, assumed Dallas would choose to hold on to the veterans. That fantasy vanished when Dallas immediately cut Stewart ("Looked like Tarzan, played like Jane," says Ackles). "They outsmarted themselves," says Johnson. "They sent us a bunch of guys they thought they could live without, thinking they were better than anything we had. Which they were. But it didn't matter."

Nelson greeted the deal apprehensively. Then he attended his first Dallas practice. "They ran a trap play," Nelson says, "and two offensive linemen trapped each other and fell over. After eight years in the league, I didn't need that." Nelson asked Johnson for a trade, and the coach barely flinched. "Fine," he said. "No problem."

Upon arriving at Valley Ranch, Howard and Solomon were pulled aside by an apologetic Jones. "I hate to say this," the owner said, "but your time here is probably short. So just sit down, play special teams, don't complain to the media, and we'll take care of you."

The two men nodded. What could they say?

Meanwhile, Walker was greeted in Minnesota with Beatles-like fervor. The Cowboys had paid him a $1.25 million "exit bonus" to accept the deal (as well as ten first-class airline tickets), and the Vikings threw in the free use of a house and a Mercedes-Benz. "Herschel," Burns said at the introductory press conference, "I want to welcome you to the Minnesota Vikings. I'd like to see [the football] going across that end zone about ten times a game."

Though the trade was difficult to analyze at the time, its impact was monumental. This wasn't Lou Brock for Ernie Broglio. This was Lou Brock, Ernie Banks, Ron Santo, and Billy Williams for Ernie Broglio. Over time Johnson, always eager to trade a high draft pick for a bushel of lower ones, turned the Vikings' package into nineteen players—including running back Emmitt Smith, cornerback Kevin Smith, safety Darren Woodson, cornerback Clayton Holmes, and defensive lineman Russell Maryland.

And what of Herschel Walker?

In his debut with the Vikings, Walker first touched the pigskin on a kickoff and returned the ball 51 yards. Minutes later, he took his initial handoff from quarterback Tommy Kramer and ran 47 yards upfield. "Not bad," a beaming Lynn said in the Metrodome press box. "Two plays, a hundred yards."

Walker produced the best rushing effort by a Viking in six years, compiling 148 yards on 18 carries in a 26–14 victory over the Packers.

Wrote Michael Wilbon of the *Washington Post:* "Maybe the Minnesota Vikings didn't give up enough for Herschel Walker. What a bargain."

The euphoria lasted for a week. Walker was the wrong back for the Vikings, whose offensive line relied on stunts and traps, not straight-ahead physicality. Minnesota finished the season 10–6 and lost its opening postseason game. Walker ended with 669 rushing yards in eleven games. A hot T-shirt in town read THE H-BOMB HAS LANDED ON MINNESOTA.

"When we brought him here, there went our Super Bowl hopes," said Vikings safety Joey Browner. "There went our future."

Months after the deal was completed, Jones and Lynn met in a conference room at the NFL owners meeting in New Orleans. Ackles had prepared a letter to NFL commissioner Paul Tagliabue stating that the Cowboys were going to release all the players acquired in the trade. A copy was presented to Lynn.

"Mike Lynn always had this nice suntan," said Ackles. "But when I gave that letter to him, the guy turned absolutely pale. He knew he had just made the biggest screwup in NFL history."

Frustrated, angry, and humiliated, Lynn told Jones to keep the damn picks and the players.

Then he flew back to Minnesota. Alone.

Even though The Trade (as the Walker deal came to be known throughout Texas) would eventually help the Cowboys win multiple Super Bowls, for Dallas players it was a Roberto Duran hook to the gut.

Au revoir, season.

With Walker, Dallas was terrible. Without Walker, Dallas was a joke. The team was already missing Aikman to a broken finger, and second-year receiver Michael Irvin would suffer a season-ending knee injury in the sixth game. In its first contest without Walker, Dallas actually ended the third quarter tied with San Francisco at 14 before allowing 17 unanswered points in a 31–14 defeat. Daryl Clack, the fill-in halfback, ran for 32 yards.

"We are making progress," Johnson said afterward. "I hate to lose, as anybody who spends any time around me knows, but I can see now that we are starting to become a football team."

An 0–6 football team. But a football team nonetheless.

The Cowboys dropped their next two games and traveled to Washington on November 5 as the NFL's only 0–8 operation.

By now, life at Valley Ranch was unbearable. Prior to the previous week's loss to the Phoenix Cardinals, Jones introduced former Cowboy Lee Roy Jordan into the Ring of Honor and was all but booed off the field. There were a season-high 2,461 no-shows, and one fan wore a sack over his head reading GEE, I MISS TOM LANDRY.

Ed Werder of the *Fort Worth Star-Telegram* summed up the bleakness with his mid-season report card, giving the quarterbacks a B, the running backs and offensive linemen Ds, and the wide receivers Fs. Wrote Werder: "The Dallas Cowboys, a team with stars on its helmets but few on the field, have spent the first half of the National Football League season losing games, fans and self-respect."

Entering the Redskin contest, there were few reasons for optimism. The Aikman-less, Walker-less, Irvin-less Cowboys were now dependent on Paul Palmer, the halfback they had recently acquired from Detroit for what amounted to three Pepsis and a jar of B&G Pickles. A former first-round pick by the Chiefs out of Temple University, Palmer possessed two professional claims to fame. First, he was a monumental bust. Second, while playing for Kansas City he once threatened to fumble intentionally.

Palmer, though, was the best the Cowboys had. And for one day, it was good enough. Dallas came out flat. The Redskins came out flatter. The Cowboys entered halftime leading 3–0, and Johnson stormed into the locker room and gave one of the most impassioned talks of his life. "We can pull this out!" he bellowed, beads of sweat trickling from his forehead. "This is something we need to do, and the opportunity is right there!" The Cowboys stormed back onto the field and, well, stunk. Walsh completed 10 of 30 passes for 142 yards. But the Redskins—14½-point favorites—were even worse. They scored only 3 points in the second half, and Johnson and Co. had its first win, 13–3. The star was Palmer, who—while wearing a wristband listing his team's plays—carried 18 times for 110 yards.

"The stress of losing those first eight games was building," says Walsh. "Nobody wants to be known as a chronic loser. We didn't want to win—we *needed* to win."

Afterward, Johnson spoke of more triumphs to come, and Jones distributed hugs as if they were Peeps on Easter Sunday. Safety Bill Bates went so far as to sneak behind his coach, place his hand in his (perfectly coiffed) hair, and muss it into a poodle cut. It was a great moment. A brilliant moment.

A fleeting moment.

The 1989 Cowboys never won again. Not once. Palmer's magic vanished, the defense was porous, and Aikman returned to take a hellish beating. He started the following Sunday against the Cardinals, threw for an NFL rookie record 379 yards, and was knocked cold for nearly five minutes before being helped off the field. "Troy earned all of our respect," says Garry Cobb, the Dallas linebacker. "He got killed and refused to cry. I've been on the field when quarterbacks cry, and it ain't pretty. Dan Marino was a crier—*'Whose man was that! Where's the blocking! Whah!'* But Aikman—never. Aikman was a man."

"Troy gave all the linemen boots as a present at the end of the season," adds offensive tackle Dave Widell. "With the job we did, we all should have given them back."

As the glow from victory number one faded, the Cowboys returned to their ornery, agitated ways. Johnson was spending seventeen-hour days in his office, suffocating beneath the dual weights of humiliation and strife. By now nearly all of the veterans had had it with their coach's collegiate stylings. The players had assigned seats on flights and were required to wear suits and ties for all travel. "He even made us take the bus together to the stadium," says Folsom, the tight end. "It seemed weird, walking onto the bus and seeing Ed Jones and Tom Rafferty sitting there like little kids going off to elementary school."

The two weeks following the Washington win evoked new lows in player-coach relations. There was a shouting match between Johnson and Everson Walls, when the coach spotted his veteran cornerback laughing it up with opposing players immediately after the Cardinals loss. There was a nightmarish practice the day before the Thanksgiving matchup with the Eagles, when Johnson had his team hitting in full pads beneath a frigid rainstorm. Says center Mark Stepnoski: "I was sitting there thinking, There's a lot I don't know about pro football. But I know this is fuckin' stupid. Right now Philly is on a plane—they're on a nice, warm, dry plane and they're taking the whole day off except for meetings. And we're sitting out here in freezing-cold rain hitting in full pads. You know what? We're gonna get our asses kicked." The Eagles not only won, 27–0, but left the Cowboys looking foolish. In his postgame press conference, a red-faced Johnson insisted that Philadelphia coach Buddy Ryan had placed a bounty on the heads of Aikman and kicker Luis Zendejas.

Was the charge correct? Sort of. Ryan had indeed offered money to any Eagle able to knock out either of the two Cowboys. But it was little more than a cheesy motivational tool—hardly different from Johnson's having his players soak in the cold rain for two hours. In the end, Johnson appeared whiny and unprofessional. Two weeks later, as the Cowboys exited Veterans Stadium after another loss to the Eagles, he was pelted by an onslaught of snowballs and batteries. "If you're going to have snow in the stands," Ryan said with a dismissive shrug, "they'll throw snowballs."

It was that kind of year.

In the final contest of the regular season, Johnson's Cowboys fell to the Packers, 20–10, for their fifteenth loss. Wrote Randy Galloway of the *Dallas Morning News:* "Sunday's futile finish for the Cowboys was an appropriate ending to a season that set back a 30-year-old franchise 30 years." Some fifteen hundred miles away, Tom Landry, a guest of Giants owner Wellington Mara at the New York–Los Angeles Raiders game, was asked to assess his old team. "Well, I wouldn't start a rookie quarterback right off—you take a chance on ruining him," said Landry. "And I'd never have traded Herschel."

The contrast was remarkable.

In New York, Landry was relaxing comfortably in Mara's luxury suite.

In Dallas, the Texas Stadium toilets had frozen.

Chapter 7

WELCOME TO THE EMMITT ZONE

Emmitt was a football messiah, delivered to Dallas by the gods of the game.
—Dennis McKinnon, Cowboys wide receiver

As HIS CAREER progressed and Emmitt Smith went on to become one of the great running backs in the history of the National Football League, different people recall different things.

For opposing tacklers, it is Smith's crowbar stiff-arms and incomparable resiliency.

For coaches, it is Smith's churning legs that refused to stop, refused to slow down.

For marketers, it is his fluorescent smile.

For buddies, it is his obsession with dominoes.

For teammates, it is the outfit.

The world's ugliest outfit.

All these years later, the memory sticks like batter to a sizzling pan. Though Smith now owns a closet stuffed with some of the trendiest threads this side of Santo Versace, it makes little difference. The outfit *is* Emmitt Smith. Emmitt Smith *is* the outfit.

"I saw what he was wearing," recalls Richard Howell, Smith's agent at the time, "and I just thought, Emmitt, what in the world . . ."

Keep in mind, the year was 1990, when big, colorful *Cosby Show* sweaters were still en vogue and larger-than-life men like Rob Van Winkle (Vanilla Ice) and Stanley Burrell (MC Hammer) were sporting pants the size of jumbo tents.

But, really, what in God's name was Emmitt Smith thinking?

As he walked toward the podium in a Valley Ranch conference room, reporters and photographers looked at Smith and snickered. His bright purple shorts and matching vest were sprinkled with gold polka dots. His T-shirt was the hue of a box of Sun-Maid Golden Raisins. He wore black loafers on his feet, minus socks. A white Cowboys cap adorned his head.

The date was April 22, 1990, and this was Emmitt Smith's introductory NFL press conference.

"You don't walk up in no professional organization in no polka-dotted two-piece short set on," says Cowboys fullback Tommie Agee. "Everybody—absolutely everybody—gave him grief for that."

Eight hours earlier Smith had been sitting on a friend's couch in Pensacola Beach, Florida, anxiously watching the NFL Draft and waiting for his name to be called. In his three years at the University of Florida, Smith had set school records with 3,928 rushing yards and 36 touchdowns. He had exceeded 100 yards in twenty-five of thirty-four games, including a 224-yard effort against Alabama in his first collegiate start. Smith *knew* he was a Top 10 pick.

And yet, there were doubters. At 5-foot-9 and 200 pounds, Smith was significantly smaller than the prototypical NFL back. Of greater concern was the speed dilemma: Smith didn't have any. In college, he was often caught from behind by cornerbacks and (egad) linebackers. To ease the minds of NFL scouts, in the weeks before the draft Howell held an open workout for Smith at Florida. His client excelled in all areas—blocking, pass catching, strength. Then he ran the 40 in a pedestrian 4.59 seconds. "Emmitt is so competitive that he's arguing when they tell him the time," Howell recalls. "Not only did they argue back, they told him he rocked the start, which makes the time faster. As he's arguing I'm thinking, Emmitt, you have to stop this."

Smith did stop—and ran another disappointing 4.59. Still, in his mind the sluggish time made little difference. Smith kept a list of his professional goals on a piece of paper back home:

LEAD NFL IN RUSHING
NFL ROOKIE OF THE YEAR
HALL OF FAME
NFL'S ALL-TIME LEADING RUSHER
GREATEST RUNNING BACK EVER!!!

The list was equal parts admirable and wacko. To many of the men involved in collegiate scouting, Smith projected as a change-of-pace back who, after some seasoning, could *maybe* get fifteen carries a game. He certainly didn't compare with Penn State's all-everything Blair Thomas, the faster, stronger, more powerful tailback who would go No. 2 to the New York Jets.

As the draft dragged on, Smith's frustration mounted. "It was scary," says Howell. "We thought he'd go between ten and thirty, but it was a deep draft. I was told the Falcons had him rated the sixth- or seventh-best running back."

When North Carolina State's Ray Agnew was tabbed by New England with the tenth pick, Smith stormed out of his friend's house and stared down at the soothing waves of the Gulf of Mexico. He was one of the first junior eligible players to apply for the draft, and perhaps it was a mistake. The negative thoughts flowed through his head. *Maybe I should have stayed in school. Maybe I made the biggest blunder of my life.*

Approximately forty-five minutes later, Smith's mother, Mary, frantically screamed for her son to return inside. Bob Ackles, player personnel director for the Cowboys, was on the phone. He wanted to talk.

"Emmitt," Ackles said, "how would you like to be a Dallas Cowboy?"

With those ten words, a team's history was forever changed. As the years passed and Smith emerged as an all-time great, we were often told that Dallas traded up from the twenty-first pick to the seventeenth to take Smith, and that everyone was gaga for him from the beginning.

If it were only so simple.

Johnson approached the draft intent on finding the best available pass rusher. His first two cravings, USC linebacker Junior Seau and Miami defensive tackle Cortez Kennedy, were off the board before Dallas picked. So, for that matter, was James Francis, the Baylor linebacker. Johnson was so opposed to the idea of selecting an offensive player that changing his mind required Joe Brodsky, the team's crusty running backs coach, to stand atop the table in the team's Valley Ranch draft room and scream, "This is the guy, dammit! Emmitt Smith is the guy!" Brodsky had studied tapes of every game Smith had played in college and high school. He loved what he saw.

Johnson relented. "One of the best decisions I ever made," he says. "How important was Emmitt to turning the thing around? He was vital."

There was just one problem: Emmitt Smith wanted money. Lots of money.

Jerry Jones, on the other hand, was still aching from the abuse he took one year earlier, when he was crucified for paying Aikman $11 million—well above market value for a No. 1 pick. Though far from thin-skinned, Jones was sensitive to criticisms that he was an overmatched Arkansas hayseed. It hardly helped that, in the immediate aftermath of the draft, Jones raved to a local radio host that the Cowboys had Smith rated "fourth overall" on their draft list. "This is a bright spot," Jones said. "It's going to make Nate Newton block better, make Troy throw better, and make that defense a lot better, having this guy on our squad."

Rule No. 1 in potential contract talks: Keep your praise to a minimum.

It didn't take long to realize that Jones's draft-day euphoria would not carry over into negotiations. As the team reported to its new training camp at St. Edward's University in Austin, Smith returned to Pensacola and bunkered down for a lengthy process. Jones's initial presentation was a five-year deal for $3.2 million—less than what picks No. 15, 16, 18, and 19 signed for. When Howell dismissed the offer as insulting, Jones went on the offensive. "Howell told me right from the start that he's a litigator," he told the *Arkansas Democrat-Gazette.* "All he's doing is dragging something out that doesn't have to be that way."

If Jones wanted to play hardball, Smith would play hardball. With the University of Florida about to begin its fall semester, Smith drove to Gainesville and enrolled in classes. A theraputic recreation major, he had long ago promised his mother that he would earn a degree. So why not be proactive?

The tactic was brilliant. In Gainesville, Smith was strolling to and from classes, basking in the laid-back atmosphere, and even making local headlines for running down two thugs who vandalized a former teammate's Corvette (EMMITT'S IN MOTION: HE MAKES THE CATCH! raved the *St. Petersburg Times*). In Austin, meanwhile, the Cowboys' top running back was Timmy Smith, the former Redskin who, less than three years earlier, had rushed for 204 yards in Super Bowl XXII. Now fat and lazy, Timmy Smith was a disaster. Shula recalls one practice in which Smith was supposed to follow a pattern called "the Choice Route," where he would run six yards and cut either left or right. Instead Smith bolted twenty yards down the field and made two or three jukes. When Shula asked Smith if he was confused, the back replied, "Coach, you said it was a choice route. I *chose* to do something different."

By the first week of September the Cowboys were desperate. Not only was Timmy Smith heading the depth chart, but the team sent two draft picks to Houston for fullback Alonzo Highsmith, a former standout for Johnson at the University of Miami who, in the wake of two arthroscopic knee surgeries, was a shell of his collegiate self. Johnson praised Highsmith as "one of the outstanding talents in the NFL," hoping his words would reach Emmitt Smith's ears.

Perhaps they did.

On September 4, 1990, one day after the Highsmith trade and five days before the Cowboys' season opener against San Diego, Smith agreed on a four-year deal worth $650,000 annually. According to Howell, the final contract was a nod to Jones's ego as much as it was about money. "Jerry was concerned about the reaction from other owners," says Howell. "So we had a little outside deal for $50,000 per year that didn't go in the main contract, we had a signing bonus of $40,000 and a reporting bonus of $40,000 and all sorts of incentives which were also gimmes."

But the key, from Jones's vantage point, was that it at least *appeared* to others that Smith was locked up for four years and a reasonable amount of money. Hence, the provision for a fourth year at $495,000 that became void when Smith so much as stepped onto the field for one game at *any* point in his career.

"Jerry was able to report a four-year deal," says Howell, "and we were able to get Emmitt in uniform and ready to play. It was win-win."

When Smith finally joined the Cowboys, he discovered a team whose roster looked vastly different from the 1–15 laughingstock of a season earlier. Dallas had brought in a league-high sixteen Plan B free agents, including safety James Washington from the Los Angeles Rams, wide receiver Dennis McKinnon from the Chicago Bears, and fullback Tommie Agee from the Kansas City Chiefs. The team also added a lightly regarded tight end from the Phoenix Cardinals named Jay Novacek. "Professionals," says McKinnon. "We were professional football players who knew how to play the game right."

On the first day of camp, well before Smith had officially joined the team, Johnson called his players together and announced, "Our goal is to get to the Super Bowl . . ."

Long pause.

". . . this season."

Was he nuts? The Cowboys had won a single game the year before. Surely, the Super Bowl was out of reach. "Yeah, it was out of reach," says Washington, the new safety. "But I bought what he was saying. He wasn't telling us that we would win the Super Bowl. He was telling us that if we don't believe, we'll *never* win the Super Bowl."

Following a 1–3 exhibition run (if the staff learned one thing, it was to pay the preseason little mind), the Cowboys opened at home on September 9 against San Diego. With Emmitt Smith watching from the sidelines for all but a handful of plays, the Cowboys slogged through three and a half quarters of mediocrity. But everything changed seven minutes into the fourth, when San Diego, leading 14–10, faced a fourth-and-6 from the Dallas 48-yard line. Instead of kicking the ball away, Chargers coach Dan Henning called for a fake punt. The ball was snapped directly to linebacker Gary Plummer, who ran two yards before being tackled by Dallas safety Bill Bates. Aikman proceeded to march his team down the field, then dive into the end zone for the 17–14 triumph. The quarterback was swarmed by teammates, who hugged and high-fived their young leader.

The Cowboys were undefeated.

Afterward, a distraught Henning took exaggerated pulls from his Marlboro. You don't lose to the Dallas Cowboys. You just don't. "I told the players, 'I called it,'" said Henning. "'It was my dumb mistake.'"

A few hours after the win, Johnson and Shula agreed that Timmy Smith—who had gained 6 yards on 6 carries versus San Diego—would be released and replaced in the starting lineup by Emmitt Smith. The following Sunday, the new starter gained 11 yards on a half-dozen carries in a humiliating 28–7 loss to the Giants at Texas Stadium. *This* was the savior? "Emmitt just wasn't that impressive," says tight end Rob Awalt. "When you first see people, you're measuring speed, size, strength, explosiveness—all the things that make up that 'Wow!' factor. Emmitt didn't look like he had any 'Wow!'" Smith spent much of the afternoon sulking along the sidelines. When the game ended, he rushed toward the locker room, frustration etched across his face. "I roomed with Emmitt, and I told everyone that I was sharing a room with the man who would make Cowboy fans forget Tony Dorsett," says Crawford Ker, the offensive guard. "Emmitt just wanted a chance to play and show what he could do. Not getting it frustrated the hell out of him."

Smith was far from the unhappiest Cowboy.

Through the ups and downs of a tumultuous rookie year, Troy Aikman believed that, inevitably, he would wind up the Cowboys' starting quarterback. Granted, Johnson's loyalty to Steve Walsh was more than a tad disconcerting. But if one thing became clear during the mono-win season, it was that Aikman was a far superior player. Teammates saw it. Assistant coaches saw it. Even Jones saw it. Aikman was simply too big, too powerful, too talented. "Steve had a lot of knowledge," says Gerald Alphin, a veteran NFL receiver, "but he had an arm like a noodle."

Johnson remained unswayed. Against the powerful Giants in Week 2, Aikman had one of the better games of his young professional career, completing 10 of 18 passes for 109 yards. Four of his incompletions were drops. "In two years Aikman will be the best quarterback in the NFL," Giants linebacker Carl Banks predicted afterward. "He's strong, he's full of confidence, and he never gets rattled."

Maybe so. But when one of Aikman's fourth-quarter passes was tipped and returned for a touchdown by Lawrence Taylor, Johnson inserted Walsh. Afterward a furious Aikman stormed from the locker room, only briefly speaking with the media.

Though he continued to publicly support Aikman, in private Johnson had little good to say about a player who, he was quite certain, would spend his career lathered in mediocrity. Johnson went so far as to call Aikman "a loser" to a handful of reporters—a scathing label for a professional athlete. When the insult reached Aikman, he was crest-fallen. "Troy was stung by Jimmy's actions and words," says Awalt. "As a result, he wasn't able to trust him."

In his five years at Miami, Johnson's starting quarterbacks were Walsh, Bernie Kosar, and Vinny Testaverde—intelligent players who could improvise with the flow of a game. Aikman did not work in such a way. He needed a play called, he needed a primary target, and he needed to know that, after eight steps and a hard cut to the right, the receiver would be in the exact spot. When all went as planned, Aikman could be brilliant. When routes were blown or the line collapsed, Aik-man could be Turk Schonert.

"Jimmy wanted Troy and me to call our own plays to see how comfortable we were with the system and to let the coaches know what we liked and didn't like," says Walsh. "I thrived under it and Troy struggled. He said, 'Y'all just call the plays. I'll execute it—but I don't wanna think about what to call.' I was always the more cerebral quar-terback, and thrived in that system of picking plays and designing ideas."

Had the option been available, Johnson would have gladly traded Aikman and handed Walsh the keys to the Cowboys. But as the No. 1 pick of the new administration, Aikman was the handsome, rich face of the franchise. No. 8 AIKMAN jerseys filled Texas Stadium. No. 3 WALSH jerseys did not. Fans were already concerned that Jones and Johnson were out of their league. To deal Aikman would confirm it. "Jimmy just needed to leave Troy alone and get the fuck out of the way," says Mark Stepnoski, the team's center. "The more he messed with his mind, the worse it was for us. We all knew Troy had a bright future. Why didn't Jimmy?"

One week after the Giants loss, the dilemma was settled. Dallas sent Walsh to New Orleans for No. 1 and No. 3 picks in 1991 and a No. 2 in 1992. The trade allowed Johnson to save face—he could say, "We always knew Troy was our quarterback" and seem to mean it. But the truth remains: Johnson wanted Walsh to be his guy, and it simply didn't happen. Couldn't happen.

With his rival off to the Bayou, Aikman was at last *the* starting quarterback of the Dallas Cowboys.

Now all he had to do was win.

Watching the Cowboys of 1990 was akin to sitting through a sixteen-week *Days of Our Lives* marathon—*while drunk*. There were brief highs followed by indomitable lows. There were breakout performances followed by unpredictable setbacks. The team won its opener, then lost three straight. It pulled out a nail-biter over Tampa Bay in Week 5 and got crushed by the hapless Phoenix Cardinals the following Sunday.

Thanks to the play of veteran safeties James Washington and Ray Horton and the emergence of third-year linebacker Ken Norton, Jr., the defense was no longer a Tiffany's box for opposing offensive coordinators to unwrap and open. Through the first ten games of 1990, only two opponents exceeded 28 points. The Cowboys' defenders were faster, younger, and significantly more determined than in recent years. "I wanted to make sure every one of my teammates hit the other players so hard their skulls would fall from their bodies," says Washington. "That's the attitude I brought."

The offense was a different story. Despite the arrival of Emmitt Smith, the Cowboys could not score. At first, the blame fell on the inconsistent Aikman, who could dazzle one week, then throw three interceptions the next. Finally, fed-up members of the team went to Johnson with complaints about a coach who, according to dozens of players, was single-handedly responsible for Dallas's feebleness.

David Shula had to go.

"The man," says Ray Alexander, a Cowboy receiver, "was a true butt-head."

Put simply, Shula was not a viable NFL offensive coordinator. He was a nice guy who, at age thirty-one, was well suited to tutor Division I-AA tight ends or, better yet, sell insurance or manage a steak house.

But there was that thing; that . . . *name.*

Within the National Football League, the surname "Shula" evokes the same awe that accompanies "Kennedy" in American politics or "Pulitzer" in the media. Don Shula, after all, was not merely David's father, but a legendary figure who, over the course of a thirty-three-year career with the Baltimore Colts and Miami Dolphins, would win an unprecedented 347 games and appear in half a dozen Super Bowls.

As a boy David roamed practices as the unofficial ballboy and, come Sunday, charted games from the stands. What he liked most was running routes with Dolphin receivers Paul Warfield and Howard Twilley, then picking their brains on technique. Twilley taught him the subtleties of pattern running. "Howard was slow," Shula later said, "but he knew exactly how he did things."

The same went for the analytical Shula, who starred for four years as a wide receiver at Dartmouth before spending the 1981 season as a kick returner with the Baltimore Colts. The following year Shula was enrolled in the University of Baltimore Law School when Wally English, the Dolphins' receivers coach, left with two regular-season games remaining to accept the head coaching job at Tulane. Dad needed a fill-in. "I was going to return [to school] the second week in January," David said. "But then we got into the playoffs, and we won the first game, and we won the second game, and then we went to the Super Bowl. Then my father asked me to stay on for the next season."

Within six years, twenty-nine-year-old David Shula's title had become "assistant head coach." But with nepotism came ridicule. Around the league Shula was deemed a lightweight. "I never thought my last name hurt me," he says. "But the age thing was tough."

In the early months of 1989, Jimmy Johnson visited Don Shula, seeking permission to hire Dave Wannstedt as his defensive coordinator. Wannstedt was Johnson's longtime friend and assistant coach, and had only recently been hired by the Dolphins. Don Shula was willing to let him go—with a catch. If Johnson wanted Wannstedt, he would also have to take David Shula as offensive coordinator. It was high time the boy made it on his own.

"Everyone knew what the deal was," says Stepnoski. "Why else would we hire that guy?"

In Miami, David Shula had been blessed with the Pro Bowl talents of quarterback Dan Marino and his two fleet wide receivers, Mark Clayton and Mark Duper. In Dallas, he had two rookie quarterbacks, no legitimate halfback, and one wide receiver, Michael Irvin (who would suffer a season-ending knee injury after six games). In his first year on the job, Shula was hog-tied. He would have loved to air it out, à la Marino's majestic bombs, but felt constrained by mediocre talent.

Consequently, Shula's schemes were simplistic, relying on a minute number of low-risk formations and calls. The players, led by Aikman, hated them. "Nobody bought into what he was doing," says receiver Kelvin Edwards. "Because he was so young, he wanted everyone to know that his way was the only way. He was trying to present himself as 'The Man.' He was 'The Man,' all right. He was the man who caused us to lose so many games."

Was Shula the sole reason Dallas went 1–15 in 1989? No. But one year later his rigidity led to problems. The tension began during training camp, when Shula urged the team to consider cutting Irvin. At his best, the self-annointed "Playmaker" was an explosive performer who used his 6-foot-2, 205-pound frame and uncommon strength to outmuscle defensive backs. But from Shula's vantage point, Irvin was all hype, little substance. He was slow, obnoxious, unreliable, and hobbled by the knee injury.

According to several team officials, Johnson thought long and hard about following Shula's advice and ridding the Cowboys of Irvin. Yes, his love for and devotion to the receiver was powerful. But was Irvin a legitimate player anymore? Would he be able to separate from cornerbacks? Could he hold up? Could he . . . ?

In the end loyalty won out. Irvin was a Miami Hurricane. The offensive coordinator was not.

Truth be told, few actually believed Shula to be a bad guy. Fellow assistants liked his mild-mannered demeanor. But he officially lost any of the players' remaining respect in the days leading up to a Week 3 clash at Washington, when instead of devoting practice time to attacking the Redskin defense, he designed a plan he considered to be revolutionary.

"We were gonna surprise the Redskins by huddling up on the sideline, calling the play, and sprinting to the line of scrimmage and running the play," says Rob Awalt, the tight end. "First of all, you feel like a goober; like, 'This is how a bad high school coach might do things.' But then, to make it worse, we'd run a goddamned fullback dive. It's bad enough when your team stinks. But when your offensive coordinator can't get out of his own way, it's brutal."

Shula's greatest misjudgment was failing to recognize the weapon he possessed in Smith. In the Week 5 win over Tampa Bay, Smith gained 121 yards on 23 carries. The following Sunday, in the setback at Phoenix, he touched the ball 12 times. Smith rebounded with 16 carries in another win over the Bucs, but then averaged 11 handles in losses to the Eagles, Jets, and 49ers (in the aftermath of the San Francisco defeat Smith blasted the game plan as "useless"). Even Aikman, who loved throwing the ball 40 times, wondered aloud why the rookie back was being ignored.

Any hope of a Shula-Smith bond died in the aftermath of the Cardinals game, when Shula told the media that a missed block by the rookie had cost the Cowboys. Informed of Shula's comments, Smith addressed the media. "Lemme ask y'all this," he said. "How many carries did I have today?"

Twelve.

"And how many yards did I average?" Smith asked.

Four.

"Well," he said, choler mounting with each word, "if a man is averaging four yards a carry, maybe they should give him the ball more often."

Finally, after the Week 10 loss to San Francisco dropped the Cowboys to 3–7, Smith approached Joe Brodsky, the grizzled running backs coach, and pleaded his case. "I'm still hearing the same things I've heard all year: 'We need to gain a hundred yards on the ground,'" he said. "You told us that before we played San Francisco. Then you gave the running backs fifteen carries."

Brodsky agreed 100 percent. Shula was lame and unimaginative, and, if the season were to be salvaged, he had to change his ways. Brodsky insisted the undersized kid from Florida was ready for a greater load. At last, in Week 11, Shula listened.

In a breathtaking 24–21 triumph over the Rams in California, Shula let loose as Dallas exploited the league's twenty-sixth-ranked defense. Aikman put up his first 300-yard passing game of the season, and Smith generated 171 yards in total offense. Michael Irvin, finally healthy after a nightmarish year, caught a pair of touchdowns. During the game, many in the press box noticed a striking sight—Johnson and Aikman chatting. "Because of all the conversation going on [about Aikman's discontent], I thought it would be beneficial for me and Troy to talk," Johnson said. "We needed to stay on the same page. We probably should have been doing it before."

Maybe it was Aikman's anger. Maybe it was Shula's enlightenment. Maybe it was the recognition that, in Smith, the Cowboys had something special. Maybe it was Irvin's return to health. Maybe it was simply the natural progression of a young football team. Whatever the case, Dallas followed up the Rams victory with wins over Washington, New Orleans, and Phoenix. The NFL's laughingstocks were 7–7 and in the thick of the NFC playoff race.

For the first time in years, the Cowboys actually had a postseason picture to consider: Win at Philadelphia and Atlanta in the final two weeks of the season, and they were in. "Nobody," says Johnson, "would have ever believed it."

On December 18, two days after the team stomped Phoenix, 41–10, Johnson had dinner with Wannstedt and offensive line coach Tony Wise. Over burgers and beers at Bennigan's, he made a bold proclamation to two men who had been with Johnson since his days coaching at the University of Pittsburgh. "I told you at [Oklahoma

State] that we'd win a national championship together one day, and we did," he said. "Well, I'm telling you now that we'll win a Super Bowl."

Leading up to the December 23 matchup at Philadelphia, the city of Dallas was alive with optimism. The water-cooler conversations were all pigskin. GO COWBOYS! signs dangled from building windows. Dallas had played six home games in a row with attendances in excess of 60,000. It was almost as if Tony Dorsett and Roger Staubach were back in uniform, rejuvenating a city in dire need of a jolt. Finally, the public was embracing Jones and Johnson. Bring on the Eagles, dammit. Bring 'em on . . .

In Philadelphia, nobody was shaking. Having beaten the Cowboys six straight times, the Eagles walked with a can't-touch-this swagger. The Cowboys were up-and-coming, but Philadelphia—loaded with menacing defensive stars like Reggie White, Jerome Brown, and Andre Waters—had arrived. "Everybody in this league knows the road to toughness runs right through Philadelphia," said Eagles running back Keith Byars. "Everybody."

Just five snaps into the game, Philadelphia defensive end Clyde Simmons stormed past left tackle Mark Tuinei and drilled Aikman, wrapping him in a bear hug before driving him into the turf. Aikman's right shoulder popped from the socket. He was done for the year—the sixth quarterback knocked out of a game by the Eagles that season.

Onto the field jogged Brandon Hugh "Babe" Laufenberg, aka The Reason Perhaps Dallas Shouldn't Have Traded Steve Walsh. A former sixth-round draft pick out of Indiana University, Laufenberg had spent the last seven years bouncing from Washington to San Diego to Washington to New Orleans to Kansas City to Washington to San Diego and, finally, to Dallas.

What was he like as a quarterback?

"Babe was a great guy," says Fred McNair, a rookie quarterback who was cut by Dallas in training camp. "Wonderful personality."

In three-plus quarters of play, Laufenberg threw 36 passes, 13 of which were completed and 4 of which were intercepted. It was one of the ugliest displays in Cowboys history. Philadelphia won, 17–3.

Amazingly, a final-week victory over Atlanta would still give the 7–8 Cowboys a wild-card birth. With Aikman at the helm, the hot Cowboys surely would have beaten up on the 4–11 Falcons. With Aikman on the sideline in a sling, however, the game rested on Babe's shoulders.

Oy.

Having not thrown a pass for most of his two seasons with the Cowboys, Laufenberg's local claim to fame was a promo spot for his weekly radio program, during which he said, "Tune in to my show and find out why I should be the starter and Troy Aikman should be driving a bus." It was classic Laufenberg, who compensated for limited skills with a disarming sense of humor. Once, upon cutting Laufenberg, Redskins coach Joe Gibbs told him he wanted his sons to grow up to be just like the Babe. To which Laufenberg responded, "What, out of work?"

The Atlanta game was brutal. Coming off three days of rain, Atlanta–Fulton County Stadium's surface was a pig trough. Though teammates said all the right things, they knew victory was unlikely. "Babe," says Awalt, "wasn't really an NFL quarterback." In his pregame speech, Falcons coach Jerry Glanville told his players that the Cowboys had dozens of cases of champagne on ice waiting in their locker room. So what if it was untrue? "Those fuckers already think they have this thing won!" Glanville screamed. "What the fuck kind of bullshit is that? Are you gonna let them get away with that?"

Blitzed mercilessly, Laufenberg finished 10-of-24 passing for 129 yards, with 3 sacks and 2 interceptions. The Falcons won, 26–7.

In the locker room after the game, Johnson was in a foul mood. Though his team could still—if you believed in miracles—clinch a playoff berth with a Rams upset victory over New Orleans on Monday night, Johnson prided himself as a realist. "The Saints can get ready to play Chicago," he snapped in his postgame news conference. "It's over."

Indeed, it was. The following evening New Orleans beat Los Angeles 20–17, assuring Steve Walsh his first playoff appearance.

Before long, though, even the hypercompetitive Johnson was able to appreciate what the Cowboys had accomplished. A team that had won a single game one year ago was now a playoff contender. Smith ran for 937 yards and 11 touchdowns. Aikman threw for 2,579 yards. The defense ranked tenth in the league.

"When we started this season, I don't think anybody had it in their minds that we were headed for the playoffs," said Johnson, who became the first man with a losing record to be named the NFL's Coach of the Year. "Now when we go into next season, it's going to be the goal for every individual that not only are we going to be in the playoffs, we're going to be successful in them."

Chapter 8

MAKING A RUN
AT THIS THING

Michael Irvin's the only guy I know who can put a sweat
suit on, look at you, and say, "Don't I look good?"
—Alonzo Highsmith, Cowboys fullback

BY THE TIME members of the Dallas Cowboys began reporting to training camp in July 1991, it was as clear as Governor Ann Richards's white mane that this was Jimmy Johnson's football team—no ifs, ands, or buts.

Of the eighty-five players on the field at Austin's St. Edward's University, a mere thirteen had worked under Tom Landry. As opening day crept closer, it looked as if that number just might drop to twelve.

Whither, Michael Irvin?

At this point in his NFL coaching career, Johnson no longer exercised blind loyalty toward his former University of Miami pupils. In private, he willingly admitted that such biased leanings had been a mistake; that bringing in overmatched ex-Hurricanes like Daniel Stubbs and Randy Shannon had damaged the team and his credibility. The greatest harm had been done the previous September, when Johnson sent second- and fifth-round draft picks to the Houston Oilers for fullback Alonzo Highsmith. Cowboy players watched in disbelief as Highsmith, a once-mighty Miami star now lacking the speed and power of his younger incarnation, started in front of Daryl "Moose" Johnston, the fullback with battering-ram shoulders and an Amtrak motor. "That was an absolute shame," says Rob Awalt, the Cowboy tight end. "Alonzo was running one-legged. Clearly Jimmy was playing him out of loyalty, not merit. It was a joke."

By the start of 1991, Johnson had come to his senses. Many of the Miami imports were gone, replaced by bigger, stronger, faster, *better* alternatives. Shockingly, it looked like the next to be set free was going to be Irvin.

When he was selected by Dallas with the eleventh pick in the 1988 NFL Draft, many personnel experts considered it another example of Tom Landry's Cowboys losing their way. Sure, Irvin had been a productive player at Miami. But (like Emmitt Smith two years later) Irvin was slow. There was also the issue of attitude. With rare exception, the NFL of the 1980s was a recluse's paradise: Shut up, put on your helmet, play hard, go home—no mess, no fuss, no pizzazz. That was not Irvin. On his first day as a freshman at the University of Miami in 1984, he was standing in a cafeteria line when a senior offensive lineman named Mike Moore cut in front of him. Instead of humbly accepting the slight as most freshmen would have, Irvin popped Moore in the head. "It was shocking," says Highsmith. "Mike didn't take no crap."

Irvin was the by-product of an upbringing that called for quick lips, creative thinking and—more than anything—hardheadedness. The third youngest of Walter and Pearl Irvin's seventeen children (Pearl had six from her first marriage, Walter had two from a previous relationship, and the remaining nine they had together), Michael was deemed "special" well before entering the world. While attending Primitive Baptist Church in Fort Lauderdale, Florida, one Sunday morning in early 1966, Pearl felt someone reach out and grab her pregnant belly. Suddenly, a jolt shot through her womb. "My whole stomach went to jumping," Pearl later recalled. "Michael leaped for joy in my stomach." Pearl looked around but failed to spot anyone. It was, she swore, a sign. "I said, 'This child is going to be blessed among all of my children.'"

From the time he arrived on March 5, 1966, Michael was treated royally. He was uncommonly strong and eternally hungry. He would eat cornflakes out of mixing bowls, and if money was tight, use water instead of milk. When the refrigerator housed neither peanut butter nor jelly nor cheese, he gladly made sandwiches of bread and ketchup or bread and mayonnaise.

Growing up in a modest three-bedroom brick house on 27th Avenue in Fort Lauderdale, Michael was poorer than poor—the Irvins were a food stamps–and–Salvation Army type of family. In elementary school he would wear black hightops purchased at the neighborhood thrift store. When his son outgrew the shoes, Walter cut the tops off and Michael would walk around with exposed toes (classmates would mockingly call them "cat heads"). "I don't know if Michael ever realized how poor we really were," says Rene, one of his sisters. "When you're in the middle of it, you just go along and live your life the best you can."

In one room of the family home slept Walter and Pearl; in another, the ten sisters; in another, Michael and his six brothers. Michael didn't have his own bed until college. "I'm gonna buy you a house one day," Irvin would tell his mother. "A big, big house. I guarantee it." Had any one of the sixteen others made such a boast, Pearl would have laughed them off. Michael, she believed.

Though Irvin was a mama's boy, he took after his father in looks, flamboyance, and determination. From Monday through Saturday Walter woke up at 4:30 A.M. and departed for some unknown destination to work as a roofer. He would be caked in mud and tar when he returned home after dark. Though exhausted, Walter made certain to play with his children before dragging his body into bed. He was an eleventh-grade dropout who spent his weekends as a Baptist preacher and insisted all his offspring attend college. "You have to understand where I came from," Irvin says. "I watched my father break his back to feed all his kids. He worked from sunup to sundown."

As a young teenager Irvin spent his summer days alongside his father. Both had large hands and powerful shoulders. Michael, though, possessed an ungodly athleticism his father lacked. At Piper High School, he starred in basketball, track, and football. He ran faster, threw farther, and lifted more than any other student. Willie Irvin, his older brother, forced Michael to run five miles per day in exchange for a daily trip to Burger King. "We saw that he was special," Willie says. "I didn't want him to waste it."

Not that Michael was a saint. During his sophomore year at Piper, he was suspended for punching a female student during a dispute. Already dissatisfied with Piper's athletic and academic opportunities, Walter tranferred his son to St. Thomas Aquinas, a private Catholic school known as the alma mater of tennis star Chris Evert. It was a seminal decision—Michael emerged as the best wide receiver in the state (he caught 59 passes for 987 yards and 12 touchdowns as a senior in 1983–84), as well as a student who grasped concepts with newfound aplomb. "I realized there were people willing to help me," Irvin said. "I was around kids who had plans. I said, 'Man, this is what I've been missing.'"

During Irvin's first year at St. Thomas, his father was diagnosed with cancer. Having grown up in a household fortified by the idea that hope and faith conquer all, the Irvin children believed—no, *knew*—Walter would overcome. He didn't. "Toward the end I'd take my father to the doctor for visits," Irvin said. "He talked about being your own man, having passion and fire for what you believe. He said being a man is having responsibilities, being a man is taking care of your family.

"One time I heard him say, 'I don't know if I can take this anymore.' That was the biggest blow to me, hearing him say that. It's like he was quitting." On a fall afternoon during his senior year, Michael arrived home to find the sidewalk in front of his house lined with automobiles. When he walked inside, Pearl hugged her child tightly. Just hours earlier Walter had told his son, "Michael, I'm going home on the morning train." Now Walter Irvin's train had left the station. He was dead at age fifty-three. Michael fled the house and ran five miles to the

St. Thomas Aquinas campus, where he cried in a priest's arms. Then he returned to his family and renewed the promise he had made long ago. "I will take care of you," he told his mother. "You won't have to worry."

Though he was recruited strenuously by Syracuse, Louisiana State, and Michigan State, Irvin chose to attend the University of Miami and stay near his family. After redshirting his freshman season, he pieced together the best three-year run in school history, setting career receiving records for catches (143), yards (2,423), and touchdowns (26). To many, what stood out most was his brashness. Irvin accented big plays with spikes and dances and taunts. In his final regular-season collegiate game, a 20–16 win over South Carolina, he caught a 46-yard touchdown pass from Steve Walsh and spent the final 15 yards brandishing the ball in front of the defender. "Mike's enthusiasm and flash was very real," says Walsh. "It wasn't an act or done for show. It's exactly who he was—a guy who loved playing football."

On the day of the 1988 draft, shortly after NFL commissioner Pete Roselle announced that the Cowboys had selected "*Marcia* Irvin," Irvin looked into the TV cameras and said, "Go tell [Cowboys quarterback] Danny White I'm going to put him in the Pro Bowl!" Upon entering Valley Ranch for the first time, Irvin spotted a life-sized cardboard cutout of Landry—arms folded, fedora tilted to shade his eyes. Without flinching, Irvin draped his arm around the cardboard coach and loudly excalimed, "He's my new daddy!"

Dallas players and officials used to the hangdog status of the franchise were immediately taken aback. Who did this kid think he was? How dare he speak in such a boatsful manner. Yet the Michael Irvin who took the field was (if possible) even brasher than the one who barked his way through press conferences and interview sessions.

In one of his first training camp scrimmages, Irvin wrestled with a veteran San Diego defensive back named Elvis Patterson and nearly tossed the Charger over a fence—old-school, don't-fuck-with-a-'Cane style. In his first preseason game as a professional, Irvin burst past Raiders cornerback Terry McDaniel while shouting, "Gotcha, bitch!"

Shortly thereafter he was lined up against Mike Haynes, the future Hall of Famer. "I'm in awe," recalls Irvin, "so I decide I've gotta smack him across the helmet real hard, just to establish myself." SMACK! Haynes's head snapped back. "Rookie," he screamed, "do that again and I will fuckin' kill you." Irvin was unmoved. He was bold, loud, and obnoxious. Wrote Bernie Miklasz in the *Sporting News*: "He arrived with a diamond earring, a gold rope chain, indefatigable vocal cords, great hands and the kind of charisma the comatose Cowboys had been missing for years."

But Irvin didn't back it up. As a rookie he caught a pedestrian 32 passes for 654 yards and 5 touchdowns. "When Michael first came to the league he dropped a ton of passes," says Kelvin Edwards, a Dallas receiver from 1987 to '89. "I wasn't impressed."

Though his sophomore season, now under Johnson, began with great promise (Irvin caught 26 passes through his first six games), the good times came to a halt on October 15, 1989, when he tore the anterior cruciate ligament in his right knee in a loss to the 49ers at Texas Stadium. While the injury clichés of "He's a fighter" and "If anyone can beat this, it's Michael" were immediately invoked, Johnson wasn't so sure. Why, back in 1988 Johnson had been dumbfounded when the Cowboys took Irvin in the first round. To visiting scouts, he would halfheartedly brag of a "big horse who makes plays and loves to win." Translation: Irvin was slow and in need of work.

Now, with a bum knee, Johnson knew Irvin would be even *slower*. Wasn't the name of the NFL speed? Weren't the new Cowboys being built on burst? "Even I was scared," said Irvin. "For the first time in my life I wasn't sure of my knee, I wasn't sure of my ability, I wasn't sure I could do the things I used to do." When Irvin finally came back for the fifth game of the 1990 season, he was apprehensive and inconsistent. Raiders owner Al Davis called with a trade offer, and Jones and Johnson listened. There were better options out there—collegiate speedsters waiting to be plucked . . . free agents . . . anyone.

Johnson resisted, and Irvin's twelve-game totals (20 catches, 413 yards, 5 touchdowns) dazzled nobody.

Michael Irvin? Who needed Michael Irvin?

Fortunately for the long-term success of the Cowboys, the answer to that question came in one four-letter word: Norv.

Not that people were jumping for joy on February 1, 1991, when the Cowboys announced that thirty-eight-year-old Norval "Norv" Turner would be taking over as the team's offensive coordinator. A former quarterback at the University of Oregon who had never played in the NFL, Turner's name elicited all the excitement of a T.J. Maxx clearance rack. Turner had spent more than half a decade as an assistant with the Los Angeles Rams, which meant he was a key decision-maker for a franchise that had gone 32–31 over the last four seasons. *Whoopee!*

If anything, Turner's arrival was greeted skeptically. Yes, David Shula was a bland thinker who for the good of the franchise had to be minimized (he was demoted to receivers coach and resigned three weeks later to take a similar position with the Cincinnati Bengals). But why rip one man's lack of hands-on experience and find a substitute with even less?

What Irvin, Troy Aikman, Emmitt Smith, and the rest of Dallas's offensive players quickly learned, however, was that in Turner, the Cowboys had unearthed a visionary. Unlike Johnson, who too often measured worth in 40-yard dashes and 350-pound bench presses, Turner viewed the football field as a chessboard. How can I best attack your defense, and what are the pieces I need to do so? If I send two receivers and a tight end *here*, what are you going to do *there*? His entire system was based on speed—not foot speed, but the amount of time it took for a play to unfold. Quick quarterback drops, five-step slants, throwing to spots—that was Turner's modus operandi. "It was obvious as soon as he got there that Norv was already the best offensive coach in the league," says Lorenzo Graham, a Dallas running back. "I had never seen a coach like him. He only had about six basic plays he'd run, but he always called them at the perfect time."

In Turner's early days, the media focused on his fantastic relationship with Aikman, a welcome departure from the strained Shula partnership. But what really set him apart—and Dallas on a new course—was his instant appreciation of Irvin. Where Johnson and Shula saw slow, Turner saw precise. Where Johnson and Shula saw injury-prone, Turner saw untapped potential. "Norv loved the way Mike used his body to catch the ball," says Tim Daniel, a Cowboys receiver. "His body was the shield between the pigskin and defensive backs." Turner was blown away by Irvin's belief that he would, without fail, catch every ball thrown his way. "Other guys have better numbers and skill, and people in the league like to evaluate a player on numbers," said Turner. "But Michael believes he is a great football player, so that's what he makes himself."

Trade Michael Irvin? Hell no. Turner was determined to make him a star.

The optimism over Turner's fresh approach manifested itself on September 1, when the Cowboys traveled to hostile Cleveland Stadium for opening day and were—for one of the rare times in Johnson's three seasons—*expected* to win.

Dallas, in the words of *Morning News* writer Rick Gosselin, "ran and passed the ball at will, silencing the Browns and leaving their notorious Dawg Pound (and first-year coach Bill Belichick) in a whimper." Smith was elated, rushing for 112 yards on a career-high 32 carries. Aikman was thrilled, throwing for 274 yards and 2 touchdowns. And Irvin . . . well, Irvin was euphoric, exceeding 100 receiving yards for just the third time in his career. The Cowboys won 26–14, totaling more yards (395) and first downs (25) against the Browns than in any game the previous two seasons. "That was the one game where I remember all of us saying, 'You know what? We're gonna make a run at this thing,'" says Dave Wannstedt, the defensive coordinator. "Cleveland had a good team, and we beat them up on their home field."

The triumph was as much an ode to Johnson's roster construction as it was to Turner's game planning. The Cowboys were loaded with fast, hungry, intense, hard-hitting youngsters anxious to make their marks. Though Jones and Johnson were ridiculed when they drafted Aikman *and* Walsh, traded Walker, and drafted collegiate nobodies from schools like Emporia State (defensive tackle Leon Lett), Texas–El Paso (defensive end Tony Tolbert), and Central (Ohio) State (offensive tackle Erik Williams), rivals no longer found humor in a franchise ready to tear apart the league.

In his first three years, Johnson accumulated a whopping thirty-eight draft picks, then used them masterfully. From the '89 draft, Aikman, Johnston, Stepnoski, and Tolbert emerged as franchise cornerstones. A year later Dallas uncovered Smith, receiver Alexander "Ace" Wright, defensive tackle Jimmie Jones, and defensive back Kenny Gant. The Cowboys traded up with New England for the top pick in 1991, hoping to land Notre Dame receiver/kick returner Raghib "Rocket" Ismail. When Ismail demanded a five-year, $15.5 million deal (and threatened to jump to the Toronto Argonauts of the Canadian Football League), the Cowboys were again mocked in league offices. Dallas "settled" for defensive tackle Russell Maryland of Miami—then landed six more draftees who would become key additions, including Alvin Harper in the first round and little-known defensive back Larry Brown of Texas Christian in the twelfth. "We had a very good system," says Bob Ackles, the team's director of player personnel from 1986 to '91. "Sure, we had excellent scouts. But our success was all about Jimmy. If he thought the guy who cut the grass could give him information on a player, he'd listen. He absorbed scouting information amazingly fast. A scout would be talking about this one player and Jimmy would just shout, 'Next!' Then, 'Next!' Then 'Next!' again. He knew exactly what he was looking for, and if a player had one deficiency—no matter how small—Jimmy would lose interest. He wanted the perfect fit."

Two days after the win over Cleveland, the Cowboys gathered at Valley Ranch to begin preparing for a Monday night home clash with the Redskins. Having just thrashed Detroit 45–0, the Redskins were the NFL's top team. Their offensive and defensive lines were bigger and stronger than the Cowboys', their wide receivers were faster and more established than Irvin, Harper, and Wright, their coach—Joe Gibbs—was a legend. Mismatch alert! warned the *Washington Times*.

But what the media failed to grasp was the newfound confidence and optimism that had permeated Dallas.

If the Cleveland victory shouted, 'We're coming!' the performance against Washington screamed, "We're here!" In front of 63,025 fans, the Cowboys put together touchdown drives of 80, 80, and 84 yards in their first three possessions, building a 21–10 lead with 5:44 remaining in the half. It was pure domination of a defense unaccustomed to such treatment, and the success of the offense was 100 percent Norv Turner—run, run, run, short pass, slant, run. *BAM,* Smith burst through the line for a dashing, twirling, spinning 75-yard touchdown run; Aikman completed 13 of his first 17 passes; the Dallas linemen talked nonstop trash to an exhausted Redskins defensive line.

It didn't last.

Dallas entered halftime with a 21–20 lead, as the two teams combined for 22 first downs and 441 yards. They swapped long field goals in the third quarter, but the Redskins took over early in the fourth, when Gerald Riggs's 1-yard touchdown scamper gave his club a 30–24 advantage. Washington upped the lead to 33–24, providing the needed cushion to absorb a last-second 6-yard touchdown pass from Aikman to Irvin. At the end of the day, the Redskins had simply worn their opponent down.

Following the game, the Dallas locker room was silent. "I'm disappointed," said Johnson. "But as disappointed as we are, everybody is encouraged with what we can do. I think we will win a lot of games."

Though the Cowboys lost to the Eagles 24–0 the ensuing Sunday, they captured five of their next eight games, including an emotional 21–16 victory over the Giants in Week 5 that Aikman called "the biggest win since I've been here." Through eleven games, Aikman was leading the league with a 65.3 completion rate, Smith needed 25 yards to crack 1,000, and Irvin's 56 catches for 874 yards topped the NFL. The Cowboy offense was an increasingly unsolvable puzzle for opposing defenses—focus on shutting down the passing game, Smith burns you; stuff the line to thwart the run, Aikman hits Irvin for one long completion after another; blitz Aikman with linebackers and safeties, and risk being picked apart with screens and slants. "We were lethal," says Irvin. "Absolutely lethal."

Defensive backs who once mocked Irvin's deficiencies were now overwhelmed by a quarterback-receiver combination that could not be stopped. In their first twenty games together, Aikman and Irvin combined for 10 touchdowns—more than Terry Bradshaw-Lynn Swann (8), Joe Montana-Jerry Rice (6), or Dan Marino-Mark Clayton (5). Away from the football field, the two Dallas players had as much in common as Kareem Abdul-Jabbar and Axl Rose. Aikman was quiet and contemplative, Irvin brash and scattered. Aikman embraced country music and cold beer, Irvin hip-hop and blunts. Aikman preferred the company of a close friend or two, Irvin surrounded himself with an ever-growing posse of childhood pals and hangers-on. Aikman kept his emotions in check, opting for a stiff upper lip over a good cry; Irvin never held back. Yet despite so many differences, the two shared a genuine affection for one another, based on a singular approach to the game. Though they were raised in completely different households in completely different parts of the country, Aikman and Irvin were taught from young ages that on the field winning—more than a good effort; more than sportsmanship; more than fun—was what truly mattered. The two men didn't merely want to win—they *had* to win. *Needed* to win. A Sunday ending in defeat was literally treated as a funeral. In the aftermath, neither man ate; neither man drank; neither man had much to say. "We're like Paula Abdul's song 'Opposites Attract,'" said Irvin, who posted a sign reading 8 + 88 = TOUCHDOWN above his locker. "But [Troy and I] get along so well because we both want it so bad."

On November 24, the 6–5 Cowboys traveled to Washington for a rematch against the Redskins.

Their season hung in the balance.

Over the previous two weeks, Johnson's team had lost a pair of heartbreakers to the Oilers and Giants that left their playoff hopes dangling from a tattered thread. So here were the Cowboys—down, battered (four starters were out with injuries), humbled (its defense was ranked twenty-fifth in the league), and forced to face the 11–0 Redskins. What had once appeared to be a year of promise was now a mounting disaster. The Cowboys trailed Detroit and were tied with the Giants, Philadelphia, and Atlanta for the two NFC wild-card spots.

Talk in Washington wasn't about defeating the Cowboys (who were 12½-point underdogs), but whether the Redskins would join the 1972 Miami Dolphins as football's only undefeated team. "How do you beat a gorilla?" Johnson preached to his players five days before the game. "You just can't hit him lightly. You've gotta hit him with all you've got."

For Dallas, the motivation was high.

The reality was bad.

With the Cowboys leading 14–7 early in the second half, Aikman dropped back to pass and was grabbed around the waist and slammed to the ground by Redskins defensive tackle Jumpy Geathers. Though the pain was not excruciating, the diagnosis—strained ligaments in his right knee—would sideline him for much of the rest of the year.

The last time Dallas had lost its starting quarterback, Babe Laufenberg entered the game and blew the season. The Cowboys had learned their lesson.

The new guy wearing No. 7 was no Babe.

As Steve Beuerlein began warming up along the Dallas sideline, he was not thinking about Troy Aikman's bum knee. He was not thinking about the Redskins' ferocious defensive line, or the fact that he had thrown but five passes in a year and a half. He was not even thinking about the rowdy fans leaning along the railing, screaming at the top of their lungs.

No, Steve Beuerlein was thinking about love.

Boy, did he *love* being here. The atmosphere. The intensity. The football spiraling out of his hand, crackling through the crisp D.C. air.

For too long, Steve Beuerlein had been a gridiron prisoner. Selected by the Los Angeles Raiders in the fourth round of the 1987 NFL Draft, the former Notre Dame star quickly learned that to survive with the silver and black, one had to kneel at the altar of team owner Al Davis.

Beuerlein was not one to kneel. Following a 1989 season during which he threw for 1,677 yards and 13 touchdowns in ten games, Beuerlein missed training camp in a contract holdout. When he returned for the 1990 regular-season opener, he was placed on the inactive list and kept there the entire year. It was Davis saying, "Don't fuck with the chief," and it was as blatant as a Big Mac at Le Bernardin. "I became Al Davis's whipping boy," says Beuerlein. "It was miserable. I'm in street clothes, watching my career slip away."

When the Cowboys acquired Beuerlein for a fourth-round draft choice on August 25, 1991, he had no expectations of wining the starting job. Beuerlein and Aikman first met when the former was with the Raiders and the latter at UCLA, and they quickly hit it off. Unlike Steve Walsh, Beuerlein knew his place. "Troy is the number-one quarterback," he said on his first day. "I'm aware of that, and I'm comfortable in that at least I know my role here."

Before jogging onto the field to replace Aikman against the Redskins, Beuerlein conferred with Turner, who insisted he relax and simply find the open receivers. On his third series, Beuerlein completed a pair of passes to Irvin, the second a 23-yard juggling, one-handed touchdown snare that gave Dallas a 21–7 lead early in the fourth quarter. "I just remember the feeling of euphoria on that touchdown," Beuerlein says. "From that point I was able to say, 'OK, let's have some fun.'"

With their new leader completing 7 of 12 passes for 109 yards and Smith rushing for 132 yards on 34 carries, the Cowboys shocked the Redskins, 24–21, spoiling their dreams of a perfect season. How big was this one? A day after the triumph Dick Armey, a Republican representative from Texas's 26th district, took time away from less important stuff like, say, governing to recite a poem on the House floor:

> *Oh, how the mighty have fallen*
> *Irvin and Smith left Redskins sprawlin'*
> *Roused from the undefeated dream*
> *By that oh-so-hated Dallas team!*
> *The 'Skins saw Johnson's bag of tricks*
> *Hail Mary passes, onside kicks!*
> *And wasn't it a sight to see,*
> *That heroic, second-string Q.B.?*
> *The loss took place at R.F.K.*
> *But evokes the words of J.F.K.*
> *Cowboy fans chant this one-liner,*
> *Say it loud: "Ich bin ein Beuerleiner!"*
> *Add to the rivalry one more game,*
> *Besides those of Landry-Allen fame.*
> *It's a tough loss, but don't be too sore,*
> *Wait 'til the playoffs, when we beat you once more.*

As the Cowboys surged behind Beuerlein, wrapping up the season with five straight victories (including a 25–13 spanking of the nemesis Eagles at Philadelphia to clinch a postseason berth), Johnson decided that, come playoff time, he would stick with what was working. This, despite a verbal promise that starters would not lose their jobs because of injury. This, despite the improved health of Aikman, who by Week 16 was ready to return. This, despite the anger of half the Cowboy roster.

Though Aikman was more reserved than Beuerlein, over the years he had developed a powerful bond with teammates—especially Irvin, fullback Daryl Johnston, tight end Jay Novacek, and the offensive linemen. At the end of each season, Aikman would purchase lavish gifts for everyone, ranging from plane tickets to ostrich boots to personal computers to golf clubs. "I was a backup receiver whom Troy didn't know from a man on the moon," says Cory Fleming, a Cowboys receiver in the mid-1990s. "But at Christmas he gave me a really nice pen with my name on it and a bottle of Dom Pérignon. That speaks volumes."

Each day after practice, Aikman and Beuerlein would return to their lockers and face a firing line of questions. "It was a constant source of discussion—me or Troy?" says Beuerlein. "It was on TV and in the papers and on the radio. People were saying, 'Is this a permanent thing? Is Steve the quarterback of the future?' It was insanity."

The Cowboys wrapped up their season with a 31–27 victory over Atlanta at Texas Stadium. Players thinking of loafing through the finale were rudely smacked in the head when, on the Friday before the game, Johnson held a full-pads practice in a heavy rainstorm. Screaming above the downpour, Johnson ripped his men. "If you guys have been reading the paper and don't think we're going to try and win this goddamned game, you're crazy!" he said. "That's what we're here for—to win games!"

It had been a memorable eleven-victory run. Smith led the NFL with 1,563 rushing yards. Irvin ranked first in receiving yards (1,523) and second in catches (93)—both team records. Three Cowboys (Smith, Irvin, and Novacek) were Pro Bowl starters. By season's end the starting lineup included three rookies on a roster that averaged 25.9 years of age.

With the completion of their 11–5 regular season, the Cowboys were scheduled to fly to Chicago to face the Bears for a December 29 first-round playoff game—the team's first postseason appearance in six years.

Coming off a 52–14 drubbing at the hands of the 49ers, the Bears were in an unusually angry mood. Chicago's players felt San Francisco had deliberately run up the score, and they were livid. "I'll live to avenge that game," said Bears quarterback Jim Harbaugh. "I plan to get revenge somehow."

Avenge? Revenge? The Cowboys were too giddy to care. Two days earlier Smith had donned a Santa Claus outfit and strolled through the locker room with a bag chock-full of expensive bottles of champagne—one for each man. "This present is to the team for the season," he said in between ho-ho-hos. "I'm spending my playoff money before I get it."

The Bears were angry and tight. The Cowboys were loose and laid-back.

It showed.

Dallas jumped out to an early 10–0 lead, then used its best defensive performance of the season to frustrate Harbaugh and his mediocre collection of weapons. Three times the Bears had the ball inside the Cowboys' 10-yard line, and only once did they score.

After Chicago cut the lead to 10–6 midway through the third quarter, the Cowboy offense awoke. Beuerlein and Co. pushed the Bears 75 yards in fourteen plays before scoring on a 3-yard touchdown pass to Novacek. With the defense playing its best game of the year, Chicago never truly threatened.

In a season of firsts, Johnson had his first playoff victory.

Cowboys 17.

Bears 13.

In his postgame speech, Johnson talked about steps: how beating the Bears was step one en route to a greater pursuit. Though the coach knew his team was at least a year away from being Super Bowl–worthy, he was a strong believer in the power of positive thought. Who knows? Maybe if the Cowboys played at a supreme level they could upend the Detroit Lions, their next opponent, and somehow sneak into the NFC Championship Game.

Or, maybe not.

At the precise moment the clock reached 0:00 at Chicago's Soldier Field, the majority of Dallas's players were satisfied. They had defied expectations by winning a play-off game, and they were worn out. Johnson could have that effect on his players—there came a point when the nonstop barking sounded less inspirational and more like Charlie

Brown's teacher: *Wah, wah, wah, wah, wah.* "Jimmy will kill me for saying this," says Craig Kupp, the third-string quarterback, "but during practice the week leading up to the Lions my sense was that it was good enough to beat the Bears, and anything else was just extra. We were content."

Complicating preparations for Detroit was Aikman's mounting resentment. By now he was 95 percent healthy and itching to play. He would arrive at practice each day hoping Johnson had changed his mind, and inevitably leave disappointed. "Troy was putting pressure on the team that wasn't really fair," says Larry Brown, the rookie defensive back. "He kept reminding Jimmy that he was ready, and Jimmy had made it clear Steve was the guy."

The distraction hardly helped the Cowboys' near-insurmountable task. Blessed with Barry Sanders, the NFL's best running back, it was seemingly logical to assume Detroit would run the ball thirty times. However, when the two teams had met in late October, Lions coach Wayne Fontes threw a wicked curveball, handing off to Sanders just twenty-one times in the Lions' decisive 34–10 rout. So what did the Dallas defense prepare for this time? Sanders left, Sanders middle, Sanders right. "I don't think we were better than Dallas," says Rodney Peete, the Lions' backup quarterback. "We just outsmarted them."

All signs pointed to a bad weekend when, upon its final descent into Detroit Metropolitan Airport, the Cowboys' charter flew directly into a hailstorm. As the plane rocked up and down and players vomited into paper bags, offensive lineman John Gesek thought, "This can't be good." The jet touched down, skidded to the side, and returned to the air. "Turns out we almost T-boned another plane," says Gesek. "Nearly dying the day before a game is never an encouraging sign."

Motivated by the paralysis suffered by teammate Mike Utley, an offensive guard who had injured his sixth and seventh cervical vertebrae in a November 17 game against the Rams, the Lions stormed the Pontiac Silverdome and overwhelmed their opponents. With seven, eight, and sometimes nine Cowboys stuffing the line in anticipation of a Sanders jaunt, Lions quarterback Erik Kramer completed 29 of 38 for

341 yards and 3 touchdowns. "That may be the only time," says tight end Rob Awalt, "that I saw Jimmy have the wool pulled over his eyes."

With the Cowboys trailing 14–3 in the second quarter, Johnson summoned Aikman from the bench. For Beuerlein, it was a slap in the face—*You remove me this early, after I've led you to six straight victories?* For Aikman, it was a slap in the face—*You put me in now, after I've been ignored for eons?*

It mattered little. The Lions were the smarter, better, more prepared team. They won, 38–6. "We were good," says Cowboys linebacker Vinson Smith, "but we weren't ready yet."

Afterward, Johnson gave what many consider to be the best postgame speech of his career. Before a downtrodden group of players and coaches, Johnson insisted there should be nothing but pride. "We have built the foundation of something that cannot be stopped," he said. "And will not be stopped. We went into Solider Field and beat the Bears. This is only the beginning. This moment—remember it. It is not an ending. It is not a defeat. It is another step on the road that leads inexorably to the Super Bowl and greatness as a football team. You are on that road."

Over the next fifty minutes, Johnson sealed two pacts. First, he pulled Aikman aside, embraced his quarterback with a long hug, and said, "This team is yours. Over and out. You are my guy."

Then, moments later, he met with his coaches. "Next year," Johnson said, "this shit doesn't happen. Next year—Super Bowl."

Chapter 9

THE LAST NAKED WARRIOR

You're from California? You must be a fucking faggot.

—Charles Haley, upon meeting a new teammate

IN THE AFTERMATH of the 1991 season, Cowboy coaches and executives congregated at Valley Ranch to assess the organization's greatest needs. In '91, Dallas defenders compiled 23 sacks, the lowest total in franchise history. Hence, topping the wish list was a disruptive, no-holds-barred defensive lineman—the type of player who put fear in the hearts of rival quarterbacks. Buffalo's Bruce Smith came to mind, as did Chris Doleman of the Vikings and Reggie White of the Eagles. But such players were the cornerstones of their respective franchises—factually unavailable.

There was, however, one man who could be had for the right price.

Dallas, meet Charles Haley.

And his exceptionally large penis.

Selected by San Francisco in the fourth round of the 1986 NFL Draft, Haley was a little-known pass rusher from Division I-AA James Madison University. Yet with 12 sacks as a rookie, the Gladys, Virginia, native quickly earned high praise as one of the league's dominant quarterback killers.

And as one of its most imbalanced.

The reputation started with the penis—a fire hose of an organ that brought Haley more pride than any game-winning tackle. As he grew comfortable in the 49ers locker room, Haley would stroll up to an unsuspecting teammate, whip out his phallus, and repeatedly stroke it in his face. Players initially laughed it off. But Haley refused to stop. He would jerk off in the locker room, in the trainer's room. He'd wrap his hand around his penis, turn toward a Joe Montana or John Taylor, and bellow, "You know you wanna suck this!" or "You only wish you had this, baby!"

"Charles used to beat off in meetings while talking graphically about players' wives," says Michael Silver, who covered the 49ers for the *Santa Rosa Press Democrat.* "It got to the point of ejaculation."

Haley was socially awkward and unflinchingly vicious. He'd been prescribed medication to treat manic depression, but would take the pills one day, then skip them the next two or three. Haley once exposed himself to reporter Ann Killion of the *San Jose Mercury News,* a pathetic attempt at gender intimidation. He rarely passed up the opportunity to verbally pounce on a teammate's shortcoming—an ugly child, a protruding mole, a lisp. "Charles was a great player," says Dexter Carter, the former 49er running back. "But there's only so much a man can tolerate." Once he got going, the words flew from Haley's mouth as if they were shot from a Browning .50-caliber machine gun. Anyone effeminate was a "faggot." African-American players who became close with the coaching staff were "house niggers" and "Uncle Toms." Whites were "honkies" and Hispanics "spics." (A joke Haley told with particular brio: What do a Mexican and a hotel have in common? A mop.) Twice, his racial barbs resulted in fights with 49er teammate Jim Burt, a white defensive lineman who decked Haley both times.

Haley's supporters (and there are two or three) insist the talk was silly banter from an unstable man. His detractors, however, point to 1991, the sixth and final year of his initial tenure with San Francisco.

The beginning of the end for Haley the 49er came in the fifth week of the season, when his team traveled to the Los Angeles Coliseum and fell 12–6 to the Raiders, who were led by ex–San Francisco greats Ronnie Lott and Roger Craig. To Haley, both men were more than mere gridiron peers. They had been mentors, father figures, role models, heroes. Hence, the emotions ran deep. As he entered the locker room after the defeat, a dehydrated Haley was immediately connected to an IV. With tears streaming down his cheeks, Haley yanked the needle from his arm, punched a hole in the wall, took a swing at coach George Seifert, and began screaming at quarterback Steve Young, who had played poorly. "I could have fucking won that game in my sleep!" he yelled. "You're a motherfucking pussy faggot quarterback! A motherfucking pussy faggot with no balls!" As the blood gushed from his arm, Haley charged toward Young, arms flailing, legs kicking. With the media waiting outside the locker room for postgame access, a 49ers official burst through the door, down the hallway, and into the Raiders' clubhouse. Seconds later he returned with Lott, a towel wrapped around his waist. When Haley spotted his former teammate stepping into the 49ers locker room, he wept uncontrollably.

Haley apologized to Young, but the truce was short-lived. In the course of the season, Haley complained that the team needed to dump all its white linebackers and "replace 'em with a Soul Patrol." He regularly ripped Seifert—to teammates, to opponents, to anyone—and once tried to strangle him during a film session. Haley's biggest enemy was Tim Harris, the Pro Bowl pass rusher in his first year with the team. "We were," said Harris, "two roosters in a henhouse." Like Haley, Harris was fast, strong, and intimidating. Unlike Haley, Harris was a decent man who got along famously with the other 49ers. Haley's resentment toward his teammate festered throughout the season until, near year's end, he cut a hole in the roof of Harris's $50,000 BMW 733i convertible, stood on the top of the car, pulled down his pants, and urinated onto the steering wheel and floor. "There are some things you just don't do," says Carter. "And that tops the list."

Shortly after the incident, Haley entered a meeting and sat backward on his chair. Defensive line coach John Marshall instructed him to turn around and show some respect. "Fuck you!" Haley screamed.

"Charles," said Marshall, "turn your damn body around now. I mean it."

"No—fuck you!" yelped Haley. "I've gotta go to the bathroom anyhow. I've gotta go take a shit."

With that Haley—clad in a gray T-shirt and shorts—rose and left the room. When he returned he was holding a small piece of scrunched toilet paper in his right hand. Before the entire defense, Haley pulled down his shorts, wiped his rear end, and threw the soiled paper at Marshall.

Upon learning of the incident, Seifert marched into the office of John McVay, the team's general manager. "OK," he said, "I've had enough. Haley's gotta go."

Like everyone else in the NFL, the Cowboys had heard about Haley's antics, just as they had been well versed in the backgrounds of other "troubled" players they'd wound up signing. Before the 1990 season Dallas had jumped at the chance to sign former Rams safety James Washington, who admittedly hit teammates during practices with an intent to injure. "Yeah, I would smash Jim Everett when I wasn't supposed to," he says of the Rams' onetime signal caller. "But I thought the bitch was a punk." A year later the Cowboys traded for Tony Casillas, an Atlanta Falcon defensive lineman who infuriated coworkers by taking off three weeks of training camp for "occupational stress." There was also the time Casillas simply decided not to show up for Atlanta's charter flight to Los Angeles. "After thirty minutes someone finally called Tony's home," recalls teammate Scott Case. "Tony's wife answers and says, 'Yeah, well, Tony doesn't feel like playing this week.'" Both Washington and Casillas came to Dallas, behaved well, and played spectacularly.

Now, in debating the pros and cons of adding a pass-rushing Tasmanian Devil who occasionally urinated in luxury automobiles, Jones and Johnson could not get beyond one undeniable fact: Without Haley, the Cowboys' defense was solid. With him, the Cowboys' defense was potentially spectacular.

On August 26, twelve days before the opener of the 1992 season, Dallas sent two draft choices to San Francisco for Haley. Those covering the Cowboys were at a loss—why would a team surrender a twenty-eight-year-old three-time Pro Bowler for so little? Johnson played along. "We can't speak for the 49ers as to why he's available and we didn't really get deeply into that," Johnson said. "Nothing we heard from San Francisco was in any way a negative."

If the Cowboys were truly unconcerned by Haley's volatility, however, why did Jones take his limousine to Dallas–Fort Worth International Airport to pick up his new star personally?

"I guess the drive back was about forty minutes," Jones said. "In that span, we covered a lot of ground. This was my main question: 'Charles, I know you're in Dallas now, but are you leaving your heart in San Francisco?'"

Haley glared menacingly at Jones. A *what-sort-of-stupid-fucking-question-is-that?* look crossed his face.

End of conversation.

In contrast to the early portion of his career, when Haley largely kept to himself, as soon as he joined the Cowboys he felt comfortable. On his first day at Valley Ranch, Haley arrived in the conference room for a defensive film session dressed only in a towel. "The next thing you know, Charles is lying naked on the floor in front of the screen, entertaining himself," says Casillas. "Hand on his penis, back and forth."

When Butch Davis, the defensive line coach, saw what was transpiring, he stopped the tape. "Haley!" he yelled. "Get your fuckin' clothes on and don't come back in until you're dressed." The room erupted in laughter.

On his second day at Valley Ranch, Haley wrapped an Ace bandage around his penis and strolled through the locker room naked, screaming, "I'm the last naked warrior! I'm the last naked warrior!"

On his third day at Valley Ranch, Haley walked past a large hot tub in which offensive linemen Mark Stepnoski, Kevin Gogan, and John Gesek were sitting. "You know what the problem here is?" Haley yelled. "It's another example of the white man keeping the black man down. Look at the three of you, relaxing as . . ."

He went on. And on. And on.

At this moment, in the infancy of the Haley Era, Gesek unlocked the key to surviving life with Charles. Instead of bowing to the barbs, instead of slinking into a mound of bubbles or turning the other cheek, the 6-foot-5, 275-pound Gesek looked Haley in the eyes and said, "Who the hell are you?

"You and I are gonna have to fight," Gesek continued. "I mean, what right do you have to talk to us that way? What do you know about us? About this team? How 'bout being here for more than a week before you open your mouth?"

With that, Haley shuffled off.

"Charles liked to push buttons and test the waters," says Kenny Gant, a Dallas safety. "He would kiss you on the mouth and say, 'Man, I love you.' He'd just put a big ol' kiss on your face, waiting to see your response. I'd be like, 'Uh, Charles, didn't you just tell me to go fuck myself two hours ago?'"

Though Haley brought a dizzy insanity to Valley Ranch (he's likely the only Cowboy in team history to refuse to wear a jockstrap during games), he was an undeniable winner who'd earned two Super Bowl championships in six seasons with San Francisco. "He knew the game better than any of us," says Antonio Goss, a 49er linebacker. "He could pick up little patterns and cues that nobody else would see. Charles might have been odd, but he was intelligent and incisive."

From Johnson's vantage point, Haley was the missing piece. When he wasn't groping his penis or damning the white man or telling a writer to fuck himself with a blowtorch or calling Jones *Massa Jerry! Massa Jerry!*" as he entered the locker room, Haley was staying late for extra film; providing instruction to rookies and young players; barking out words of encouragement.

On one of the final days before the season opener against Washington on September 7, 1992, Johnson gathered his team and gave a tone-setting talk. "I want y'all to remember something very important," he said. "What many of you have in common is the one thing that should drive you—nobody wanted you." He looked around the room. There was Haley, dumped by the 49ers. There was Emmitt Smith, bypassed by sixteen teams in the '90 NFL Draft. There was Nate Newton, the 340-pound offensive lineman routinely dismissed as too fat. There was Stepnoski, the undersized center. There was Irvin, who'd barely avoided being cut. There was cornerback Larry Brown, a twelfth-round pick. There was tight end Jay Novacek, left unprotected by the Cardinals. Sure, the Cowboys had a golden boy in Aikman to plaster on billboards and brochures. But by and large, it was a team of misfits. Of Charles Haleys.

"There were so many pieces thrown into a stew," says Washington. "But it wasn't any ordinary stew. It was the Southern Country cooking stew, and it just tasted *soooooooo* good."

For the Cowboys, it had been a good offseason. No, a *great* offseason.

First, the league confirmed that Dallas was America's Team again, placing the franchise on an unheard-of five nationally televised games.

Then, in early April, the Cowboys learned that Air Force's Chad Hennings, the 1987 Outland Trophy winner, might be available. Dallas had initially used an eleventh-round pick on Hennings in 1988, figuring that, once his military commitment was fulfilled, the defensive tackle might give the NFL a shot. Though Hennings was an armed services loyalist, he started to think differently when President Bill Clinton announced massive cuts in the national military budget. Hennings wanted out.

At 6-foot-6 and 272 pounds, Hennings was bursting with potential. But he was also rusty. Having spent much of the past half decade deployed in England, flying A-10 Thunderbolts in Western Europe (and in the Gulf War, in which he earned two medals for flying forty-five relief missions to support Kurdish refugees), Hennings had not touched a football in four years.

On the night of April 25, 1992, he boarded a plane at London's Heathrow Airport and landed in Dallas nine hours later for a tryout. His internal clock was eight hours ahead and he hadn't slept in a day. "I thought I'd come in, run the 40 in front of my position coach, then talk," he says. "It was nothing like that." With Jones, Johnson, and ten to fifteen others in attendance, Hennings went through a bevy of tests and drills. He was equal parts nervous, exhausted, and exhilarated—and his performance dazzled the masses. Football depended largely on speed and size. Here was the merging of the two.

"I like what I see," Johnson said. "When can you get out of the Air Force?" Three weeks later Hennings was a Cowboy.

Dallas used three of its first four picks in the NFL Draft to select players who, like Haley and Hennings, would put the final touches on Johnson's dream of a blitzkrieg defense. With the seventeenth selection the Cowboys landed Texas A&M's Kevin Smith, a badly needed shutdown cornerback with flypaper hands and Deion Sanders reaction time. With the twenty-fourth pick they grabbed Robert Jones, an East Carolina middle linebacker considered to be the draft's best pure athlete. And with the ninth pick of the second round, they selected a linebacker-turned-safety out of Arizona State named Darren Woodson.

"During Darren's senior year of college he'd line up for two games at defensive end, then the next week he'd be out in space on man coverage, then he'd be an inside linebacker," says Jeff Smith, a Dallas scout. "He was a marvelous athlete—a physical freak of nature—whom a lot of teams probably didn't know what to do with. But we believed he was worth a shot."

Smith and Jones would start immediately, and within three years Woodson—a product of the Phoenix projects who was raised by a single mother working two jobs—would emerge as the best safety in the NFL.

The Cowboys were loaded.

And Johnson was miserable.

Not just miserable. Tyrannical. Not one veteran could recall a more vicious Jimmy Johnson than the one who stalked the sidelines in Austin during training camp. For Irvin, whose relations with the coach dated back to Miami, the behavior was predictable. Johnson was often his most laid-back and nurturing when he knew he had a team that wasn't up to snuff. At Oklahoma State, for example, many recall Johnson the teacher and my-door-is-always-open communicator.

But the 1992 Cowboys were built to win, and Johnson felt the pressure of meeting his own high expectations. His philosophy was simple: *I beat the crap out of you, I humiliate you, I dehumanize you—and you turn into a cold, hard gridiron machine.* "That was Jimmy in a nutshell," says Maurice Crum, a free-agent linebacker who had played for Johnson at Miami. "When I was a freshman in college I'd had a root canal, and I was hurting pretty bad. I asked Jimmy if I could sit out a practice—I mean, I could barely talk. He said, 'Well, do you wanna play for this team?' I said, 'Yes.' So he says, 'See you at practice.'"

In the summer of '92, Johnson screamed at every mishap, error, and (oddly) good play that rubbed him wrongly. During a team meeting he hollered "Harold Heath!" and demanded the rookie tight end from Jackson State report to the front of the room. "He cut me right there," says Heath. "In front of everybody. It was just wrong."

Johnson made it clear to his players that some (Aikman, Emmitt Smith, Irvin) would be treated with greater dignity than others—and if you didn't like it, you could find another line of work. A glaring example of this fanaticism came during the second week of August, when Kevin Smith, the first-round pick, snuck out of his dorm room after curfew and didn't return until 7 the following morning. Accompanying Smith was a rookie free-agent cornerback named Michael James. When Johnson learned of the misadventure, he called the two into his office. "I know I can't cut you," he said, pointing toward Smith. Then he turned to James. "But you," he growled, "better play your ass off this weekend, because you might not be here Monday morning." That

Saturday James was the Cowboys' best defensive back in a 34–23 loss to the Houston Oilers. He was active. He was aggressive. He was fast.

He was cut two days later.

"Jimmy liked to fuck with your head," says Stepnoski. "He wanted the mental edge."

Ever since arriving in Dallas as a third-round pick out of Pittsburgh in 1989, Stepnoski had felt unloved by his coach. The feelings were on point—Johnson didn't like Stepnoski's long hair and casual demeanor and it's-all-a-load-of-garbage approach to gridiron discipline. "I'm a nonconformist when it comes to football," Stepnoski says. "I believe in hard work, but I don't like being treated like a child. That's what happens in a football setting—you're treated like a five-year-old." In their first three years together, Johnson and Stepnoski were like Arafat and Netanyahu. Stepnoski refused to move to Dallas for offseason conditioning; Johnson refused to pay him well-earned fitness bonuses. During the '91 preseason, Stepnoski suffered a severe bruise in his right calf and had to miss several days of practice. Johnson responded by accusing Stepnoski in front of the entire team of faking the injury, then making him *walk* a 100-yard sprint—"just to fucking embarrass me," the center says. For the entire year, the head coach and starting center failed to exchange a single pleasant word to one another.

Stepnoski had hoped to return in 1992 with a fresh start, but when Jerry Jones refused to meet his contract demands he held out and missed the entire preseason. Johnson coolly greeted his center upon his eventual return and did not activate him for the first two games. Other veterans—notably James Washington, Tony Tolbert, Michael Irvin, and Jay Novacek—had also held out, but none faced such hostility. "He insisted on punishing me for the audacity of challenging his authority," says Stepnoski. "It was typical bullshit."

Despite Stepnoski's feelings, the Cowboys were primed for big things. Not only did the '92 edition look to be significantly more talented than past editions, but there was also a camaraderie that had not existed before. In late June a whopping eighty-eight players attended the team's *optional* quarterback school—a showing unprecedented in the history of the franchise. The cohesion carried over into training camp. In contrast to past years, dozens of players would remain at the practice facility long after workouts had ended to study films over pizza and Gatorade, then hit the Austin nightlife for beers, shots, long legs, big breasts, and lap dances galore at Sugar's Uptown Cabaret or the Yellow Rose or another of the city's better strip clubs. With the Cowboys often drawing 15,000 to 20,000 fans for workouts, they didn't have to do much to receive special treatment. Sure, thirty-something veterans like Jim Jeffcoat and Bill Bates avoided the party scene. But for the young, cocky, on-the-verge Cowboys, Texas was theirs for the taking.

Chapter 10

RETURN TO GREATNESS

Our toughest games were practices. After going through a week against Michael Irvin and Alvin Harper and Russell Maryland and Nate Newton, Sundays were easy.

—Kevin Smith, Cowboys cornerback

HERE ARE TWO things you should know about the 1992 Dallas Cowboys:

A. Nearly everybody had a nickname.
B. They weren't especially flattering.

Emmitt Smith was "Bushwick" because of his (apparent) physical resemblance to Bushwick Bill, the 3-foot, 8-inch Geto Boys rapper who had recently shot himself while drunk. (He lived.) Offensive lineman Kevin Gogan was "Red Bone," a colloquial term for a light-skinned black woman. "He was a white dude who loved those sisters," says cornerback Kenny Gant. "He had a cute little white girlfriend, but it didn't matter to him." Wide receiver Alvin Harper was "Freaky Harp" because of the freaky women he'd do freaky things with in freaky places at freaky times. Defensive lineman Tony Casillas was "Pretty Tony" because of his belly-button ring and girlish mannerisms. Safety James Washington was "Drive-By" because of his street upbringing and thuggish disposition. Offensive lineman Nate Newton was "The Kitchen" because of his 340-plus-pound girth and mounds upon mounds of Jell-O-firm fat. Wide receiver Tyrone Williams was "Big Bird" because of his gawky 6-foot, 4-inch frame.

"We all were called something," says Kevin "Pup" Smith. "If you were a Cowboy you had a nickname."

Some had two.

Cornerback Larry Brown was initially dubbed "Bone Brown" because of his high cheekbones but, says one teammate, "it was actually meant to be a joke, because on the field Larry was soft like a pussy, not hard like a bone." Soon enough Brown's moniker was changed to "Phyllis Diller" because of the facial similarities between the African-American football player and the wrinkly, unfunny white comedienne.

Rookie cornerback Clayton Holmes was first anointed "Chip Head" by veteran defensive back Ike Holt, who thought the dent in Holmes's high-top fade (hey, it was the '90s) looked like a chip. When that lost steam, Holmes was anointed "Half Man, Half Horse."

"Clayton walked with his ass sticking way out," laughs Gant. "Sorta like a horse, sorta like a man." He pauses. "Really more like a horse."

Of all the nicknames, the most original was bequeathed upon Ken Norton, Jr., the fifth-year linebacker out of UCLA. Best known as the son of the former world heavyweight champion, Norton was fast, strong, engaging—and possessor of a Jay Leno–esque chin. Just how elastic was Norton's mandible? During one game he was preparing to rush the quarterback when Charles Haley screamed from the sideline, "Kenny, back the fuck up! Your chin is offsides!" The laughter could be heard from Texas Stadium's highest seats. Teammates took one glance at Norton and came up with every imaginable insult ("Big Chin," "Face Boner," etc.) before tagging him "Mac Tonight" after the McDonald's commercial featuring a long-chinned moon crooning "It's Mac Tonight."

The Cowboys were funny. Personable. Engaging. Tight-knit. Though players had initially bonded in their antagonism toward Johnson's devilish workouts, a brotherhood had evolved. Many still laugh at the time Mark Tuinei, the Pro Bowl offensive lineman, used tweezers to remove the slip of paper from a coach's fortune cookie and inserted one reading, CONFUCIUS SAY YOU WILL BE BALD, FAT, AND UGLY. With a roster chock-full of wannabe models, there were unofficial fashion shows after every game. Players would stroll through the locker room in their purple and green and orange suits and elicit cheers or catcalls from the peanut gallery. "Yo, Barney," someone would yell when Irvin dared break out the purple Armani, "go back to Happy Land!" In surviving the 1–15 debacle together, many of the Cowboys knew an unusual sort of kinship. Anything could be said. Absolutely anything. "Hey," Washington would bellow to any teammate within earshot, "how's your wife and my kids?"

Now, with golden days on the horizon, the cohesion was immeasurable. Players would report to Valley Ranch and find their lockers outfitted with bottles of wine or backpacks or leather jackets or digital cameras—courtesy of "Mr. Jones." Free cars for the season were available to any player in need. Gift certificates floated from the sky. Those who wanted to play golf after practice could walk into a supply closet and grab anything from spikes to visors to khaki shorts. "Dallas was all about class and treating players like royalty," says Kenny Gant. "You were a king." As a result, in a sport ruled by pain and turmoil, Dallas players were downright giddy. "If you were black or white, offense or defense, a partyer or a family guy, you were one of us," says Newton. "There was no division in that locker room. We were one."

Veteran Cowboys took special pleasure in torturing first-year players. The hazing began during training camp, when rookies were forced to take the veterans out for a $250-per-head dinner at Papadeaux's Restaurant. (In anticipation of the feast, players would chant, "Run those hos to the Papadeaux's!") Holmes still gets chills when he thinks about the time he was sitting on a toilet in the locker room when—*WHOOSH!*—the Great Flood arrived. "A huge bucket of ice water comes raining down upon my head," says Holmes. "Boy, was I pissed. But what could I do? I was a rookie."

That was nothing compared to the day Kevin Smith forgot to pick up the defensive players' sandwiches for Wednesday morning practice. As soon as the workout ended, Newton, Jim Jeffcoat, and a handful of others bum-rushed the unsuspecting rookie, stripped off his entire uniform (save for his helmet and jockstrap), carried him to a practice field, and used rolls upon rolls of ankle tape to affix him to the goalpost. Newton turned to Holmes and his fellow plebes and barked, "If any of you remove even one piece of fucking tape from his fucking body, you'll get yours!" For the next hour, Smith wiggled and tugged, yanked and pivoted, until he finally escaped. "It was cold as hell out there," says Holmes. "Pup came back into the locker room and half the hair on his body was torn off by that tape."

To officially become a Cowboy, a player had to run at least once with Michael Irvin, who was equal parts big brother, party host, and torture administrator. Though he missed the preseason in a contract holdout, Irvin deemed it his duty to welcome new players into the fold, be they first-round draft picks or unknown rookie free agents. At bars, all drinks were on The Playmaker. At strip clubs, Irvin would unroll a wad of one- and five-dollar bills and dish them out like cookies on a Camp Kiwi field trip. To the Cowboys who longed to live on the wild side, Irvin was a model ringmaster. First, he paid for everything. Secondly, he stayed out late without condemnation from Johnson, who was familiar with the cravings of his star wideout.

Most important, Irvin was a Hall of Fame hoochie magnet. "I was Mike's right-hand man when it came to picking up the women," says Anthony Montoya, a team employee who ran errands for Irvin and several other players. "We'd have a practice and then we'd go straight to the titty bar—the limo driver, Michael, and myself. Mike would pick out who he wanted and then tell me what time to come back and pick him up. Happened hundreds of times." Though he was "happily" (in his words) married to Sandy, a former cosmetologist and Miami Dolphins cheerleader whom he had met on a McDonald's line while at the University of Miami, Irvin never thought twice about slipping off the ol' wedding band and hitting the clubs. It was who he was; what he did. "There was a lot of I, I, I, me, me, me," Sandy said. "Because he was The Man. Just because of how easy it came—the women, the drugs—it was available wherever they turned."

Irvin took great pleasure in removing his clothes, standing before a mirror, and saying "How can I allow only one woman to have a body this good?" or parading nude before rookies and lecturing, "This is the body you will aspire to have. This is the body you will aspire to achieve. You will not achieve it, but this is what you will strive to achieve." Boasting a Magic Johnson smile and the uncanny ability to make any-one feel important, Irvin bedded all whom he coveted. "Man, Mike was something," says one Cowboy teammate. "He was incredibly cocky. Before a game he'd have the people from Versace enter the locker room and measure him for a suit. He wanted to pick a feather from some exotic animal and put it in his derby hat. He wanted crocodile shoes with the tongue raised. Mostly, it was the women. Mike literally had a swarm of women at his beck and call in every NFL city. And I'm not talking about eights or nines. These girls were twelves."

For younger Cowboys like Gant, Holmes, Harper, and Erik Wil-liams, Irvin was a god. He would take them out, buy them dinner, point to a girl at the bar, and say, "I'm gonna give her to you." Moments later Irvin would be whispering in her ear, one hand cupping his mouth, the other placed gently on her thigh. He'd eventually nod to-ward an awaiting teammate and—*BAM!*—game over. "Mike got more Cowboys laid than touchdown catches," says one reporter who covered the team. "It was his present to teammates."

"Truthfully, I never drank in high school or college, never even cursed in high school or college," says Gant, who was raised in tiny Lakeland, Florida. "So when I got to Dallas and met guys like Mike it was '*Whooooooooooosh!*' Women? Drinking? Parties? Everything for free? I'll take it all!"

Irvin would load young teammates up on shots and mixed drinks until they were throwing up in an alley. They'd report to practice the next morning with bloodshot eyes, dizzy minds, and a greenish tint to their skin. "What the fuck!" Irvin would yell so all could hear. "Pussy can't handle a little water?"

Amazingly, even players like Troy Aikman and Jay Novacek, white country-and-western lovers with all the sparkle of Tulsa parking meters, considered Irvin an exemplary teammate. For one thing, he might have stayed out until 4 A.M., but come 8:30, Irvin was in the weight room, outlifting half the offensive line. "His drive and determination was second to none," says Tim Daniel, a Dallas receiver. "Sometimes you see somebody and say, 'That guy's super-fast' or 'That guy's super-strong,' and it explains everything. But Mike wasn't super-fast, and his strength came from working out. He was just the one who wanted it worse than anyone else in the league."

These were the Cowboys of '92—loose but intense, wild but dedicated, unproven but convinced the Vince Lombardi Trophy was theirs for the taking.

That confidence soared on Thursday, September 3, when—just four days before the Monday night opener against the Redskins—Irvin agreed to a two-year, $2.75 million contract to rejoin the Cowboys. When Stepnoski signed shortly thereafter, the Cowboys were whole again. But were they as good as advertised? One week earlier *Sports Illustrated* picked Dallas to win the Super Bowl. When Johnson saw the magazine, he neither smiled nor frowned. What had *SI* said that he didn't already believe? Damn right the Cowboys would win the Super Bowl.

Despite reigning as defending Super Bowl champions, Washington came to Dallas in less-than-jovial spirits. They were furious that the NFL's story du jour was not the possibility of a Redskin repeat, but rather the up-and-coming Cowboys. Having been burned repeatedly in his last matchup against Irvin, cornerback Darrell Green summed up his teammates' agitations, guaranteeing that "somebody is going to pay."

The Redskins paid dearly.

Six hours before game time, Emmitt Smith snuck into an empty Cowboys locker room, opened up his duffel bag, and placed $7,500 Rolexes in the locker of every offensive lineman. On the back of the jewelry was an inscription: THANKS FOR THE 1,563 RUSHING

YARDS: NFL RUSHING TITLE. EMMITT SMITH. "Talk about a way to start the season," says Alan Veingrad, an offensive tackle. "I won't speak for the other guys, but I was pumped."

On Washington's opening offensive play, nine Cowboys stormed Redskin quarterback Mark Rypien, who pedaled backward before falling beneath the weight of linebacker Vinson Smith. Of the two thousand or so plays that take place in a typical NFL season, 98 percent are immediately forgotten. This one wasn't. With a singular rampage through Washington's vaunted offensive line, Johnson had issued an unambiguous statement to the rest of the league: *Fear us—we're coming.*

As Vinson Smith rose from atop Rypien's battered body, a new sound overtook Texas Stadium. During Landry's best days, the place could get loud. But there was always a certain respect-thy-neighbor restraint. This was different. These Cowboy fans—now loyal to the Jones-Johnson way—were wild boars in search of prey. Their roars were of the throaty, blood-in-the-esophagus ilk.

The game was never close. On the second play, Redskins running back Earnest Byner was thrown for a 3-yard loss. On third down, Charles Haley charged past tackle Jim Lachey and forced Rypien into a rushed incompletion. On fourth down, Ike Holt blocked Kelly Goodburn's punt for a safety.

The ensuing noise was deafening—a fleet of Amtraks meets *Frampton Comes Alive!* With Emmitt Smith rushing for 140 yards and Irvin catching 5 passes for 89 yards, the Cowboys rolled to a 23–10 triumph. Here was a landmark win for the new-era Cowboys, proof that they could stare down the antagonists from Washington and not flinch. As the season progressed, players would look back at this game as a turning point. No longer would the Cowboys be bullied. "I just remember Jimmy having this fire in his eyes," says Clayton Holmes, the rookie defensive back. "He looked at me and I knew, 'Whoa. We're not losing.'"

Though he ended the game with a modest 216 passing yards, Aikman had officially arrived. With a ferocious Washington defensive line blitzing frequently, Dallas's quarterback hung in the pocket until the last possible second while firing one pinpoint bullet after another. Having long boasted one of the league's most powerful cannons, Aikman was now armed with something even more vital than physical gifts—his coach's confidence. By season's end he would rank near the top on the league's leaderboards with 3,445 passing yards and 23 touchdowns.

"Troy," said a giddy Johnson, "is coming of age."

While the city of Dallas celebrated one of the biggest wins of the post–Landry Era, the two men who had facilitated the turnaround were beginning to drift apart.

Wait. Hold on. Perhaps this is overly dramatic. After all, some would say the wedge between owner and coach first came to be on February 25, 1989—the day Jerry Jones announced he had purchased the Dallas Cowboys. They were never as close as it seemed, of course, but there was a mutual need. Jerry Jones *needed* Jimmy Johnson to win football games. Jimmy Johnson *needed* Jerry Jones to purchase the chess pieces.

But until 1992—until success was not a *hypothetical,* but an *inevitability*—the egos of two men with grandeur in their horoscopes coexisted well. Yes, the coach was exasperated by the owner's buffoonery—his desire to drag celebrities into the locker room after games; his tendency to name-drop and brag of a gridiron knowledge that, quite simply, didn't exist. And yes, the owner wondered aloud why his coach was so guarded; so secretive; so damn stubborn. Why he refused to let the man paying the bills into his inner circle? *Dammit,* Jones thought, *I own this team, not Jimmy.* But again, before 1992 everything was under control.

And then, during the '92 preseason, it started. The *I* Syndrome.

Where once there was "We" in the Cowboy-themed sentences of Jones and Johnson, now—suddenly—it was all "I." When the Cowboys traded for Haley, Johnson intoned, "*I* thought Charles could bring a lot to the table." When the Redskins were battered and bruised, Jones bragged, "The way *I* built this team . . ." The two not only noticed each other's linguistic transformations, but raised the ante with comical regularity. There might be no *I* in T-E-A-M, but there was plenty of it in J-O-N-E-S and J-O-H-N-S-O-N.

Though Jones was often irritated by Johnson's need for control, it was the coach who fumed—and rightfully so. Why was it that whenever the media wrote about Dallas's rejuvenation, it was always HOW THE JJ TWINS TURNED AROUND THE COWBOYS (*Newsday*, July 14, 1991) and JONES, JOHNSON REVIVE COWBOYS FAST (*Washington Times*, September 6, 1991)? When it came to seeking out oil, Jones's accomplishments could not be denied. When it came to football, however, Jones was a dolt. Sure, Jones could watch a Herman Moore and understand why the Detroit wide receiver was a star. But in terms of the nitty-gritty—in deciding whether a Division II nose tackle could transition to NFL linebacker or whether an opposing team was disguising its blitz package—he was no more insightful than the schlub at home in his Barcalounger.

When Bob Oates of the *Los Angeles Times* wrote that Jones "makes the calls in the Cowboys front office while Johnson replaces Landry on the practice field," he was eating out of the owner's hands. Because he played collegiately, and because he had paid $150 million to purchase a team, Jones considered himself Johnson's football equal. He took credit for moves in which his sole contribution was an official sign-off. Jones bragged about the 1990 trading of Steve Walsh to New Orleans, even though Johnson had brokered the deal. He talked about how he ironed out the Haley blockbuster, when it was Johnson and the team's advance scouts who did 99.9 percent of the grunt work. And for Christ's sake, how many times did Johnson have to hear about Jones's draft-day genius? Were it up to the coach, Jones would spend the two days of the NFL Draft relaxing on a beach in Bermuda or climbing Mt. Washington or . . . something. *Don't call us, Jerry. We'll call you.*

Instead, Jones had treated the most recent draft as if he were planning his own bar mitzvah. Having invited ESPN's cameras into the team's "war room," Jones surrounded himself with friends, family members, and associates—all to make him appear presidential. Inside the room were Jones's two sons, his business partner, his treasurer, his marketing director, and a gaggle of corporate sponsors.

"I can't control that," an exasperated Johnson told writer Skip Bayless. So, ever the brawler, Johnson invited his own entourage. While most teams had, oh, six or seven men in their draft bunkers, the Cowboys' room contained nearly forty.

More than anything, Johnson blamed Jones—whom he considered to be excessively tightfisted—for unnecessary training camp holdouts. He found Jones's rip-the-agent-to-the-press tactic during the Emmitt Smith negotiations of 1990 to be juvenile. This year was even worse. During Irvin's holdout Jones refused to offer the receiver more than $700,000 per year—and it was baffling. Hadn't Irvin just caught 93 passes for 1,523 yards? Hadn't he emerged as the team's leader and spark plug?

So, as the Cowboys prepared to travel to New York for a Week 2 meeting with the Giants, Johnson upped his efforts to shut Jones out. To players, Johnson complained their owner's meddling was damaging morale. To the scouts and coaching staff, Johnson moaned that, because of the owner, they were all underpaid. "Jimmy kept his coaches and players as far away from Jerry as he possibly could," says one team official. "It was sad, because Jerry meant well and wanted to help in any way he could. But in Jimmy's mind it was *his* team, not Jerry's."

The most impressive attribute of the '92 Cowboys? None of it mattered. Contract holdouts, coach-owner disputes, Haley's penile Olympiads, late-night clubbing with Michael Irvin and twelve strippers—distractions came, distractions went. Dallas stormed into Giants Stadium and, before New York coach Ray Handley could blink, attacked the hosts with unrivaled ferocity. Dallas drove 72 yards on its first possession to build a 7–0 advantage, then followed with a blocked punt by linebacker Robert Jones. When Cowboy defensive back Robert Williams rovered the ball in the end zone, Dallas was up 14–0—and the rout was on. By the end of the second quarter the score was 20–0, and New York had yet to achieve a first down. At halftime the scoreboard read 27–0.

As they entered the locker room, Dallas players behaved as if they were planning a week at Club Med. Under Johnson's hypercompetitive guidance, rarely was any lead big enough. But here they were, up big and already thinking of the week ahead.

Uh-oh.

When Aikman hit Irvin with a 27-yard touchdown pass early in the third quarter, the score was 34–0 and the stadium broke out into a chant of "Ray Must Go!" (Having replaced Bill Parcells, the charisma-deprived Handley was reviled in New York.) The Cowboys' defense came out relaxed, and New York—unburdened by the expectations of victory—pounced. Quarterback Phil Simms led his team to consecutive touchdown drives of 80, 80, 62, and 55 yards, and a once-mute Giants Stadium crowd turned wild. In the history of the NFL, no team had ever overcome a 34–0 deficit. Now here were the Giants, down 34–28 late in the fourth quarter. Up in the coaches' box, defensive coordinator Dave Wannstedt was losing his cool. At one point, with New York facing a second-and-7 at the Dallas 21-yard line, he looked at the field and screamed into his headset, "Who's got the tight end?"

Again—"Who's got the tight end?"

Nobody answered. "Fuck! Fuck! Fuck!" Wannstedt yelled. "Nobody's got the tight end."

Moments later, Simms found receiver Ed McCaffrey for a 19-yard gain.

In the end, Dallas held on—barely. With 3:42 left in the game, the Giants had the ball on their own 19-yard line. Simms coolly jogged onto the field, a wave of noise drowning out his play calls. Panic reigned along the Dallas sideline. *What if we lose this game? How will we ever recover?* On first down, Haley charged through the line, forcing Simms to toss an incomplete pass. On second down, Simms completed a pass for 1 yard. On third down, another completion, this one for no gain. New York punted. Wannstedt praised Jesus. Dallas hung on.

Afterward, Tony Wise, the offensive line coach, put the afternoon in perspective: "We've got a lot of young guys," he said, "with shit stains on their underwear."

Ghosts are unpredictable. According to mediums, they arrive when they want and haunt as they please. Throughout history there have been millions of sightings, at venues ranging from the White House to the Kremlin to a Toys "R" Us in Sunnyvale, California.

On October 5, 1992, a specter would appear before the most unlikely of places—the Dallas Cowboys defensive.

Unlike your clichéd, run-of-the-mill spirit, cloaked in either invisibility or a king-sized sheet, this specter wore a helmet, shoulder pads, and the white-and-green home uniform of the Philadelphia Eagles.

His name was Herschel Walker.

In the three years since Dallas had hoodwinked the Minnesota Vikings, Walker had become an NFL cautionary tale. He was Exhibit A in the no-single-player-is-worth-all-those-picks rule of thumb to franchise building. When a team talked about swinging a trade, someone inevitably would note, "We don't want to end up with a Herschel." *Ha, ha, ha.*

It was all fun and games for everyone but Walker, who had gone from the featured back on America's Team to a joke. "He's a con artist," one NFC personnel director told *Sports Illustrated.* "Nobody has made more money and done less." Following a 1991 season in which Walker ran for just 825 yards, the Vikings exhausted every effort to trade him. Only the Eagles showed any interest. They signed him as a free agent and found themselves with an angry, motivated thirty-year-old. "People have questioned my heart," he said early in the season. "Go ahead and get in the ring with me. I'll tear your head off."

Walker spoke in general terms, but his target easily could have been the Cowboys. Following the victories over Washington and New York, Johnson's team beat up on the Phoenix Cardinals, 31–20, to post its first 3–0 start in nine years. After a bye in Week 4, Dallas traveled to Philadelphia for a Monday night dance with the Eagles and their new tailback.

Though coach Buddy Ryan had been replaced by the mellow Rich Kotite, and All-Pro nose tackle Jerome Brown had died in a car accident, Philly appeared as physical as ever. Quarterback Randall Cunningham was healthy for the first time in months, and Walker was pounding opposing tacklers. In anticipation of the Cowboy game, the *Philadelphia Daily News* ran a twenty-page pullout section on the matchup. WIP sports radio began its pregame show fifteen *hours* before kickoff. Tickets were being scalped for $225 a pop. This was big.

An hour or so before the game, Jimmy Johnson strolled to the Eagles' side of the field to seek out Walker. Though the Cowboys coach was never a fan of his former halfback, he'd always had respect for the man. Walker was, after all, a kind and decent soul, hard to root against in even the most heated of rivalries. "I'm glad to see you doing so well," Johnson told Walker. "You deserve the success."

If Johnson was trying to soften Walker up, it didn't work. In what surely goes down as one of the most gratifying days of his life, the Eagles running back scored on second-half touchdown runs of 9 and 16 yards in a resounding 31–7 victory. Long ripped for possessing the dexterity of a boot, his first score—the 9-yard bolt out of the I-formation—was a thing of beauty. Walker took the handoff from Cunningham, broke Ken Norton's tackle in the backfield, shifted from left foot to right, and followed a block into the end zone.

Meanwhile, Emmitt Smith—beloved by Dallas fans in a way Walker never was—was held to 67 yards on 19 carries. That, along with Aikman's 3 interceptions, was more than enough charity for a fierce Philadelphia defense. The game was never close.

"All this misery for Dallas," wrote Randy Galloway in the *Morning News,* "and even Herschel gets to rub it in."

In the wake of the Eagles loss, Johnson looked over his men and insisted this was "a test."

"We'll see who you are," he said, "champions or pretenders."

In a 27–0 rout of Seattle the following Sunday, the Cowboys answered, blitzing and battering Seahawks quarterback Dan McGwire until he could be blitzed and battered no more. The younger brother of Oakland A's slugger Mark McGwire, Dan was a 6-foot-8, 243-pound oak tree, prime for chopping. The Cowboys hit him high, low, helmet-to-helmet, helmet-to-back. They told him that he sucked, that he was a punk, that he was theirs for the taking—and his mama, too.

The Cowboys defense sacked McGwire four times, knocked him out in the third quarter, then sacked backup Stan Gelbaugh three more times. Seattle lost yardage on five of its first fourteen offensive possessions and averaged 1.3 yards per snap, gaining 62 total yards and only 8 on its final thirty-one plays. Tony Tolbert and Jim Jeffcoat each had two sacks and safety Ray Horton returned an interception 15 yards for a touchdown. "This," said Jeffcoat, "was the best defense I've ever seen us play."

On a wall in Wannstedt's office hung a chart featuring the record of the 1976 Pittsburgh Steelers defense. With quarterback Terry Bradshaw battling neck and wrist injuries, the unit carried the franchise to a 10–4 record, pitching five shutouts, holding one team to 6 points, and limiting two other teams to single field goals. "Eight games without allowing a touchdown," Wannstedt raved. "Now that's a dominating defense."

The chart was not mere wall fodder, but a message to his troops of what they could accomplish. "And it began," Wannstedt says, "with the defensive line." On most teams, there was a clear order: Starters started, backups came in occasionally to provide a breather. Under Wannstedt, however, the Cowboys shuttled linemen as if they were commuters on a train platform. The starters were Haley at right end, Casillas and Russell Maryland at the tackles, and Tolbert at left end. But there was almost no drop-off when the reserves—Chad Hennings, Jimmie Jones, Leon Lett, and Jeffcoat—entered. "Those were the hardest-working guys I've ever been around," says Hennings. "We challenged each other to be great."

Although Haley was the star and Tolbert and Lett on the rise standouts, the heart of the line was Jeffcoat, who at age thirty-one possessed maturity most teammates lacked. When the Cowboys initially signed

Haley, Johnson called Jeffcoat into his office. "We got Charles Haley, and eventually he's going to be the starter," Johnson explained. "You've got two ways you can look at this: You can become more valuable to us because of the things you can do in the pass rush, or we can cut you."

Silence.

Had Jeffcoat asked for his release, at least half the teams in the league would have jumped at the opportunity to add a proven quarterback crusher. In the nine seasons since he was drafted out of Arizona State, Jeffcoat had compiled 586 tackles and 70 sacks. "He knew the NFL game, he knew all the techniques," says Maryland. "Jim was a true professional." So here he was, sitting on Johnson's couch, staring down an uncertain future.

"The more I thought about it, the more excited I became," says Jeffcoat, who would lead the '92 Cowboys with $10\frac{1}{2}$ sacks. "Charles was a great player who needed to start, and I was comfortable being a sixth man. If anything, it would extend my career."

With a loaded defense playing its best football in years, the Cowboys were suddenly unstoppable. They followed the Seattle thrashing by beating the Chiefs and Raiders (limiting the teams to a combined 23 points), and on November 1 the Eagles came to town for the highly anticipated rematch. This time Dallas's defense relentlessly hounded quarterback Randall Cunningham, holding him to a trio of completions through the end of the first half. With 163 yards on 30 carries, Emmitt Smith became the first runner since 1989 to exceed 100 yards against the Philadelphia defense. Dallas won, 20–10.

Although his team suffered a humiliating 27–23 home setback to the lowly Rams on November 15, Johnson could not have asked for more. The Cowboys traveled to Washington, for a December 13 meeting with the Redskins, sporting an 11–2 mark. They had the league's hottest defense, its top running back (Smith was first in the NFL with 1,309 yards), its elite possession receiver (Irvin had 62 catches for 1,156 yards), and—after years of struggling—its best young quarterback.

Far removed from his days of fighting with Steve Walsh for work and with Johnson for respect, Aikman was poised, mature, and—on the streets of Dallas—a burgeoning legend. So, for that matter, were his teammates. "We could do no wrong," says Kenny Gant. "We were on top of the world, and it was a beautiful thing. We were on a roll, and no one was gonna stop us."

No one—with the possible exception of their head coach.

Chapter 11

TURBULENCE

If you tell your kid, "If you don't stop messing around, I'll spank you," and then you don't spank him, he'll never stop screwing up. When Jimmy Johnson threatened to spank, you damn well better believe he was gripping a paddle.
—Lin Elliott, Cowboys kicker

WHEN ROBERT JONES was three months old, his father pointed a shotgun at his mother's stomach and pulled the trigger.

As she fell backward onto a mattress in the family's Blackstone, Virginia, home, Pearl Jones—blood spewing from her abdomen—landed atop her youngest child and died. She was thirty-six years old.

In hindsight, the murder may well have been inevitable. Bennie Jones was a man with violence running through his veins. He beat Pearl frequently, never held a steady job, and drank regularly. Pearl had recently moved out to live with a neighbor, further fanning her husband's rage. Though Robert does not remember his mother's body landing on top of him, rarely has such a minute moment in time—the hundredth of a second it took for the bullet to launch and land—made such a dramatic impact on a child; on a family; on a way of being.

"I have one picture of my mom," says Jones. "One picture."

Sitting in a Cheesecake Factory near his home in Austin, Texas, Jones is a bundle of emotions. As he speaks, tears well in his eyes. Convicted of second-degree murder, Bennie was sentenced to twenty years in prison. (Years later Robert visited his father and asked why he committed the crime. Bennie Jones replied coldly, "Because she wouldn't listen.") With nowhere to go, Robert and his eight siblings were scattered throughout the state of Virginia. Six of Robert's seven brothers have served jail time. One died of a cocaine overdose. Another hung himself. Another was sentenced to life in prison for murder—he bashed a man's skull with a pipe wrench and left the body on the railroad tracks.

Robert was taken in by his aunt Betty and uncle Ernest, and when he turned seven his uncle was sent to jail for eight years. Though Betty Watson raised her nephew to the best of her abilities, she was a far cry from Aunt Bee. Betty partied deep into the morning hours and left Robert home alone. Sometimes he'd wake up to an empty house, a seven-year-old boy scared to death. "She had food on the table for me, but that was about it," says Robert. "I can't blame her, though. This is what she knew."

With nowhere to turn, Robert found a family in the parking lots and alleys of Blackstone. "The streets became my daddy," he says. "To fit in, you start giving in to what society says you should do." Located in the middle of Nowhere, Virginia, the Blackstone of Robert Jones's youth featured three traffic lights, winding dirt roads, and a hopelessness that permeated like a cancer. There was a bleak sense of we-have-no-future-so-don't-kid-yourself among the blacks of his environs. "I called it the 'Country Ghetto,'" he says. "No hope allowed." With his mother dead, his father and uncle in prison, and his siblings . . . wherever, Robert turned to booze and marijuana. He used both with striking nonchalance, as a way to fit in and to numb the pain of a joyless existence.

At age twelve, Robert was approached by one of his brothers, Bennie, Jr., and asked to participate in the armed robbery of a liquor store. (He wisely declined.) He attended school because his aunt insisted, but did so with little vigor. He skipped classes, blew off homework assignments, ignored his teachers.

"There was one reason I kept at it," he says. "Football."

In an ocean of darkness, the sport was Jones's lighthouse. From the time he enrolled at Nottoway High School as a freshman, Jones was faster, stronger, bigger—*angrier* than the others. He played with the intensity of a boy coated in scars; as if, when bulldozing opposing ball carriers, he was, in fact, bulldozing his father. Before he ever envisioned football as a gateway to a better life, Jones loved Saturdays for the temporary escapism. On the field, he wasn't Robert Jones, victim. He was Robert Jones, superstar.

In Billy Boswell, one of Nottoway High's football coaches, Jones was embraced by an adult who actually believed in him. Boswell encouraged Jones to pay attention in classes; to make something of himself. Because he lacked the grades to attend college, upon graduating from Nottoway Jones (with an emphatic push from Boswell) enrolled in Fork Union Military Academy, a boarding school with a track record of turning kids around. Boasting a report card of Bs and Cs, Jones graduated from Fork Union and was recruited by nearly every big-time Division I school in the country. Wanting to stay close to home, he chose East Carolina University.

In his four years as an undergrad Jones excelled as both student and football player, landing on the honor roll as a criminal justice major and earning all-America status as linebacker. Perhaps the most profound role college played in Jones's life was exposing him to friends and teammates who grew up with loving nuclear and extended families. With harrowing emptiness, Jones watched the parents of others visit campus and embrace their children with hugs and kisses.

"My number one goal in life was to have a big family of my own," he says. "I wanted to sit down for breakfast with a wife and lots of kids and talk about what we were going to do that day. I wanted to have a huge Christmas tree with all the gifts underneath, and on Christmas morning we'd all gather around and be together. Imagine yourself as a kid, never being able to sit down and jump in your dad's lap or just being secure in the knowledge that you had a dad at home. That was me."

Jones pauses, takes a long, prideful breath. He now has a wife of his own. Six children, too. But he is lost in the past. "Most people want to play in the NFL because of the fame or the money or whatever," he says. "I saw it as a way to have a family."

Beginning with his arrival in Dallas as a 1992 first-round draft pick, Jones struggled to fit in. On the field, he was a 6-foot, 2-inch, 236-pound physical specimen who lacked *spark*. He was fast, quick, strong—but a wee bit off. Johnson named him the Cowboys' starting middle linebacker early in camp, then stewed week to week as Jones played . . . *well*. Not amazing and not terrible—just . . . *well*. "I loved the guy, and his intangibles were very good," says Dave Wannstedt, the defensive coordinator. "But in all honesty, he was not ready to do what we needed him to do."

Though Wannstedt's assessment rings true, it fails to explain the entire story. By the time the Cowboys opened the '92 season, Jones had married Maneesha Richardson, his college sweetheart, and was committed to staying faithful. Yet here he was, in an environment littered with temptation. With rare exception, the Cowboy who didn't hit the strip club circuit wasn't an accepted member of the team. The same goes for the Cowboy who didn't drink heavily and stay out late; the Cowboy who didn't slink toward the big-breasted hottie in the tight leather pants and strapless top; the Cowboy who didn't smoke a joint every now and then (or, in many cases, just *every now*). "We were like movie stars," said Erik Williams, the offensive tackle. "We were like rock stars. If it was a day game and we would get done around six or seven, we would go to a bar. I would call the females that I dated. Most of them were strip club women, because that's what I did all the time. It was like a fish market. I'd view the women and pick one." If you were going to be a Dallas Cowboy—a *real* Dallas Cowboy—you needed to live The Life. That meant partying hard, partying late, and, if you had the misfortune of being married, leaving your wife at home and screwing the hell out of whoever caught your eye. It meant loading up on $100 bills, heading straight for the Men's Club of Dallas, and purchasing the longest, wettest, nastiest lap dance money could buy. It meant turning in your scruples at the door. "If you have a weak constitution, Dallas isn't for you," says Ray Horton, the longtime safety. "I mean, we were holding position meetings at strip clubs. *Position meetings!*"

Robert Jones was conflicted. He didn't want to go to strip clubs; certainly didn't want to cheat on his wife. But the women were everywhere, as hot and as loose as he'd ever seen. "It was hard," he says. "Real hard. Because all these guys are acting a certain way, and you're trying to fit in but also maintain your sense of what's right." Early in the season, the rookies were required to treat veteran Cowboys to a night on the town. The team would feast on a steak dinner, followed by dessert at a strip club. The Cowboys rented a private room and had dozens of dancers thrusting and feeling and slinking in a buffet of raunchiness. The liquor was flowing, the blunts burning. "I went along and kept it from my wife," Jones says. "Eventually she found out and we had a big argument. It's sad, but I was only trying to be accepted."

Such was the difficulty Jones faced as a Cowboy, and it affected him profoundly. His anxiety was akin to that of a gay man trying to keep his homosexuality a secret. Jones did not want his teammates knowing he was—*what?*—honest? Decent? A loving husband? He said nothing of his commitment to his wife, let alone his family's murderous past. Instead he talked trash and cracked stupid jokes about women and lived Shakespeare's "All the world's a stage" to the hilt. Only his stage was the Cowboy locker room, and he starred as the typical chauvinistic athlete.

The result was a rigid man who fell far below the expectations he had been burdened with by Johnson. After drafting Jones, Bob Slowik, an assistant defensive coach with the team, raved, "He'll give Dallas a dimension of pursuit from sideline to sideline that probably hasn't been there in a long time." Johnson felt the same way, then watched in dismay. To the head coach, Jones symbolized his least-favorite breed: the gifted athlete who lacked a motor. He had no idea that Jones was confused . . . conflicted . . . embarrassed. It was hard enough playing linebacker in the NFL without having a mind clouded by doubt. Jones was lost, and it showed.

As a result, Johnson made Jones's life miserable. He mocked him in practices, chewed him out during games, tried to coerce the kid into becoming the player he wasn't.

Everything came to a head on the afternoon of December 13, 1992, when the Cowboys fell apart against the Redskins at RFK Stadium. Leading up to the game, a palpable bitterness consumed both teams. Though hailed as the defending Super Bowl champions, the 8–5 Redskins were three games behind the 11–2 Cowboys, and fading fast. They were a forgotten franchise, lost in the revival of America's Team. With a win, the Cowboys would clinch their first NFC East title in seven years.

"I'm going after the arm," Michael Irvin responded when asked how he would treat the cast-encased broken right forearm of Washington cornerback Darrell Green. "I'm not joking. I'm going after his arm. I don't think the arm is healed yet. I don't think the guy's healthy and I'm going after that arm on every running play. I'm not making threats. Those are facts."

Green initially refused to believe Irvin would utter such a classless statement. The words crossed a line of decency, and served as powerful motivators to the already agitated Redskins. *First we're disrespected by the media . . . and now you threaten our best player?*

After controlling the first three quarters of the game, the Cowboys unraveled in a defeat that Jim Jeffcoat called "the weirdest." The drama began early in the fourth quarter, with Dallas leading 17–10 and facing a third-and-goal from the Washington 2-yard line. Aikman took the snap, dropped back, rolled to his left, and locked eyes with receiver Kelvin Martin, who was slashing through the end zone. Though only in his fourth season, Aikman was already one of the league's best at looking off the defense: darting his eyes left and right to keep the intended target a mystery. This time, he and Martin stared at one another like Ali MacGraw and Ryan O'Neal in *Love Story,* passionately gazing into each other's eyes . . . lovingly . . . long-ingly . . .

WHOOSH!

In came Redskins linebacker Andre Collins, who intercepted the ball and ran 59 yards to the Dallas 42. "That," said Richie Petitbon, the Washington defensive coordinator, "was the biggest play of the game."

Though the Redskins managed only a field goal, the Cowboys officially handed the night away with 3:14 left in the fourth quarter. That's when Aikman, preparing to throw on second-and-7 from the Dallas 5-yard line, was twisted to the ground by defensive lineman Jason Buck. As Aikman began his release, the ball popped loose and rolled backward. Attempting to make something of nothing, Emmitt Smith snatched the pigskin and inexplicably tossed it toward Redskins safety Danny Copeland, who grabbed the ball in the end zone. Touchdown, Washington.

Game over.

Redskins: 20.

Cowboys: 17.

Jimmy Johnson: indignant.

As is ritual, after the game the Cowboys met for a few moments as a team, showered, spoke with the media, dressed, and bolted for the airport, where they boarded a chartered airplane for the return to Dallas.

Win or lose, the postgame flight is an opportunity for players and coaches to wind down, reflect, and begin the recovery process. After the requisite fifteen-minute keep-it-down-because-we're-supposed-to-be-devastated silent time, men open up. They joke, laugh, play dominoes, play cards, talk smack, eat dinner.

Upon boarding, Johnson walked toward his seat near the front of the airplane and spotted the flight attendants preparing dinner. "Don't give my guys anything to eat!" he roared. "I mean it! Nothing!" Johnson sat down and cracked open a Heineken. Then another Heineken.

Then another. Unlike the teetotaling, God-fearing Tom Landry of Cowboy lore, Johnson's off-the-field cravings encompassed the music of Barbra Streisand, violent movies, white shag carpet, and—most of all—cold beer.

When the plane reached cruising altitude, players quietly scattered about. Like most teams, the Cowboys sectioned their airplane. The front five rows belonged to the coaching staff and executives. Behind them sat a handful of broadcasters and media types. Finally, taking up the rest of the jet's space were the Dallas players. Each row of the American Airlines jet had four seats. Every player claimed two seats to himself.

While gazing out the window, Robert Jones felt a tap on his shoulder. It was Charles Haley. "Do me a favor," Haley said. "Let me sit here so I can play cards with these guys." Haley nodded toward the nearby trio of Thomas Everett, Tony Tolbert, and Kevin Smith, the team's regular Tonk players. "So I get up, and I'm just sort of leaning on my seat, watching the guys play," says Jones. "What else did I have to do?"

Jones stood facing the rear, unaware as to why the airplane suddenly went silent. When he turned his head, he understood. There was Jimmy Johnson, eyes the color of maraschino cherries, breathing down his neck. "I didn't think he was setting up to jump me, because I'm quiet, I'm not causing a scene—I'm just standing there looking," says Jones. "So when I saw him, I stood straight up so he could get by. I figured he was going to the bathroom or walking the plane or something." Jones pressed his body toward his seat to make room for Johnson to pass. He held the position for two seconds . . . three seconds . . . four seconds . . . five seconds. Nothing.

Johnson looked into Jones's eyes and yelled, "Where's your fucking seat?"

Quiet by nature, the linebacker stammered, "Uh, Charles had to use it because they were playing cards."

"You know what?" said Johnson. "You're the weakest fucking middle linebacker I've ever come across. You play an entire game at middle linebacker and you make one fucking tackle? Find your damn seat!"

Jones paused.

"Find your goddamned seat," Johnson said, "before you don't have a fuckin' job."

Gulp.

Jones stumbled around before falling into Haley's lap. From three rows up, Frank Cornish, the backup center, laughed softly. Johnson's head spun like an owl tracking a vole. "Stop smiling!" he hollered.

"Coach," said Cornish, "I'm not smiling. Nothing's funny."

Johnson shuffled back to the front of the plane, slurring angrily. As the players whispered, *"What an asshole"* and *"What's up his ass?"* he reappeared. Cornish, who had stood to use the bathroom, saw Johnson scowling at him again. "Coach," he said, "we're all disappointed that we lost. Nobody is taking it for granted."

Johnson's lower lip quivered. "Frank, are you challenging me?" he said.

"No," responded Cornish. "Not at all."

The center quickly exited, stage left, into the bathroom.

A former sixth-round draft choice, Cornish was a solid, dependable, eminently disposable reserve. If Johnson felt the itch, he would cut him in a second. "I never liked that about Jimmy," says Robert Jones. "Think about the guys I was with when he jumped on me—Charles Haley was a star, Thomas Everett was the starting safety, Kevin Smith was a shutdown corner, Tony Tolbert was a great defensive end. He chose me and he chose Frank because we were guys he could pick on and not worry about. He never messed with his bread-and-butter guys, because he was a bully. Bullies only pick on the guys they can mess with."

In a final dose of brutality, Johnson—again retreating to the front—walked past fullback Tommie Agee, who was sitting on the armrest of his seat because Emmitt Smith was cramping and needed to stretch his legs. "Tommie," he said, "what are you doing out of your seat?"

Agee tried to explain, but his coach didn't want to hear it. "Sit down!" he said. "Sit the fuck down!"

And then Johnson left to drink another Heineken.

In the rear of the plane the players were outraged. Here were the Dallas Cowboys, 11–3 and manhandling the NFC East. They had the league's best record, best running back, best quarterback, best possession receiver, and one of its best defenses. And their coach felt the need to treat them like four-year-olds. "Fuck this!" said Irvin. "I know we lost, but he shouldn't have come back here like that." Haley patted Jones on the shoulder. "Man, that was so wrong," he said. "I took your seat and he didn't say nothing to me." Players were fed up with Johnson's insensitivity.

The following day, the Cowboys were scheduled to gather at noon for a meeting at Valley Ranch. Horton was sitting alone outside the weight room when Johnson approached. "Ray," he said, "how are the guys?"

An elder statesman who knew this would be his final season, Horton lacked the insecurity to sugarcoat an answer. "Coach," he said, "they're really pissed at you."

Johnson failed to flinch. "That's fine," he said, "as long as they play for me."

Moments later Johnson entered the team meeting, stood before the room, and made an announcement. Horton knew what was coming— Johnson would apologize and the organization would move on. *Right?*

"I know some guys are mad at me," Johnson said, "but I just want to win."

And that was that.

"Typical Jimmy," says Horton. "He was single-minded and he was hard, and all he cared about—I mean, the only thing—was winning football games. It's probably not the healthiest way to be, but it made him a successful coach."

In the ensuing days, players bitched about Johnson to one another.

They whined and moaned and questioned the decency of a man who would treat "family" (as Johnson often referred to his players) in such a disrespectful manner. But there was little they could do. He was the boss, they were the employees. Anyone who wanted to quit a team heading for the playoffs was more than welcome to do so.

On the following Sunday, the Cowboys traveled to Atlanta and trounced the Falcons, 41–17. Still fuming at their coach, players took it out on the overmatched Falcons. Aikman completed 18 of 21 passes for 239 yards and 3 TDs, and Emmitt Smith added 174 rushing yards and his NFL-high seventeenth and eighteenth touchdown runs. With the victory, Dallas clinched both the NFC East title and a first-round playoff bye. Shortly after the game, CPC/Environment, the company responsible for those cheesy commemorative coins recognizing everyone from JFK to MLK to the 1986 New York Mets, announced that it would be issuing "a limited edition of 5,000 pure silver commemorative medallions honoring the Cowboys!" (With each one-troy ounce pure silver medallion individually numbered!)

Were the Cowboys back on top? The coins sold out in less than a day.

Ever nervous of a letdown, Johnson deemed it vital to destroy any potential pre-playoff complacency. The Cowboy players averaged a league-low 25.3 years of age. They were pups among men, and the coach didn't want a postseason berth to swell their heads.

What he needed was a scapegoat.

What he had was Curvin Richards.

Growing up in the Trinidadian town of Laventille Village, Richards hated running. *Hated* it. As his friends spent their days playing soccer, darting up and down a grassy patch of earth, young Curvin sat back and watched. Or slept. Or stayed home. When he was nine, his father, Kevin, was hired as a welder in the United States, and the family relocated to Houston. It was here, at LaPorte High School, that Richards discovered his calling.

Though he might have found soccer to be dull, Richards was smitten with the pigskin. "There's almost something magical about being on a football field," he said. "Running with the ball." Upon graduating from LaPorte with 1,159 rushing yards and 14 touchdowns as a senior, Richards enrolled at the University of Pittsburgh. After three seasons he ranked only behind Cowboy great Tony Dorsett on the school's all-time rushing list. When Richards declared early for the 1991 NFL Draft, the Cowboys gladly used their fourth-round pick on a 5-foot, 10-inch, 190-pound power back with untapped potential. "He's a great, great tailback," said Syracuse coach Dick MacPherson. "Curvin Richards is what everybody looks for when they need a running back."

But Richards had one fatal flaw—mindlessness. Before the opening game of his first season with Dallas, veterans told the rookies that the team's charter flight to Cleveland was departing from Dallas Love Field Airport, not Dallas–Fort Worth International Airport. The lone plebe not to double-check, Richards missed the plane. Later in the year, a veteran Cowboy posted a sign in the locker room reading GO TO KROGER'S BEFORE NOV. 20 FOR YOUR FREE TURKEY! It was the oldest clubhouse trick in the book—and Richards eagerly darted to the supermarket. "Curvin was a fuckup," says center Mark Stepnoski, his teammate both at Pitt and in Dallas. "If a guy is going to screw up repeatedly, why would you trust him to do anything?" Richards would arrive late to practices and forget little things like, oh, his helmet. In team meetings he refused to take notes, an inexplicable stubbornness that infuriated running backs coach Joe Brodsky.

What especially irked Johnson was Richards's inability to hold on to the football. As a rookie he only received two carries, so fumbles were a nonissue. But during the 1992 season Richards was a disaster. He fumbled 3 times in 52 rushing attempts—compared with Emmitt Smith's 2 fumbles in 432 chances. His slippery hands especially stood out in practice, where three days rarely passed without Richards coughing it up. Johnson could tolerate a bad week. He could tolerate occasional distractions. He could even tolerate failure (well, at least to some degree). He could not tolerate fumbling.

"It's a shame, because physically Curvin was a carbon copy of Emmitt Smith," says Tony Jordan, a running back who spent two years in the NFL and attended training camp with Dallas in 1992. "But culturally Curvin was a little different. He had a laid-back approach that didn't lend itself to the intensity of pro football."

To eradicate the fumbleitis, Johnson would insert Richards into rushing drills and implore defenders to imagine themselves as pigeons and Richards the world's last bread crumb. "We'd do this drill where nobody was there to block the safeties," says safety Darren Woodson. "It was the toughest drill on the running backs, because a hole would open up and the safeties would just kill whoever was coming through. We knew it was a running drill, and they would put Curvin Richards in and Jimmy would say to us, 'Come down hard and smack the shit out of him.' Then he'd turn to Curvin and say, 'Make sure you hold on to the ball.'" Sometimes Richards held on. Oftentimes he didn't. "When that happened," says Woodson, "you are talking about the wrath of God coming down. *Goddammit! Motherfucker! What the hell!*'"

Dallas's final game of the season was a home contest against the lowly Chicago Bears. With 10:59 remaining in the fourth quarter, Dallas held a 27–0 lead that had the 63,101 fans dancing in the aisles. Needing 109 yards to surpass Pittsburgh's Barry Foster for the league rushing lead, Emmitt Smith clinched the crown with a 31-yard touchdown scamper early in the third quarter. Defensive tackle Russell Maryland scored his first career touchdown when he snagged a bobbled pitchout, rumbled 26 yards into the end zone, and celebrated with a belly flop. It was a good day. A great day. A celebratory day.

Until Curvin Richards entered the game.

In 13 carries, Richards fumbled twice. His first was returned 42 yards by Chicago lineman Chris Zorich. "Man, Jimmy was *mad*," says wide receiver Tim Daniel. "I was standing right there when he turned to Curvin and said, point blank, 'If you fumble again, your ass is cut and you'll never carry the ball for the Dallas Cowboys again.'"

To celebrate his purchase of the Dallas Cowboys, Jerry Jones *(right)* took Jimmy Johnson to Mia's, one of the city's best Mexican restaurants. Little did the men know that they would be spotted by a *Morning News* reporter—and that Mia's was the favorite eatery of Tom Landry *(below)*, the soon-to-be-fired legendary coach. *J. Mark Kegans/Dallas Morning News*

Neil Leifer/Sports Illustrated

Jerry Jones *(left)* and Jimmy Johnson strategize in the team's "war room." Though Jones often demanded credit, it was the Cowboys coach who was largely responsible for turning the franchise around with one dazzling personnel decision after another. *Peter Read Miller/Sports Illustrated*

Though blessed with myriad athletic gifts, Herschel Walker was the type of running back Johnson didn't want—uninstinctive and robotic. When the Vikings offered a bushel of players and draft picks in 1989, Johnson eagerly traded his star halfback. The deal was the key to the Dallas revival. *Manny Milan/Sports Illustrated*

Cowboys receiver Alvin Harper soars high into the air after scoring a touchdown in his team's Super Bowl XXVII rout of the Bills. Though Harper was as athletically gifted as Michael Irvin, his addiction to the nightlife kept him from living up to his potential. *Peter Read Miller/Sports Illustrated*

Jimmy Johnson receives the ceremonial Gatorade bath near the end of Super Bowl XXVII. Though he considered the victory the crowning achievement of his coaching career, the obsessive, intense Johnson never truly relished the accomplishment. *Jim Gund/Sports Illustrated*

Thanks to back-to-back Super Bowl titles, Jimmy Johnson and Jerry Jones were often all smiles (and drinks). Behind the scenes, however, the two men shared a distant, oft-heated relationship, burdened by Jones's jealousies and Johnson's insecurities. *Al Tielemans/Sports Illustrated*

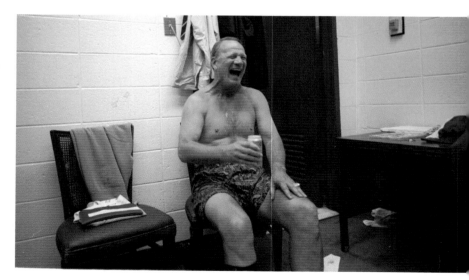

When Jones could no longer tolerate Johnson, he turned to an old friend—former Oklahoma coach Barry Switzer. Though Switzer was a charming man with a cheerful disposition, his time in Dallas was burdened by one unalienable truth: he wasn't an especially competent coach. *Lynn Johnson/Sports Illustrated*

Once as determined and team-oriented as any other Cowboy, Emmitt Smith turned increasingly self-centered with success. "He didn't give a shit about us anymore," says one teammate. "He was all about Emmitt, Emmitt, Emmitt." That said, Smith was a four-time NFL rushing champ who cleared 1,000 yards for eleven straight seasons in Dallas. He made the Cowboys offense go. *Robert Beck/Sports Illustrated*

Never exactly humble, Michael Irvin reached new heights of arrogance with the fame and the Super Bowls and the money. Says one teammate: "Before a game he'd have the people from Versace enter the locker room and measure him for a suit. He wanted to pick a feather from some exotic animal and put it in his derby hat. He wanted crocodile shoes with the tongue raised." Irvin's drug and woman problems helped bring down the dynasty. *Bill Frakes/Sports Illustrated*

Deion Sanders's arrival in Dallas after the 1994 season was accompanied by much fanfare and talk. Yet Sanders's lazy practice habits and indifference to details helped poison the locker room. *Bill Waugh/Associated Press*

Though Troy Aikman was initially optimistic about the arrival of Barry Switzer, he quickly learned to despise the man who, in his opinion, was destroying what Jimmy Johnson had worked so hard to build. *Lynn Johnson/Sports Illustrated*

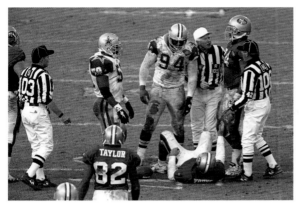

Defensive end Charles Haley was both a dynamic force on the Cowboys defensive line and seemingly psychotic. Shown here looming over former teammate Steve Young, Haley was known for exposing himself to peers and once urinating in a teammate's car. *V. J. Lovero/Sports Illustrated*

Tipping the scales at a whopping 360 pounds, Nate Newton was a dynamic—if not wee bit slow—offensive lineman who was partially responsible for the fabled White House. His most famous quote as a professional athlete: "We've got a little place over here where we're running some whores in and out, trying to be responsible, and we're criticized for that, too." *Al Tielemans/Sports Illustrated*

Though little more than an excellent special teams player, Kenny Gant started a Dallas phenomenon with his Shark Dance celebration after big plays. Before long, Gant was performing at birthday parties and bar mitzvahs. *Peter Read Miller/Sports Illustrated*

Emmitt Smith looks for a lane against Pittsburgh in Super Bowl XXX. The underdog Steelers held the NFL's rushing champ to 49 yards, but couldn't overcome two costly interceptions by quarterback Neil O'Donnell. Dallas won, 27–17. *Robert Beck/Sports Illustrated*

Less than two months after the glory of Super Bowl XXX, police found Michael Irvin in a Dallas hotel room with strippers, cocaine, drug paraphernalia, and sex toys. When Irvin wore a mink coat to the ensuing grand jury appearance, it came to symbolize all that was wrong with the decaying Dallas dynasty. To date, the franchise has not returned to the Super Bowl. *Bill Waugh/Associated Press*

Then Richards fumbled again. Johnson yanked him. As he jogged toward the sideline, Richards surely expected to be browbeaten by Johnson. Instead, the coach said the worst thing possible: absolutely nothing.

The Cowboys held on to win, 27–14, and entered the locker room with a franchise-best 13–3 record; an NFC East title; a bye week—and a coach *again* on the brink of a meltdown. Two weeks after the airplane incident, Johnson was even angrier. In his postgame press conference, he struggled to look directly at the assembled reporters, muttering, "The team is to be congratulated on winning thirteen games. [But] I was not happy with the sloppy play." Johnson furiously chewed out his players, pinpointing each miscue as if it had occurred in the final minutes of a deadlocked Super Bowl.

"This is crazy," Tony Wise, the offensive line coach, said. "Whether anybody around here believes it or not, we beat a pretty good football team today." Aikman was equally disturbed. "What really concerned me is that he didn't congratulate us at all," he said. "That was really hard on a lot of guys. There was a lot of bitterness."

After addressing (and undressing) the team, Johnson headed straight for Jerry Jones's suite to let his owner have it. With a quarter remaining in the game, Jones had escorted Prince Bandar bin Sultan, the Saudi ambassador to the United States, onto the sideline. When Johnson spotted the smiling owner and prince (as well as Bandar's *six* bodyguards), he flipped. "What the fuck are these guys doing here?" he yelled at Jones. "In the middle of a game that we're blowing?"

After Johnson calmed down, he told Jones that Richards had to be cut. The owner insisted they sleep on it, but the following morning the coach's mind was unchanged. In the history of the NFL postseason, teams won scoring a lot and scoring a little. They won with good defense and adequate defense. They won with clutch kickers and nervous kickers. They *never* won turning over the football.

When the Cowboys informed the league of the transaction, Joel Bussert, the NFL's senior director of player personnel, was shocked. "Jimmy," he said, "I just want to make sure you know that you'll have to pay this guy full playoff money and that you can't replace him now on the postseason roster."

"Fine," said Johnson. "I just want Richards away from us."

Upon learning of his fate from Johnson, the low-key Richards nodded his head, cleaned out his locker, and quietly departed Valley Ranch. His teammates were saddened, but hardly surprised. "Jimmy gave Curvin plenty of warnings," says James Washington. "What else was he supposed to do?"

The Cowboys were heading to the playoffs—one man down.

Chapter 12

HOW 'BOUT THEM COWBOYS!

Someone sent Mark Tuinei palm leaves back from his home in Hawaii. Before the game against the 49ers, Mark looked at me and said, "I wanna give you a Hail Mary with these leaves." I said, "Brother, I'll take whatever you've got."
—Tony Casillas, Cowboys defensive lineman

WHEN FANS LOOK back at the Dallas Cowboys of the 1990s, they tend to think of the glamour boys—Aikman, Emmitt, Irvin, Haley. Even Jimmy Johnson and Jerry Jones.

Truth be told, one of the most important—and overlooked—Cowboys also happened to be the only *real* Cowboy.

That's right. Along with emerging from relative obscurity to become Aikman's most reliable target, Jay Novacek was a true, honest-to-goodness cowboy. During offseasons he lived in a brick cabin on 3,500 acres in Gothenburg, Nebraska. The closest paved road was seven miles away. To reach the nearest city (Omaha) took three and a half hours by car. Among his closest friends, Novacek counted the 150 head of cattle roaming across his property. He wore a hat that read, simply, REDNECK.

"All he wanted," says Lin Elliott, the Cowboys' kicker, "was to go dove hunting."

Raised in a cornucopia of midwestern towns, young Jay watched and learned from his father, Pat, who coached high school football in such outposts as Martin, South Dakota, and Wyoming, Iowa. Pat was a quiet man who abhorred flashiness and stressed the virtues of hard work and precision. If Pat Novacek's receiver ran a 15-yard route, it damn well better have been *exactly* 15 yards. The father also taught the son about self-sufficiency. As the Novaceks sat down for dinner each night, they knew that the meat on their plates had been shot, killed, and skinned by dear ol' dad.

When Jay was in seventh grade, his family settled into Gothenburg and he settled into becoming an elite youth basketball and football player. Though he was an all-state signal caller at Gothenburg High, Jay was ignored by his dream college, the University of Oklahoma. Instead he signed with the University of Wyoming. When Nebraska coach Tom Osborne called the following day, Jay easily could have snubbed his prior commitment in favor of the mighty Cornhuskers. But that wouldn't have been the Novacek way. "He had given Wyoming his word," said Pat.

In four years of college, Novacek rose from obscurity to stardom. As a senior all-American he averaged 22.5 yards on 33 receptions. In track and field, he won the 1984 Western Athletic Conference decathlon title and was invited to the U.S. Olympic Trials.

Convinced they had stumbled upon a raw Kellen Winslow prototype, the St. Louis Cardinals used a sixth-round pick in the 1985 draft to select Novacek, turned him into a wide receiver/tight end hybrid—then barely used him. In five seasons, Novacek never exceeded 38 receptions or 4 touchdowns. "It was stupidity," says Cliff Stoudt, a former Cardinals quarterback. "Gene Stallings was our coach, and I used to think, 'If this guy's such a brilliant leader, how can he keep our best player off the field?'"

The Cardinals let Novacek walk after the 1989 season, and Dallas was the only team to offer a contract. Though Jones and Johnson would have you believe they saw magic in the 6-foot-4, 231-pounder, truth is Novacek was a low-risk shot in the dark who couldn't have been any worse than the incumbent, Steve Folsom.

"No one else wanted me," says Novacek. "I was a nobody. But when I arrived in Dallas, I found a team with a cockiness and drive I'd never seen before. There was this belief that the Super Bowl was inevitable. I loved that."

With the Cardinals, Novacek went through signal callers like Prince goes through backup singers. From Stoudt to Gary Hogeboom to Timm Rosenbach to Tom Tupa, St. Louis offered defenses a buffet of mediocre, lead-footed stiffs.

Then Novacek found Aikman.

The chemistry was undeniable. Both fans of country music, cowboy boots, pickup trucks, cold beer, and spotlight avoidance, the quarterback and tight end felt an immediate kinship. Aikman supplied Novacek with the one thing he craved—a quarterback robotic in his ability to pinpoint exact locations, time after time. "Early on when I was playing with Troy he'd come out of a break and the linemen and linebackers would be blocking the visual path between he and me," Novacek says. "All of a sudden I'd see this hand rise up and throw the ball my way. It'd get to me every time. I'd say, 'Did you even see me?' He'd say, 'No, but I knew you'd be there.' I'll take that sort of trust over a Super Bowl title any day."

Aikman was even more euphoric. Here was a new breed of tight end. Sure, Novacek was far from a bruising blocker. But he utilized angles and body leverage to keep pass rushers at bay. Most important, he was uncoverable. Too fast for linebackers and too big for defensive backs, Novacek ran the 8-to-10-yard buttonhook with unrivaled effectiveness. "I called Jay 'Superman,'" says Vinson Smith, the Cowboys linebacker. "He might have been the best athlete on the team. You looked at him and thought, 'No way.' Then you'd cover him and he'd catch everything."

In 1990 and '91 Novacek caught 59 passes, and in 1992 his 68 receptions set a team record for the position. Where other offensive coordinators deemed Novacek undersized, Norv Turner salivated at the never-ending matchup problems. No longer did a tight end have to be burly, slow, and excessively rugged.

Following a bye week, on January 10, 1993, the Cowboys would open the playoffs by hosting—of all teams—the loathed Philadelphia Eagles, the one franchise Johnson preferred *not* to play. Although the Cowboy coach knew his team was far superior to the Eagles, there was something about Philly that brought out the yips. Back when Aikman was a first- and second-year quarterback, the Eagles took pleasure in beating him senseless. One couldn't help but wonder whether such poundings stuck with Aikman, especially after Philadelphia sacked him 11 times in a 1991 contest.

Though the Eagles under second-year coach Rich Kotite were less intimidating than the snarling, growling Buddy Ryan incarnation, they were still an 11–5 club with a swarming, cheap shot–taking, trash-talking defense. As if this point needed to be reinforced, Philadelphia safety Andre Waters—aka "Dirty Waters"—placed Emmitt Smith atop his I-will-hit-you-late-and-below-the-knees list, telling the media, "Two of us are going to walk onto the field, but only one of us is going to walk off."

Instead of shuddering, the Cowboys clipped the safety's words and added them to a locker room bulletin board layered with articles about the Eagles. Philadelphia had talked much trash over the years, and perhaps the words once had an impact. But these were the new Cowboys. The *better* Cowboys. Even if the Eagles could contain Smith, pressure Aikman, and blanket Irvin with cornerback Eric Allen, they lacked anyone with the skills to stick Novacek. He would make a difference—Turner was quite certain of it.

As the Eagles sprinted into Texas Stadium before the start of the game, they were greeted by venomous spewings that laid to rest the gentlemanly reputation Landry had once established. Fans heckled Waters, insulting his mother, his father, his ugly face, and his upright style of running. They screamed and yelled and shouted and hollered—and relished one of the biggest routs in either team's playoff history.

Before a sellout crowd of 63,721 (many of whom paid in excess of $1,000 for scalped tickets), the Cowboys opened up a 7–3 lead on

Aikman's touchdown pass to Derek Tennell, and late in the second quarter extended the lead to 14–3 when the quarterback hit Novacek with a 6-yard bullet across the middle of the end zone. Though he caught only 3 balls for 36 yards, Novacek was an obsession for Philadelphia's defenders. They shadowed him with a linebacker; had the strong safety cheat up—and were meticulously shredded by Smith (114 rushing yards), Irvin (6 catches, 88 yards), and Aikman (200 passing yards, 2 touchdowns). The Cowboys jumped out to a 34–3 lead and laughed all the way to the final whistle, winning 34–10.

"There was a lot of talking before this game," said Cowboys linebacker Ken Norton, Jr. "We did our talking on the field. I don't think they have too much they can say right now." The greatest joy for Dallas came in mocking Waters, who spent the afternoon flailing at opposing receivers and missing tackles. During a stop in play, Waters jogged up to Smith and whispered, "I'm gonna break your fuckin' leg."

Smith laughed. "Whatever," he said. "Whatever."

After the game, an eager media throng gathered around the safety's locker, anxious for an assessment.

For one of the few times in his thirty years, Waters had nothing to say.

In general society, eleven years can be an eternity. It's the difference between a seventeen-year-old kid and a twenty-eight-year-old man—high school and college graduations, marriage, home ownership, children, mortgages, investments, loans.

In sports, however, eleven years passes like the flicking of a light switch.

Such was the feeling in Dallas when it came to the Cowboys, the 49ers, and "The Catch." Though eleven long years had passed since Joe Montana avoided the rush, rolled right, and found Dwight Clark skying through the back of the end zone for the NFC Championship, the pain remained as raw in Dallas as vinegar atop a paper cut. The Cowboys should have played in their sixth Super Bowl in 1982. It was there for the taking. Right there. Just stop Montana one last time and . . .

Sigh.

With the rout of Philadelphia, the Cowboys were rewarded with a trip to San Francisco, where the 49ers once again stood in the way of a Super Bowl berth. But whereas the '81 49ers were out-of-nowhere up-starts featuring a blossoming quarterback (Montana) and dozens of no-names, the team Dallas now prepared for stood as an undisputed dynasty. These were the high-flying Niners of Steve Young, Ricky Watters, Brent Jones, John Taylor, and, of course, the incomparable Jerry Rice. With a 14–2 regular-season record, then a 20–13 win over Washington in the Divisional Playoffs, Coach George Seifert's club was the smart-money pick to win its fifth Vince Lombardi Trophy. The Niners were 4-point favorites over Dallas, and with good reason.

Jimmy Johnson made a career out of talking the talk and walking the walk, but any confidence he projected in the week leading up to the game served only to mask a harrowing reality: He wasn't quite sure his team could win. "They were better than us," says Johnson. "And not only slightly better. They had more talent, they were more experienced, and they were more complete. We were the youngest team in the league and they had four Super Bowl trophies."

Johnson feared the 49ers' talent, but he was truly petrified by the field. Even at the start of the season, Candlestick Park was a below-average NFL playground, what with its surface being battered for eighty-one games every year by baseball's San Francisco Giants. Now, after five months of abuse, Candlestick was the Everglades. "[The field] was abominable," wrote Brian Hewitt of the *Chicago Sun-Times* following the Redskins game. "Footing was a rumor. And every time anybody made a cut, the movement produced a large divot. By the end of the game it looked like a Civil War battlefield." The NFL flew in grounds consultant George Toma to resod the field, a Herculean task akin to seeding the Sahara. He and twenty-six cowork-ers replaced the grass in the middle of the field, and at one end repaired the gridiron from sideline to sideline. "This," Toma said, "is hands down the worst field I've ever seen." Making matters worse, the weekend forecast called for torrential rains.

"I'm not gonna lie—we were nervous," says Kevin Gogan, the veteran offensive lineman. "I knew they had a great team, but I was mainly worried about not falling on my ass in a puddle."

As soon as it was determined that Dallas and San Francisco would meet for the NFC Championship on January 17, 1993, members of the media began predicting how badly Jerry Rice would burn Larry Brown and Kevin "Pup" Smith, the Cowboys' young cornerbacks.

While the mild-manned Brown responded to such a slight with a shrug, Smith took it personally. A first-year player with a mere seven starts to his résumé, Smith genuinely believed he could manhandle the legendary Rice. "Kevin didn't back down," says Darren Woodson, the Dallas safety. "He and Michael Irvin would go at it in practice with these knock-down, drag-out, one-on-one drills that convinced Kevin he could play with anybody."

Beneath a pewter late-afternoon sky (but no raindrops), the two teams took the field for warm-ups with unusual intensity and emotion. While the 49ers tended to be significantly more low-key than Dallas, San Francisco's players were screaming, pointing, jumping up and down, barking like starved dogs. The team's star running back, Ricky Watters, jogged toward the Cowboys and began taunting—"Y'all are nothing! Y'all gonna get your asses kicked!" Kevin Smith decided he'd heard enough. Upon spotting Rice, he laughed aloud and screamed, "Gonna be a long day for you, motherfucker!" The receiver did a double take. He was Jerry Rice, dammit. Who the hell was Biff Smith? Or was it Pete Smith? "Jimmy used to say that cockiness borders on confidence, because if you're unwilling to take chances you won't get to where you want to go," says Jim Jeffcoat. "He wanted players who believed they could beat anyone in the league on any given day. That was Pup."

Technically, Smith *wasn't* up to the challenge: Rice had one of his better *statistical* games of the season, catching 8 passes for 123 yards and a touchdown. But in a sport of emotion and heart and physicality, numbers have limited reach. Beginning with the 49ers' first offensive series, Smith was in Rice's face and head all day, talking nonstop trash, kicking him in the calves, elbowing his ribs, knocking his shoulder pads. "All that shit I saw on TV is bullshit!" Smith yelled. "If you're the best in the league, I'm gonna have a *looooong* damn career." This was Rice's eighth year in the NFL, and no other cornerback—not Darrell Green, not Mike Haynes, not Rod Woodson, not Deron Cherry—had ever treated him with such disrespect. Though the press had spent much of the week hyping Charles Haley's revenge against his old franchise, it was the rookie defensive back who provided the jolt. After one too many "motherfuckers," Haley pulled Smith aside and said, "Man, that's Jerry Rice. You can't talk to him like that."

"Fuck you!" Smith yelled. "Who the fuck are you playing with? You might as well go put on your little gold helmet, you little fucking pussy!"

As it turned out, Smith had every right to talk trash. The Cowboys didn't beat the 49ers so much as they thugged them. After spending all week publicly fretting about the threat of mud and rain, Johnson came out and attacked. The first half ended in a 10–10 tie, but Dallas pounded the 49ers at every opportunity. As Steve Young scrambled from the pocket in the second quarter, Russell Maryland lassoed him from behind and ripped his helmet off. When Haley knocked down a Young pass, he cursed his ex-teammate out. It was no-holds-barred football, and the dirtier the Dallas uniforms, the dirtier the attitude. "We were not going to lose that game," says Kevin Smith. "No way."

Dallas broke the halftime deadlock with its first long touchdown drive of the afternoon. Starting from their own 22-yard line, the Cowboys methodically marched down the field, using eight plays to move 78 yards. On third-and-7, Aikman dropped back and zipped a 16-yard completion to Irvin, putting his team in 49er territory. On the next play, Aikman went for broke, hitting Alvin Harper down the sideline for a 38-yard gain to the San Francisco 7. Two snaps later, fullback Daryl Johnston stormed into the end zone, handing Dallas a 17–10 advantage.

The 49ers responded with a field goal, but on their next series the Cowboys scored again, this time on a 16-yard pass to Emmitt Smith. With 12:25 remaining in the game, Dallas held a 24–13 lead.

Then the Cowboys coaching staff outthought itself.

Norton intercepted Young on the ensuing possession, and Emmitt Smith's 28-yard scamper through the San Francisco defense gave the Cowboys a first-and-10 from the 49er 16-yard line. But Dallas struggled to move the ball, and found itself facing fourth-and-1 on the 7 with 7:13 left to play. Johnson looked down the sideline toward Lin Elliott, the rookie free agent kicker who'd missed 9 of 35 field goal attempts. Johnson liked Elliott; thought the boy would have a solid NFL career. But now was not the time to test the mettle of young kickers—it was the time to put a knife to the 49ers' throat.

Norv Turner called for Aikman to hand the ball off to Emmitt Smith, who had run for 1,713 yards in the regular season and surely could grind his way to one more. Johnson signed off.

But with the Candlestick Park faithful screaming and the field looking like a half-baked cake mix and the future of two franchises in the balance, Smith took the handoff, cut behind right tackle—and met a brick wall: Mike Walter, linebacker. No gain.

On the sideline, Johnson was dumbfounded. Did that just happen? The 49ers offense charged back onto the field, and with 4:22 remaining Young hit Rice with a touchdown pass, cutting the Dallas lead to 24–20. It was not hard to predict what was about to transpire: The 49ers' defense would stop the Cowboys, then Young would strut back onto the field, guide his team to glory, and take the greatest franchise in modern football history to a fifth Super Bowl. Wrote Paul Zimmerman in *Sports Illustrated*: "The momentum had switched, all right, and when you're a coach caught in a momentum shift, you do one of two things: You ride with it and pray, running the ball and working the clock in the hope that the other team won't have enough time to beat you, or you try to switch the momentum back in your favor and put the game away."

Johnson was no wimp. He chose the latter.

The Dallas coach sent Aikman onto the field with instructions to win a trip to the Super Bowl. On first down from the Cowboys' 21-yard line, Turner called for Ace Right 896 F Flat—a crossing pattern to Irvin, who had spent much of the day manhandling the 49er secondary. Dallas had already run the play successfully five or six times, with the ball always going to Harper, who, as the second option, would run 10 yards and curl. "Michael got greedy," said Aikman. "He was tired of running [the cross] and not getting the ball. So as we're breaking the huddle, Michael says to Alvin, 'You take the [cross], I'm taking the [curl].'" Aikman dropped back and immediately checked on Irvin, who was blanketed, so he looked for Harper. "We rarely threw the ball to Harper on the slant because he's got those short 'alligator arms,'" said Johnson. But as Irvin's understudy crossed the middle of the field, Aikman hit him in dead stride, cornerback Don Griffin slipping a couple of yards behind. Throughout his first two years in the league, Harper had earned the reputation as an undisciplined route runner with a low football IQ. This time he was perfect. Harper angled across Candlestick's battered turf, mud and muck leaping from his heels. When he was finally tackled, it was at the 49ers' 9-yard line.

The stadium, euphoric seconds earlier, was now a winter's crypt. No noise. No emotion. The 49ers were about to lose, and the Bay Area's denizens seemed to know it.

On third-and-goal Aikman hooked up with Kelvin Martin on a 6-yard touchdown pass and, even with a blocked extra point, the Cowboys held a commanding 30–20 lead. When safety James Washington intercepted Young's pass to Mike Sherrard, the Cowboys could finally celebrate. They had overcome the weather, the naysayers, the Team of the '80s, and the specter of "The Catch" to reach the Super Bowl for the first time since 1979. For Kevin Smith, the capper came late in the fourth quarter, when a beaten-down Rice cut-blocked him from behind *and* flashed the middle finger.

"You don't do that," laughs Smith, "if you're winning."

As his team stormed into the locker room, hugging and whooping, a relieved, exhausted, *giddy* Johnson praised the men he had tormented, tortured, loathed, and loved. Aikman, the quarterback he had once called a loser, completed 24 of 34 passes for 322 yards and 2 touchdowns. Emmitt Smith, the running back he wasn't interested in, ran for 114 gutsy yards. Irvin, the receiver he considered cutting, caught 6 balls for 86 yards. Robert Jones, the linebacker he humiliated, made several key tackles. Three years after their 1–15 debacle, the Cowboys were heading to the Rose Bowl, site of Super Bowl XXVII.

Surrounded by his players, Johnson beamed from ear to ear. "Everybody," he screamed, "you did one helluva job! And all I've got to say is, how 'bout them Cowboys!"

Yeah!

Fuck yeah!

Let's get 'em!

Hell, yes!

The Buffalo Bills awaited.

Chapter 13

SUPER BOWL XXVII (AKA: DON'T KISS JULIE BROWN!)

Our team partied that Super Bowl week.
Boy, did we ever party.
—Darren Woodson, Cowboys safety

THE DALLAS COWBOYS spent much of the next six days bunkered at Valley Ranch. They finally flew to Los Angeles on the afternoon of Sunday, January 24, eager to dive into an ocean of pre–Super Bowl XXVII goodies but equally intent on avoiding the unavoidable pitfalls.

Yes, the Buffalo Bills awaited them.

But so did temptation.

Super Bowls are tailor-made for mishaps. Take forty-six horny, handsome, athletic, twenty-something-year-old men, place them in a city known for sexy women, late-night clubs, and rock-your-world drugs . . . then shake and serve. Only two Cowboys—Charles Haley and Ray Horton—had experienced a Super Bowl before. For the rest, this was Mardi Gras.

Though it would be six more years before an Atlanta Falcons safety named Eugene Robinson was arrested the night before the Super Bowl for offering an undercover female police officer $40 for oral sex, Jimmy Johnson made certain his players comprehended—or at least *seemed* to comprehend—what they were in for.

Before allowing his troops to hit L.A. for a Sunday night of all-out debauchery, Johnson called a meeting to issue a stern warning. The Cowboys had no curfew their first three nights, then an 11 P.M. room check the rest of the week. "When you lay down a two-by-four board in the middle of a room, most everybody can get on that board and walk across it and not fall," Johnson said. "Now take that board up ten stories high between two buildings. Some of the people aren't going to make it across that same board because they let themselves get distracted.

"If you let it overwhelm you that this is going to be the single-most-watched sporting event in the entire world this year; if it overwhelms you that there are three thousand media people here; if it overwhelms you because of how much money is involved, it will be a distraction. Don't be distracted by the fact that there are other things going on here besides football this week."

As soon as they were dismissed from official team duties, the Cowboys stormed Los Angeles like ants upon a picnic basket. Headquartered in the luxurious Loews Santa Monica Beach Hotel (as opposed to the Bills, who were shacked up at the Hyatt Regency in boring, deserted-at-night downtown L.A.), members of the team *might* have thought they'd hit it big when they headed down to the lobby bar and spotted the likes of Gene Hackman, Tom Berenger, Whoopi Goldberg, and Betty White (Yes, *Betty White!*). But they *knew* they had it made when it was learned that a who's who roster of models from a New York City agency were pitching tent in the hotel for a week of photo shoots.

Such potential conquests were why, in the days after the San Francisco triumph, the Cowboys held a vote as to whether wives should be allowed to come immediately or be forced to wait until later in the week. Nary a player raised a hand in favor of an early arrival.

"I'd say most of the women knew what was going on and sort of accepted it as a trade-off for the lifestyle," says Lisa Holmes, the spouse of Clayton Holmes, a defensive back. "As a wife, you'd find phone numbers in your husband's pocket, find pictures of half-naked women with CALL ME notes on the back, know he was going to a strip club with the guys. I guess we all wanted to believe the best, but we knew."

With rare exception, the majority of the Cowboys viewed getting married as an annoying-yet-required obligation that men in their mid-twenties did because, uh . . . hmm . . . well . . . nobody was quite sure why. Some married their childhood sweethearts. Others wed college girlfriends. The vast majority of WOCs (Wives of Cowboys) were long-legged, big-breasted beauties with résumés chock-full of homecoming queen anointments. Yet the vast majority of their husbands cheated on them with reckless, indifferent abandon.

"I was a terrible husband—the worst there ever was," says Nate Newton. "I loved my wife, but I didn't want to be just with her. She'd be lying if she told you I said it'd be any different. My wife knew who I was. Oh, she'd say, 'But you were gonna try!' Maybe, but this is who I am and this is how I act."

"What can I tell you?" says James Washington. "A lot of us were addicted to *it*."

To what?

"To the pussy."

In Los Angeles, *it* was everywhere. At the hotel bar, where women in miniskirts and leather pants paraded their wares like peacocks at a petting zoo. At the clubs, where "Oh my God—he's a Cowboy!" spread from lips to ears to lips to ears. "Being a Cowboy—the women came easy," says Lin Elliott, the scrawny 6-foot, 180-pound rookie *kicker*. "I was a slightly-out-of-shape balding guy who wore glasses, but the star on the helmet works magic. If I had practiced kicking footballs as hard as I worked on chasing girls and drinking beers, I'd have had a fifteen-year career."

Throughout a week that, according to the pundits, was all about gridiron supremacy and the American game and football immortality, Dallas's players overtook the town. There were parties atop parties, from singer Babyface's gala at Club Escape to a ten-women-for-every-guy shindig hosted by rapper Heavy D. The ultimate blast was NBA star Ron Harper's twenty-ninth birthday bonanza, featuring a wall-to-wall army of celebrity men and half-naked women. "Man, I met *a lot* of people in that one night," says Kenny Gant, the reserve safety. "I met Magic Johnson; I met the chicks from [the TV show] *Martin* and danced with them. It was insane."

In what may well be an NFL record, Michael Irvin escorted approximately a dozen women to his hotel room in a four-day span—and his wife didn't get mad. Not once. Of course, she didn't know, either. "The one thing I feel guilty about is helping Mike lie so many times to Sandy," says Anthony Montoya, Irvin's assistant and a team gofer. "He cheated on her nonstop, and we always had to make sure she never found out. It hurt me, because she deserved better."

"Mike had more pussy stories than anyone I've ever met," says Jean-Jacques Taylor, the longtime *Dallas Morning News* writer. "He was legendary." Others—Alvin Harper, Nate Newton, and Charles Haley among them—were near legendary. If Irvin had a dozen women, the nine or ten Alvin Harper latched onto wasn't so shabby, either (his wife, Jamise, was in the dark, too).

In storming their way through Los Angeles, the Cowboys somehow managed to escape the gossip columns. This was due in large part to Bills linebacker Darryl Talley, who on that first Sunday night accompanied some teammates to a Sunset Boulevard club called Roxbury and found himself face-to-face with Magic Johnson's bodyguard. According to witnesses, Talley, a ten-year veteran and two-time Pro Bowler, and Bills quarterback Jim Kelly drank excessively and teased Johnson—who is HIV-positive—about his nightclubbing ways. The ribbing went too far. Johnson's bodyguard—a mountainous man nicknamed "Big Anthony"—first advised Bills lineman Bruce Smith to have his teammate "cool it down," then punched Talley in the face, flipped him to the floor, and said, "Let's stop it here." The *Fort Worth Star-Telegram* termed it "the first unofficial contact drill of Super Bowl XXVII."

Although Dallas's players were significantly wilder than the relatively mild Bills (a handful of Cowboys were at Roxbury when "Talleygate" took place), the hundreds of media representatives in attendance found the incident too juicy to ignore. Talley was forced to hold a redemptive press conference, but when his answers came off as unrepentant ("What would *you* do in a bar?" he snapped when asked if drinking was involved) Bills coach Marv Levy tried to defend his player. The succeeding twenty minutes were even more disastrous. "The report is untrue," Levy said. "It didn't happen. It's a lie! It's a lie!"

In addition to finding the whole Talley affair uproarious, the Cowboys were encouraged that, in the heat of the action, not one Bill came to the linebacker's defense. As he sat bloodied and humiliated on the Roxbury floor, teammates failed to gather around Talley. "No chance that happens with us," says Kevin Smith. "Absolutely no chance. We looked out for each other."

Had this incident been insufficient to convince the Cowboys that they would walk all over the Bills, then a final week of practices and tape sessions did the trick. Making their third straight Super Bowl appearance (and still without a win), Buffalo was a solid, talent-laden ball club that committed a lot of mistakes and, according to Johnson, played tissue-soft football. In an early-week meeting with his players, Johnson implored the Cowboys to smack Kelly around—even when there was no reason to do so. "Make sure he knows you're there," Johnson said. "Touch his uniform, tap his helmet, step on his foot—make him *feel* us. Make him scared." The coach assured his team that the Bills, fearful of dropping yet another Super Bowl, would inevitably unravel. "Capitalize on mistakes," he said, "and we can't lose."

The youthful Cowboys were portrayed as the team more prone to nervousness, and nothing could have been further from the truth. Take Tuesday's Media Day, when Dallas's players and coaches gathered on the Dodger Stadium infield and set the press ablaze with a charm, charisma, and swagger last seen at a Super Bowl seven years earlier, when the Chicago Bears of Jim McMahon, William "The Refrigerator" Perry, and Walter Payton dazzled the masses.

The star of the show was Johnson, who seemed to enjoy escaping from his cave after a season of eighteen-hour workdays. Runner-up was Johnson's hair, famously coiffed to take the form of a light brown lady-bug shell. Throughout his years as the Cowboy coach, Johnson had faced an endless stream of questions about his trim—*What do you use? How come it never moves?*

Now, Johnson reveled in the attention, especially when a sexy MTV veejay named Downtown Julie Brown ran her hands through his scalp and smiled devilishly. "What's the one rule of thumb you've given to the players?" she asked, shoving a microphone in the coach's mug.

"Don't kiss Julie Brown!" Johnson yelped—then smooched her on the lips.

The Buffalo Bills came to Los Angeles sporting a 14–5 record and featuring a high-flying, no-huddle offense. Led by Kelly, running back Thurman Thomas, and 65-catch receiver Andre Reed, the Bills scored the third-most points in the league, regularly overwhelming opposing defenses.

But while the Cowboys enjoyed a week of good times and crisp practices ("In my four years with the team, we'd never, ever looked that sharp," says receivers coach Hubbard Alexander. "I don't think we dropped a pass all week"), Buffalo appeared tight. The team's workouts were unusually quiet and stiff. Banter was kept to a minimum. Such was the by-product of repeated big-game failure. Drop one Super Bowl—no biggie. Drop two in a row—trouble's brewing. Drop three—you're Greg Norman.

But the Bills were more than tight. They were anxious. Paranoid, even. On the Monday before the game, the Bills practiced in jerseys without numbers—an effort by Levy to confuse the imaginary spies he believed to be watching Buffalo's every move. Two days later, Bill Polian, the team's general manager, demanded security investigate a pair of binoculars peeking out from a nearby window (nothing was uncovered). On Thursday, three days before the game, Polian ordered that security confiscate the film of an Associated Press photographer. Every move the Bills made reeked of nervousness. "Apples to apples, I think we were the better team," says Bills safety Kurt Schulz, a rookie at the time. "But they had something that allowed them to play at a higher level. Maybe the monkey on our back was too heavy. One thing I know—the pressure we put on ourselves was greater than what the Cowboys felt."

Especially at ease was Aikman, the former UCLA quarterback who felt at home practicing on his old campus in his old city. Save for a highly publicized dinner date with actress Janine Turner of the TV show *Northern Exposure,* Aikman kept the week simple. A few days before the game, he was driving along the Pacific Coast Highway with Mike Fisher and Richie Whitt of the *Fort Worth Star-Telegram* when a radio DJ cracked the joke, "What's the difference between a football and a gallstone?"

Lengthy pause.

"Jim Kelly can pass a gallstone."

Aikman smiled. "Don't laugh too hard," he told the scribes. "Come Sunday they could be making that joke about me."

But they wouldn't be, and the Cowboys knew it. On the Saturday night before the game, Johnson relocated his team from the hopping Loews Santa Monica Beach Hotel to the quiet Beverly Garland Hotel, where they could peacefully reflect in the final hours. In his address to the players over dinner, Johnson spoke of "planting the seed."

"I know that your thoughts are that you'd like to do this for certain individuals," he said. "The best way to honor those individuals is to go out there and play your ass off for yourself. Because this is something that all of us will have with us for the rest of our lives. The best way for those people to remember you and remember this game is with a Super Bowl ring on their finger, remembering the feeling of the win."

The room fell silent. Players looked at one another, almost in a sort of reverential meditation. "We loved each other—all of us," says Newton. "The last thing we wanted to do was let our teammates down.

We were gonna win the motherfucking game for each other. For our brothers."

For the first time since the team's arrival in Los Angeles, that night not one player violated curfew or hit the town for a few beers or invited three strippers onto the premises. Instead, the Cowboys congregated in their hotel rooms and played cards, watched movies, ordered room service, and talked shop. "That was something special about that night," says Kenny Gant. "I was Alvin Harper's roommate, and we just sat there with Clayton Holmes and Derrick Gainer, unable to sleep, planning for the biggest game of our lives. Just talking."

Aikman, who had spent most of the week holed up with his new Mac Apple PowerBook 160, hung out with John Gesek, Jay Novacek, and long snapper Dale Hellestrae and watched *Unforgiven*, the Academy Award–winning Clint Eastwood film. In one of the more memorable scenes, the characters portrayed by Eastwood and Gene Hackman fight beneath a driving rainstorm.

"Is that lightning coming from outside?" Aikman said, turning toward Gesek.

"Nope," Gesek said. "It's the movie."

"No . . . no," said Novacek, peeking out the window. "The rain's coming down in buckets."

Aikman's face went blank.

"Shit," he said. "I can't throw a wet ball."

He stood up and left the room.

The most important kickoff of Aikman's life was less than twelve hours away.

The weather would clear.

His nerves? Well, that remained to be seen.

"What the fuck?"

Dave Wannstedt repeated himself. "What the fuck?"

Here he was, sitting in the press box above the Rose Bowl, looking down upon a splendid stadium packed with 98,374 fans (the largest crowd to ever see a Cowboys game), and everything was off. A man wed to routine, the Cowboys defensive coordinator had a minute-by-minute approach to football preparation. There was an exact time to leave the locker room, an exact time to take the elevator up to the box, an exact time to double-check his equipment.

But this Super Bowl . . . this damned Super Bowl . . .

"I get up there and go through my final checklist," he says. "And someone yells out, 'Fifteen minutes until kickoff!' I was livid." Actually, Wannstedt was anxious. Anxious to start the game. Anxious to win. Anxious to move on.

Unlike the other Cowboy assistants, eight of whom would return to the team in 1993, a new gig awaited Wannstedt. Twelve days earlier the Chicago Bears had hired him to replace Mike Ditka as head coach. It was a noteworthy accomplishment for a blue-collar kid from Pittsburgh who scrapped his way up the coaching ladder. Wannstedt was professional, hard-nosed, and disciplined, and his players felt a unique loyalty. "The respect Dave earned was forged out of his honesty," says linebacker Vinson Smith. "If Dave told you something, you knew it was true. In the NFL that's pretty rare."

In the aftermath of the Bears' announcement, friction formed between Johnson and his defensive coordinator. As they prepared for Buffalo, coaches speculated about who would follow Wannstedt to the Windy City. On a Wednesday afternoon Johnson walked into a coaches' meeting and overheard his assistants debating whether to flee for Chicago. "Fuck all of you!" he snapped. "Why don't you just all get the fuck to Chicago!" Though Johnson was respected by his staff as a quick mind and unrivaled delegator, his moodiness could wear thin. Johnson demanded the same of his assistants as he did of himself—100 percent commitment to the game of football. While Wannstedt was equally intense, he possessed an empathy Johnson lacked. One evening Johnson and his coaches would be gorging on nachos and beer at On The Border, the Dallas restaurant where they congregated every Friday night, and the next he would be cold and dismissive. "Jimmy was not always easy to grasp," says Hubbard Alexander, the receivers coach.

"He had some mystery to him." On the flight to Los Angeles, Johnson and Wannstedt—the closest of pals—did not sit next to each other. It was a first in their four years in Dallas.

So as he sat atop the stadium, looking down at *his* Cowboys for the final time, Wannstedt desperately wanted the game to begin. Instead, there was hoopla. The famed Rockettes performed a tribute to Hollywood, music, and the movies. O. J. Simpson flipped the opening coin. Garth Brooks sang the national anthem. As he wrapped up the song, a soft rumbling filled the stadium. *Whooooooosh!* Five F-15 fighter jets soared above. The players felt the energy. Nervous energy. Excited energy. A record 133.4 million viewers watched on televisions around the world. "I just couldn't believe I was standing there, playing in the Super Bowl," says Robert Jones. "One year ago I was watching the dang thing on TV from my dorm room. Now here I was." Gesek stood alongside Chad Hennings, the former Air Force pilot, who gazed longingly at the jets. "Man," Hennings yelped, "those are sure fun to fly!" Irvin walked along the sideline, encouraging . . . motivating . . . directing. "This is what it's all about!" he said. "This is what we've been waiting for! Let's do it! Let's do it! Let's do it!" James Washington and Ken Norton, pals dating back to their days at UCLA, uttered the same prayer they'd recited for years—"Lord, don't move a mountain, but give us the strength to climb it." Growing up in the rough Watts section of L.A., Washington would watch his hero, Raiders cornerback Lester Hayes, and think, "If Lester can get to the Super Bowl, one day I will, too." Now he was trembling with emotion.

Backup tight end Derek Tennell, another UCLA grad, gazed into the stands and couldn't believe his good fortune. Less than one month earlier he'd been unemployed and considering law school. Then, because of a knee injury to Alfredo Roberts, the Cowboys signed Tennell. Despite never fully learning the playbook, he'd appeared in two games with Dallas, and now he was sixty minutes removed from a Super Bowl ring. Five seasons earlier, Tennell had been a replacement player with the Cleveland Browns, an unforgivable sin in the eyes of most NFL veterans. But the Cowboys took Tennell in and embraced him. "All I'd ever wanted was to win the Super Bowl," Tennell says. "It was right there in front of me." Immediately before the game Haley— being Haley—walked up to Tennell and started ripping into him about not belonging with Dallas. "You're a nobody!" Haley said. "You're . . ." Haley was messing with the wrong guy. "Charles," said Tennell, "I don't care who you are or how much money you make—I will break your nose and your jaw if you keep talking."

Haley slinked away.

With sweaty palms and pounding hearts and racing minds, the Cowboys' kickoff team jogged onto the field for the start of a game they expected to own. Johnson's earlier words echoed in their ears: *"Buffalo is not a physical team, they're a finesse team. They put the ball in the air, so punish them every time a wide receiver or running back touches the ball. Rip the ball away. Hit them repeatedly. I recruited Thurman Thomas at Oklahoma State, and he will put the ball on the ground. Swarm him. Don't give him a crack."*

"We knew we were better," says Kevin Gogan, the offensive lineman. "We had no doubts about winning that game."

It did not begin well. After limiting the Bills to five plays on their opening possession, Dallas received the ball, picked up a mere 1 yard, then lined up in punt formation on fourth-and-9 from its own 16-yard line. Because of an injury to linebacker Dixon Edwards, Robert Jones was forced to play special teams, something he had not done all season. When the ball was snapped, Steve Tasker, Buffalo's special teams wizard, snaked inside of Jones, soared through the air, and smothered Mike Saxon's punt. As the Cowboys jogged off the field, the action was replayed on the stadium JumboTron. Johnson watched, tracked down Jones, grabbed him by the uniform collar, and ripped him to pieces. "Rightfully so," says Jones. "I blew it." When, five plays later, Thomas ran for a 2-yard touchdown, the Bills sideline was euphoric. "That was a huge play," says Steve Christie, the Bills kicker. "We were sure the momentum was about to swing our way. This was our game. *Ours.*"

The Cowboys' offense struggled for most of the first quarter, failing to pick up Buffalo's blitzing linebackers and allowing the Bills' mediocre cornerbacks to sag in and take away corner routes from Irvin and Harper.

Then, in a flash, everything changed. With five minutes remaining in the quarter, Buffalo had a first-and-10 at midfield when safety Kenny Gant charged untouched through the middle of the offensive line, forcing Kelly to uncork a throw toward tight end Pete Metzelaars. In stepped Washington, who picked off the ball at the Dallas 40-yard line. Six plays later Aikman dropped back three steps, looked straight down the field, and hit Novacek with a 23-yard touchdown pass to tie the game and steal the momentum. "The problem with having a history like we had is doubt creeps in quickly," says Rob Awalt, the Bills' tight end. "We didn't handle adversity particularly well."

As a former Cowboy, Awalt knew all too well that if Aikman got on a roll, the Bills were roadkill. "So many weapons on that team," Awalt says. "We had to control the ball to win. The problem is that we weren't disciplined. Jimmy told his guys that, and he was right. We made too many mistakes at too many inopportune times."

On Buffalo's next series, Haley swooped around tackle Howard Ballard and clobbered Kelly. As the ball popped loose at the 2-yard line, defensive tackle Jimmie Jones plucked it from midair and stepped in for the score: 14–7, Dallas. This was exactly what Wannstedt had imagined throughout the previous two weeks, when he prepared obsessively for the rapidity of the Bills' vaunted no-huddle attack. The Cowboy defense practiced consecutively against its first-team and scout-team offenses. One offensive unit would run a play, then the other offensive unit would dash onto the field and run a play. *Bam! Bam! Bam! Bam!* "We were ready for it," says Wannstedt. "I assumed we would be." Whereas most teams that faced Buffalo tried to sneak linemen in and out between snaps, the Cowboys—blessed with eight top-flight players at the position—simply kept their troops on the field until there was a prolonged stoppage. The Bills thrived on wearing out opposing defenses until they were forced to rely on scrub backups. The Cowboys had no scrub backups.

Early in the second quarter the Bills faced a first-and-goal from the Dallas 4-yard line and failed to score. On their next series, Kelly dropped back and was nailed in the right knee by Norton. Kelly screamed in agony—both from the pain and the instant recognition that his Super Bowl was kaput. "Have somebody grab a baseball bat and hit you in the leg for a good amount of time," says Kelly. "That's what I felt."

Though Kelly was too erratic to be considered the NFL's best signal caller, he was the soul of the Bills. In his place came backup Frank Reich, a soft-spoken Maryland product who eight years earlier had rallied the Terrapins from a 31-point hole to shock Johnson's Miami Hurricanes. The return from the dead was Reich's specialty—in the Bills' wild-card playoff game against Houston, Reich relieved an injured Kelly and erased a 32-point deficit for an NFL comeback-record 41–38 triumph. But these Cowboys were neither the Hurricanes nor the Oilers. In the second quarter Reich led the Bills to a field goal, cutting the Dallas advantage to 14–10. Then he sat back and watched a Super Bowl rout noteworthy for its stark lopsidedness. On the ensuing possession Aikman capped a five-play drive with a 19-yard touchdown pass to Irvin. Thomas, bothered by ankle and shoulder maladies, fumbled two plays later, and Dallas recovered and scored again, this time on an 18-yard Aikman-Irvin hookup. The Cowboys held a 28–10 halftime advantage, and the crowd—covered in blue and white and decidedly pro-Dallas—roared with glee.

As he jogged off the field Emmitt Smith turned to Leo Armbrust, the team's guest chaplain, and casually said, "Father, I'd give anything to watch the halftime performance." Alas, Smith missed out on Michael Jackson. But the Cowboys were the real show. They led 31–17 at the end of three periods and, thanks to a Super Bowl–record nine turnovers by Buffalo, cakewalked to a 52–17 triumph. "We just beat them up," says Tony Casillas. "I didn't know we'd throttle them that badly, but once we took out Kelly the game was over."

Before Dallas could officially claim its first Vince Lombardi Trophy in fifteen years, something was needed to make an eminently forgettable blowout Super Bowl at least moderately memorable. Yes, Aikman would win the MVP with 273 passing yards and 4 touchdowns. And yes, Emmitt Smith ran for 108 yards on 22 carries. And yes, both Irvin and Harper caught touchdown passes. But what this game required was personal humiliation.

What it required was Leon Lett.

A second-year defensive lineman out of Fair Hope, Alabama, and tiny Emporia State (enrollment: 6,194), Lett was slightly less country than a plate of chicken fried steak with a side of okra. Lett's father, Leon, Sr., had worked at a local printing company and believed strongly in the disciplinary effects of a good belt whipping. As a result Leon would grow into a *timid* 6-foot-6-inch, 297-pound giant. "The first away trip he ever took with the team, he missed the pregame meal because his nose was bleeding and he was afraid to show up and be laughed at," says Johnson. "His coaches at Emporia State ripped him because he wouldn't go to class. The reason he didn't go to class was because he was embarrassed that he didn't know the material." Teammates still recall Lett's fear of the media, and the reservoirs of sweat that formed beneath his armpits during interviews. "The Big Cat just didn't want the limelight," says Hennings. "He was really soft-spoken, and the last thing he needed was a big moment on the biggest stage."

With the Cowboys leading 52–17 late in the game, Lett picked a fumble off the ground and rambled 64 yards toward glory. In the era of mounting me-me-me attitudes, Lett was the last guy to showboat. Yet as he approached the end zone, Lett stuck the football in his right hand and held it down low, as if he were carrying an attaché case weighted with bricks. From nowhere (well, from 90 yards behind) emerged Bills receiver Don Beebe, who swatted the ball milliseconds before Lett crossed the goal line. Touchback, Bills.

Had the game been tight, Lett surely would have found himself yanked, cut, and working at any one of the Greater Dallas/Fort Worth area's five thousand Olive Gardens. Instead, Cowboy players laughed until they cried. The only moderately irked member of the team was kicker Lin Elliott, who was one extra point away from setting a Super Bowl record. "Oh, well," says Elliott. "Leon was a good guy. No harm."

"He made a mistake, that's all," says Beebe. "We met up a few months after the Super Bowl, and I asked how his life had changed. He told me people were very hard on him. For God's sake, they won the dang game."

Indeed, the Cowboys were world champions. As the final seconds ticked off the clock and Johnson's hair was de-crusted by the requisite Gatorade bath, euphoria set in. Irvin walked up and down the sideline, hugging everyone in sight. Ike Holt and Tommie Agee rolled along the ground like puppies, screaming, "We won the Super Bowl! We won the Super Bowl!" Emmitt Smith had tears flowing down his cheeks— the goal of becoming a world champion could be checked off his list. Jerry Jones paced back and forth, muttering, "Dallas Cowboys, world champions." Aikman was about to make the world's easiest $50,000 for reciting nine words—"I'm going to Disney World!" and "I'm going to Disneyland!" He was the MVP, and nobody could argue. Inside the locker room, players were shocked to find—of all people—Jesse Jackson shaking hands and posing for pictures. "I was like, 'What the hell is Jesse doing here? What kind of affirmative action is he looking for in the Cowboys locker room?'" says Newton. "'Why aren't you in the locker room with Buffalo trying to soothe their ache?'"

Yet of the cornucopia of images, the one that lingers is the visible emotion of a man who didn't even play. Safety Bill Bates had joined the Cowboys as an undrafted free agent in 1983, and through the darkest of days during the Tom Landry Era he maintained a belief that the Super Bowl was in his future. Sadly, in the fifth game of the '92 season Bates tore his ACL. Though he took in the action from the Rose Bowl sideline, Bates felt distant, almost as if he were a ballboy.

When the final whistle blew, however, he was overcome with emotion. He entered the Dallas locker room, curled up on the floor, and wept. "That's when I realized how much winning the Super Bowl meant," says Darren Woodson. "Here was Bill, a veteran who'd been through it all, crying like a baby. He was finally a champion, and he couldn't believe it."

Knowing the hell he had been through, Jerry Jones pulled Bates from the locker room and asked if he'd like to ride back to the team hotel. Moments later, Bates found himself soaring above Los Angeles in the owner's private helicopter. "We just circled the city," Bates says, "looking down on the thousands of lights. It was spectacular."

Three years after finishing 1–15, the Dallas Cowboys were atop the world.

Chapter 14

NUT-HUGGERS

My first road game with Dallas, we walk into the hotel lobby and there are four hundred people waiting—grown men, beautiful women, kids. It's a circus and a rock concert rolled into one. My first road game with the Rams, the only people waiting are the bellhops.

—Jim Price, Cowboys tight end

WHAT HAPPENS WHEN a team wins a Super Bowl?

Lunacy.

Absolute lunacy.

Prior to the thrashing of Buffalo, most members of the Dallas Cowboys were mere football players—admired to some degree, but far from household names (outside of Troy, Emmitt, Michael . . . and maybe Nate Newton—he of the 360-pound Shamu physique). But would anyone have recognized, say, Jay Novacek or Tommie Agee or Alvin Harper or Tony Casillas were they strolling down Emerald Lane on a sunny weekend afternoon? The NFL is not the NBA, where players *are* the brand—endorsed, publicized, and plastered atop billboards. No, in professional football anonymity reigns supreme.

In the aftermath of Super Bowl XXVII, however, the Cowboys became the most omnipresent group of athletes the country had seen since 1987, when the New York Giants beat Denver for the title and promptly had five players release autobiographies (one has not lived until he reads *Simms to McConkey: Blood, Sweat, and Gatorade*).

Cowboy players made paid appearances at supermarket openings and at shopping malls; at dance clubs and at roller rink birthday parties. They did radio spots, hosted TV specials, served as MCs. Jimmy Johnson wrote a "tell-all" book that told little. Tom Vanderveer, mayor of Troy, Texas, announced that the city council was considering changing the town's name to "Troy Aikman."

In what surely goes down as one of the most questionable decisions of his otherwise wondrous career Aikman, along with Novacek, special teams coach Joe Avezzano, and former Cowboys Randy White and Walt Garrison, formed a country music group, The Boys. Their album, *Everybody Wants to Be a Cowboy*, mixes horrific songs and horrific singers into one uniquely horrific package. The first single, "Oklahoma Nights," was sung by Aikman, whose vocal stylings are reminiscent of a cat choking on a lug nut.

Of all the events that merged to form Cowboy Mania, the one that remains most curious is the rise of Kenny Gant, a third-year defensive back from Albany State who led all nonstarters with 54 tackles during the '92 season and tied for the team lead with 3 interceptions. Though Gant excelled on special teams and as a nickel back, he was little more than an average NFL player. "Truthfully, I just wanted to hang on," he says. "When I was drafted I went to a Wendy's in Albany, Georgia, to celebrate with a hamburger. I was small-scale like that."

What Gant did possess, however, was perfect timing.

During practices early in the 1992 season, Gant noticed that Kevin Smith, his fellow defensive back, would celebrate a good play by bending an arm at the elbow and holding it up to his helmet. Smith termed it "the Shark Fin," and said the defensive backs at Texas A&M, his alma mater, used it to show off. "In practice all of us started flashing the fin, just sorta goofing around," says Gant. "But it wasn't like there was anything to it." That is, until the fifth game of the '92 season, when Gant sprinted down the field on a punt, charged Seattle's Robb Thomas, and hammered him with a forearm to the head. As Gant leapt to his feet, he bent his right arm, held it to his noggin, and swayed it back and forth while bobbing his rear end. The Texas Stadium crowd roared with delight.

After the game Gant was surrounded by reporters, intrigued by the newest dance sensation. Gant smiled. He was a fun-loving guy who enjoyed jogging onto the practice field wearing only a jock or riding naked through the locker room in the laundry cart or hopping over a fence to sneak onto safety Bill Bates's ranch for a quiet evening of fishing or hitting the clubs with teammates. Now, there was the Selachimorpha thing. "I just had my shark fin up," he told the press with a chuckle. "We weren't letting nothing get by."

A craze had arrived. In the aftermath of the Super Bowl, Gant's celebrity reached a whole new level. He was now, officially, "The Shark." There were Shark Dance posters. Shark Dance T-shirts. A local player hangout, the Cowboy Sports Café, served the Sharkbite—a blue-tinted Long Island Iced Tea. Gant would visit a shopping mall and hear people holler his name while making a fin. "I'd be in restaurants eating and I'd look up from my food and some guy or some kid would be doing the Shark Dance," says Gant. "It's funny how one day you're anonymous and the next day you're huge. I loved it."

A couple of months after the Super Bowl, Gant was hired by a Dallas attorney to appear at a pool party for his son's thirteenth birthday. Gant arrived in a suit and tie and performed his Shark Dance to the delight of the approximately thirty youths in attendance. He then turned to the father and asked to borrow a pair of swim trunks.

"Kenny," the man said, "you don't have to . . ."

The Shark insisted.

"I had on a pair of this guy's nut-huggers," laughs Gant, "and I jumped right in."

The strangest request came from the Jewish family that hired Gant to appear at their son's bar mitzvah. A deeply religious Pentecostal from the decidedly non-Jewish town of Lakeland, Florida, Gant grew up attending church on Sundays, Mondays, Wednesdays, and Fridays, serving as a drummer in the congregation's band, and watching in awe as many around him spoke in tongues. *Brad Mitzvee? What the heck was a Brad Mitzvee?*

"Man, was that fun," says Gant. "I helped light the candles, I wore a yarmulke, I did the Shark Dance, I line-danced. I got paid but I would have done it for free."

Beyond the Shark appearances and country albums and Brad Mitzvees, what best symbolized the Cowboys' rise from contenders to superstars was the Hoopsters, the team's offseason "charity" basketball squad. Formed in the early 1970s by wide receiver Drew Pearson, the Hoopsters' initial mission was to travel the state of Texas promoting the Cowboys, rewarding fans for their undying support during the season and making some cash on the side. The Hoopsters would come to town, play the River Oaks Volunteer Fire Department or the Lubbock Police Department or the faculty of Atlee Parr High School and donate most of the proceeds to charity. The games would be competitive, but never crossed the line.

Any lingering philanthropic intentions dissipated in the mid-1980s, when a linebacker named Eugene Lockhart took charge of the Hoopsters and ran the operation less like a goodwill tour and a bit more like a Hollywood agent. The Hoopsters began demanding exorbitant appearance fees for their participation. Instead of COME OUT AND SEE THE COWBOYS RAISE MONEY FOR A GOOD CAUSE! promotional signs should have read COME OUT AND SEE THE COWBOYS RAISE MONEY FOR A GOOD CAUSE—MINUS THE $30,000 WE'VE GOTTA PAY THEM TO BE HERE, THE FOOD WE'RE REQUIRED TO SUPPLY, AND THE FIRST-CLASS HOTEL SUITES THEY PROBABLY WANT, TOO. "Lockhart was not a good guy," says Anthony "Paco" Montoya, who managed the Hoopsters and worked as a gofer for several players through the 1990s. "He was a bully who did things the wrong way." In 1988, a basketball-loving rookie named Michael Irvin led a Hoopsters revolt, literally wrestling control of the team from Lockhart in an Odessa, Texas, hotel room. "When it was over there was lots of broken furniture," says Montoya, "and the Hoopsters had a new leader."

Yet the sex-seeking, money-hungry, fame-addicted wide receiver was hardly a Saint. Irvin had no trouble putting the Hoopsters to his own use, whether that meant demanding a $10,000 personal appearance fee for a two-hour "charitable" basketball game or securing perks that would have put the Rat Pack to shame. On May 10, 1993, the Hoopsters were scheduled to play a Friday night exhibition at Baylor University that was to raise money for the resurrection of Paul Quinn College, a small, traditionally black school. As the game was set to begin, an organizer informed Irvin that he did not have the $25,000 check the Hoopsters required. Instead of staying and, say, playing for less money to entertain the 240 spectators, Irvin, Harper, Kevin Smith, Jimmie Jones, and the rest of the Cowboys bolted. Such behavior came as no surprise to Rodney Dodd, president of the Little Dribblers in Fairfield, Texas, who had presented the Hoopsters with a $5,600 check for a March 5 appearance. Less than a week before the game, Dodd was told the fee had increased to $7,000, plus expenses. "I called [Irvin] back and told him we didn't want them," said Dodd at the time. "To this day we've never seen our fifty-six hundred dollars."

Unlike the old Hoopsters of Pearson and Everson Walls, Irvin's priorities were money, winning, and postgame sexual pursuits. Whether playing a bunch of beefy marines at a military base or a flabby gaggle of middle-aged teachers in a dimly let gymnasium, the Hoopsters *had to* win. That's why, in a May 1991 game against the staff of a Dallas radio station, KKDA-AM, Irvin became so incensed by a questionable foul call that he allegedly grabbed the referee—an unpaid volunteer named Willie Summerling—and showered him with obscenities. When Summerling warned Irvin to dial back his antics, the player slugged him in the mouth, knocking loose a dental plate. There were two thousand spectators in attendance, many of them children.

With the Cowboys' on-field successes came increased Hoopster requests. They flew to Mexico City for a game, flew to Las Vegas for another. They played the Redskins in Washington, engaged in two or three mini-brawls, and left with a hard-fought 3-point triumph. "Once we played these soldiers in Killeen and we needed an escort out of the stadium," says Kevin Smith. "The other team wanted to fight some Cowboys to prove their manhood, and as time ran out I hit a three-pointer for the win. That was pretty darn sweet."

Though players generally joined the Hoopsters in the spirit of camaraderie, what proved to be the greatest perk—especially in the shadow of the '92 season—was a dazzling postgame buffet of booze, marijuana, cocaine, and sex. Whether the Hoopsters won or lost, following each contest they headed either for the hottest nightspot in town or to their hotel, which would be transformed into Club Hoopsters. Though the Cowboys were a big deal in Dallas, they were larger-than-life in smaller towns across the state and country, where a visit from the Super Bowl champions was akin to a return of Elvis. Kids turned out to see their sports heroes. Men turned out to see their sports heroes too. But women—well, mounds of women came out to gain a firsthand physical experience. "It didn't matter if you were a dope dealer, a Channel 5 TV reporter, a judge on the U.S. District Court," says Newton. "You weren't getting the women the Cowboys were."

If you were hot, you might get to spend the night with a player. If you were sexy, you might even end up on the Hoopsters' private airplane. If you were two lesbians looking to put on a show, you might be allowed to fly the jet. "That's when it really got crazy," says Montoya, who traveled with the team. "To call those flights 'off the hook' doesn't do anything justice. I don't think there's a word for what went on. We filled those planes with more women than we did players, and they were willing to do anything."

Anything?

"Absolutely anything."

It was here, 30,000 feet above the ground, that Alvin Harper earned the nickname "Freaky Harp." Though married to Jamise, his college sweetheart from the University of Tennessee, Harper never met a groupie, a stripper, a cheerleader he wouldn't have sex with. In a feat that left teammates stunned, Harper was banned from the Men's Club of Dallas for having sex in a phone booth. To be a Cowboy star in the 1990s and have someone demand you leave his strip joint—well, that took work.

On the Hoopsters' chartered airplane, there were no bouncers, no wives, no coaches. Just loose women looking to party with the Super Bowl champions. Cowboy players would have sex in the main cabin, sex in the bathrooms. Irvin, the ringleader of all things erotic, would direct various arrangements—women on women, two women on a teammate, three women on a teammate. "There was nothing Mike couldn't think of," says Montoya. "He had quite the imagination."

"I'll tell you one thing," says Clayton Holmes, a defensive back and Hoopsters guard. "If you were employed by the Cowboys, it didn't take much to get whatever it was you craved. And we craved a lot."

As the Dallas players were reaping the benefits of a Super Bowl victory, Jerry Jones and the team's brass weren't having quite so much fun.

The problem: Emmitt Smith—and his ego.

Though he was publicly hailed as a quiet, humble, levelheaded cornerstone of the Cowboys' offense, on-field success had drastically changed Smith's demeanor and sense of self-worth.

Coming out of the University of Florida after his junior season, Smith was an uncomplicated kid who deferred to his mother, Mary, on nearly all issues. If Mary said UF was the best school for her Emmitt, then, by God, UF was the best school for Emmitt. If Mary believed Richard Howell, a little-known agent, was the best choice, then Richard Howell it would be. Young Emmitt was blessed with neither profound intelligence nor sound judgment, but he happened to have a mother possessing both.

Now, however, in the wake of three straight Pro Bowl appearances, two straight NFL rushing titles, and 108 yards in a Super Bowl, Smith was a new man. In February 1993, he and some business associates traveled to Atlanta to attend the Super Show, an annual sports merchandising bonanza that draws anyone who's anyone in the world of professional athletics (for a refresher, think back to the scene in *Jerry Maguire* when the character played by Cuba Gooding, Jr., Rod Tidwell, is approached by a kid and asked, "Are you Hootie?"). In past years, Mary Smith's Emmitt would have been humbled by such a celestial gathering. This time, however, as he cruised through town in his stretch limo, his Louis Vuitton handbag atop his lap, Smith gazed out the tinted window and spotted enormous billboards featuring Michael Jordan—Nike's standard-bearer. "I need to be bigger than him," he said.

Those surrounding Smith laughed—until they realized he was serious. Such was the new mentality of the NFL's rushing champ, who, according to one teammate, "began to separate from the rest of us." Smith imagined himself not as a football player, but as lord of all things. He wanted to endorse sneakers (he became a Reebok spokesman) and write books (his autobiography, *The Emmitt Zone*, would be published in 1994). He fancied himself a TV personality and was euphoric when, during Super Bowl week, Howell had him booked as a guest on *The Arsenio Hall Show*. (Enraged at not being invited as well, Irvin refused to speak to Smith for two days.) "He had a huge ego that made him sort of a dick," says Mike Freeman, the former *New York Times* NFL writer. "Teammates respected him, but they also thought he did a lot of things for personal attention."

Smith talked up his basketball talents—then played with the Hoopsters and stunk up the court. He bragged of his ability to drive a golf ball, and played 18 holes with Craig Neal, a former NBA journeyman who worked for Howell. "I probably shouldn't say this," Neal told Howell, "but Emmitt lost so many balls in the woods that I had to start chasing them. I wound up getting a poison ivy shot."

Coming on the heels of a banner season, Smith licked his chops over the expiration of his three-year contract. Though he was a restricted free agent, meaning Dallas could match any other offer, Smith believed he was the engine that powered the machine. While Aikman was a superb quarterback and Irvin, Harper, and Novacek were dangerous receivers, the Cowboys were nothing without No. 22 lined up in the backfield. Just about the only player Smith deemed equal to his status was Detroit's Barry Sanders, regarded by most as the NFL's best running back. Smith both admired and envied the Lion, whose shiftiness and stop-on-a-dime control he desired and whose status he craved. So smitten with Sanders was Smith that, midway through the '92 season, Jerry Jones called his running back into the team's executive offices. "Emmitt," Jones said, "there are probably two people alive who consider you on a par with Barry Sanders, and they're both in this room." Jones proceeded to reach into a drawer and pull out a stack of papers. "My partners aren't going to like this," he said, "but I'm going to give you Barry Sanders's contract, and I'll give it to you as is."

Smith was floored.

"We don't need disharmony," Jones said, licking his proverbial chops. "We don't need to get agents involved. By giving you this contract, the Dallas Cowboys are saying to the world that Emmitt Smith is every bit the running back Barry Sanders is."

Smith interrupted. "Jerry," he said, "I appreciate it. But I really have to speak with my agent first."

With that, Jones nodded and smiled. But his heart sank. Sanders's contract—a five-year deal for $5.9 million—was widely regarded as one of the league's worst. When Howell informed his client of this, Smith fumed. Screw Jerry Jones and screw the Dallas Cowboys. If they wanted to play that way, he would play that way too.

On March 27, 1993, Ed Werder of the *Dallas Morning News* reported that Smith and Howell had scheduled a meeting with the Miami Dolphins. "You can never close the door on a player that good, so we're pursuing him to an extent," said Tom Heckert, the Dolphins' director of pro personnel. In his piece, Werder noted that it would take a contract of "at least" $3 million per season (or about $2.5 million more than Smith made in '92) to avoid having Dallas match. Miami was interested, said Heckert, "[but] we definitely want to make sure this isn't a ploy [to force the Cowboys' hand]."

Four days later—convinced that it was, in fact, a ploy—Miami coach Don Shula canceled the meeting. Smith was unbowed. He and Howell contacted every other team in the league, dangling before them the chance to sign a twenty-three-year-old workhorse entering his prime. Nobody bit. "We'd offer Emmitt four million a year," one general manager told Howell, "but what's the point? We know Jerry will match." On May 14, Jones made what he termed "the final take-it-or-leave-it offer"—a laughable incentive-and-signing bonus-free four-year deal with annual salaries of $2 million, $2.2 million, $2.2 million, and $2.5 million. "That's all you'll get," Jones told Howell. "Not a penny more." The difference between the offer and what Smith desired ($17 million over four years) was staggering. When Smith declined, Jones went on the offense, slamming Howell to the media as a sleazy, greed-obsessed agent out to take advantage of a client. It was classic hypocrisy. Did Jones really want to get in a battle over greed? The Cowboys—a franchise valued at $165 million—had already announced a 23 percent increase in ticket prices for the upcoming season. Just a few weeks later, Jones arranged a beneath-the-table merchandising deal that would have netted him 20 percent of every Apex One–produced Cowboy garment sold by JCPenney. The agreement went squarely against the NFL's collective bargaining agreement—greed personified, in the view of rival owners.

Come the start of training camp on July 15, Smith was home with his family in Pensacola, 687 miles from Austin. Though Johnson was consumed with an array of nagging issues—ranging from the herniated disk that would keep Aikman sidelined for six to eight weeks (he suffered the injury lifting weights during the offseason) to reserve tight end Alfredo Roberts's broken foot to a handful of rookie holdouts—it was Smith's absence that caused him the most distress. While Jones was assuring the press that Smith would be back with the Cowboys by opening day, Johnson wasn't so sure. Throughout his dual careers in oil and football, Jones maintained the belief that he could overcome all obstacles. No gusher? Let's drill to the east. No Emmitt? Someone else can run the ball.

In the Cowboys' case, that *someone* turned out to be a 5-foot-10-inch, 194-pound rookie from the University of Alabama whose claim to fame was a celebratory dance. In a game against Florida as a senior,

Derrick Lassic crossed the goal line, placed his hand over his heart, and fell to the ground, feigning a heart attack. It was an ode to Redd Foxx's character in *Sanford and Son,* and—like the old sitcom—it was a huge hit.

As the Cowboys' fourth-round pick, Lassic had few expectations thrust upon him. Yet as the preseason progressed and neither side budged in the Jones-Smith stare-down, Lassic emerged as the front-runner to start the September 6 Monday-night opener at Washington.

Wrote Ed Werder in the August 20 edition of the *Morning News:*

This is what Derrick Lassic is not:

He is not the first running back to win the league rushing title and the Super Bowl championship in the same season. He is not the Cowboys' running back with the chance to become the fourth in league history to win three successive NFL rushing crowns. He is not the player who set Cowboys records for yards and touchdowns in a season last year. He is not the player who is missing training camp for the second time in four seasons.

Derrick Lassic is not Emmitt Smith.

Much of Lassic's preseason was spent as Johnson's bull's-eye, and he came to strongly resent the coach. "I never liked how he treated players," says Lassic. "The way he played favorites was horrible. Maybe I'm saying that because I wasn't one of his favorites. Clearly I wasn't." Lassic ran for 34 yards on 10 carries in his exhibition debut against the Vikings on August 1, then gained 35 yards on 16 attempts versus the Lions in the London-based "American Bowl" a week later. He lost fourteen pounds midway through the preseason while suffering from prolonged dehydration, and cautiously tiptoed through the same type of holes he burst through as a member of the Crimson Tide.

On August 10 Smith reenrolled at the University of Florida, and on September 4, two days before the opener, the *Morning News* reported that Howell called Jones to demand a trade to a franchise that would hand his client $4 million annually.

"Totally out of the question," Jones told the newspaper.

As a boy growing up in Haverstraw, New York, Derrick Lassic never felt especially nervous before the start of sporting events. Really, why would he have? From the time he first played Pop Warner at age eight, Lassic was the fastest . . . the strongest . . . the best. He was a three-sport star at North Rockland High School who ran for school records of 1,787 yards and 31 touchdowns as a senior.

At Alabama, Lassic was on the fast track to a noteworthy collegiate career when, on March 25, 1990, a young man with everything in front of him came face-to-face with mortality. He was watching the NCAA basketball tournament in his dorm room when the telephone rang. It was a nearby hospital, informing Lassic that his girlfriend, Cherlintha Miles, had been involved in a serious car accident while driving from Montgomery to Tuscaloosa for a visit. "I was thinking something happened to the car," said Lassic, "and that she needed a ride home."

Tragically, the news was much worse. Miles, twenty, had died in a one-vehicle accident. For the next week Lassic refused to leave his room. He lost twenty pounds and his will to continue playing sports. Lassic packed his bags and prepared to head back to New York—only to be talked out of it by his father, Preston. "I had never lost anyone close to me," said Lassic, "and I was ready to give up everything."

Instead, Lassic remained in Dixie, found his way out of the darkness, and, as a senior, ranked fifth in the SEC with 905 rushing yards. He officially anointed himself a Crimson Tide legend by running for 135 yards and 2 touchdowns in Alabama's 1993 Sugar Bowl upset of Miami, thus clinching the school's first national title in fourteen years. When the Cowboys selected him in the draft, it was an ode to talent and resiliency. "I was thrilled," Lassic says. "I'd won a national championship and now the defending Super Bowl champs wanted me. Plus,

I was well aware that I wasn't ready to start in the NFL. They had Emmitt Smith for me to learn from. Perfect situation."

So here were the Cowboys, reigning titleholders, waiting to open their season in the dank, smelly, cramped visitors' locker room of RFK Stadium, and here were two contrasting sounds. On a television blaring from a side office, a tape was playing of Smith's Sunday interview with *The NFL Today*, in which he claimed he might be done playing football. "I got plenty of money saved away," he said, "so I think I can live continually, live healthy, and continue to live happy." Meanwhile, in a neighboring bathroom, the team's new starting running back was violently upchucking into a toilet. The fierce, throaty echo bouncing off the porcelain filled the room and overtook Smith's voice. Had it been Aikman or Irvin or—*pretty please*—Smith experiencing pregame nausea, Cowboy players would have laughed the moment away. Nobody was laughing now.

Of all teams, the Redskins were not going to use a nationally televised *Monday Night Football* encounter to look sympathetically upon the Emmitt-less Cowboys. Not after Dallas took the '92 NFC East crown. Not after Irvin had threatened to snap Darrell Green's broken arm. Not after a rivalry that dated back thirty-three years. Certainly not after the *Washington Times* set up a Cowboys "hateline" the week of the game, inviting Redskin backers to offer their reasons for despising Dallas. A whopping 270 messages later, the point was clear. From "Johnson's Liberace-styled hair" to "my ex-wife is a Cowboys fan" to "Emmitt Smith spit on me when I asked for an autograph," apparently nobody in Washington could stand the arrogant Super Bowl champs.

Before a hostile crowd of 56,345, the Cowboys were flattened, 35–16. Dallas fumbled the ball three times in the first half, dropped two interceptions, and botched an extra point. Redskins defenders took special delight in taunting the lippy Irvin, who no longer seemed so tough (or loquacious) without the threat of a handoff to Smith.

The snap judgment was that Dallas without Smith was only a so-so operation. Yet the truth ran deeper. The real issue here was shattered team morale. As Smith stayed away, Jones spoke openly—and, it seemed, eagerly—about renegotiating Aikman's contract, which still had two years remaining. Led by Haley, a number of the African-American Cowboys wondered aloud why a black man like Smith had to beg for the money he deserved while the white, sandy-haired quarterback could have riches thrown at his feet. As far as Haley was concerned, it was business as usual in the NFL, a league without an owner or general manager of color and only two black starting quarterbacks (Houston's Warren Moon and Detroit's Rodney Peete). "We were saying, 'Wow, you're not gonna take care of Emmitt!'" says Larry Brown. "This guy works hard, he's at practice, he's in the weight room. Our whole thing was that if Mr. Jones didn't care about Emmitt, he wasn't gonna care about any of us. The frustration among us wasn't just the money—it was lack of respect for a guy who played all out, who worked his ass off, who never complained."

Though he was but an innocent bystander, Lassic paid dearly. In his first game as a pro, Lassic actually played well, gaining 75 yards on 16 carries against one of the league's better defenses. He blocked adequately for Aikman, ran precise routes, and did as he was told. But the Cowboys' offensive line—big, tough, tops in the NFL—blocked with neither the intensity nor the efficiency of past years. "I asked Erik Williams, 'E, what the hell is going on here? Why aren't y'all blocking for this kid?'" says James Washington. "He said, 'Well, he runs too fast. We have a flow and he isn't able to see it.' It was totally unfair to Lassic."

The mounting friction especially irked Johnson, who was painfully aware the team's punch bowl had been poisoned. With increased urgency Johnson urged Jones to reach an accord with Smith. So what if the NFL would be incorporating a $31 million salary cap beginning in 1994? "The problem was that I fell into the same trap I was trying to get players to avoid," Johnson said later. "I was paying [too much] attention to Emmitt not being there and knowing that we weren't going to be as good a football team without him. I lost focus. We were working, but we weren't focusing in on what we needed to be doing."

The bottom fell out in Week 2, when the Buffalo Bills came to Texas Stadium and recorded a 13–10 win before a visibly agitated crowd. Elliott missed two field goals and, two days later, lost his job. Lassic fumbled twice while gaining a mere 52 yards on 19 carries.

Though Cowboy fans had come to embrace Jones in the post-Landry years, no one seemed to agree with his stance regarding Smith. In a stadium accustomed to adoring signs like I LOVE TROY and EMMITT FOR PRESIDENT, the fans were now expressing their furor.

JERRY JONES: TRADE YOUR EGO, SIGN EMMITT

JONES, DO THE RIGHT THING, NOT THE WHITE THING SIGN EMMITT

WHAT IS THE DIFFERENCE IN ARKANSAS CLASS AND FIRST CLASS—EMMITT

Immediately after the game Haley stormed into the locker room, tears streaming down his cheeks. He fumed aloud, "We're never gonna win with this fucking rookie!" When Jones entered, Haley picked up his helmet by the face mask and whizzed it ten feet through the air, past the owner, and through a wall. *THUD!* "You need to sign that motherfucker now!" he screamed. The silence was deafening. "I thought that thing was gonna kill me," says Jones. "Nobody was happy, and I understood why."

A bawling Haley proceeded to approach Jones, lean into his ear, and whisper, "Sign Emmitt! I don't care how you do it. Cut me. Take the money out of my check. Just sign Emmitt!" It was a new type of crazy for Haley, who—in a career chock-full of nutty moments—had never before whipped a helmet at the man signing his paychecks.

Lassic, meanwhile, sat quietly at his stall. It wasn't his fault Smith remained unsigned—but it sure felt that way. "The fans showed no class," he said of the merciless booing. "But it really bothers me when one of my teammates says something like that. That hurts bad. I only heard it from one person, but it makes me wonder what everybody else is thinking."

Prior to the opener against the Redskins, Tony Wise, the offensive line coach, had held a meeting to tell his minions that it was they, not Smith, who made the Dallas rushing attack work. "We're gonna block our asses off and this kid is gonna have a huge day!" Wise yelped. "It's about time you guys started getting the attention you deserve! It's not Emmitt who makes this thing work. It's you!" Immediately following Wise's plea, the linemen studied a tape from a 1991 game, during which Smith spun, dipped, and charged to 100-plus yards. "Guys were like, 'Yeah, Tony. Right,'" says John Gesek. "We knew how good Emmitt was." By the time the Bills game had ended, nobody was fooling himself any longer.

"Tony couldn't pull that shit on us, because the truth was so damn obvious," says Nate Newton. "Lassic was a nice kid, but if we expected to get back to the Super Bowl, we needed Emmitt in the lineup. It was as clear as motherfuckin' day."

The day after the Bills debacle, the PLO and Israel signed a peace accord on the South Lawn of the White House. The news was the talk of the world—save for Dallas, Texas. When a local radio station asked listeners for their opinion about the breakthrough, the only thing callers wanted to discuss was Smith's absence. Forget Yasir Arafat's plan—what was Jerry Jones's?

On September 16, four days after the Cowboys dropped to 0–2, Howell and the Cowboys agreed to a four-year, $13.6 million deal that made Smith the NFL's highest-paid running back. At a press conference that evening, Jones smiled, handed his star a check for $2 million, and flashed a rare dose of humility. "Some might wonder who the winners and losers are in this," he said, standing alongside Smith. "When he signs his contract for four years, then the Cowboys are big winners. And when I sign this bonus check—it's a big one—then he's a winner."

Dallas's Pro Bowl rusher smiled politely, but he had learned a lesson. "I spoke to Emmitt at that time and I told him, 'Always remember this,'" says Dennis McKinnon, a former Cowboys receiver. "No matter how big you get, the color issue never changes. You're always black first and foremost to those doing the paying." For many Cowboys, the contract squabble resulted in the continued shift in Smith's outlook and priorities.

Where joy and passion once served as his motor oil, now there was a palpable need to look out for No. 1 first, everyone (and everything) else second.

Smith returned to practice that Friday, and the debate began as to whether he'd be ready to play against the Phoenix Cardinals on Sunday night. In earlier times Smith would have been one of the first to practice, anxious to reestablish his status. But this was a different Emmitt—in the eyes of running backs coach Joe Brodsky, a *disappointing* Emmitt. Smith arrived late for practice, jogged at half speed, and seemed more interested in gloating over his financial windfall than in preparing for action. He was flabby in the stomach and soft in the legs. If Smith had lifted anything since the Super Bowl, it was a glazed donut. "I'm mad at him," Brodsky said. "He needed to be in my office at seven this morning getting himself ready for the mental game. I don't know what he was doing. I don't know whether he was putting money in the bank or trying to take money out of the bank."

The Smith who spent the following days treating his return to the NFL as if it were a spa retreat was not a player Brodsky wanted to deal with. He scowled at Smith; barked at him and told him money had already changed his work ethic. The Cowboys flew to Phoenix and beat the Cardinals 17–10 for their first victory of the year, but Smith was a nonfactor. He carried the ball 8 times for 45 yards.

Yet whether Brodsky wanted to admit it or not (he didn't), Smith's signing represented more than the addition of a lazy, overpaid slacker. With his return came hope. Although Dallas had lost a few free agents from the '92 roster, the only striking difference from the world champion Cowboys and the 0–2 Cowboys was the running back from Florida.

"We had some hosses on our offensive line—guys who could dominate the defense," says center Frank Cornish. "But it takes a great back to set up good blocks and take an offense to a different stratosphere. We had our guy back in the fold, and we were dangerous again.

"With Emmitt, we were in a different stratosphere."

Chapter 15

GOOD TIME?
LET'S MEET @ 12

Remember North Dallas Forty? *We made that look like fuckin' kindergarten.*
—Nate Newton, Cowboys offensive lineman

Joe Fishback liked sex.

No, let's amend that. Joe Fishback loved sex. *Loooooooved* it. He loved it with black women, with white women, with short women, with tall women, with thin women, with fat women. He loved it once a day. Twice a day. Ten times a day. "I couldn't go to sleep unless I had *at least* three sexual encounters," says Fishback, a Cowboys defensive back. "Some guys might say, 'I have to smoke.' Some guys might say, 'I've gotta drink.' I had to find women. I was addicted."

Fishback is hardly exaggerating. He was, in the most clinical of determinations, a sexual addict—one of the estimated 9 million residing in the United States. "It got so bad for me that the night before home games we would go to the hotel and go over everything, and then we could go home for a couple of hours. I would go home and have someone waiting on me. I just *needed* it."

For the first two years of his career, split between the Atlanta Falcons and New York Jets, Fishback's sexual addiction was, if not under wraps, restrained. Though the Falcons and Jets certainly had their groupies, they were relatively limited in scope and size. Then, on October 12, 1993, he was claimed off waivers by the Cowboys.

Mr. Cocaine Addict, welcome to Colombia . . .

On the road, the Cowboys' team bus would arrive at a hotel, the players would file into the lobby and—*WHOOSH!*—females aplenty. Much like a junior high classroom, there would be a series of note passings. A piece of paper slipped to the leggy blonde—COME TO ROOM 222 @ 11:30. Another one handed to the brunette and her redheaded friend. GOOD TIME? LET'S MEET @ 12. Vixens who arrived too late for the grand entrance would wait until later in the night and pull the hotel fire alarm. "That way," says Rob Geiger, a KRLD radio reporter who traveled with the team, "they could stalk the players as they filed out."

Although many organizations discouraged salacious behavior, Jerry Jones chalked it up to boys being boys. It was the Dallas owner, in fact, who approved one of the more tasteless plans in recent sports history. When Jones purchased the Cowboys and agreed to have American Airlines continue to serve as the team's transportation provider, the deal came with the caveat that a Dallas representative be allowed to select the airplane crews. According to an American employee, airline supervisors were told to approach beautiful flight attendants, make certain they were single, and solicit them to work Cowboy charters.

Under the Jones reign, American maintained a book with the photographs and measurements of the most attractive flight attendants. Cowboy employees would then flip through the pages and select who they wanted to fly with the club—long legs and enormous breasts a priority. "We did a cross section, because you had redheads, brunettes, blondes," says the American employee. "The understanding was that the flight attendants would get to go to the first half of the football games, then at intermission go back to the charter and get the planes ready."

This was the type of organization Fishback was joining—and now, with the team back on top, the adulation was greater than ever.

"The Cowboys were hot, hot, hot," Fishback says. "Everyone wanted a piece of us." Within the first three weeks of Emmitt Smith's return to the Cowboys, righteousness was back in Big D. Following the victory over Phoenix on September 19, the Cowboys ran off wins against Green Bay (featuring 5 field goals from the team's new kicker, veteran Eddie Murray) and Indianapolis. Despite initial accusations of laziness, Smith quickly regained form, grinding out 71 yards versus the Packers and 104 more against the Colts. "With Emmitt back there," says Jay Novacek, "the other team always had to be afraid."

Any humility gleaned during the 0–2 start was now overtaken by a familiar swagger. The Cowboys were rock stars—Kiss, Aerosmith, and the Stones rolled into one. When they hit the town, they hit the town in a pack—twenty, twenty-five Cowboys sitting at a table in the hottest gentleman's club, slinging $100 bills and screwing dancers and ducking into back rooms for pulls on bongs and snorts of cocaine. "It was bananas," says one Cowboy rookie from the '93 season. "I was a complete nobody on that team, and I'd get back to my hotel room after a game and have two or three gorgeous women leaving me messages on my machine. I hooked up with girls in the stands, I hooked up with girls waiting outside the locker room. In college you might hook up with a couple of eights and nines. With the Cowboys they were all tens and even some elevens. It wasn't like taking candy from a baby, because a baby might put up a fight. It was too easy."

Dallas was riding high, with its biggest test to come. On October 17 San Francisco arrived at Texas Stadium intent on exacting revenge for the prior season's crushing loss in the NFC title game. In the days before the contest, 49er star Ricky Watters told the *San Francisco Chronicle* that he—not Smith—was the league's best running back. "I heard what he said," responded Ken Norton, Jr., the feisty Dallas linebacker. "He'll pay for it on Sunday."

The Cowboys walloped the 49ers, 26–17, inspiring the *Dallas Morning News* headline, THE REMATCH IS NO MATCH. Smith gained 92 yards, Watters a paltry 32. More noteworthy was that Michael Irvin seemed to be making a run at Jerry Rice's longtime reign as the NFL's top receiver. At the same time Irvin was catching 12 balls for 168 yards and a touchdown, Rice was held to a couple of catches in the first half and 7 for the game. The striking difference, however, was not statistics, but attitude. With increased fame, Rice had become a whiner and moper. Win or lose, if Steve Young was not throwing the ball his way with sufficient frequency, Rice would pout, brood, and vanish from the game. Though he, too, demanded the football, Irvin's priority was winning. "I once counted that I played with eighty-eight Pro Bowlers in my career," says Hugh Millen, a Cowboys backup quarterback. "Michael was easily the most driven, most victory-oriented player I'd ever seen. That's what separated him from his peers—the desire to win Super Bowls above all else."

Although the hard-playing Cowboys were clearly relishing their status as defending-champs-on-a-roll, Jimmy Johnson was not. In his first four years as Dallas's head coach, Johnson viewed the Super Bowl as some sort of Holy Grail: Reach it, and a wondrous world of riches and happiness awaits.

What Johnson discovered, however, was that there was no Grail; no magic. In the immediate aftermath of the romp over Buffalo, Johnson held the Super Bowl trophy aloft, basked in its luminous glow, felt the rush that comes with achieving a lifelong dream.

Then, after a few days off, he returned to the grind.

The Johnson who came back to the Cowboys for the '93 season was more fierce and biting than ever. Instead of embracing the title of "Champion," he was burdened by the stress to repeat. After the team lost to the Vikings in an exhibition game, Johnson held the toughest practice of the summer, then had the players remain for an extra hour of drills that Millen, the reserve quarterback, calls "suicidal." Johnson was screaming like a general in the midst of battle, spittle splattering from his lips. "Guys are doubled over, throwing up," says Millen. "And Jimmy was running up and down the field, angry as any coach has ever been. I still don't understand why." What irked Johnson was how, immediately after the Super Bowl, the most-asked question was not "How does it feel?" or "What was your greatest moment?" but "Can you do it again?" *Can I do it again? Are you friggin' kidding me?*

Johnson was unhappy, and he let those around him know it. He would snap viciously at the nearest lingerer, be it a player, an assistant coach, or even Jones. Whereas in past years he would at least attempt to handle personnel moves with a certain tact and decency, now it was all business. During training camp Michael Payton, a rookie free agent quarterback from Marshall, played well for a month before walking into the training room one day and collapsing to the floor. He was diagnosed with compartmental syndrome, a condition in which increased pressure in a confined anatomical space affects circulation and—in Payton's case—results in severe numbing of the legs. Payton returned to his hometown of Harrisburg, Pennsylvania, to be operated on. For the ensuing three weeks Payton worked voraciously, running and lifting weights until his doctor cleared him to return to football.

"My first day back I had a meeting with Jimmy," says Payton. "He released me." As Payton headed toward the practice field to bid adieu to teammates, Aikman gave him a heads-up that a quarterbacks meeting would begin in ten minutes.

"Not for me," said Payton. "I've been cut."

Aikman's jaw dropped. "That," he said, "is cold."

Not nearly as cold as when Johnson cut linebacker John Roper a day after the 49er victory. A former second-round draft pick by Chicago, Roper had arrived in Dallas as part of a five-person preseason trade with the Bears. At his best, Roper was a deft pass rusher who compiled 8 sacks in 1991. At his worst, he had the reputation for being moody and indifferent. "John was very talented, and he could really get after the quarterback," says Kelly Blackwell, a Cowboys tight end who came to Dallas with Roper. "But he was a *me* guy, not a *team* guy." Roper's talent was such that, heading into the 49ers matchup, Butch Davis, the new defensive coordinator, planned to highlight him in several specially designed schemes. Two days before the game, however, Roper violated one of Johnson's etched-in-stone commandments: Thou shall not fall asleep at a team meeting and expect to keep thy job.

With the lights dimmed in a Valley Ranch conference room, Joe Avezzano, the special teams coach, was briefing his players on the ins and outs of San Francisco's kickoff return patterns. As Avezzano was speaking, in walked Johnson. The head coach grabbed a chair and sat directly in front of Kenny Gant, the defensive back. "I was a little late to the meeting because I went to McDonald's," says Tim Daniel, the second-year wide receiver. "I was about to walk into the room with my Big Mac and fries when I saw our equipment manager, Buck Buchanan. Buck said, 'Tim, you *do not* want to go in there. Jimmy is not in a good mood.'"

Inside the room, the coaches were showing a tape of the 49ers' recent victory over the Vikings. Players sat in their chairs and feigned interest. "A bunch of us had gone out hard the night before, so I was exhausted," says Gant. "I had alcohol on my breath; my eyes were opening and closing, opening and closing." Johnson spun around in his chair, turned away, spun around again, turned away, then spun around a final time. *Oh, shit,* thought Gant. *He's looking at me.* He wasn't. Sitting eight or nine rows behind Gant was Roper, head nestled against his elbow, a light snore emanating from his lips. "Turn the lights on! Turn the lights on!" screamed Johnson. Ninety-nine percent of the players in the room snapped to attention. Roper did not. "John Roper!" screamed Johnson. Roper failed to wake. "John Roper!" he screamed again. This time, Roper opened his eyes and propped himself up in his chair. "John Roper!" said Johnson. "You can go on and sleep through Sunday's game! Now pick up your shit and get the fuck out of here!" Roper sat still, stunned. "Did you hear what I said?" Johnson said. "Get the fuck out of this meeting!"

The 6-foot-1, 232-pound linebacker left the room. Three days later he was cut.

What Johnson did not know was that Roper's need for shut-eye had nothing to do with partying or laziness and everything to do with the sleep deprivation that accompanies early parenthood: Roper and his wife had an infant daughter. "That baby had been keeping John up all night long," says Kevin Smith, Roper's friend and former Texas A&M teammate. "He was getting three hours of sleep per night. Dude was just exhausted."

Roper tried explaining to his coach that he loved being a Cowboy, but Johnson would not hear it. Roper's Cowboy days were over. "If that were Emmitt, there's no way he would have been cut," says Daniel. "But John Roper was the perfect guy to make an example out of. Was it cool? No. But it was vintage Jimmy Johnson."

The Dallas Cowboys were just fine without John Roper. After beating the 49ers on October 17, Johnson's ball club ran off consecutive wins over the Eagles, Giants, and Cardinals—all NFC East rivals, all convincingly outclassed. For Jerry Jones, the most meaningful of the triumphs came on the afternoon of November 7, when Dallas slammed the Giants 31–9 and finally inducted Tom Landry into the sacred Ring of Honor.

While most professional sports franchises recognize past legends by dangling their numbers from a wall or rafter, the Cowboys—always eager to separate themselves from the pack—have the Ring of Honor. The tradition began on November 23, 1975, when the team hosted Bob Lilly Day and unveiled a sign featuring the former defensive lineman's name and uniform number beneath the press box. In the fourteen ensuing years the names and numbers of six more players were added, forming—for lack of a better phrase—a Ring of Honor inside Texas Stadium.

In the four years since his firing, Landry had avoided returning to Texas Stadium, and any mention of Jones or the Ring was met with a quiet-yet-pointed dismissal. Landry and his wife, Alicia, were proud people who never accepted the way Jones had handled the axing. "I felt worse for the folks around me than I did for myself," Landry said. "My family was really upset. Then you see something like Tex's [Tex Schramm's] situation. He had so much to do with building the Cowboys, but that night on TV after he introduced Jerry as the new owner, Tex had to stand back in the corner. There wasn't even a chair for him on the podium. That bothered me."

Jones initially told Landry he would like to induct him into the Ring in 1989, but the bitterness was too raw. Gradually, the ice thawed. By 1993 the two men had worked out their differences, and Tom Landry was ready to be a part of the Dallas Cowboys once again.

As he walked through the Texas Stadium tunnel toward the field, a CBS camera flashed the haunting silhouette of Landry and his famed fedora. Once he reached the 50-yard line, the old coach was cheered like Neil Armstrong returning from the moon. Surrounding him were past Ring inductees—Lilly, Don Meredith, Don Perkins, Chuck Howley, Roger Staubach, Mel Renfro, and Lee Roy Jordan. Booed at the start of the ceremony, Jones turned toward Landry and spoke from the heart. "Thirteen playoffs, twenty straight winning seasons, five NFC championships, five Super Bowl appearances, and two Super Bowl wins," he said. "We honor you here today. Our Ring of Honor stands for the men who built this franchise and had it called 'America's Team.' This would not be the Ring of Honor without you, Coach Landry."

"The forgiveness began for Coach Landry right there," says Staubach. "It was very meaningful for him."

As he walked off the field, Landry looked to the stands and smiled. A man who was revered for his sense of righteousness had, in the end, done the right thing.

Of America's major professional team sports, none offers the unpredictability of football. While baseball's pennant race is exciting and the NBA presents unmatched flair, the NFL is the lone entity where today's Super Bowl favorite can be tomorrow's cellar dweller.

For this, there is a single reason: injuries.

From the garden-variety sprains and bruises that happen twenty or twenty-five times per game to the torn rotator cuffs and snapped femurs that wipe out entire seasons, the NFL team that finds itself unprepared for maladies is the NFL team that has a season doomed to be flushed down the toilet.

In 1993, the Dallas Cowboys seemed doomed.

With nine minutes, thirty seconds remaining in the third quarter of the November 7 Giants game, Aikman was being chased by defensive end Keith Hamilton when his left shoe stuck to the artificial turf. With a scream, Aikman collapsed and grabbed for his left leg. "We're treating it with ice," Robert Vandermeer, the team's physician, said afterward. "We hope it's not too bad."

In the following days Aikman could be seen limping around the locker room, an armful of ice packs strapped to what was diagnosed as a strained left hamstring. He was out for the upcoming game against Phoenix, and perhaps for several more weeks as well.

If Jones and Johnson had learned anything from their early failures, it was the value of a top-notch backup quarterback. With the laughable Babe Laufenberg at the helm for the final two games of 1990, the Cowboys flopped. With Steve Beuerlein filling in for Aikman the following year, Dallas went 6–0 and beat Chicago in the playoffs. Unfortunately for Johnson, Beuerlein had signed a lucrative free agent deal with the Cardinals after the '92 season. In his place Dallas traded for Millen, a seventh-year veteran who had spent much of the past two seasons starting for New England. Millen was a laid-back Seattle native who arrived in Dallas with a higher annual contract than Aikman's. When Jones called him into the Valley Ranch offices and told him, "You're making more money than Troy, and we can't reconcile that," Millen smiled and cracked, "Well, I have no problem with Troy getting a raise." Millen's salary was promptly slashed to backup level, and he spent the preseason playing bargain-basement football. "I wasn't happy with how I performed, and neither were they," Millen says. "I struggled."

Hence, when Aikman went down against the Giants Johnson decided Dallas's new starter would be a freckle-faced redhead whose résumé was highlighted by unexceptional stints with the Ottawa Rough Riders of the Canadian Football League and the San Antonio Riders of the World League. Jason Garrett didn't even have much in the way of a college background—he played at Princeton, where he was named the 1988 Ivy League Player of the Year. When he walked through the locker room at Valley Ranch, teammates often serenaded Garrett with chants of "Roo-dee! Roo-dee!"

To make matters more confounding, five days before the Cardinals game Dallas signed Bernie Kosar, the former University of Miami quarterback who had been released by Cleveland earlier in the week. Though only twenty-nine years old, Kosar seemed to have aged overnight. His passes lacked zip, and his mobility was nonexistent. Despite such concerns, Jones agreed to pay Kosar $1 million for the remainder of the year. "They talk around here about how they don't have the money," snapped an agitated Emmitt Smith, still licking the wounds of his contract war. "But they get a new quarterback and they give him big money. I don't understand it."

Smith quickly came to understand it when Garrett took the field at Texas Stadium on November 14, strolled into the huddle, and showed the poise and moxie of a six-year-old. Garrett's eyeballs were the size of silver dollars. Across the line of scrimmage, Phoenix's defensive linemen took pleasure in filling his head with the vilest of threats. They were going to break Garrett's legs and tear off his head. "When you looked at Jason, it was obvious he wasn't an amazingly gifted athlete," says Rich Bartlewski, a Dallas tight end. "He relied on intelligence and doing things right at the right times."

On this day, Garrett was all wrong. He attempted six passes in three offensive series, completing 2 for 25 yards. By late in the first quarter Johnson had seen enough. The gawky Kosar trotted into the game and connected on 13 of 21 passes for 199 yards and a touchdown. He was methodical in approach and Aikman-esque in demeanor, and Dallas beat the lowly Cards, 20–15. Following the 0–2 start, the team had won seven straight.

"We're hoping Troy will be back with us," Johnson said afterward. "If not, we'll be a much-improved team next week with Bernie Kosar."

As it turned out, the Cowboys were *not* a much-improved team with Bernie Kosar the following week. They weren't even a good team, falling to the Falcons, 27–14, at Atlanta. But while the loss was disconcerting to Johnson and Co., in Dallas it ranked a distant second to the biggest news since the Kennedy assassination.

Troy Aikman was in love.

In a city that cherished its heartthrobs, Aikman was the biggest to come along in decades. To start with, he was the star quarterback of the Cowboys—a 6-foot, 4-inch, 220-pound custom-made classic with a crooked smile and freckled skin that reddened in the sun. Aikman was everything white Dallas looked for in its leading men. He eschewed sneakers for cowboy boots and sweatpants for tight Wranglers. His car of choice was a pickup truck and his favorite band Shenandoah. In an era where a wad of chewing tobacco was no longer the status quo, Aikman pulled it off with aplomb. He made spitting sexy.

Not that Aikman went out of his way to endorse the image. Following the '91 season he was asked to appear on an episode of *The Oprah Winfrey Show* celebrating fantasy dates. "When you walk onto the stage, come out in jeans and boots," a producer told him. "It'll be great." Aikman did as he was instructed, only to find the other men decked out in snazzy suits and ties. "I think they wanted me to look like a hick," he said. "I may have grown up in the country, but to simply describe me as a country boy is rather narrow-minded. I'd like to think there's more to me than that."

Aikman was intelligent and contemplative. Though raised in all-white environs that bred a certain degree of prejudice, he maintained open-mindedness toward teammates of different races and ethnicities. While his best friend on the Cowboys was fullback Daryl Johnston, his brother—the man he'd have taken a bullet for—was Irvin. "Troy valued loyalty more than any other quality," says Brad Sham, the Cowboy announcer. "He'll always have loyalty toward Michael, because Michael is loyal toward him."

What Aikman lacked, but craved, was that sort of bond with a member of the opposite sex. Although he'd dated a steady stream of women during his first four years in Dallas, nothing stuck. Like many athletes, he was suspicious of those interested in spending time with him. Did they want his money? His fame? An experience to brag about to their friends and coworkers? He once returned to his house to find a couple of strange women eating pizza on his patio (they had scaled the fence). Another time a woman licked Aikman's face as he bent down to help her pick up a napkin. "Troy had to fax his grocery list to Tom Thumb Market because when he shopped there it'd cause a near-riot," says Rob Awalt, the former Cowboys tight end. "He was the Elvis of Dallas." Aikman even had a code—"Eight ball"—that translated to friends and companions as, "Let's get the hell out of here. It's too crazy."

Dale Hansen, the Cowboy radio announcer, still recalls a night during the 1990 season when he, Aikman, and Kevin Gogan went to Borrowed Money, a popular country-and-western bar. As soon as Aikman walked through the door, a tidal wave of humanity surged his way. "Troy agreed to sign autographs for thirty minutes," says Hansen. "I mean, girls were on all fours, crawling under a rope to get a piece of him. He could have slept with any number of drop-dead gorgeous women there that night. But that generally wasn't Troy's way. He wasn't looking for that."

No, he was looking for love. And here it was—here *she* was.

Throughout much of the season, there were ever-intensifying reports of Aikman's involvement with Lorrie Morgan, the sexy blond country music star whose hits included "Five Minutes" and "What Part of No." Though modestly accepted in Nashville for her passable vocal skills, Morgan was best known as a pre–Shania Twain sex symbol—one who made form-fitting outfits and low-cut shirts a prime component of her image. In August, Morgan even wrote a guest review for the *Morning News* of Aikman's song, "Oklahoma Nights." ("We all know Troy's not a professional singer . . . but I think he did a real good job. It's possibly a very sexy voice over candlelight.") Never was Aikman's attachment to Morgan more visible than before the Cowboys-Cardinals game, when Morgan sang the national anthem, walked toward the injured quarterback, and embraced him in a kiss. A day later, Aikman and Morgan walked arm-in-arm to a sports memorabilia auction benefiting the Troy Aikman Foundation. To male fans, the news of Aikman's attachment was greeted with a sort of "Way to go, bro" collegiality. Morgan, after all, was a blond bombshell. Women, though, were devastated. Troy Aikman was the ultimate fantasy, and as long as he was single, there was always a chance.

"They only wound up dating about a year, but it was a huge deal in Dallas and Nashville," says Susan Nadler, Morgan's former spokesperson. "Every day there seemed to be a different sighting in the newspaper. There'd be Troy and Lorrie eating, Troy and Lorrie walking, Troy and Lorrie kissing. But you know how football fans get. When Troy got hurt or didn't play well or the Cowboys lost, Lorrie would get blamed."

As Aikman became moderately comfortable with the celebrity of his romance, he was more willing to be spotted with Morgan (who was in the process of divorcing her third husband and would later date Fred Thompson, the 2008 presidential candidate). Yet over time, with her music career calling her to Nashville and his football career keeping him to Dallas, the relationship frayed. By the end of the season Aikman would be single once again.

Women across the state of Texas let out a cheer.

In the months that followed his fumble near the end of Super Bowl XXVII, Leon Lett received enough venomous letters to fill the combined mailboxes of Howard Stern and David Duke. Gamblers enraged over his flub's impact on their bets would track down Lett's home phone number and threaten to lodge a bullet through his temple. Fans would see him in the grocery store or a movie theater and crack jokes. Kids would point his way and snicker, "He's the guy who blew it."

Lett tried to brush it off; to pretend the words didn't wound. But they did. Dating back to his youth in Fairhope, Alabama, Lett was the athletic star who preferred invisibility to the limelight. "I think everyone has met a guy like Leon," says Darren Woodson. "A big guy, a huge guy, tough as nails and nice enough, but he could not talk to people. It probably took me three years to have a conversation with him. He just wanted to be left alone."

If the Super Bowl gaffe was hell to Lett, what next transpired was an endless loop of *Joanie Loves Chachi*. Aikman returned from his two weeks off to lead the 7–3 Cowboys into a Thanksgiving Day matchup with Miami at Texas Stadium. At 8–2, the Dolphins were the class of the AFC. Prognosticators hyped the game as a potential Super Bowl XXVIII matchup—Jimmy Johnson versus Don Shula; Michael Irvin versus Irving Fryar; Troy Aikman versus um, well, thirty-nine-year-old Steve DeBerg (Dan Marino was injured).

To the surprise of few, the Cowboys jumped out to a 14–7 lead on two big plays courtesy of rookie Kevin Williams—a 4-yard touchdown reception and a 64-yard punt return, also for a score. Unfortunately, the Dolphins' defense, ranked twenty-fourth in the league, held the Cowboys scoreless in the second half. The biggest factor was the fierce sleet that pelted the field. "Sunshine is nice," said Miami fullback Keith Byars, "but when the elements come into play, that's when we find out which players can step up."

With two minutes, sixteen seconds remaining in the game and Dallas leading 14–13, the Dolphins took over on their own 20-yard line. Dismissed throughout the years as someone who would break a coach's heart with boneheaded decisions, DeBerg coolly guided his team into Dallas territory, completing 8 of 11 passes, including a clutch 16-yard connection with Byars. With fifteen seconds remaining and Miami out of time-outs, kicker Pete Stoyanovich lined up for a 41-yard field goal attempt. Under normal circumstances, Stoyanovich ranked as one of the league's best. He'd converted 81 percent of his attempts in 1992, and 84 percent in both '90 and '91.

But with the sleet and the snow and the cold and the wind, a kicker's odds (especially a Miami-based kicker) dropped precipitously. When the ball was snapped, Stoyanovich leaned forward, whipped his leg back, kicked the ball, and—*THUD!* From the middle of the defensive line, Jimmie Jones had raised his arm into the air and knocked the ball to the ground. It rolled and rolled and rolled toward the 7-yard line. "Peter!" yelled Dallas safety Darren Woodson, shouting the code for *Don't touch the damn football!* Others joined in. "Peter! Peter! Peter!" (Explained Joe Avezzano, the special teams coach: "That term 'Peter' originated years before because it means, uh, don't play with it.")

Out of nowhere came Lett, barreling into the football like a moose on Rollerblades. Well aware that with Lett's contact the ball was now live, Dolphins center Jeff Dellenbach slid through the ice and snow and recovered the ball in the end zone. Miami players screamed, "Touchdown! Touchdown!" while Dallas's defenders looked on in befuddlement.

Officials initially placed the ball at the 7-yard line, then moved it to the 1, the spot where Dellenbach made the recovery. Given the second chance, Stoyanovich nailed the kick.

Dolphins win, 16–14. Texas Stadium, alive with snowy pleasure seconds earlier, falls silent.

"If you're a professional, [the rule] is something you're supposed to know," said an agitated Kevin Smith. "I know the rule. Ten other guys out there knew the rule. We get paid a lot of money. Leon is supposed to know the rule."

Lett bolted into the locker room and straight to the trainer's quarters. He refused to come out—not for teammates, not for friends, certainly not for the media. Stripped down to his thermal underwear, he cradled his head in his hands and sobbed. It was one thing to botch a meaningless play at the end of the Super Bowl. It was another to blow an entire game.

"I never held that against Leon," says Johnson. "I was shocked, but that was our fault. Leon hadn't worked on special teams all season, and because of the snow and his height we put Leon on field goal block team. If anything, I felt bad for him."

In a rare moment of empathy, Johnson approached Lett and engulfed him in a hug. "Don't get down over this," he said. "It's just one game. We need you."

Lett was shocked. The same coach who had cut Curvin Richards and John Roper; who had chewed out Robert Jones on the airplane; who had exercised unparalleled ruthlessness . . . was human.

It was a kindness the player would never forget.

Chapter 16

COURAGE

Emmitt was the most instinctive runner I've ever seen.
Now combine that with all the guts a human being can
possess and you're talking all-time great.

—**Alan Veingrad, Cowboys offensive tackle**

FOR MANY TEAMS, a nightmarish loss like the one to Miami changes everything. Confidence wanes. Doubts creep in. The shadows of conference rivals—in this case, the New York Giants—loom even larger. Through Week 13 the 7–4 Cowboys actually trailed 8–3 New York in the NFC East standings. Could the franchise preordained by *Sports Illustrated* as "the team of the '90s" fail to capture its own division? Could a team led by Troy Aikman, Emmitt Smith, and Michael Irvin fall to the anonymous, uninspiring Giants?

Maybe.

To their credit, the Cowboys rebounded from the Miami debacle to win their next four contests. They clinched a playoff birth, but entered the final week of the regular season tied with New York for first place in the NFC East.

Their last game was a visit to the Meadowlands with not only a division title on the line, but a first-round bye and home-field advantage throughout the playoffs.

Leading up to the clash, Jones signed Aikman to an eight-year,

$50 million contract. It was the most lucrative deal in NFL history, and while few could argue with the quarterback's worthiness, the news served as a slap in the face to Smith. How was it, he and other African-American players wondered, that Aikman barely had to sweat for a new deal while Smith bled a kidney? "Arguably, Troy Aikman is considered . . . maybe *the* star of the NFL," raved a giddy Jones. "Certainly, the Dallas Cowboys have had our success and have our future based upon the way Troy Aikman is as a player and as an individual." The giddiness was a a stark contrast to the pained expression Jones wore upon re-signing his star halfback (with an invisible gun pointed to his head) following the 0–2 start.

This just wasn't right—and Smith was about to prove it.

Entering the showdown with New York, Smith had regained his status as one of the league's top running backs. With 1,318 yards, he led Rams rookie Jerome Bettis by a mere 35 yards in the race for the league rushing title. Yet despite the numbers, there was an increasing sense that Smith was more image than substance. He wanted to be a star—a huge star. He craved endorsements and fame and a showbiz résumé, and if that meant ripping off his helmet so the camera could catch his glowing portrait, so be it.

"Emmitt," says Kenny Gant, "was different. Just different."

Teammates were torn. Some loved Smith for his toughness. Others resented him for his selfishness and arrogance. He often refused to sign autographs. He would walk past fellow Cowboys without saying a word. When players opened their Christmas gift from Smith the following season, they were less than shocked to uncover a copy of *his own* autobiography. Aikman gave golf clubs, Irvin gave bubbly, Smith gave . . . *The Emmitt Zone*? "Emmitt would score a touchdown from the two-yard line, keep the football, and sell it at his souvenir shop back home in Pensacola," says Dale Hansen, the Cowboys radio announcer. "I thought that was both odd and selfish." Cornerback Clayton Holmes never forgot an incident that took place during the Super Bowl XXVII after-party, when he approached Smith about signing an autograph for his mother,

Claudia. "Man, I ain't signing shit!" Smith barked. "If I sign that, I have to to sign for everybody else in here." Holmes's mother was standing nearby, mortified and embarrassed. "Emmitt has those moments," says Holmes. "And you just think, 'Why be like that? Why?'"

Now, on January 2, 1994, Smith and the Cowboys were trying to win in the most hostile of environments. Save for Philadelphia, no American city had tougher fans than New York—especially when it came to the Cowboys. With the mere mention of Aikman or Irvin or Smith from the public address announcer, Giants Stadium turned into an avalance of boos and hisses. On this day, the hostility was louder and more passionate than usual. "Man," says Kevin Smith, "those fans just detested us."

Nonetheless, Dallas jumped out to a 13–0 halftime lead, gaining 238 yards on 41 plays while limiting the Giants to 15 offensive snaps (and silencing the masses). As they walked off the field for intermission, Dallas's players could be heard laughing. It was a beautiful 41-degree day in northern New Jersey, with the sun and a soft northeastern breeze, and the Texans were living it up. Meanwhile, in the Giants' locker room linebacker Lawrence Taylor, who was playing the final regular-season game of his spectacular thirteen-year career, was incredulous. He stood up and, with tears streaming down his cheeks, delivered a message of empowerment. "This is it!" he said. "The last game, and these guys are giving you no respect! Let's go out there and be the bullies! Let's smash their mouths in! This ain't Dallas! This is New-fuckin'-York!"

Perhaps it was Taylor's words. Perhaps it was the crowd. Perhaps it was good old pride. Whatever the case, New York charged the field and played magnificently. Giants fullback Jarrod Bunch scored on a 1-yard touchdown run to cut the lead to 13–7 early in the third quarter, and a pair of David Treadwell field goals—the second coming with ten seconds remaining in regulation—turned a potential blowout into an evolving classic.

For Dallas, the worst blow had been delivered well before

Treadwell's kicks. On his nineteenth carry late in the second quarter, Emmitt Smith broke free on a 46-yard run when he was slammed by Greg Jackson, New York's hard-hitting fifth-year safety. As he fell Smith protected the ball with the left side of his body and landed on his right. He literally felt his right arm detach from his shoulder, and the pain reverberated through his body. (For those who have never experienced such an injury, close your eyes and imagine your arm being ripped in half, set aflame, and placed in a wood chipper.)

Smith walked to the sidelines grasping his shoulder and grimacing in anguish. The immediate fear was that Smith was done and Derrick Lassic would have to carry the team into the playoffs.

Two snaps after departing, however, Smith walked back onto the field. He had already exceeded 100 yards, and he wanted more. "I was faster than Emmitt and I was quicker than Emmitt," says Lassic. "But you're talking about a man who refused to be stopped. That was his greatest strength—he would not be denied."

Come halftime, Smith entered the training room, popped a couple of Vicodins, and had the shoulder X-rayed. He was diagnosed with a grade-two separation, a dislocation severe enough for most players to take an afternoon off. "The trainers asked me what we could do," says Buck Buchanan, the team's longtime equipment manager. "So I grabbed a redundant pad, which looks like a big donut, and attached it under his shoulder pad but above the shoulder. I did it with string, so it wasn't especially sturdy. I just hoped it could reduce the pain."

Though Smith ran for 168 yards, each hit felt like a hot coal to the flesh. When Treadwell's kick forced overtime, Smith sighed deeply. Would this game *ever* end? "Emmitt knew we needed him," says Johnson. "And he wasn't about to pass up the challenge."

In one of the most courageous displays in NFL history, Smith dominated the overtime, carrying 5 times for 16 yards, catching 3 passes for 24 yards, and setting up Eddie Murray's game-winning kick for a 16–13 victory. Throughout the period Smith calmed himself by repeatedly muttering, *"It's nothing but pain—just block out the pain.*" But it wasn't just pain. Cowboy linemen still recall Smith's horrifying screams from the bottom of piles as he absorbed shots that would have landed others in the ER. Afterward columnist Skip Bayless, who published his own Cowboys newsletter, *The Insider,* would accuse Smith of faking the severity of the injury—a ludicrous claim considering Smith had literally bitten through his mouthpiece. Following the game John Madden, the CBS announcer and former Oakland Raider coach, visited Smith in the training room. The Cowboy star had just won his third straight NFL rushing title with 1,486 yards and—despite the anguish—was beaming with pride. "My entire career I've never come down to the locker room," Madden said. "I came down today to shake your hand. I've never seen a better performance than that."

Smith spent the next fifteen hours at Baylor University Medical Center, connected to an IV and pumped full of pain medication. It was the most uncomfortable night of his life.

And one of the happiest.

The Cowboys were back in the playoffs, yet Jerry Jones was far from euphoric.

Three days before the Giants game, Johnson was asked by ESPN whether he would be interested in becoming the head coach of the expansion Jacksonville Jaguars, who were to begin play in 1994. Considering the fact that the Cowboys were fighting for the division title; that Johnson was only midway through a ten-year contract; that Johnson had routinely preached loyalty and togetherness, the wise answer—the only answer—should have been "No."

Instead, Johnson said he was "intrigued."

Later, when pressed by Ed Werder of the *Dallas Morning News,* Johnson elaborated. Sort of. "I was asked about Jacksonville and what I said instead of the standard line was that anytime you have a job, you're willing to listen to other opportunities."

Jones was indignant. Sure, he and Johnson had had their difficulties. But hadn't he provided Johnson with everything he'd wanted? Money, players, the Super Bowl. To Jones, Johnson's words were treasonous. In a New Year's Eve telephone interview from a hotel room in New York, Jones—about to head out for a bash at the famed 21 Club—brushed aside Johnson's comments, noting to a reporter, "It's up to me. I have no intention of making a coaching change. To have this as an issue is a joke."

But it wasn't a joke. The Cowboy coach had already met twice with Jacksonville owner Wayne Weaver, and while the initial topic of conversation was Johnson's endorsement of Norv Turner to lead the Jaguars, talk soon turned to Johnson himself taking the job.

"Jimmy's giving speeches to his players about how everyone's in this together and the value of teamwork, then [Jaguars owner] Wayne Weaver calls to get a recommendation for Norv and Jimmy sells himself," says Mike Fisher, the veteran Cowboy beat writer for the *Fort Worth Star-Telegram*. "Jimmy fucked Jerry, he fucked Norv. While he's telling his team, 'One for all, all for one,' he's lifting his skirt toward the Jaguars."

For his part, Jones was sick and tired of his so-called best friend. Johnson warned his players not to change with success . . . *but what about him?* When was the last time Johnson had given credit to anyone but himself? Jones was especially upset by the way Johnson browbeat his coaching staff—a collection of twelve good men who worked long hours for moderate salaries. He'd heard reports that, with the regular season winding down, Johnson had strolled into a coaching meeting, looked over his assistants, and barked, "You fuckers get it together or not a one of you will be around next year."

Who was this man? And why was he such a jerk? And, most important, why didn't he afford Jones the respect he deserved? For that matter, any respect at all?

"I bought the team and took all the risks," Jones said. "And then I came in here and gave Jimmy all the security in the world. I personally guaranteed him a ten-year contract. If he had never coached another game, if he got hit by a truck and got disabled, or if he never won another football game, he was still going to make six or seven million dollars. The reason for the ten-year contract was I wanted more of a proprietary feeling. I don't want to make the decisions in a vacuum that make me basically the sole keeper of the shop for the future around here. I want somebody else also standing right there, thinking about the future of the team. I didn't want somebody around here helping me make decisions who just had a short-term attitude. I didn't want a lame-duck coach."

Now, it seemed, he had one.

After an invaluable bye week that helped (soon-to-be-named) league MVP Emmitt Smith heal his shoulder and Jimmy Johnson and Jerry Jones cool their heels, the Cowboys learned their first playoff opponent, on January 16 at Texas Stadium, would be the Green Bay Packers.

Coming off a wild-card win over Detroit, the 10–7 Packers hardly inspired fear in the hearts of Dallas's players. In the week leading up to the game Dale Hellestrae, the Cowboys' long snapper (and offensive lineman), spent portions of his practices trying to snap footballs into moving cars. A bunch of offensive linemen dressed a candy machine in Cowboys garb and placed it in front of Erik Williams's locker. "You see," Haley told the media, "you kick Erik in the ass and candy falls out."

To few people's surprise, it was a nightmarish afternoon for the Packers. The Cowboys' 27–17 victory was relatively effortless. With a still-hobbled Smith held to 60 yards on 13 carries, Aikman took over, completing 28 of 37 passes for 302 yards and 3 touchdowns. Early in the game he zoomed in on tight end Jay Novacek, an expert at locating holes in the defense. As his quarterback continued to settle for dunks and dinks, Irvin walked toward the Packers sideline and demanded coach Mike Holmgren cover Novacek more intently. "That was typical Michael," laughs Novacek. "He wasn't saying it so they'd really cover me tighter. He was saying it out of respect—'No matter what you do, Jay will get open.' I was on the field laughing my head off."

He had good reason to—the Packers were out of their league.

Three days before the Cowboys and 49ers were to meet yet again in the NFC Championship Game, Johnson and his girlfriend, Rhonda, were driving to Campisi's restaurant. The radio dial was turned to WBAP, where *Morning News* columnist Randy Galloway was hosting his *Sports at Six* show with special guest Dan Reeves, coach of the New York Giants. For several minutes, Galloway and Reeves debated the upcoming Cowboys-49ers clash, comparing the histories and roster makeups of the two franchises. Finally, Johnson had heard enough. He called the show, itching to lay down the law for all listeners. "We are going to beat their rear ends," Johnson said. "We will win [the ball game]. And you can print that in three-inch headlines.

"In my opinion—and I am a biased person—I think we're going to go out Sunday and that crowd is going to be going absolutely wild. I think we're going to have a very, very tight game for about three quarters. Then before it's over I think we're going to wear them out. We're going to beat their rear ends, and then we're going to the Super Bowl. That's my personal opinion."

Looking closely at the two teams, the boast was, from a pure football vantage point, logical. Playing in the subpar NFC West, San Francisco struggled to finish with a 10–6 record, wrapping up the regular season with embarrassing losses to Houston and Philadelphia. Though they still featured superstars like quarterback Steve Young and receiver Jerry Rice, the 49ers were thin in the secondary and offensive line. In the year since the teams had last played for the conference title, there was a profound separation. This time Dallas, which would host the game at Texas Stadium, was the more prepared, more confident, more talented operation. With a Super Bowl defense comes a swagger. And the Cowboys had plenty of it.

Somewhat surprisingly, Johnson's words did not go over well with his team. For veteran Cowboys, Johnson's shtick had worn thin. His tough-love, I won't-treat-all-of-y'all-the-same mojo worked wonders with young, naïve players just entering the league. But as the Cowboys grew together, they came to tune out Johnson's chest-thumping rhetoric. "I majored in physical education, not psychology," Newton told the *Boston Globe*, "so all I know is he put our asses in the frying pan now."

"Jimmy really depended on the dangling carrot principle," says Kevin Smith. "Let me just give them enough to be happy, and dangle a little more. Because if you give a player too much he's not going to work out as much, he's not going to do the offseason things he needed to do, he's not going to do what he must. You don't get it as a kid. But the more stable you are financially, the less you're going to just follow along."

While the 49ers came to Dallas carrying a grudge from the previous season's setback, they also found themselves caught up in an unhelpful sideshow. That's because Jerry Rice had neither forgiven Kevin Smith nor forgotten the unyielding trash talk spewed at him in the January 17, 1993, game. Rice was normally impenetrable, yet something in Smith brought out his inner Biff Tannen.

Hence, three days before the game Kevin Smith was more than happy to answer reporters' questions about his rift with Rice. "It's all Jerry," Smith said slyly. "I was just playing him tough last year, and he comes along at the end of the game and flashes me the middle finger. I don't know why, but he did." The quotation was an instant goat getter. Upon spotting Rice before the start of the game, Smith approached and reached out his hand. "Good luck," he said. "Let's have a good game."

Rice muttered a slur, again flashed the finger, and jogged past. "Truthfully, I was just messing with the man," says Smith. "I knew he probably wouldn't shake my hand. But I thought I'd try and make a home in his head again."

There was a scuffle between the teams. At the coin toss, San Francisco's captains refused to acknowledge Dallas's players.

The game was on.

(Pause)

And then it was done.

In what had been hyped as the "Game of the Year," the Cowboys trounced San Francisco, 38–21. The biggest—rather, most noteworthy—play of the game came on the first series, when Kevin Smith clipped Rice's leg during an out route, and the receiver responded by throwing a punch and shouting, "Fuck you, bitch!" Penalty, unsportsmanlike conduct—15 yards. That the legendary receiver was held to 6 catches for 83 yards only added to Smith's glee. "Ah," he says. "To get under the skin of an opponent, then see it work. Nothing's better."

Unlike the previous year's contest, Dallas made certain there would be no dramatic ending. The Cowboys scored four touchdowns in their first five possessions, roaring to a 28–7 halftime lead. When Aikman left the game with a concussion early in the second half (asked to name the site of the upcoming Super Bowl, a woozy Aikman responded, "Henryetta, Oklahoma"), Bernie Kosar stepped in and zipped a 42-yard touchdown pass to Alvin Harper.

"We have not often been this humiliated," 49er coach George Seifert said afterward. "It hurts."

Once again, Dallas was going to the Super Bowl.

Once again, Dallas would face Buffalo.

But a cakewalk, this would not be.

Chapter 17

SUPER BOWL XXVIII (AKA: WE WANT THE BALL! WE WANT THE BALL! WE WANT THE BALL!)

*Super Bowls act as a big headache pill for the city of Dallas.
No matter how we behaved, no matter how many things
we did wrong, the people would forgive us. Why?
Because we gave them Super Bowls.*

—Kevin Smith, Cowboys cornerback

BILL BATES WAS garbage.

How else to describe a rookie free agent who possessed everything required to play safety in the National Football League—save for speed, athleticism, and pedigree? As a senior at the University of Tennessee in 1983, Bates was named second-team All-Southeastern Conference, but his claim to fame came in a game two years earlier, when he was brutally run over by Georgia tailback Herschel Walker. That was the lasting impression Bates left on NFL scouts: solid collegiate player; can't stick with the big boys.

When the 1983 NFL Draft began and ended with nary a sniff in his direction, Bates wondered whether he had a future in the game he loved. On the following day Dallas scout Bob Ford contacted Bates and invited him to try out, telling him, "If there were thirteen rounds in the draft instead of twelve, you'd be the thirteenth pick of the Dallas Cowboys."

Bates was ecstatic. *Me! Really?* "Ever since I was a boy my dream was to play for Dallas," says Bates. "And when you're given the chance to pursue a dream, I believe you have to go for it."

What Bates didn't realize at the time was that the Cowboys were telling literally every semi-talented undrafted collegiate player that he would have been the team's thirteenth-round selection. When he arrived at camp in Thousand Oaks, California, Bates was surrounded by dozens upon dozens of thirteenth-round picks.

The one-legged nose tackle? Thirteenth-rounder!

The legally blind kicker? Thirteenth-rounder!

The pack-a-day smoker from Anne Arundel Community College? Thirteenth-rounder!

But it didn't take long for Tom Landry to see that, in the unathletic rookie with the southern twang and Grover nose, he had something. Bates was the type of player who annoyed the hell out of complacent veterans, most of whom cringed at the gosh-golly-gee rookie pouring his heart and soul into every play. Bates was a square peg in the Cowboys' round hole of a locker room—squeaky clean, authentically Christian, loyal to his wife, Denise, and 100 percent intense even in the waning seconds of a blowout. Before long teammates mockingly nicknamed him "Master," prompting the rigid Landry to tell reporters earnestly, "Wow, those guys must really respect Bill." (Writer's tip: Place Bates's nickname before his last name and say it aloud.)

With the 1989 upheaval, Bates—who thrived as a safety and special teams standout for six years under Landry—assumed that his days in Dallas were numbered. He barely survived Johnson's first season, and in 1990 was relegated primarily to special teams. As other thirty-something contemporaries gradually vanished from the NFL, however, Bates excelled. He was, in many ways, reborn. On kickoffs and punts, Bates would dart down the field like a bull after a red cloth, charging through blockers, battering over bigger players, single-minded in his determination to destroy the ball carrier. "I remember coming to the sideline once," says Kenny Gant. "Bill had broken his wrist and the trainers told him, 'Game's over.' Bill said, 'No, tape it up.' As a young guy coming in, I never saw a player who cared less about his body."

Having survived the depressing late-Landry years, Bates was elated when, in 1992, the Cowboys played like Super Bowl contenders. Sadly, in the fifth game of the season Bates tore his ACL trying to make a play on special teams. He planned to stand along the Rose Bowl sideline for Super Bowl XXVII, but the idea of watching his team play without him on the world's largest stage was too much to bear. As soon as all his healthy teammates left the locker room, Bates turned to a trainer and pleaded, "There's a lot of tape left here. You can still tape me!"

"I don't think that's a good idea," the trainer replied. Bates sighed—the sideline it was.

Thanks to the rigid rehabilitation regimen of Cowboys strength coach Mike Woicik, Bates returned bigger, stronger, and faster in 1993, leading the club with 25 special team tackles. Having previously topped out at 4.6 seconds in the 40, Bates now ran a 4.58. The improvement was unheard of, especially for a thirty-two-year-old. "Three weeks ago I would have given you ten-to-one odds that Bill Bates wouldn't have a chance to make the team," Johnson said during training camp. "But it really is incredible what he's done."

When the Cowboys beat San Francisco to advance to Super Bowl XXVIII, nobody was more gleeful than Bates. "That was very, very meaningful to me," says Bates. "I felt like everything I'd worked for and overcame over the years was finally paying off."

Equally elated for another shot at glory was James Washington, like Bates a veteran safety who appreciated what it meant to play in such a big game. With the emergence of second-year safety Darren Woodson during the '93 season, Washington had been reduced to a nickel back. He was twenty-nine years old and certain his time in Dallas was nearing an end. "In the first Super Bowl I was driven by winning that ring," says Washington. "But I understood in the second that this was my opportunity to put my name on the market and scream, 'This guy can still play!'" On the Wednesday before the game, Johnson pulled Washington aside and told him he was going to start. First off, the coach liked his veteran poise. But more important, Johnson needed to utilize his three safeties—Washington, Woodson, and Thomas Everett—to stop the Bills' no-huddle, multireceiver offensive sets. If Woodson was the young up-and-comer and Everett the savvy professor, it fell on Washington to do what he did best: smack the daylight out of people. "I'm not trying to kill nobody, but I'm trying to limit my threats," says Washington. "When I'm saying I want to tear up your vertebrae, I literally want to jeopardize you at that point in time. I attack you like you stole my mama's purse."

Unlike past Super Bowls, the NFL decided, this year's game, to be held in Atlanta's Georgia Dome, would be played just one week after the conference championships. As a result, neither the Cowboys nor the Bills would party with the same vigor as they had in the lead-up to Super Bowl XXVII. Sure, there were shindigs and ladies and large doses of fruity alcohol. But the nightlife in Atlanta was relatively tame. For the Cowboys, who were accustomed to living like rock stars, the subdued atmosphere was a bit unusual. For the Bills, who in 1992 held a clinic entitled "The Super Bowl: How Not to Approach One," it was a blessing. "They were much more prepared for what we had to offer the second time," says Woodson. "We thought we'd walk all over them, but then it was sort of like, 'Uh-oh.'"

Unlike the previous year, when the Rose Bowl served as a classic Hollywood setting, the whole Georgia Dome scene was just, well, off. Super Bowls are not meant to be played indoors on artificial turf beneath bright lights in a relatively nondescript southern city. Even with 72,813 fans in attendance (most of whom once again supported the Cowboys), the joint lacked buzz . . . spark . . . greatness. It felt like a big game, not THE big game.

To Bates, however, this mattered little.

In the moments before kickoff, the captains of the Bills and Cowboys met at midfield, where legendary quarterback Joe Namath was on hand to conduct the coin toss. Standing alongside Michael Irvin, Kevin Gogan, Ken Norton, Jim Jeffcoat, and Eddie Murray, Bates watched the silver dollar rise from Namath's palm and disappear in the Georgia Dome lights. "Tails!" he shouted—a call Bates had debated for hours with his wife. When the coin indeed landed on its tail, Bates was giddy. "We want the ball!" he squealed for all to hear. "We want the ball! We want the ball!"

"That was really embarrassing," he says now. "But that was everything pent up—missing the previous game, coming from nothing, joy, energy, excitement."

Yet while certain veterans like Bates and Washington were anxious to make the day memorable, the Cowboys seemed to approach the game with a casualness befitting the venue. Having battered the Bills so decisively in Pasadena the year before, Dallas's players assumed they would do so again. "There were no ifs, ands, or buts about the Super Bowl. I knew we would win," says Kevin Smith. "We all did." So did the prognosticators, 95 percent of whom predicted the Cowboys—favored by a whopping $10^{1/2}$ points—in a blowout. Even *Sports Illustrated*'s Paul Zimmerman, who had picked the Bills to win the three previous Super Bowls, changed his tune.

Such outlooks infuriated the Bills, who with each Super Bowl letdown grew increasingly defensive. On Media Day, Buffalo linebacker Cornelius Bennett was asked by a reporter whether he thought his team could win. "What kind of fucking question is that?" Bennett railed. "No, we're going to fucking lose. Excuse my language, but don't ask me that kind of question. Hell yeah, I think we're going to win. You think we came here just to lose the thing? You think we came to the previous three Super Bowls to lose? No, OK, so don't ask me that damn question. That's fucking stupid. I'm pissed off about you asking me that, all right? So print that. I didn't fucking come here to lose, I never come to the Super Bowl to lose, I don't fucking play this game to lose."

Like their star linebacker, the Bills were fired up. The Cowboys, on the other hand, were bad. Really bad. Still feeling the effects of his concussion, Aikman looked Ken O'Brien–like in his inability to leave the pocket or throw the ball away. He misfired low to Jay Novacek on an early 4-yard dump-off, and two plays later missed a wide-open Kevin Williams crossing the middle. Because the Cowboys had done their best to conceal the severity of his injury, the 134.8 million viewers watching the Super Bowl assumed Aikman was off his game. What they didn't know was that he was still suffering from headaches, nausea, dizziness, and disconcerting memory lapses. "It was scary," said Leigh Steinberg, Aikman's agent, who spent the night of the concussion in the hospital with his client. "We sat there, he and I alone in the dark, and his head was kind of in a cloud. He kept asking me the same questions over and over."

Normally a master of precision, Aikman was strikingly erratic. On the Buffalo sideline Bills coach Marv Levy saw an opening. The Cowboys without a sharp Aikman were good, but hardly unbeatable. This was his team's best shot. "We came right at them," says Jim Kelly. "And we had them on the ropes."

Though the Cowboys held Buffalo's offense in check, Aikman could generate little first-half action against a defense inspired by the sight of a wobbly quarterback. The Bills stuffed the line against Emmitt Smith, eliminating the effectiveness of his favorite play, the lead draw. "I remember looking across the field at their sideline and they were spazzing a little bit," says Rob Awalt, the Buffalo tight end. "They were yelling at each other, trying to figure out what in the world was going on. I'm pretty sure they came in thinking they were going to throttle us 40–0." Instead, at the end of the first half, the Bills led 13–6, having scored on a couple of field goals and a 4-yard run by Thurman Thomas. Dallas, meanwhile, managed only a pair of field goals, with Aikman throwing for an empty 121 yards and Smith gaining just 41.

"We were flat," says Kenny Gant. "But as we were jogging into the locker room at halftime, I couldn't believe what I was seeing and hearing." A handful of Bills veterans were spewing trash talk at the Cowboys, an odd display of chutzpah considering Buffalo had been humiliated in the three preceding Super Bowls. "It was almost as if they wanted to piss us off," says Gant.

In his five years with the team, Johnson had often reacted to half-time deficits by calling out players and intimidating his men into performing better, harder, faster, stronger. This time Johnson leaned against a table and spoke in a relaxed tone. "Look, we're gonna win this game," he said. "We're gonna start hammering them with Emmitt up the middle, we're gonna force mistakes, and they're not going to be able to respond. I promise you."

What Johnson could not have predicted was that the team's savior would be the bone-crushing, trash-talking, do-rag-wearing Washington. To his fellow defensive backs, Washington was a cagey leader, smarter than the average NFL player and willing to call out coaches and team executives. To others (Aikman, his former UCLA teammate, included), Washington was a nonstop headache. "He wouldn't shut up, and he saw himself in a light that wasn't realistic," says one teammate. "He was a slow, uninstinctive player whose only skill was hitting. James thought he was a leader, but to lead, people have to listen to you." Defensive coordinator Butch Davis so reviled his veteran safety that he said no more than ten words to him throughout the entire season.

On the first play of the third quarter, Washington made a solo tackle on Bills running back Thurman Thomas at the Buffalo 34-yard line. On the next play, Washington tackled wide receiver Bill Brooks on the Bills' 43. Then, in a flash, *it* happened. On first down and 10, Kelly stood six yards behind center, with Thomas lined up to his left. One day earlier, Davis and a handful of players had been watching TV when they stumbled upon an ESPN interview with Levy. As the Buffalo coach chatted away, behind him the Bills offense was walking through a play that culminated in a direct snap to Thomas. "He would line up predominantly on Kelly's right in the shotgun, maybe seventy-five to eighty percent of the time," Davis recalled. "Well, as we're watching he's on the left. We'd never seen them do that. Ever."

Now, as Thomas stood to the left of his quarterback, Cowboy

defenders knew what was about to transpire. At the snap, Thomas stepped in front of Kelly, snared the ball, and sped to the right, where—*SMACK!*—he was immediately pancaked by an expectant Leon Lett. The football popped free and bounced toward Washington, who had often faced ridicule from teammates for the intensity with which he practiced picking up footballs off the ground. Now here he was, lifting the ball from the turf and weaving his way 46 yards for a touchdown.

Full of vigor and cockiness minutes earlier, the yapping Bills were muted. The Cowboy sideline, meanwhile, erupted in high-fives and screams of elation. Though the score was 13–13, the game was over. "From that point on," says Don Beebe, the Bills receiver, "we mentally tanked it."

"I never, ever thought we gave up in the two Super Bowls I played in with the Bills," says Awalt. "But when Thurman lost that ball, it was like, 'Oh, shit. Here we go again.'" On Buffalo's next series, the Bills faced a third-and-8 from their own 39 when Charles Haley and Jim Jeffcoat barreled through the offensive line and hammered Kelly for a 13-yard loss. The Cowboys took over and commenced upon a 64-yard touchdown drive behind the churning, grinding, determined legs of Emmitt Smith, who lowered his head and bounded into Bill defenders like an anvil slamming through a concrete wall. On six of the eight snaps the Cowboys ran "Power Right," where Smith would follow linemen Kevin Gogan, Erik Williams, and Nate Newton (combined weight: 968 pounds) into daylight. Smith gained 61 yards on the series, capped off by a 15-yard scoring run. Dallas led 20–13, an advantage that held up through the end of the third quarter. "People forget that that was a heckuva game," says Bates. "They played us very tough. It wasn't clear that we were going to win until that last quarter, when stuff started to happen."

"Stuff" was Washington. On the first play of the fourth quarter, the Bills were facing third-and-6 from their own 35-yard line. With four receivers lined up along the line of scrimmage, Kelly dropped back and looked toward Beebe, who crossed the field and had a step on Kevin Smith. Kelly cocked his arm and launched a bullet. The throw was artistic—a textbook spiral rotating through the air, Beebe's hands rising in anticipation of making the catch. Then, *swoosh*, Washington—old, slow, a backup—stepped in, snagged the pigskin from mid-air, and returned it to the Buffalo 34-yard line. As he jogged toward the sideline, Washington pumped his fists in the air. "It was over," says Awalt. "O-V-E-R. You could honestly look around and go, 'We're done.' All three Super Bowl losses compounded to that moment. I had never noticed it prior to that. The guys took great pride in, 'We're back! We'll piss the league off.' But when that turnover happened it was 'Well, we've lost three in a row and we just lost our fourth.'"

Nine plays later, Emmitt Smith sealed the victory with a 1-yard touchdown run. The Cowboys went on to win, 30–13—the blowout that wasn't.

In the immediate aftermath of the game, the Buffalo locker room felt less like a gathering of defeated jocks, more like a cemetery. Though the obituary had yet to be written, the Bills were boxed and buried. Kelly had bad knees. Andre Reed's speed was in decline. Thomas—one of the game's greatest backs—had immortalized himself as an inconsistent big-game performer. And Marv Levy, the beloved head coach, was sixty-eight years old and, dare one say, overmatched. "Our team adopted the good-guy mentality of Coach Levy, and sometimes that worked," says Anthony Fieldings, a Buffalo linebacker. "But at the championship level it helps to be mean, and those Cowboys were mean. They hit you while you were on your way down and made sure to get in every possible lick. I saw the Dallas players laughing and joking as they came out for the second half, and our guys were arguing about nonsense."

Members of the Bills insisted that they would one day win a Super Bowl. As of 2008 the team has not been back. "The worst thing about losing a Super Bowl is the postgame party," says Steve Christie, the Bills kicker. "The losers have a preplanned party, and you literally sit there in a conference room at a hotel, depressed beyond belief. You're eating your sandwich, drinking your beer, desperate to be anywhere but there."

Somewhat surprisingly, many Cowboys also failed to elicit euphoria from Super Bowl XXVIII. Although Bates could be found kneeled over before his locker, crying joyfully, his emotional overload was isolated. As opposed to the triumph one year earlier in Pasadena, this victory was coupled with an emptiness. "There is nothing like the first one," says Irvin. "We all thought we were a Hollywood team, and that first Super Bowl was in Hollywood. So now you're gonna tell me the next one is in Atlanta? Against the Bills *again*? When people say, 'Was the second as good as the first?' I laugh. It couldn't be. Not possible."

Most demoralized was Washington, who in the wake of the game of his life couldn't believe what he was being told. Despite 11 tackles, an interception and a fumble return for a touchdown, the media had voted Emmitt Smith (30 carries, 132 yards, 2 touchdowns) Super Bowl MVP. The decision begged the question of what, exactly, the writers had been watching.

After the reporters had cleared the locker room and Johnson gave a congratulatory speech, talk among Cowboy players turned to legacy. Who knew how many more Super Bowls this young, aggressive, energetic, talented team could win. Two? Three? Four? Hell, why not five? They had the perfect quarterback, the perfect running back, the perfect tight end, the perfect pair of receivers, and a ferocious defense.

"And we had the best head coach in the NFL," says Gant. "Nobody doubted Jimmy Johnson would lead us to even greater glory.

"We were," says Gant, "unstoppable."

Chapter 18

DIVORCE

Great coach, humongous jerk at times. Not too many
tears when Jimmy Johnson walked out the door.
—Mark Stepnoski, Cowboys center

THE ARTICLE RAN on page 2B of the February 18, 1994, *Dallas
Morning News*—a seemingly ordinary offseason football piece on an
otherwise ordinary day in Texas. Beneath the headline JOHNSON,
BACK AT WORK, MAKES NO WAVES ABOUT JONES, writer
Frank Luksa detailed the thought process of the Cowboys head coach,
straight off of a ten-day vacation and preparing for his sixth year on
the job.

Never one for the exotic or, for that matter, adventurous, Johnson
spent his time away from football snorkeling and fishing (he caught a
large kingfish) to his heart's content in the Florida Keys. He gorged on
all the seafood he could stuff in his (oversized) belly, downed one Heineken after another, basked in the sun, and thought of everything *but*
the Dallas Cowboys. "For the first time in about six or seven years I
didn't read a newspaper," he said. "I might have watched *SportsCenter*
once or twice in two weeks. I had a fantastic, relaxing time."

Now, back at Valley Ranch, Johnson seemed a new man. When
asked by Luksa about his dealings with Jerry Jones, rumored to be (kindly
speaking) strained, Johnson spoke optimistically. "Our relationship is

the best now that it's been since we've been with the Cowboys," he said. "We understand each other better than ever and as I've said before, we have a good working relationship."

For his part, Jones said that he and Johnson were getting along swimmingly.

It was a loving time to be a Dallas Cowboy.

The atmosphere was cheerful.

Everyone was happy.

Everything was . . . garbage.

Throughout the 1993 season, as fans and the media focused primarily on Emmitt Smith's contract squabble and the dramatic triumph over the Giants and Troy Aikman's concussion and, finally, the march to a second straight Super Bowl, a pair of oncoming tornadoes swirled. In one vortex was Jerry Jones, a man with an ego as large as the Great Pyramid of Cholula; a man who, within the past year, had told reporters he was quite certain he could coach the Cowboys were he inclined to do so; a man who resented his coach's privacy issues and need for authority and—*goddammit!*—the nonstop credit he received from the local media. "Jerry's head," says Denne Freeman, the veteran Cowboys beat writer, "was larger than any benevolent dictator the world has ever known." Mostly, Jones resented Johnson's declared interest in the Jacksonville Jaguars coaching position. Where was the loyalty? The . . . gratitude?

"I knew as early as 1991 that I might want to make a change with Jimmy," Jones said. "My attitude at the time—and I told this to Jimmy—was 'You're doing a good job, but don't let the door hit you in the ass on the way out.' There were a couple of times during the 1992 season that he practically invited me to make the change. There were two times when I had to sit him down and tell him that this is how it's going to be or else." Well before Jones versus Johnson had begun to trickle into the mainstream media, Jones would confer with his family over how little respect he was afforded from his coach. "I'm going to fire his ass," he'd say. "I can go out and find myself another coach."

In the other vortex was Jimmy Johnson, a man with an ego as

large as the Qinghai-Tibet Plateau; a man who detested his boss's incessant need for attention and mocked his limited, unimpressive, uninspiring knowledge of the game.

Wasn't it Jones who, before the '93 season, invited a twenty-seven-year-old defensive tackle named Fletcher Rudisill to training camp, sight unseen? Wasn't it Jones who raved that Rudisill—a former starter at Hudson Valley Community College whom Jones had met *in a bar*—was a diamond in the rough who could prove to be another Cowboy steal? Wasn't it Rudisill who couldn't jog twenty feet without stopping to vomit? Wasn't it Rudisill who was cut after two weeks? "This," sneered Johnson to a handful of writers, "is the guy Jerry sent me."

Why, for God's sake, did Jerry insist on sticking his nose in the business of running a football team? *Spend your damn money, put butts in the seats . . . and leave me the hell alone.* "It was a joke," says Larry Brown, the veteran cornerback. "Jerry placed the coaches in bad positions by pretending he didn't want power but then doing everything to control every piece of the team. Jimmy didn't go for that." Johnson still regularly thought back to the 1991 postseason, when he wisely chose Steve Beuerlein over Troy Aikman as his playoff starter, then watched as Jones intruded by telling the *Fort Worth Star-Telegram* that Aikman was—without question—the future of the franchise. So furious was Johnson that he stormed around Valley Ranch, a copy of the newspaper in hand, screaming, "Maybe I'll just get out of here and take this staff with me to Tampa Bay! Who's coaching this football team anyway?"

To Johnson, the deterioration of a once-cordial relationship reached critical mass on the day before the 1992 NFL Draft, when the Cowboys called the Browns and offered five draft picks in exchange for two of Cleveland's. Later in the day, after Jones had departed from Valley Ranch, Browns coach Bill Belichick called back to sign off on the deal, and Johnson announced it to the media. Jones was furious that he was not informed, and on draft day the owner and coach exchanged words in a heated closed-door meeting. According to *Sports Illustrated*'s Peter King, five minutes before the draft Jones told Johnson, "You know the ESPN camera is in the draft room to-day. So whenever we're about to make a pick you look at me, like we're talking about it."

An irate Johnson stormed from the room and ducked into his office.

"You okay?" he was asked by Bob Ackles, the director of player personnel.

"Yeah," Johnson snapped. "He's an asshole. Fuck him."

"Jimmy," Ackles said, "he owns the team."

"Fuck him," Johnson said.

Johnson headed for the parking lot, where he was lassoed by Wannstedt. "Don't let him get to you like that," Wannstedt said. "It's not worth it."

Though Johnson eventually returned, he stewed for the entire day.

In the follow-up to two straight Super Bowl victories, those observing the Cowboys from a distance applauded an owner willing to win at all costs. But perception was far from reality. Jones's obsession with squeezing every last penny out of Texas Stadium (fans be damned) was legendary within the team's offices. Allan Cariker, the team's information systems manager, still fondly recalls how employees under the Murchison and Bright regimes were allotted free tickets for home games. "As soon as Jerry arrived he took back all the tickets and sold the right to have them for insane prices," says Cariker. "Where was the decency in that?" Heading into the '93 season the owner installed a new front row into the upper stadium deck and sold the seats at premium prices (thus resulting in a lawsuit from six longtime season-ticket holders who had purchased front-row seats decades earlier and now found themselves in row two). He replaced two thousand west end zone seats with "luxury" (aka: offensively expensive) Platinum Club chairs. "You've got loyal fans who bought seats when the team wasn't doing well," said John Gardner, a twenty-eight-year-old fan who, as a result of Jones's policies, considered discarding his season tickets. "Now, it's like making money is the most important thing, not what the fans think."

Such income-generating strategies were tasteless, but in Johnson's mind hardly compared to Jones's inability to treat people righteously. First off, there was the ongoing issue of the Dallas assistant coaches, one of the lowest-paid groups in the league (running backs coach Joe Brodsky, for example, was making $78,000). Furthermore, Johnson was still incensed with the way Jones's stubbornness had resulted in Smith's two-game holdout to start the '93 season—especially as the team's merchandise generated an NFL-high $695 million in sales. Johnson knew opposing franchises would flock after the Cowboys' pending free agents, and he feared Jones would let one and all willingly depart. (Indeed, on March 3 the Los Angeles Rams signed Jimmie Jones, an underrated defensive tackle, to a four-year, $7.7 million deal.)

Nothing speaks more poignantly of Jones's ode to penny-pinching than the saga of Bobby Abrams, the backup linebacker who played with Dallas for parts of the 1992 and '93 seasons. After appearing in four games with the Cowboys in 1992, Abrams was released and signed by the Cleveland Browns. Shortly after Dallas won the Super Bowl, a team representative called Abrams and offered him either a Super Bowl ring or $65,000. "Having earned a ring with the Giants in 1990, this time I took the cash," says Abrams. "I just didn't feel like I was that big a part of things."

Abrams returned to the Cowboys the following year. He went through training camp and was active for the first eleven regular-season games, performing primarily on special teams. Upon being released yet again, he was signed by the Vikings. When Minnesota's season ended Abrams found himself glued to the TV, rooting intensely for his old team. As Dallas won yet another Super Bowl, Abrams knew he'd take the ring. "I felt like I was a part of it," he says. "Even though I wasn't there at the end, it was a meaningful accomplishment." When he called the Cowboys to request the hardware, however, he was greeted by hmms, haws, and—eventually—rejection. "They told me that since I signed with an NFC team that I wasn't entitled to a ring or the money," he says. "So even though I was a contributor to a championship, it meant nothing."

The decision came directly from Jones, and it was laughable.

But that was the boss, a person Johnson no longer had affection or patience for. Johnson could only laugh when he heard that the Cowboy owner had allegedly instructed a private investigator to follow Jim Dent, the famed Dallas sportswriter, as he was researching a Jerry Jones biography. Was he that insecure? That pathetic? "Both Jerry and Jimmy had such tremendously huge egos," says Larry Lacewell, the team's director of college and pro scouting. "I think what it came down to was the stage just wasn't big enough for both of them. They both lacked the intelligence to give the other guy the credit and respect he deserved. So instead of harmony, it became a mess."

The Jerry-Jimmy soap opera was best surmised in a *New York Times* editorial titled, appropriately, J.R. AND BOBBY, PART II:

> The problem seems to be who gets the credit for Restoring the Dynasty. The sportswriters gave it straightaway to Mr. Johnson, who took the team from 1–15 to two consecutive championships. Mr. Johnson nodded his perfectly combed head at the sportswriters and said, yes, I think you have got it about right.
>
> Mr. Jones, for his part, pointed out that he was the fellow who stacked up the $60 million or so needed to pay Troy Aikman and Emmitt Smith. Mr. Jones was said to feel that with that kind of talent on hand, he could probably coach the Cowboys himself. Mr. Johnson began to muse that it did not seem right to have an acknowledged Lombardi-style Football Genius like himself make only $1 million a year and maybe the Jacksonville Jaguars might like to play their first game in 1995 under the tutelage of a wizard of the sport.
>
> It is not yet clear which of these athletic-dorm siblings will rise up and symbolically slay the other. But the spectacle reminds us that there is one story older than Iron John. It involved Cain and Abel.

The beginning of the end came on the night of March 21, 1994, when Jones, Johnson, and a contingent of current and former Cowboy coaches and executives converged upon Orlando for the annual NFL meetings. Sitting at a restaurant table within the confines of Walt Disney's Pleasure Island, Johnson began recounting Jones war stories with two of his former assistants, Dave Wannstedt (who'd become head coach of the Chicago Bears) and Norv Turner (who'd recently been hired as head coach of the Washington Redskins), their wives, as well as Roz Dalrymple, wife of the team's media relations director, and Rhonda Rookmaaker, Johnson's girlfriend. Also present were Brenda Bushell, Johnson's former TV coordinator, and Bob Ackles, the Cowboys' former director of player personnel—both of whom had been fired by Jones—and Ackles's wife, Kay. With the drinks flowing, Johnson described his boss as, among other things, a buffoon, a liar, a jerk, and an incompetent. He recounted the '92 draft fiasco, when Jones insisted Johnson make him look good for the ESPN cameras. "We were all telling stories, having a good time, and we were ten feet away from a free bar, so everyone was feeling pretty good," says Ackles. "That's when Jerry and Larry Lacewell walked up."

Basking in the glow of another Super Bowl title, Jones was hovering ten feet above the ground, accepting the handshakes and congratulatory salutes of his league-wide peers. As the prime dealmaker in the NFL's recently signed $4.4 billion television contract, Jones was now officially one of the big guns. Any owner who had initially been skeptical of this quirky outsider from Arkansas now had to acknowledge Jones's moxie.

Carrying large plastic cups of Scotch, Jones and Lacewell walked up a grassy hill and spotted Johnson and Co. "Here's to the Dallas Cowboys," cackled Jones as he raised a glass, "and here's to the people who made it possible to win two Super Bowls!" With that, Ackles spun toward wife Kay and grinned. Ever since May 4, 1992, when he was fired by Jones, Ackles had retained a bitter taste in his mouth. The owner, after all, had once promised that he would be a Cowboy for life. Now, Jones finally seemed to be acknowledging his contributions. It was almost enough to . . .

"Oh, B-b-b-b-ob, K-k-k-kay," said Jones, interrupting his own toast. "I didn't see y'all sitting there."

Dead silence.

"It was just incredibly rude," says Ackles. "Jimmy was looking at the man like he had an asshole in the middle of his forehead."

Jones acted as if nobody had heard him, and he repeated the toast. Not only did the participants refuse to raise their glasses, but Johnson shot Jones an unequivocal *what-the-fuck-are-you-doing-here?* glare. "It was embarrassing," says Lacewell. "With the exception of Jimmy, these were people who either left the organization or were fired. They didn't want to hear a toast from Jerry." Jones slammed down his glass and snarled. "You goddamned people just go on with your goddamned party," he said, storming off to a chorus of snickers. How dare no one respond to his words. How dare no one invite him to sit down. He was hurt, humiliated, and, most of all, tired. Tired of the hostility. Tired of the disrespect. Just plain tired of feeling like a guest of the Dallas Cowboys.

An enraged Jones immediately returned to the nearby Hyatt Grand Cypress, plopped himself down atop a stool inside Trellises, the lobby bar, and railed against Johnson to friends. "I should have fired Jimmy and brought in Barry Switzer a *long* time ago," he said. Sitting nearby were a handful of sportswriters. Jones greeted the journalists and left the bar with Lacewell. Within minutes most of the scribes departed too. The four who remained—Rick Gosselin and Ed Werder of the *Dallas Morning News,* Joe Fisaro of the *Tampa Tribune,* and Geoff Hobson of the *Cincinnati Enquirer*—sat drinking with Ackles, who had ambled up to the bar. "The place cleared out until it was just a few of us," says Gosselin. "Then Jerry and Larry came back in and Bob said, 'That's my cue to leave.'"

Without skipping a beat, Jones grabbed Werder by the left pants leg and said, "Why don't you guys sit down a while. Let me buy you a drink. You sure as hell don't want to go to bed and miss the biggest story of the year."

Werder looked at Gosselin. Gosselin looked at Werder. This absolutely, positively had to be their scoop. "Guys," said Gosselin, "I'm heading off to bed."

"Me too," said Werder.

Fisaro and Hobson followed their colleagues to the elevator banks. The two non-Dallas writers retreated to their rooms. The two Dallas writers returned to the bar, where Jones and his loose lips awaited. Thus began *the* interview. "I think it's time that I let you know I'm thinking of firing Jimmy," Jones said. "I think it's really time that I go ahead and do it before we run into more trouble. Now, I think, is the time to go ahead and get rid of his ass."

Gosselin and Werder were stunned. This wasn't quite what they had anticipated.

"You know, you may laugh at me for this one," Jones said. "But I could step out and hire Barry Switzer as coach of the Dallas Cowboys tomorrow and he'd do a better job than Jimmy. Hell, I could probably get Lou Holtz over here. I might just step out tomorrow and hire either one of them. You know that Barry and I have been friends for thirty years. I think he'd do a great job in the NFL.

"Let me point out one thing before you go to bed tonight," Jones said. "I think there are five hundred people who could have coached this team to the Super Bowl. I really believe that. Shit, I could have coached the hell out of this team.

"You know," he added, "I should have gone and fired that little sonofabitch a year ago. I can assure you this right now: I'm going to fire that sonofabitch and I'm going to hire Barry Switzer!"

For the next hour, Gosselin, Werder, Lacewell, and Jones sat and continued to speak of all things Jimmy, Jerry, and the future of the Cowboys. "Lemme ask you boys a question," Jones said to the table. "Can you win a Super Bowl without a franchise quarterback?" The answer, of course, was yes. "Can you win a Super Bowl without a franchise running back?" Yes, again. "Well," he said, "can you win a Super Bowl without a fucking great coach?"

Indeed, you could.

"People have said that Jerry was drunk or Jerry was out of his mind or Jerry was just venting at the wrong moment," says Gosselin. "None of that is true. He was almost talking himself into firing Jimmy. He knew exactly what he was saying and what he was doing." The owner of the Dallas Cowboys wanted to win in the worst way—but he didn't want to win *this* way.

In a nod to proper journalism, Gosselin and Werder double-checked that everything Jones said was on the record. It was 5 A.M., after all, and Jones's bloodshot eyes and half-empty glass of Scotch told the story of an owner lacking momentary judgment. "Print it," Jones said. "Print fuckin' all of it." No, said Werder, let's meet for breakfast and review the information. When the three men parted ways, Werder rushed to his room to start typing while Gosselin began his mad-dash reporting. Luckily for the scribes, earlier that morning Lacewell had filled Johnson in on Jones's feelings, and now Johnson had caught wind of Jones's rant. As Johnson wandered the hallways of the hotel, looking for Gosselin, he encountered Don Shula, the legendary Miami Dolphins coach. Johnson's face was blank. "Jimmy, what's wrong?" Shula asked.

"It's nothing," Johnson said. "I think I've just been fired as the head coach of the Dallas Cowboys."

Moments later Johnson found Gosselin. "I am really dumbfounded," he told the reporter. "For the simple reason that I don't know what I did.

"It concerns me when he says to a group of reporters that he's not only going to fire me, but even says who the replacement is going to be. This wasn't a statement to one person behind closed doors. This was a statement made in a bar with a lot of people around."

Come 9 A.M., the two reporters and Jones met in the lobby. A more subdued Jones reviewed his quotes and restated his initial declaration: Print it. "That's one thing about Jerry—he's always good to his word," says Gosselin. "Say what you want about him, if he says something, he never backs off."

On the morning of Wednesday, March 24, readers of the *Dallas Morning News* walked to the end of their driveways, picked up their newspapers, pulled off the rubber band, and gasped. POST-SEASON SCRIMMAGE, screamed the front-page headline. The story read:

> ORLANDO, Fla.—Jimmy Johnson said he is reconsidering his future as coach of the Super Bowl champion Dallas Cowboys after learning that team owner Jerry Jones made repeated threats about firing him early Tuesday morning.
>
> Mr. Johnson confronted Mr. Jones with his concerns in a midday meeting.
>
> "I met with Jerry, and I'm still coach of the Cowboys," he said later. "This particular incident makes me pull back and reassess things."
>
> Mr. Johnson abruptly left the NFL's annual spring meetings two days before their scheduled conclusion. He will miss his principal media commitment—a Wednesday morning coaches' breakfast.

"By the time the story came out, it was pretty clear to me that Jimmy's tenure was over," says Gosselin. "It wasn't official, I suppose, but the relationship was torn apart. There was a lot of negativity behind everything, and it all exploded in Orlando. They were two men who could no longer coexist."

Later that day, Jones held a thirty-minute press conference at the hotel, refusing to apologize for his threat while chalking everything up to "just another day in the life of the Dallas Cowboys."

He went on, "[The bickering] is something that happens all the time. It never does affect any decision-making on my part, and I know it won't affect any on Jimmy's."

As Jones spoke, his coach was sitting in his convertible, driving back home to the south Florida coast, thinking about escaping a job he no longer wanted and an owner he could no longer tolerate. Jones had gone too far, and Johnson knew he would never again work for the Dallas Cowboys. "It was over," he says. "I really knew it was over."

Four days later, on March 28, the owner of the Dallas Cowboys dipped into his notebook of phone numbers and dug out the ten-digit extension for a man living a remarkably humdrum life in the college town of Norman, Oklahoma. "Barry," said Jones, "it's Jerry. I have two questions for you. First, do you still want to coach? And second, how would you feel about coaching the Dallas Cowboys?"

In the history of America's Team, here was a truly historic moment. This was Clint Murchison hiring Tex Schramm and Tom Landry in 1960. This was selecting Roger Staubach in the tenth round of the 1964 draft. This was . . .

"Jerry, do me a favor," Switzer said. "Can you call back in a couple of hours? I just got home from the hospital and I'm still sorta groggy. They did one of those damn colonoscopies on me."

Chapter 19

ANAL PROBE

It's been almost twenty years since Barry recruited me to Oklahoma, and if you ask him today who Reggie Barnes's parents are, he'll still say Wilmer and Ruth. Still."
—**Reggie Barnes, Sooners and Cowboys linebacker**

IN LIFE, THERE are things that make perfect sense and things that make no sense at all.

Ghostbusters made sense.

Ghostbusters II did not.

Kiss's *Destroyer* made sense.

Kiss's *Music from "The Elder"* did not.

Chocolate-covered raisins make sense.

Chocolate-covered ants do not.

Jimmy Johnson coaching the Dallas Cowboys made sense.

Barry Switzer coaching the Dallas Cowboys did not.

The whole thing had to be a joke, right? Jerry Jones would *not* hand over the reins of America's Team to a man who had been away from the game for five years; who had left the University of Oklahoma in disgrace after a scandal-pocked career resulted in probation for the school because of his failure to "exercise supervisory control"; who didn't even watch the NFL and, for the life of him, couldn't tell you what division the Cowboys played in; whose area of expertise was the friggin' *wishbone offense;* who had spent his most recent days operating an insurance agency.

"There was sheer disbelief when Barry's name came up," says Jim Dent, the legendary Texas sportswriter. "Here was this man who had coached the hated Oklahoma Sooners, a team no self-respecting Texan could stand, and the rumor was he was coming to Dallas. I couldn't fathom it."

Neither, for that matter, could Switzer. Back in 1989, when Jones was closing in on purchasing the Cowboys, he had considered Switzer a long-shot possibility to replace Tom Landry as head coach. At the time Jones wanted Johnson, and knew he'd likely have him—but the soon-to-be Cowboy owner loved Switzer's bravado; his open-mindedness; his personal touch; and his understanding and appreciation of the African-American athlete. Mostly, he loved his 157–29–4 record in sixteen seasons with the Sooners, whom he coached from 1973 to 1988.

"Barry Switzer is a winner," Jones said. "That's the bottom line. He wins."

Now five years later here was Switzer, fresh off of a colonoscopy, standing in his living room and wondering what the world was coming to. *Coach the Dallas Cowboys? Me?* Three hours after Jones's initial phone call, Switzer dialed the Cowboys owner back. "I had one of those anal probes, but I'm a little more clearheaded now," he told Jones. "Did you say you wanted me to coach the Cowboys?"

Indeed.

"This is not an interview," Jones said. "You don't have to prove yourself. I know who you are. I know what you stand for. I'm firing Jimmy tomorrow, so consider this an offer—if you want it, you've got the job."

The day was March 28, 1994, and professional football was spinning on its head.

In Norman, home to the University of Oklahoma, Switzer was treated as a merging of mayor and favorite son. He was making appearances on behalf of this car dealership and that bakery, shaking hands and kissing babies and eating like a king at his favorite local restaurant, Othello's. He had even made a handful of trips to Italy with his three children—Greg, twenty-five, a concert pianist; Kathy, twenty-four, a senior at Oklahoma; and Doug, twenty-one, a quarterback at Missouri Southern. "I didn't need the work," he says. "I really didn't." And yet, in his soul Switzer was a football coach. A whistle around the neck, the crisp green grass of a practice field, helmets shining beneath a boastful sun: *That* was heaven.

Switzer thought and thought and thought. "OK," he finally said to Jones. "I guess I'll do it."

"Football's been my life, and it was an opportunity to do what I love," says Switzer. "It was close enough to Oklahoma for my family to be a part of it, and I knew enough people with the Cowboys to think it'd be enjoyable."

A sporadic reader of the newspaper, Switzer was only mildly aware of the volcanic eruption that had taken place 1,278 miles away in Orlando. He knew that Jones and Johnson had had their issues, but he also knew they'd won the last two Super Bowls together. "Great coach, great owner, great organization," says Switzer. "I couldn't understand why those guys weren't working out. But some problems are irresolvable."

In the aftermath of the debacle, nothing had been healed. Troy Aikman and Emmitt Smith spoke out against Jones, with the tailback threatening, "If you fire Jimmy, fire me," and the quarterback going so far as to say, "If I could have anticipated something like this happening, I would have been hesitant about signing a long-term contract." On the morning of Monday, March 28, the *Dallas Morning News* reported that Jones and Johnson would meet that day to maybe—just maybe—sort out their differences and pursue a third straight Super Bowl crown. Wrote Tim Cowlishaw: "Both sides believe anything is possible this week." Little did Cowlishaw know that on that same morning Jones would call to offer Switzer a chance at coaching redemption.

On the afternoon of Tuesday, March 29, with Switzer's official hiring still a well-kept secret, Johnson and Jones held an awkward, bizarre, surreal joint press conference at Valley Ranch, announcing their divorce. With contorted faces and pursed lips, the two men sat side by side. It was like watching an old episode of *Moonlighting*, knowing damn well that when the cameras stopped rolling, Bruce Willis and Cybill Shepherd couldn't stomach each other. Randy Galloway of the *Morning News* accurately termed the scene a "lickfest."

"You will never witness anything more fraudulent in all of sports," Galloway told KERA radio. "Not even in a Don King press conference."

He was right.

Jones's words: "This is so ironic, because it was just five years ago that a lot of us were here in this room and certainly a lot of us here in Dallas, when basically I said that I thought that Jimmy Johnson would prove to be worth five Heisman Trophies, or worth five number one draft picks, or all of it combined. There's no question that that's what has proven to be. Jimmy has done everything in his power and has done it successfully for you, as fans, to be a part of something that really had not been done before, if you really look at where it came from."

Jones's thoughts: *Thank God I fired this asshole.*

Johnson's words: "Over the last five years, Jerry Jones and myself have been able to do some things that a lot of people would have said couldn't be done. Because of our relationship and how we were able to do things in a quick, decisive way, we were able to take a team that was the worst in the NFL to winning two Super Bowls. We've had probably the most candid discussions the last couple of days that we have ever had and I can sincerely tell you that I feel better about Jerry Jones, as a friend, for understanding me today than I ever have in our entire relationship."

Johnson's thoughts: *Thank God I quit this asshole* (and snagged a $2 million buyout to boot).

As the aftershocks worked their way through the hallways of Valley Ranch, Jones exited the facility and went about his business.

Though he had feigned sadness during the press conference, the Cowboy owner felt about as sentimental as a tote bag. Johnson was gone—praise Jesus.

On the afternoon of Wednesday, March 30, the Dallas Cowboys officially introduced Switzer as the team's coach. Nearly 150 media representatives attended the Valley Ranch press conference—an ode to both the aura of America's Team and the lunacy of the move. "Nothing is going to change," Switzer told the assembled journalists. "Get ready to watch the Dallas Cowboys be the best in the NFL.

"I give Jerry my commitment of loyalty," Switzer said. "I promise you I don't have an ego that allows me to put myself in a position to damage the relationship. I'm not attacking Jimmy here, but when it comes to getting credit, what the hell difference does it make?" Jones was beaming from ear to ear. Switzer was, too.

Did he have a message for the fans? someone asked.

"Yeah," Switzer said. "We've got a job to do and we gonna do it, baby!"

Uh . . .

"Barry Switzer, head coach of the Dallas Cowboys?" wrote C. W. Nevius in the *San Francisco Chronicle*. "Kind of has a ring to it, doesn't it? Like Regis Philbin, ambassador to China. Somewhere Tom Landry has just decided that he will skip dinner and is going to lie down for a while."

In the wide swath between scumbag and saint, there's a place for Barry Lane Switzer. Depending on who you ask, the third head coach of the Dallas Cowboys is either a brave leader or a brazen cheater; a proponent of opportunity or a proponent of opportunism. "Barry," says Larry Lacewell, his longtime friend and coworker, "is everything to everybody and nothing to nobody."

To those who supported his hiring in Dallas, Switzer was the genius behind an Oklahoma program that had dominated the collegiate landscape for much of his sixteen seasons. More than just a coach,

Switzer excelled at loyalty. If you played for Switzer, you almost certainly came to love him. "He's a great, *great* man," says Dean Blevins, Switzer's former quarterback at Oklahoma. "When Barry was recruiting me out of high school he found out that I played golf every afternoon. So he'd drive out there, strap my bag on his shoulder, and be my caddy. To this day, I'd do anything for him."

Yet to the masses who bemoaned his hiring by the Cowboys, Switzer was the worst kind of heathen. Sure, he'd won national championships in 1974, '75, and '85. But what good is victory void of integrity? In the early '80s Switzer was charged with insider trading by the Securities and Exchange Commission. Although the case was dismissed for insufficient evidence, he and two partners were asked to repay $1.5 million in loans. In 1984 he was arrested for driving while drunk. Four years later, the Sooners were placed on three years' probation for "major violations," including offers of cash and cars to recruits and airline tickets to players.

Those who believed it could get no worse only had to wait until early 1989, when, within a two-month span, Sooners defensive back Jerry Parks shot and wounded a teammate, three players were charged with rape in the athletic dorm, and star quarterback Charles Thompson was charged with selling cocaine. Switzer had allegedly alerted Thompson to the fact that he was under investigation, forcing the FBI to call off a larger probe and move against Thompson before it intended. "Barry's biggest problem throughout his career was he didn't have any interest in nuts-and-bolts discipline," says Brad Sham, the longtime Cowboys announcer. "That doesn't work as a father, it doesn't work as a boss—and it certainly doesn't work as a football coach."

Unlike the majority of his coaching peers, whose stories of lifelong gridiron glories read like dime-a-dozen *Inside Sports* profiles, Switzer's background spoke of a man saved by the game; a man who easily could have been dead or in jail or selling used cars.

Born in tiny Crossett, Arkansas, on October 5, 1937, Switzer grew up in a shack without electricity or running water. He was raised in a "shotgun house," so named because, he once said, "you could shoot a blast through one end and out the other without hitting a thing."

"We didn't have a telephone until I was in college," Switzer said. "I went through junior high studying under coal-oil lamps and listening to battery radios because we didn't have electricity. We had the old privy out back, the three-holer with the Sears, Roebuck catalog and the lime sacks in the corner. At night I used to take my grandmother and mother to the privy carrying a coal-oil lamp and a .22 pistol to shoot the copperheads. My granddaddy planted tomatoes behind that very same privy, and I'll tell you something else—they were the best darned tomatoes in the country." To take baths, Barry and his younger brother Donnie would use barrels to catch rainwater. To keep the mosquitoes away in the summer, Barry would fog his bedroom with toxic Real Kill spray.

With that inextinguishable smile, Switzer can make his youth sound downright Opie Taylor–esque. Yet not only were Frank and Mary Louise Switzer dirt-poor, both were alcoholics. As Mary Louise stayed home to raise Barry and Donnie, Frank failed at one business venture after another before turning to bootlegging. If there was a bright spot to an otherwise down-in-the-dirt childhood, it was that, unlike most other white children growing up in America in the 1940s and '50s, the Switzer boys came to ignore skin color. In his career as a bootlegger, the majority of Frank's customers were poor and black, and their children served as young Barry's closest confidants. Wrote Switzer in his 1990 autobiography, *Bootlegger's Boy*: "[One] particular black settlement was a dozen or more shanty houses. The people who lived there raised cotton and sugarcane and had an old sorghum mill, and an old black mechanic named Sam Patton had a garage of sorts. In the fourth grade I used to pick cotton for a black man, and I'd go swim in the creek with the black kids. They had a barrel stay we used for a basketball hoop. Other than my big collie dog, Major, black kids were my best friends." Later on, as rival coaches scratched their heads over Switzer's ability to recruit minorities, it became clear that his advantage was empathy. Switzer wasn't black, but he knew what it was to *feel* black.

He also knew what it was to feel pain. Though Barry worshipped his father in the way boys naturally do their paternal role models, Frank Switzer brazenly cheated on his wife, with little regard for her emotional stability. When she wasn't minding her boys, Mary Louise spent her days reading novels and sinking into a depression fueled by her husband's infidelities and nonstop drinking. There was no joy in Mary Louise's life; no momentary sparks. She was sad, poor, listless, and married to a man who broke the law to line his pockets and violated the vows of matrimony to sow his wild oats. She took barbiturates by prescription and, according to her oldest son, "would kind of glide through the day with a glaze around her."

Barry's escape from a tortured home life came via sports. He entered Crossett High School in 1951 and soothed feelings of inadequacy with athletic brilliance. He played football, swam freestyle, and excelled in the shot put, setting a regional record with a 53-foot, 4-inch toss. For a boy who had always seen himself through the prism of his parents' shortcomings, the fields and pools of his youth allowed for mental and physical liberation. During Barry's senior year, the Alcoholic Beverage Control Commission came to the Switzer household and arrested Frank. As his father was being cuffed, Barry watched one of the agents smash Frank in the mouth with a gun butt. "You sons of bitches!" Frank yelled. "You broke my teeth!" He was sent to the Arkansas State Penitentiary. His wife and sons were ashamed, but visited every other Sunday.

The opportunity for a different life came to Barry Switzer in the form of a football scholarship from the University of Arkansas in Fayetteville, which he attended from 1956 to 1960 and where he excelled as an offensive lineman and linebacker. For Barry, college wasn't about football so much as it was about personal development, confidence, and a sense of self. As a boy, Barry could not escape his father's shadow, and often feared that he was doomed to follow his path. "[At college] I learned to express myself well in public," he wrote in *Bootlegger's Boy*. "I learned to be a leader and get along with people at the same time. My social experiences and maturing meant as much to me as my degree."

But if there is a defining moment that explains Barry Switzer, it occurred on the night of August 26, 1959, when he was twenty-three years old. Lying in bed, an electric fan blowing the mosquitoes off his face, Barry was approached by his mother, who was loaded up with alcohol and prescription drugs. "Mother," he said, "I would rather not ever see you again, and know you are safe and well taken care of, than to see you like this all the time." Beaten down by a life short on love and high on abuse, Mary Louise bent to kiss her son's cheek. He turned his head away. Barry was mad, frustrated, distraught—disgusted. Mary Louise rose from the bed, removed a pistol from the closet, walked to the back porch, and shot herself. Barry dashed down the hallway and found her lifeless body. He carried her into the house and placed her atop her bed. The sheriff soon arrived and confirmed what the son had known: Mary Louise Switzer was dead.

"I felt like I was the one who had caused her to pull the trigger," Switzer wrote. "All she wanted was my love and I turned my face away. I have carried this guilt with me the rest of my life."

Upon graduating from Arkansas in 1960, Switzer enlisted in the U.S. Army Reserves for six months before being asked by Razorbacks coach Frank Broyles whether he would return as an assistant.

Broyles was initially drawn to Switzer's intelligence and work ethic, but what he uncovered was the best recruiter he'd ever seen. Borrowing the gift of schmooze his father used in peddling booze, Barry could walk into a home and immediately grasp the needs of the player and—more important—his mother. Barry was a fast talker, but not an offensively slick one. He was young enough to relate to high school seniors and wise enough to speak of educational needs. When Arkansas ran off twenty-two straight wins in 1964 and '65, much credit went to the players Switzer had helped bring in. Two of the Razorbacks' linemen were, in fact, Jerry Jones and Jimmy Johnson. "Nobody had anything but respect for Barry back then," says Jones. "It was easy to see he had a future."

When Jim Mackenzie was hired to coach Oklahoma in 1966, he tabbed Switzer as his offensive line coach. Upon Mackenzie's death from a heart attack on April 28, 1967, Oklahoma named Chuck Fairbanks the new coach. Not only did Fairbanks retain Switzer—he promoted the twenty-nine-year-old to offensive coordinator and had him dump Oklahoma's two-back offense and replace it with the wishbone. By season's end the Sooners were college football's No. 1–ranked team.

Fairbanks departed for the New England Patriots after the 1972 season, and the Oklahoma Board of Regents agreed to hand the job over to the thirty-five-year-old Switzer. He arrived in Norman as an obscure assistant hoping to maybe, just maybe, make a career out of this coaching thing. He left sixteen years later as one of the most legendary, polarizing figures in the ninety-four-year history of OU football. Though nobody accused Switzer of being an ineffective football coach, a state known for its church-per-block convictions finally tired of the man. In his 1988 autobiography, *The Boz,* former Sooners linebacker Brian Bosworth said Switzer "turns his back" on his players' off-the-field transgressions. According to Bosworth, such behavior included extensive freebasing of cocaine and the acceptance of lavish gifts from team boosters. When Oklahoma's 1949 national championship team said it would cancel its fortieth reunion if Switzer was retained, the university had no choice. Switzer resigned under pressure, damned to an eternity of seeing his name alongside the words "outlaw" and "scoundrel."

Then Jerry Jones came calling.

The Cowboys owner had always possessed a soft spot for Switzer; for his vulnerabilities and pain as much as his compassion and football knowledge. Jones saw Switzer for who he was—the type of guy who would give a stranger the shirt off his back and wash, iron, and fold it, too. So what if Texans despised Oklahoma as college football's anti-Christ? Jones believed they would learn to love Switzer the way he did. "So many people in this business have a big ego," says Lacewell. "Well, Barry Switzer has about as little ego coaching as anybody I've ever known. He wanted good players and he was willing to spread the credit around."

Now Jones was giving the world's most unlikely coaching reclamation project a second chance. He was betting a five-year, $5 million contract that it would work. "Jerry wanted somebody to be loyal to him," says Switzer. "Someone who he would be comfortable with in his own house. He didn't have that with Jimmy, what with all the undercurrents and the inability of his coach to share success. But Jimmy is an insecure person. I'm not."

Switzer, Jones believed, would ably coach the Cowboys, and without Johnson's attitude. So what if Switzer was inclined to make the occasional moronic statement about strippers or boosters or helping players out with a little bit of pocket change? So what if Switzer's ethics lapsed from time to time? So what if Switzer would soon be diagnosed with ADD (hardly a shock to those familiar with his here-one-minute-gone-the-next mannerisms)? "The day after I signed Jerry insisted, 'Tear up the contract. I'm going to redo it,'" says Switzer. "I said, 'Why?' Jerry said, 'Because I got up this morning, I looked at myself in the mirror, and I liked myself.'"

Best of all, now Jones would serve as his own general manager. On March 31, 1994, the Cowboys released tight end Alfredo Roberts, a trusty reserve who had played for Johnson at the University of Miami. The next day Switzer was asked what he didn't like about Roberts. "I'll be honest with you," he said. "I heard it on the radio a few minutes ago while I was out looking at some houses. I guess the general manager made a decision to release him and didn't consult the coach. Hell, it's OK with me."

Chapter 20

WALKING INTO A BUZZ SAW

I don't care what anyone says—Barry Switzer was the exact right guy to take over the Cowboys. A coach who pushes and punches only lasts so long. Barry soothed and coddled. It's weird, but we needed that.

—Dale Hellestrae, Cowboys offensive lineman

THE ASSUMPTION AROUND Dallas was that Barry Switzer was doomed to walk into a buzz saw; that the players who had followed Jimmy Johnson to two straight Super Bowl titles were stubborn loyalists who would never give their hearts, minds, and bodies to this renegade from Oklahoma.

The assumption was wrong.

To kick off the first meeting with his new players, Switzer, standing at the front of a conference room at Valley Ranch on April 4, 1994, glanced from man to man and asked, "Dammit, where's Charles Haley? Where the hell is Charles Haley?"

Haley, squatting in the back, stood and raised his hand.

"I'm mad at you!" Switzer yelled. "I heard you flicked your dick at everybody, and you didn't do it to me! What am I, chopped liver?"

The room broke out in laughter. This was no Jimmy Johnson.

Oh, there were ominous signs of rebellion here and there. When he learned of Switzer's hiring, Michael Irvin, Johnson's most vocal supporter, said he could not play for the new coach and threw a garbage can toward television reporters. Then, at the conclusion of the initial twenty-minute meeting, Irvin stormed out with smoke billowing from his ears. What enraged Irvin was not Switzer, the man, but the words emerging from his lips. "I've known Jerry Jones for a long time," Switzer told his new players, "and I think we all owe him for what he's built here. Without Jerry, the Cowboys—"

"Fuck that!" screamed Irvin. "Barry, do you have any idea how many players he's fucked over money? Do you?"

Switzer was unbowed. "Mike, lemme finish," he said. "Just gimme a chance to . . ."

Irvin left.

"I wasn't mad at Barry," Irvin says. "I was just disappointed at losing a man I had come to love."

Switzer could have handled the uncomfortable incident in any number of ways. Wisely, he stepped back and did nothing. "Michael doesn't know me, but I know Michael," Switzer told reporters the next day. "I know what a great leader he is on the field, I know how he practices. I respect his fierce loyalty to [Jimmy Johnson]."

The words resonated with Dallas players, many of whom had spent three or four years under Johnson's 10,000-pound thumb. Though few thought Switzer would match Johnson as a pure football coach, he arrived in Dallas with a much-needed air of casualness. "Jimmy kept that pressure on everyone all the time, and it could beat a person down," says Jay Novacek. "The way he ran practices, the way he hammered guys—there's no way we could have survived much longer. Barry's style was important. He changed the pace when the pace needed to be adjusted."

By the aftermath of Super Bowl XXVIII, most Cowboys had had it with the hypocrisy of Jimmy Johnson. Throughout his final two seasons, Johnson preached the concept of one-for-all-all-for-one. "Ego and selfishness have no place here," he said repeatedly. "No place at all." Yet when push came to shove, why had Johnson departed? Because he was unwilling to share credit with Jerry Jones. Because of ego.

"That was the biggest disappointment with Jimmy—ego took precedence over everything," says Mark Stepnoski, the Cowboys' veteran center. "The thing I didn't understand was that Jimmy used to talk repeatedly about how if we all have success, there'll be enough credit to go around to everybody. Which is true. And sure enough, we got better every year and the more games we won the more attention guys got, the more guys made the Pro Bowl, the more money guys made, the more coaching awards Jimmy received. Then—BAM!—Jimmy and Jerry split up. I can't really fathom what it would take to make a guy walk away from a situation that good. But he did."

While there would always be the sense that he was Jones's bobo, Switzer won over his new minions not by establishing himself as the anti-Jimmy, but by being smart enough to leave things alone and stay out of the way. With the exception of Norv Turner—who departed to coach the Washington Redskins and was replaced as offensive coordinator by Ernie Zampese—Switzer kept the on-field staff intact, and even stuck with Johnson's old playbook. Though he failed to garner the support of Butch Davis, the arrogant defensive coordinator, this was hardly Switzer's failure—Davis had campaigned for the head coaching job and was outraged when he was overlooked. (As Davis would later prove in his four disastrous years guiding the Cleveland Browns, it was a solid no-hire.) Most of the other assistants found Switzer refreshingly easy to work for. In his first meeting with his new staff, Switzer laid out his manifesto. "I'm gonna let you coach," he said. "You do your job, I'll do mine. But if I find any one of you motherfuckers being disloyal I'll fire you on the spot." To Davis, this amounted to a threat. To his coworkers, it was heaven. In a league overstuffed with egomaniacal sideline blowhards, Switzer merely desired professionalism. "There was talk in the media that the coaches were against Barry, and it was complete garbage," says Dave Campo, the defensive backs coach. "He made it clear early on that he saw himself more as an overseer than a hands-on guy, and that was very wise. He put a lot of trust in us. Personally, I loved Barry."

If Switzer faced a grueling uphill battle, it was with a press corps sprinkled with lazy homers willing to take one or two misguided sources at their word. At its best, the Dallas media market offered writers like Rick Gosselin, Frank Luksa, Ed Werder, Randy Galloway, and Denne Freeman—true professionals who accurately depicted the goings-on with America's Team. At its worst, though, fans were subjected to so-called radio and television "journalists" who viewed the job as a chance to make friends with the players and gain a level of fame themselves.

Most egregious was the approach taken by Dale Hansen, the longtime Cowboy radio analyst. As far as professional football broadcasters went, Hansen was one of the nation's elite. On KVIL-FM he played well off of partner Brad Sham and knew the game with unquestioned insight. The problem, though, was that at the same time Hansen doubled as a journalist (he was a sportscaster for Channel 8), he maintained questionable personal relationships with the men he covered. For example, Hansen was thrilled to be included in player-only poker nights, during which illegal drug usage took place. "One time I remember three of the guys lighting up a joint," says Hansen. "They looked at me and said, 'You're not gonna report this, are you?'" Of course he wouldn't report it—hell, he wanted to be invited back. "But then I looked one of the guys in the eye and said, 'But if you fuck up Sunday, I might have to blow on you.' My theory was 'Guys, this is not my job. But if you don't play well and I know you were drunker than hell and left with a hooker Saturday night, I'm going to report that.'"

The approach was inane—especially when it came to Troy Aikman, the object of Hansen's puppy love. The crush dated back to the final days of 1988, when Aikman and UCLA were preparing to battle Arkansas in the Cotton Bowl. In a radio interview held at a Tony Roma's in Dallas, Hansen caught the senior quarterback's attention with quirky questions like, "How long until you replace Steve Pelluer?"

"Troy laughed all the way through the interview," says Hansen. "Then he came to training camp and he and I became great friends. We started to hang out a lot, doing things together." Though it did not strike Hansen as odd that he was a forty-year-old journalist befriending a kid half his age, others in the media found the bias laughably transparent. Aikman could play like Steve Pisarkiewicz on ice skates and Hansen would refuse to rip him.

When Switzer was first hired, Hansen sought input from the golden boy, who had spent parts of two seasons as a quarterback at Oklahoma. "You're gonna love this guy," Aikman raved. "He's smart, he's funny, and he understands the press."

Yet by the early days of training camp, Aikman was reminded why, while he liked Switzer at Oklahoma, he didn't especially respect him. During practices the new head coach would walk around the fields, whistle dangling from a shoelace around his neck, a vacant look in his eyes. When he spoke, it wasn't with the authority of a Jimmy Johnson, but the distant casualness of an onlooker who wasn't quite sure whether his team played in the NFC or AFC. Famously, there was an on-field incident with trainer Kevin O'Neill, a prideful man who didn't take kindly to unneeded interferences. Once, as Switzer tried to offer advice before a gaggle of players, O'Neill turned and screamed, "Don't tell me how to do my fucking job!" The coach slinked away.

Part of Switzer's trepidation was due to newness; one doesn't make the jump from five years of autograph show appearances to running the Dallas Cowboys without stumbling. But there was something more—Switzer's apparent need to be one of the guys; to establish himself as a chum, not an overlord. As a collegiate player Switzer never encountered a curfew he didn't break, and that modus operandi reigned as his players hit Austin's 6th Street bars until the wee morning hours without consequences. "Curfews," he once said, "are rat-turd things made to be broken." Once, after several players arrived in the morning with reddened eyes and reeking from the scent of Jack Daniel's, Switzer sauntered toward the 50-yard line and yelled, "If any of you sons of bitches ain't in the pool in the next ten minutes, you're gonna have to practice today!" Ninety-nine percent of the Cowboys cheered with delight. Aikman did not. To the regimented quarterback, Switzer's casual approach seemed ineffective and his practices disorganized.

"Switzer was prone to saying erratic stuff in meetings that would drive Aikman insane," says Michael Silver, the former *Sports Illustrated* football writer. "He would give a speech to the team and he'd start talking about 'my daddy's black mistress.' It drove the real serious guys who won under Jimmy nuts."

As Aikman soured on the head coach, so, too, did Hansen, his broadcaster lackey. He heard the tales of Switzer's lackadaisical ways, then turned to assistant coach Butch Davis, who—after watching Switzer aimlessly roam practices—was happy to slam his new boss. On the morning of the final Thursday of camp, Hansen was interviewed by KLIF's Norm Hitzges. When Hitzges asked if there were any concerns for the season, Hansen said that Switzer was having trouble with his assistants, and that he needed to immediately work it out. The words emerged from Hansen's mouth, but derived directly from Aikman and Davis. "I thought it was a very innocent comment," says Hansen. "Innocent but true."

That night, at exactly 10:34 P.M., Hansen and Switzer sat down for what initially seemed to be an ordinary on-air TV chat. Both men were dressed casually—Switzer in shorts and a blue golf shirt, Hansen in a red-and-blue golf shirt. With the Channel 8 camera rolling live, Hansen began with a run-of-the-mill question about training camp. Switzer responded, "I loved it. If I had orchestrated it any better it couldn't have gone better. Because I didn't orchestrate it. It just happened."

Quickly, things turned nasty. Hansen asked Switzer about the team's recent trip to Mexico City for an exhibition game against the Houston Oilers, which was plagued by travel issues that included a four-hour runway wait.

HANSEN: "A lot of players are unhappy that you haven't spoken out more saying that Jerry Jones was at fault for more of the problems we had down there. Aren't you concerned that you run the risk of losing the respect of your players?"

Game on.

SWITZER: "I didn't know [Jerry] was a Mexican official. That's the next thing we're gonna accuse him of. He had nothing to do with it. Nothing to do with it. I think—I know—that Jerry is a great guy, but I've gotta convince you and some other people . . . But it really doesn't matter."

HANSEN: "You don't have to convince me, but I think you have to convince some of your players."

SWITZER: "As long as he pays them, it doesn't make a difference. I wanna ask you. You made a phone call on the Norm Hitzges show and you said that we had a controversy on our staff down here today and discord . . ."

HANSEN: "A power struggle . . ."

SWITZER: "A power struggle? On our staff?"

HANSEN: "You're saying that's not true?"

SWITZER: "What are you talking about?"

HANSEN: "I'm talking about your assistants are all fighting . . . As some have said to me, you have like five head coaches."

SWITZER: "Dale, you know better than that. I've got the second-fastest gun on the team. You know why? Because Jerry's got the one and I've got the other, and I can fire any player on this squad, other than the ones that got the great contracts and make all the money."

HANSEN: "Jimmy Johnson said 1984 was his worst year in coaching, and the worst mistake he made was taking over a football team with an inherited staff. Aren't you making the same mistake?"

SWITZER: "No, not at all. Those guys and I get along great. All you've gotta do is interview them. We get along fine. And Kevin O'Neill, when you said we had a screaming match . . . an altercation . . ."

HANSEN (finger raised): "I said players told me that happened."

SWITZER: "Well, I don't know what players you're talking to, but it certainly didn't happen. I asked Kevin—what are they talking about? I asked the coaches, I grabbed the reporters. You guys fabricate things. You can't think. Read the *Dallas Observer*—where do you get that crap? Tell me about it. Where's it come from?"

Until this point, there had remained a paper-thin layer of civility. Now it had vanished. *The Dallas Observer*, an alternative weekly newspaper, had recently run a piece on Hansen's after-hour activities that proved terribly embarrassing to the broadcaster. Switzer knew there was a bruise, and he chose to slam it with a hammer.

HANSEN (raising a finger and his voice): "I know where my sources come from. You don't have to take a cheap shot at me."

SWITZER (smiling, grabbing Hansen's hand): "Hey, I've had as much heat as you've had. We're on the same team, we come from the same school. Lemme ask you something—"

HANSEN: "Let me say something. I've never said an assistant coach has a problem with Barry Switzer. What I'm saying and what a lot of players are saying is and what a lot of coaches are saying is that assistant coaches are having problems with assistant coaches, and players want you to step up and stop it."

This was Hansen the journalist at his worst. Did he have "a lot of players" and "a lot of coaches" confiding in him, or did he have one or two players or one or two coaches telling him the alleged mood of the team? Was he speaking to Leon Lett and Alvin Harper, or just Troy Aikman, a close friend who could use Hansen as a mouthpiece?

SWITZER: "I think they don't know what they're talking about, and you don't either, Dale Hansen. There's no problem here on this staff on the Dallas Cowboys. I promise you that."

Hansen seemed to take a step back. He was losing control of the interview. What followed were some innocent questions—one about the opening game against Pittsburgh, another about Robert Jones's ability to start at middle linebacker, where he was replacing free agent defector Ken Norton, Jr. Then Hansen seemed to offer an olive branch, asking about Switzer's enthusiasm for the job. The coach was not having it.

SWITZER: "They know who the boss is, and I'm the boss. Don't you ever question that, and Jerry Jones knows that too. Because if I wasn't I'd say, 'Jerry, this is your team, I'm your coach.' But if I don't like it and it comes down to a decision between me and a coach or a player—not the guys like Aikman or Emmitt—but hey, it's me or them, handle that, because I can go back and sit on my couch any day [punches Hansen hard in the left shoulder and raises his voice to a scream], because I came to Dallas with more money than Jimmy left with!"

HANSEN (rubbing his shoulder): "This is starting to hurt a little bit, but it hasn't changed what I believe. I gave you the forum. I still think you have dissension among your staff . . ."

SWITZER: "Aw, you don't know what you're talking about. You guys fabricate . . ."

HANSEN (sarcastically): "We make it all up . . ."

SWITZER: "You do! You do! [hits Hansen again] You're the guy who last week walked up to Jerry and you said [hits Hansen again] that Tony Casillas had a brain tumor! You guys manufacture everything! Oh, I've got a radiologist that saw the film! You guys manufacture everything!"

During camp it was rumored that the Cowboys were interested in re-signing Casillas, their former nose tackle, but that he was enduring a "personal problem." A rumor circulated around the league that Casillas had a brain tumor. Hansen asked Jerry Jones if it was true—a fair question. When Jones said no, Hansen killed the story.

HANSEN: "Did you ever see that story on the air or in print?"

SWITZER: "No, but you walked over and told Jerry that."

HANSEN (raising a finger): "I did not tell him that."

SWITZER: "Yes you did!"

HANSEN: "I did not do that. I asked a question."

SWITZER: "Yes you did! Yes you did! Are you getting good ratings tonight?"

HANSEN: "I'm getting very good ratings. But don't start questioning—"

SWITZER: "You told Jerry he had a brain tumor."

HANSEN: "I did not. I did not!"

SWITZER: "Did you tell *someone*?"

HANSEN: "I did not tell anybody. Barry, I'm giving you the forum. But let's play fair. I did not tell anybody any such thing. I ask a lot of questions, I ask a lot of tough questions, I try to ask tough questions."

SWITZER: "But you were false about that. Now you talk about our coaching staff having dissension. That's ridiculous."

HANSEN: "I never reported [the tumor]."

SWITZER: "I think I'll go call Kevin O'Neill. I'm gonna have a screaming match with Kevin. Send your camera over [grabs Hansen's left arm and laughs]."

HANSEN (smiling): "Start hitting my other arm . . ."

As far as local television went, the duel was classic. But while Switzer's points on Casillas and the *Dallas Observer* article were ill-gotten, they were obscured by Hansen, who came off as stubborn and misguided. Troy Aikman did not like the way things were going under Switzer. Butch Davis did not like the way things were going under Switzer. But Hansen was wrong—most players loved the man.

"I had Barry sit at a table with Clayton Holmes and myself and tell us, 'The organization wants me to cut one of you sons of bitches, but I'm gonna find a way to keep you both,'" recalls Kenny Gant, the special teams wizard. "That was in the preseason, and it was straight-up. I'll never forget that."

"I was the odd man out when I was with the Cowboys, so Coach Switzer called me into his office and told me straight-up, 'Son, I'm going to have to release you,'" says linebacker Reggie Barnes. "And he turns around and the man has a tear in his eye."

"I've never met a more honest, decent football coach," says Darren

Studstill, a rookie defensive back. "You could disagree with some of his decisions, but not who he was as a person."

Lost amidst a training camp gone crazy was that the Cowboys looked pretty good. Though the club went only 2–3, the first-team offense performed well, and a defense that had ranked second in the NFL in points allowed in '93 seemed ready for the regular season. "I like everything I see," Switzer raved before the September 4 opener at Pittsburgh. "I believe this team is Super Bowl–worthy."

In hindsight, if there was one disappointment it was that the media missed the feel-good story of training camp. In October 1993, a ten-year-old Dallas boy named J. P. O'Neill was diagnosed with Burkitt's lymphoma, a rare form of childhood cancer that results in large tumors in the facial or abdominal regions. Like many kids his age, J. P. was a sports fanatic. His room was covered with posters of baseball, hockey, and football players, as well as one featuring the Dallas Cowboy cheerleaders. "He loved climbing trees," says Kim O'Neill, J. P.'s father. "He would climb a tree in my parents' backyard and just sit up there and stare into the woods."

By the summer of 1994, J. P.'s health had deteriorated. The tumor in his stomach refused to go away, and the boy weakened daily. When a Channel 5 sportscaster named Scott Murray learned of J. P.'s plight, he arranged for the O'Neills to attend the Cowboys' training camp. Throughout the day, J. P. was treated like a king. He met players, collected autographs, basked in the glow. "They were all so nice to him," says Kim. "Made him feel incredibly special."

Of all the Cowboys, Aikman stood out. He chatted with the frail boy for several minutes before posing for pictures. This type of generosity was a side to the reclusive quarterback far too few people had witnessed. (When the wife of offensive lineman Dale Hellestrae was pregnant with the couple's first daughter, Aikman was the only Cowboy—heck, the only male—to attend the baby shower. When an equipment manager named Al Walker had trouble with his battered truck, Aikman bought him a new one. "No one else went out on a limb for Al," says Kevin Smith. "Aikman drove the truck up there to Valley

Ranch, gave Al the keys, said, 'This is your truck, Al. Just go get insurance.' He did stuff like that all the time that nobody knew about.") So now, as the quarterback prepared to walk away from J. P., Kim reached for the star's shoulder and said, "I know this is a lot, but J. P. was wondering if you'd throw a touchdown pass for him." Aikman looked at J. P., sitting in his wheelchair beneath a blue-and-white Cowboys cap, and said, "I'll do you one better. I'll score a touchdown for you and send you the ball." When J. P. was out of earshot, Aikman whispered to Kim, "I know your son doesn't have long. If I don't do it this week [in a matchup with the Vikings], I promise I'll score for him against the Raiders in next Sunday's exhibition."

On the night of August 7, J. P. O'Neill sat in front of his TV and watched the Cowboys fall to Los Angeles, 27–19. He didn't care about the final score. He didn't care about the standout performance of Raiders center Don Mosebar. No, all he cared about was the Cowboys' opening series, when Aikman did what no quarterback is supposed to do in a meaningless preseason game: He scrambled half a dozen yards into the end zone.

"We knew the touchdown was just for him," says Colleen O'Neill, J. P.'s older sister. "He had to tell everyone who would listen that the touchdown was his. It meant everything to my brother."

Nineteen days later, J. P. O'Neill died. He was buried at Restland Cemetery in Dallas, holding the football that Troy Aikman had sent him.

Chapter 21

ANARCHY ON (AND OFF) THE GRIDIRON

*You mean to tell me there are places where women
get naked? And they serve food there, too?*
—**Kenny Gant, Cowboys safety**

FOR ONE WEEK, everything seemed right.

The Dallas Cowboys opened the Barry Switzer Era by traveling to Pittsburgh's Three Rivers Stadium on September 4, 1994. Before his team took the field, Switzer offered up an emotional, heart-tugging speech on his life as a bootlegger's boy; of watching his mother kill herself; of having to hustle for every opportunity. The room went silent as the new coach spoke. This wasn't about winning. It was about *life*. "You men have a chance today to continue a path of greatness," he said, his voice trembling with nervous energy. "Don't let that pass you by."

Before a black-and-gold-clad crowd of 60,156 and dozens of national media outlets, the Cowboy defense battered Steelers quarterback Neil O'Donnell, sacking him 9 times (4 by Charles Haley, 3 by Jim Jeffcoat) in a one-sided 26–9 romp. "[O'Donnell] was holding the ball because he didn't have anybody to throw to," said James Washington, the Dallas safety. "But then he was scared he was going to get the crap kicked out of him."

No one was more euphoric than Jones, who afterward roamed the Cowboys locker room and looked toward the assembled media with a *Y'all-can-bite-me* grin the size of the Smithfield Street Bridge. "We dismissed a lot of the potential naysayers [who said] that this team had really hurt itself by the changing coaches," Jones said. "I feel very strongly that our best chance to win in '94 were with the changes we made."

It was a great moment for the new Dallas Cowboys. Great, but illusory.

In a far corner of the locker room, Irvin was quietly complaining to Bill Nichols of the *Morning News* that, despite the lopsided score, the Cowboys had performed woefully. "We did not look sharp," he said. "We have a lot of work to do." Though the comments were pooh-poohed by most teammates, Irvin knew whereof he spoke. A closer look at the game tape showed blown coverages, sloppy routes, and less-than-maximum intensity. "In the NFL, talent can prevail for a while," says Darren Woodson, "but not for long without something extra."

The Cowboys won their home opener the following week, squeaking past the Houston Oilers, 20-17, then lost to Detroit on *Monday Night Football*, again by a 20–17 margin. Though the game was memorable for a spectacular 140-yard performance from Lions running back Barry Sanders, what stands out in hindsight is Switzer's violation of expected NFL coaching behavior. On the Saturday night before the game Switzer skipped meetings to fly to Little Rock, Arkansas, on Jones's private jet to watch his son Doug quarterback the Missouri Southern football team. Although the trip immediately qualified Switzer for Dallas Parent of the Year, it was unheard-of behavior for an NFL coach (and a far cry from Johnson, who struggled to remember he had children). While his players and assistants planned for the following day's battle, Switzer was watching the big Missouri Southern–Missouri Western clash, standing along the sideline with a hot dog and a Dixie cup of Coke. His absence was deemed all the more galling the next day when, in a critical short-yardage situation on fourth down against the Lions, Switzer was at a loss for a play call. "It was sometimes hard to take Barry seriously," says Woodson. "You wondered where his priority was." Even as the team proceeded to perform well, Switzer's behavior screamed an unnerving message: *Accountability no longer matters.*

Over the course of his twenty-nine years guiding the Dallas Cowboys, Tom Landry was as deft an image manipulator as he was a football maestro. With one playoff berth after another, Landry was somehow able to peddle the idea that the Cowboys were as wholesome as a backyard barbecue on the Fourth of July.

Behind the image was a darker reality. Throughout much of the 1970s and '80s, the Cowboys' locker room held more than its fair share of steroid abusers, pot smokers, and cocaine addicts. The most renowned was Thomas "Hollywood" Henderson, the All-Pro outside linebacker who famously snorted coke on the sideline during Super Bowl XIII. Numerous Cowboys lived the high life, protected by the stardom that comes with performing in Texas Stadium and the reputation of a flawless head coach. It is no coincidence that such behavior took place in Big D, a city that has long fancied itself as a fast-moving, high-rolling mecca of excitement. To the rich and famous, Dallas meant long-legged blondes, high-stakes poker, and two lines of coke before an all-night free-for-all.

Under the reign of Jimmy Johnson, members of the Cowboys partied plenty hard, but were mindful that their head coach wouldn't hesitate to cut someone who seemed more interested in Q rating than TD ratio. When push came to shove, the Cowboys were all business.

With Switzer's arrival, everything changed. Not only was the new coach indifferent to whether his players stayed out late—he was often out late too, drinking hard, sitting front and center for lap dances at the Men's Club of Dallas (Switzer once even endorsed the Men's Club on his radio show, a first for NFL coaches). Upon his being hired by the Cowboys, many wondered how he would coexist with Larry Lacewell, the team's director of college and pro scouting. Why? Because after the 1977 season, following two decades of friendship dating back to their youths in southern Arkansas, Lacewell learned that Switzer had been sleeping with his wife, Criss. (In a delicious bit of irony, Lacewell's best man at his wedding had been none other than Jimmy Johnson.) Switzer paid Lacewell $25,000 to ensure that word of the affair never reached the press. "Barry likes to let his hair down and have a good time," says Lacewell, who remained married and again counts Switzer among his pals. "I was determined not to carry that animosity toward Barry my entire life, because what good is anger? Barry is who he is."

The same went for Jerry Jones, who felt socially liberated by Switzer's arrival. The Dallas owner longed for a running buddy, something he had hoped to find in Johnson (but didn't). Like Switzer, Jones considered himself a family man, deeply in love with his wife, Gene, and their three children. Like Switzer, Jones talked of compassion and times at home in front of the fireplace. Like Switzer, Jones walked the wild side.

During Jones's first few years in charge of the Cowboys, team staffers quietly wondered whether Gene knew of her husband's reputation as an unabashed skirt chaser. He maintained a well-known affair with Susan Skaggs, a long-legged thirty-something employee of the Texas Stadium Corporation, and did little to hide it. According to Todd Cawthorn, the pilot of Jones's private jet, the owner and Skaggs utilized the plane as their own mile-high Love Shack. "A Lear 35A is not exceptionally large," wrote Cawthorn in his biography on life with Jones. "We could feel the airplane moving and shaking. It didn't move and shake that long."

Jones was the type of man who looked at breasts first, rear second, breasts third, legs fourth, breasts fifth and sixth. When, in 1991, his son Stephen was engaged to be married, Jerry threw one of the raunchiest bachelor parties Las Vegas had ever seen, highlighted by a buffet of gorgeous women with *Hustler* and *Penthouse* résumés hired to dance naked. Wrote Cawthorn, an attendee: "The best part was that each and every one of the goddesses would be 'available' later in the upstairs suites—guaranteed to provide all the loving we could handle, and then some."

At an Austin bar named the Copper Tank, Jones was scheduled to sit down with Kristi Hoss, a Houston-based radio reporter, for a '94 training camp interview. "He was already three sheets to the wind when I got there," recalled Hoss, who said Jones made multiple passes at her. "He reeked of tequila. He tried to grab me around the waist. I'd start to get up and he'd pull me back down, or he'd pull me onto his lap. He kept saying, 'Darlin', you are just way too beautiful to be on the radio. You are the epitome of the Texas beauty queen. You have the most beautiful legs I've ever seen. Why don't you come on and be a Cowboys cheerleader.'"

Rob Geiger, a former reporter for KRLD in Dallas, still laughs over the time he and a particularly fetching female friend named Cici went out to dinner and ran into Jones. "He invited us to his table with thirty or forty other people," says Geiger. "As we were leaving I saw him whisper something into Cici's ear and her eyes popping wide open." What, Geiger wondered, had Jones said?

"Two things," Cici stated. "First, he asked me if I had any panties under my skirt."

And then?

"And then he told me, 'Give me five minutes with you and I'll take you to heaven.'"

If the coach and owner of the Cowboys was allowed to exercise such public audacity, what was to stop the players? Hence, as never before, Dallas's football heroes descended upon the city. The starting point was usually the Cowboys Sports Café, a seemingly unremarkable bar located in a strip mall five minutes from the Valley Ranch practice facility. Owned by a gaggle of former Cowboy players, including legendary running back Tony Dorsett and All-Pro linebacker Eugene Lockhart, the Café was initially a laid-back watering hole to visit after a long day of practice. There were some TVs, a pool table, Thursday night karaoke, double-dip chicken wings (the brainchild of Irvin, who once complained the wings were not sufficiently crispy), and a bottomless tap of cold beer.

Yet with the team's success, the Café went from quiet, around-the-corner comfort zone to groupie-stalker central. Anyone who wanted a piece of the Super Bowl champions knew where to find them. Women in tight pants and bikini tops waited by the bar. Celebrities like Steve Perry, Paula Abdul, and O. J. Simpson stopped in on their way through town. Members of the team upheld a strict rule that no one dared violate: Spouses could eat lunch at the Café, but they were not permitted to enter the premises after sundown. "I literally would have been thrown out," says Lisa Holmes, the former wife of corner-back Clayton Holmes. "It was pathetic. The only person on that team I had respect for was Emmitt Smith, because he wasn't married and if he wanted to be a *playa* it was his right. But the married guys—ninety percent of them were spending all their time at the Café and the strip clubs, thinking they were so important."

"The girls were the worst," says a former Cowboys Café waitress. "They would do absolutely anything just to say, 'I was sitting at a table with . . . whoever.' It was disgusting. And there were also the die-hard fans who'd bug players for autographs even if they were eating. It became too much."

Under Johnson, the Cowboys Café could often serve as the beginning and the end of an outing. Under Switzer, night after night the sky was the limit. Players would meet up at the Café, then plot an evening of strip club hopping and groupie banging. Most alarming was the reckless approach a small number of players took toward cocaine, which had snuck its way into the team's subculture. That members of the Cowboys smoked marijuana came as no surprise to Jones or the coaching staff—football was a painful sport, and a joint or two eased the trauma. Coke, however, was a different monster—addictive, harmful, engulfing. "You get caught up in the lifestyle and it sort of takes over," says Cory Fleming. "At least I did."

A rookie out of the University of Tennessee, Fleming was a rugged wide receiver who impressed Switzer with his size and instincts. Though he certainly knew how to enjoy a good party while in college, Fleming had never touched drugs until a line of coke was presented to him during a shindig in training camp in 1994. Intimidated by the idea of saying no, Fleming leaned over a coffee table, picked up a small straw, and snorted away. *Damn,* he thought. *That's not bad.* As the '94 season progressed and Fleming found himself on the bench (he appeared in only two games), his off-the-field activities increased. When someone said, "Fleming, we're going out!" Fleming went out. When someone said, "Fleming, we're doing shots!" Fleming did shots. When someone said, "Fleming, snort that line!" Fleming snorted that line. "It's not like I was leaving the games and there'd be someone in a car pointing a gun at my head and saying, 'If you don't snort cocaine and sleep with hookers, I'll shoot you,'" says Fleming, who was later suspended by the league for failing a drug test. "No, every mistake I made was a conscious, ill-advised decision. I was a twenty-two-year-old football player who drank and did cocaine, and I couldn't stop."

"We had a lot of guys," says a team employee, "who just couldn't resist."

When Clayton Holmes was selected by the Cowboys in the third round of the 1992 draft, he was sitting in his father's house in Florence, South Carolina, desperate to escape the childhood he describes as "one long nightmare." Holmes was raised in a trailer, the son of a stern, belt-whipping father and a stern, extension cord–whipping mother who delivered four sons from four different men. His parents never married, and struggled to put food on the table. Holmes was painfully shy and athletically unimpressive—hardly the prototype to grow up to be a Dallas Cowboy. "My life changed when I was twelve years old," he says. "I was the kid with the dirty clothes and the snotty nose who never had enough food to eat. I was picked last in everything, and I sucked. I was playing Little League baseball, but I never swung because I was afraid of looking stupid." One day, Holmes's team, Trinity Baptist Church, was trailing late in the game and the count was 3 balls, 2 strikes. "I wasn't swinging once again," says Holmes. "And my coach yells, 'Clayton, just swing the bat!'" The next pitch was a fastball over the heart of the plate. Holmes swung and tipped the ball foul. His teammates cheered wildly. "Then I swung again and hit a triple," he says. "Something just went through me right then and there. I could play!"

From that point, Holmes's confidence soared. He starred in baseball, football, tennis, and track through high school, setting a state record in the long jump with a 24-foot, 9¾-inch leap. He didn't merely love the success that came with sports—he *needed* it. The games took him far away from Florence; from the pain of being poor and beaten and "always hungry"; from the embarrassment of tattered dungarees and hole-pocked shirts; and, most tragically, from the terror of being sexually abused. As a young boy Holmes was repeatedly molested by his older brother Bam, who at night would slide into Clayton's bed and fondle him from behind. "When he would touch me, it changed who I was . . . what I felt," Holmes says. "It brought a lot of anger out of me. Look, I was a kid who was supposed to be having fun, going to school, playing sports. Instead, I had a mother and father who beat me and a brother who molested me." Though the abuse ended once he reached high school, Holmes carried the guilt for most of his life. Overwhelmed by the mental burden, he eventually attempted suicide, swallowing eight trazodones and closing his eyes. As he started to drift off, Holmes came to his senses and dialed 911. "Does anyone who hasn't been molested know what it's like?" says Holmes. "It's humiliating, it's terrifying. You feel like you did something wrong. If you want to truly fuck up a child, sexually assault him and watch what happens."

Despite the charred upbringing, Holmes rose above. He touched neither alcohol, cigarettes, nor drugs, and after two years of junior college earned a scholarship to Carson-Newman College in Jefferson City, Tennessee. "My dad used to drink and smoke marijuana," says Holmes. "He called me in the den one day and said, 'You see what I'm doing? I better not ever hear of you drinking or smoking. When you're a man making his own money you're welcome to it. But not until then.'"

When Holmes arrived in Dallas in 1992, he was a wide-eyed, small-town bumpkin who had never written a check or opened a bank account. Uncommonly shy and thin-skinned, Holmes was humiliated when, while waiting on line to meet President Clinton at the White House after the Super Bowl XXVII triumph, Jimmy Johnson yelled, "Clayton, get your ass in the back where it belongs!" Holmes severely injured his right knee early in the 1993 season, and free time invited trouble. Haunted by a victimized past, he sought an escape. "That's when I started drinking and going to the strip clubs," he says. "I was hurt, and I found that Vicodin and Tanqueray Tom Collins helped ease the pain." Following a couple of lap dances one night at the Dallas Gentleman's Club, a bouncer handed Holmes a box containing a plump joint. "First time I ever smoked one," he says. "I dug it."

The cocaine didn't come until 1994, when the team's disciplinary infrastructure was nonexistent and Holmes, like Fleming, was coaxed into trying something new. He hardly resisted. Holmes felt eight thousand pounds of pressure. From the sexual abuse. From fathering a son, Dominique, at age seventeen. From his wife, Lisa, whom he wed out of guilt. From his white in-laws, who temporarily disowned their daughter for marrying a black man. From Cowboy coaches disappointed by his performance. "I was with a whole bunch of guys, and they gave me a primo," says Holmes, referring to a blunt sprinkled with cocaine. "Two or three months later I was with some guys and I said, 'I wanna go get me some coke!'" It was the first time Holmes had initiated the outreach toward drugs. There was no turning back. "I love sex, but I *love* sex on coke," says Holmes. "So did a lot of the guys. It's more intense. More intimate." From that point, Holmes was hooked. He would seek out cocaine whenever a vacant block of time presented itself. He dabbled with Ecstasy as well. Parties that began on a Friday would stretch through the weekend. One night his wife, Lisa, entered a Dallas club and spotted her husband in the VIP section, lounging in a chair as a woman performed myriad sexual acts. "He was wigged out on Ecstasy, lost in the moment, just not the same person he used to be," says Lisa, whose marriage to Clayton ended in divorce. "When he spotted me he came running, but I didn't have any use for him. The drugs and the fame had turned him into a man I no longer knew."

Oddly, the Cowboy players who used drugs seemed largely unaffected come Sundays. Irvin was a five-time Pro Bowler. Leon Lett was a two-time Pro Bowler. Mark Stepnoski was the NFL's best center (and an unabashed stoner). Mark Tuinei was as powerful as any NFL offensive lineman. Fleming says drugs never took away from his skills. Holmes, in fact, says the best practice of his life came the day after that initial joint. "I was so relaxed and free," says Holmes. "I picked off Troy three times that day, and he was looking at me like, 'Damn, what's up with this dude?' Of course, that only convinced me that I needed to smoke even more."

Holmes agrees drugs were prevalent in the lives of too many Cowboys. So, for that matter, was alcohol, which under Jones and Switzer's new no-holds-barred approach flowed with the ferocity of Victoria Falls. If you were a Cowboy who didn't get in at least one embarrassing brouhaha, you were either an outcast, a Troy Aikman follower, or a purveyor of the extreme straight and narrow (like Bill Bates, Jim Jeffcoat, and Chad Hennings). One of the most memorable rowdy moments of the '94 season took place on a Friday night at Randy White's Grill and Bar, owned by the legendary Dallas defensive lineman. With the scent of alcohol wafting from his pores, Charles Haley rode his Harley-Davidson through the front door and into the eatery's lobby. Just days earlier Haley had thrown a world-class tantrum in the Valley Ranch training room after someone had tossed his dominoes into the garbage. That was nothing compared with an incident from the previous training camp, when Haley approached the Pathfinder belonging to rookie linebacker Anthony McClanahan, grabbed its underbelly, and single-handedly flipped the vehicle upside down. "Charles could snap at any given moment," says Robert Jones. "You never knew when that volcano would erupt."

Now here he was, on a motorcycle in the middle of the lobby, revving the engine to ear-numbing decibels. Staring on in shock were Jerry Jones and Tuinei, who happened to be dining. An aghast Jones approached Randy White. "Whatever you do," he whispered, "don't let Charles ride that thing out of here." White wrapped his arm around

Haley and said, "Listen, don't worry about driving home tonight. We'll get a car, a limo—whatever it takes." Haley shoved the restaurateur in the chest and drew back his fist. "And Randy White is the only person crazier than Charles," says Jody Dean, the Cowboys' entertainment coordinator and a witness to the altercation. "He just coldcocked Charles. I mean, knocked him right out. Then they loaded Charles in the car and took him home." Dean laughs. "Typical stuff."

Fortunately for Dallas, the debauchery had little on-field impact. Though Irvin was correct in his assessment that the team lacked the crispness of prior years, the Cowboys' talent overwhelmed. They followed the Detroit loss by pounding Washington 34–7 and Arizona 38–3, then outclassed the Eagles, 24–13. On October 23 the Cowboys visited the Cardinals and, under a relentless Tempe sun, defeated Arizona again, 28–21. Despite the woeful Cardinals' 2–4 record, the game was a brutal affair that opened with linebacker Wilber Marshall flying through the air and slamming Aikman in the head. As he was carted to the sideline with the fourth concussion of his professional career, the star quarterback was asked by team doctors to recite the day, date, and year. "Sunday," he groggily moaned.

New backup Rodney Peete entered and saved the day, throwing for 186 yards and 2 touchdowns. But by the time the Cowboys' plane landed in Dallas early Monday morning, the players—more battered than usual—needed a release. Several of the team's stars, including Michael Irvin, Emmitt Smith, Kenny Gant, and Erik Williams, jumped into their vehicles and headed for a club, Iguana Mirage, where they spent a couple of hours pounding drinks and recapping the game. At approximately 3 A.M. Williams, the Pro Bowl right tackle, rose from his seat, hollered "I'm gone, fellas," exited the front door, and climbed into his Mercedes-Benz. Though Williams had downed his fair share of alcohol, nobody was especially concerned. The Cowboys drank hard. It was how they lived.

Minutes after Williams's departure Gant followed, steering his car onto Interstate 635. Upon approaching the exit for the Dallas North Tollway, Gant spotted a twisted pretzel of metal and tire steaming by the guardrail. "That looks like *some* accident," he thought before realizing—*Oh my God!*—it was Williams's Benz. Gant skidded to a halt and ran toward the wreckage. Slumped onto the passenger's seat, Williams was breathing softly. Blood covered his body. Gant grabbed his arm. "Man, don't you die on me, motherfucker!" he screamed. "Don't you die on me!" Williams weighed 324 pounds, far too heavy for the 189-pound Gant to carry from the car. "Kenny?" Williams gasped, his eyes half opened. "Kenny?" Gant began to weep.

When the ambulance arrived, Gant removed Williams's bloodied Rolex and jewelry and drove to Parkland Memorial Hospital. Several of the Cowboys met Gant in the waiting room, where they sat and prayed until eight o'clock Monday morning. Williams, doctors told them, would live—but his body was decimated. He'd suffered a broken rib, multiple cuts on his face, a torn ligament in his left thumb, and a sprained right knee. Known to teammates as a voracious drinker, an obsessive collector of firearms, and an unpredictably moody man, Williams was a harrowing sight as he lay listless.

"The thing I remember most is his face," says Derek Kennard, the offensive lineman. "The skin was torn from his hairline all the way down to his nose."

Police later determined that Williams was driving 75 mph with a blood alcohol level of .17—well above the legal limit of .10. He would return the following season, but not as the same dominant player.

In the immediate aftermath of the accident, the Cowboys' PR machine did its all to keep the media at bay. First, the wreck never happened. Then, it wasn't serious. Finally, when it became clear that Williams had nearly died, the team could no longer hide the information. "They tried to keep it quiet," says Rob Geiger, a reporter for KRLD in Dallas. "That's how the organization operated. Very secretively."

After the Cowboys returned from Cincinnati the following Sunday, a reporter from the *Fort Worth Star-Telegram* camped out at the Iguana Mirage, curious as to whether the supposedly still-grieving players would return. They did, and the reporter—notebook hidden—sat by and kept count of the tab. "He wrote that Nate Newton had like twenty drinks, and asked why anyone would need that much booze," says Geiger. "The next day Nate decided I was the one who wrote the story. Later on I go to the Cowboys Café, and Nate walks in with a group of guys, and he comes over and is staring at me. I'm thinking, 'This guy can pound me.' He came over and stood at the table and said, 'I just got a beer . . . you better write that down.'"

Geiger gulped. "OK, Nate," he said. "I got it."

If anyone believed the Williams tragedy would serve as a sedative for the Cowboys, they were badly mistaken. Dallas's players were as arrogant as ever, and after they improved to 7–1 on October 30 with a too-close-for-comfort 23–20 victory overly the lowly Bengals (poorly coached by David Shula, the former Dallas offensive coordinator), there was little doubt that a third straight Super Bowl was headed their way.

Wherever Cowboy players went they were saluted as conquering heroes. Free food. Free drinks. Free drugs. Free sex. The Cowboys Café had taken on a living, breathing, groupie-centered life of its own. "The ego boost is amazing—and unhealthy," says Holmes. "You start thinking you're this holier-than-thou god who can do no wrong. It's fun, I guess. But it leads to some really bad errors in judgment."

On November 7 the New York Giants came to Texas Stadium for *Monday Night Football*. On the final play of the first half, Aikman launched a Hail Mary into the end zone. As Alvin Harper leapt for the ball he was slammed in the chest by safety Tito Wooten. Harper crumpled to the ground with a sprained left knee. When the play ended Hubbard Alexander, the Dallas receivers coach, charged into the end zone and screamed obscenely at Giants safety Jarvis Williams, who shoved him aside. Irvin popped Williams, then removed his helmet and swung it at the Giants. As the elbowing turned to punching, a group of child musicians readying to perform at halftime scrambled away. That's when James Washington, the Cowboys' safety, yanked a camera and monopod from photographer David Leeson of the *Dallas Morning News* and pointed it, swordlike, near the heads of opposing players. "C'mon, motherfuckers!" he yelled. "Bring it the fuck on!"

Dallas won the game (a 38–10 romp) and the brawl, but came off looking silly and out of control. Irvin was fined $12,000 by the NFL, Washington $10,000. It hardly helped that two days after the game Harper crashed Irvin's Mercedes—the third Cowboy-related automobile accident in a month.

From afar, Jimmy Johnson followed his old organization and refused to hold his tongue. Now working as an analyst for Fox Sports, Johnson took sadistic pleasure in watching the Cowboys unravel. Yes, they were 8–1 and the class of the NFL. But Johnson saw the lack of discipline; the defensive breakdowns; guys taking a play off here, another play off there. Mostly, he saw Switzer wearing *his* headphones, standing in *his* spot on the sidelines, giving *his* pregame pep talks and postgame interviews. In Johnson's mind, Switzer coaching the Cowboys was Dan Quayle taking over the presidency. "The problem with Jimmy and Barry was that they had this old, long history of just acting crazy together when they were young coaches," says Michael Silver, the former *Sports Illustrated* football writer. "After Barry came and replaced Jimmy, Jimmy got all holier than thou and acted like Barry was this lunatic and that Barry and Jerry were out of control, while Jimmy was the respectable one. And Jerry and Barry were like, 'Jimmy, it's us! You can't fucking bullshit us!' But to Jimmy, Barry became the symbol of anyone being able to coach this team. And Barry didn't like Jimmy because he was sensing this crazy condescension that he thought was so disingenuous, given that Jimmy was as bad as he was."

In the shadow of the Detroit loss earlier in the season, Johnson struck the opening salvo, telling *USA Today*, "A couple of players have told me they better not be criticized for not focusing when their coach doesn't focus." By "a couple," Johnson actually meant Aikman, who—despite Switzer's protestations—spoke with his old coach on a near-weekly basis. The discussions fueled both men's opinions that Switzer was ruining the Cowboys. "I inherited Jimmy's staff, took over a team that won two Super Bowls in a row—that is not easy," says Switzer. "For him to rip me wasn't right."

From Jerry Jones's standpoint, the lowest of blows came in the week after the Giants game, when the Cowboys were preparing for an encounter with the 7–2 49ers. Not only did Johnson continue to dump on Switzer, but he actually picked San Francisco to win. "As much as I like the Cowboys," Johnson said, "the 49ers are at home and they've been thinking about this game for a long time."

Unfortunately for the Cowboys, Johnson was right—the 49ers were ready. Having lost the last two NFC title games to Dallas, San Francisco played with an urgency the Cowboys lacked. In the days leading up to the matchup Dallas's players talked a good game. "We've beaten them three times in a row," said Haley. "This is probably their Super Bowl. The pressure is on them . . . It's time to put up or shut up." But when the showdown arrived, Dallas played listlessly. In winning 21–14 before a record 69,014 spectators at Candlestick Park, the 49ers—to quote *San Jose Mercury News* writer Clark Judge—"exorcised a past that had them renting Avises for their annual drive to the Super Bowl."

In five years under Johnson there had been enough so-called big games that players knew dropping one wasn't the end of the world. Dallas bounced back to win its next three contests, hightlighted by a 42–31 Thanksgiving Day triumph over Green Bay that Switzer wrapped up with one of the shortest postgame speeches in Cowboy lore. "I've never been any damn good," said Switzer, "but I could always get the best damn players. Happy fuckin' Thanksgiving!"

"We just had so much confidence inside of us, nobody ever thought we'd lose again," says Darren Woodson, the safety. "But if you look closely, we weren't that good. We had a bunch of injuries, our coach was inexperienced, we lacked a little fire. It was the worst team since I'd been there. Success can do that."

Dallas concluded the regular season with a 12–4 record and a home playoff game against the Packers. Yet no matter what Switzer accomplished, he was damned. Had he led the team to a 16–0 mark, writers would have complained that a Johnson-coached club could have scored more points. Had he revolutionized offensive football in the NFL, writers would have said he was messing with a good thing. Having spent his first season leaving well enough alone, he was ripped for being passive and indifferent. "Barry was probably lacking when it came to discipline," says Peete, the reserve quarterback. "But it was a can't-win. He wasn't coaching against other teams—he was coaching against the legend who had preceded him."

Switzer made his playoff debut on Sunday, January 8, 1995, and Dallas routed Green Bay, 35–9, behind Aikman (337 passing yards), Jay Novacek (11 catches, 104 yards), Alvin Harper (a magnificent 94-yard touchdown catch), and halfback Blair Thomas.

Yes, *that* Blair Thomas.

The No. 2 pick in the 1990 NFL Draft, the Penn State all-America was selected by the Jets fifteen spots before Dallas landed Emmitt Smith. The decision remains one of the most egregious in New York sports history. Thomas ran for 2,009 undistinguished yards in four years with the Jets before being allowed to walk. When the Cowboys came calling in November 1994, they offered $10,125 per game and a chance to carry Smith's dirty laundry. "Bottom line," says Thomas, "was that I needed work."

He was added strictly as a backup, but Thomas seized the opportunity late in the first quarter of the Green Bay contest when Smith went down with a hamstring injury. Despite his delusions of grandeur ("If I had been given the same opportunities Emmitt had, I'd be in the Hall of Fame right now"), Thomas was no Emmitt. Yet against the Packers, he carried 23 times for a solid 70 yards and a touchdown as Smith cheered from the sidelines. "My career didn't turn out like I'd expected," says Thomas. "But I'll always have that afternoon."

With the victory, the Cowboys would travel to San Francisco on January 15, 1995, and face the 49ers for the third straight NFC Championship Game. Having posted a 13–3 regular season mark, San Francisco was a well-deserved 7-point favorite. Not only had it stolen linebacker Ken Norton, Jr., from the Cowboys, but its new starting cornerback was Deion Sanders, the one man capable of eliminating Irvin or Harper from a game plan. Most important, the 49ers were led by quarterback Steve Young, who at age thirty-three was the league MVP, with 3,969 passing yards and 35 touchdowns.

As was the case two years earlier, California had been hammered by rain throughout the preceding week, turning thirty-four of its counties into federal disaster areas. Dallas had beaten San Francisco in the muck and mud two years earlier, but this was a different 49ers team. In a nod to the new world of expressive football players unafraid to display all their feathers, the Niners had replaced stoicism with flamboyance, inward confidence with outward cockiness. In the minutes before kickoff, Sanders, fullback William Floyd, and halfback Ricky Watters danced in the end zone, pumping their fists and loudly rapping the 69 Boyz's "Tootsee Roll." Bill Walsh, the legendary 49er coach, would have cringed. George Seifert, his replacement, begrudgingly accepted it.

"Just looking at those guys and looking at the enthusiasm they had for the game, it made you laugh," Brent Jones, San Francisco's tight end, said. "And that kind of takes the pressure off."

For the Cowboys, it was (yawn) a chance to return to (yawn) another (yawn) Super Bowl. Most of the team's players stood and watched San Francisco's *Dance Fever* antics with bemused indifference.

"Truthfully, San Francisco was loaded and hungrier than we were," says Woodson. "That happens when you lose for a couple of years and you want to get back. But even going into that game, I personally had the feeling of, 'We're gonna kick your ass. You can do whatever you want to do and it's not going to work.' I just wanted the game to start."

It started.

"Then," says Woodson, "I immediately just wanted the game to end."

On the first Cowboy possession of the afternoon, 49er cornerback Eric Davis intercepted a pass and returned it 44 yards for a touchdown. 7–0, San Francisco.

"The second I let it go," said Aikman, "I knew I was in trouble."

On the second Cowboy possession of the afternoon, Irvin caught the ball and fumbled it away in Dallas territory. Shortly thereafter the 49ers scored on a 29-yard swing pass from Young to Watters. 14–0, San Francisco.

"We were digging ourselves a pretty big hole," says Gant. "Against a team like that, it ain't easy to dig out."

On the third Cowboy possession of the afternoon, Kevin Williams fumbled the kickoff and the 49ers again recovered. Floyd capped a 7-play, 35-yard drive with a 1-yard run. 21–0, San Francisco.

Exactly seven minutes and twenty-seven seconds had passed.

"That was a horror movie," says Switzer. "If they had listened to me they wouldn't have turned the damn ball over and we wouldn't have been down by 21 five minutes into the game. But a coach can only do so much."

Actually, a coach can do a great deal. He can inspire. He can instill discipline. He can make sure his men are prepared for the biggest game of the season. He can recognize mistakes and make adjustments. Switzer, however, was overmatched and overwhelmed—the wrong man to develop an on-the-fly game plan against the relentless 49ers.

Sitting above the stadium in the Fox broadcast booth, Jimmy Johnson could not help but grin. Yes, the Cowboys still wore stars on their helmets. But these were not his collected, well-oiled Cowboys. No, these were Barry Switzer's Cowboys. And they were embarrassing themselves.

Dallas committed five turnovers, missed a short field goal, botched a punt, and decided on one baffling play call after another. Yet whereas some teams would have accepted fate, Dallas valiantly refused to die. "Guys, you know what's great about being down 21–0 after seven minutes?" Switzer asked his players along the sideline. "We've got fifty-three minutes to get back in this SOB. Now do something about it."

Slowly, methodically, the Cowboys clawed their way out of the hole. They trailed 24–14 late in the first half and should have headed into the locker room with an infusion of positive energy. Instead, Switzer—to cite defensive back Joe Fishback—*did his thing.*" With the ball at their own 16-yard line and 1:02 remaining, the Cowboys called three straight failed pass plays, then watched punter John Jett shank a 23-yarder off the side of his foot.

With eight seconds on the clock, Young spotted Rice bolting down the left corner of the end zone and hit him with a breathtaking 28-yard touchdown pass. That the magnificent Rice was covered one-on-one by the mediocre Larry Brown was yet another glaring coaching gaffe. "Larry is a great guy and a decent NFL corner," says Jim Schwantz, the Cowboys linebacker. "But every Tuesday we'd practice the two-minute passing drill late in the day, and every single time Larry would cover Michael Irvin and Mike would just kill him with a double move. Jerry did pretty much the same thing."

Dallas trailed 31–14 at the half to a team that was hungrier, feistier, and better coached. "I don't think we were ready," says Gant. "In the course of that game I started thinking, 'Is this going to be my last year with the Cowboys?' and 'Where should I go on vacation after we lose?' I know I wasn't the only guy with that stuff in his mind."

Not all of Dallas's players were distracted. Although his interceptions accounted for 3 of the team's 5 turnovers, Aikman was courageous under fire, completing 30 of 53 passes for 380 yards while being sacked 4 times and knocked down 19 more. He was taking one of the worst beatings of his life. "Troy was talented and poised, but more than anything he had guts," says Peete, the backup quarterback. "Great signal callers aren't afraid to take a hit or two. Troy was never afraid."

A fitting capper to a rotten afternoon came midway through the fourth quarter, when—with his team trailing, 38–28—Aikman launched a pass to Irvin near the 49er goal line. As Irvin ran down the field, Sanders intentionally (and blatantly) interfered by tangling up the receiver. When no penalty flag was thrown, Switzer charged head linesman Sid Semon and thrust his hip into the official. Semon flagged the coach for a 15-yard penalty. Instead of a third-and-10 at the San Francisco 43, the Cowboys faced a third-and-25 from their own 42.

"I lost control," says Switzer, whose repeated refusal to take responsibility for the loss still infuriates Cowboy players. "But I didn't lose the game. Our sloppiness lost it; our poor play lost it."

The final score was San Francisco 38, Dallas 28. As the last seconds ticked off the clock, Candlestick Park vibrated like an old lawn mower; 69,125 fans celebrating a new reign. On the Cowboys sideline, Irvin and Emmitt Smith embraced until the scoreboard clock read 0:00. Irvin had caught 12 passes for 192 yards. Smith ran for 74 yards on 20 carries before leaving the game with a right hamstring pull. Neither had an ounce of energy remaining.

"I don't even know how to tell you how disappointed I am," Irvin said later. "I can't sit here and cut open my chest and show you my heart. But I'm eaten up by this." Aikman would call it both the worst setback and the proudest moment of his career. "All people had ever really seen of us was Dallas enjoying great success," he said. "It was the first they'd seen us struggle. But that game illustrated the type of team we were, how we continued to fight."

Afterward, rookie kicker Chris Boniol boarded the team bus, sagged into his seat, and looked as if he were about to cry. He had missed a 27-yard field goal. "Hey, kid, you can't let it bother you," said Nate Newton, patting Boniol atop the head. "Shit happens. You'll get 'em next year."

Two weeks later, the 49ers won their fifth Super Bowl, routing the San Diego Chargers, 49–26, at Miami's Joe Robbie Stadium. As Woodson, Irvin, Smith, Switzer, and the other Cowboys watched the game from various spots across the country, a singe thought crossed their minds:

That should have been us.

"I'll say what a lot of guys probably think," says Woodson. "If Jimmy Johnson is still our coach in 1994 we win the Super Bowl. We lacked Jimmy's swagger and confidence and belief that we would always find a way to win. We weren't as structured or motivated. We didn't play with any fear. That doesn't mean Barry was a bad coach, because he wasn't.

"But," says Woodson, "we were never quite the same."

Chapter 22

PRIME TIME

Deion Sanders was a great football player. But the perception was that we needed him to win the Super Bowl. That just wasn't true.
—Larry Brown, Cowboys cornerback

FOR THE FIRST time in three years, the Dallas Cowboys would enter the offseason as merely another team. There would be no parade; no ring ceremony. Just as fans lavish affection upon champions, they are equally willing to ignore losers. Especially losers whom they expected to win.

Such was the status of Jerry Jones's franchise in the aftermath of the San Francisco defeat: a strange, Twilight Zone-esque merging of disappointment, confusion, disbelief, and disarray. To the young player who knows only victory, the assumption is that the good times will last forever. Yet the dwindling number of veterans who had been with the Cowboys since 1989 were forced to come to terms with the stark reality that a window was quickly closing. This was no longer a franchise of naïve pups trying to make names for themselves. Troy Aikman and Michael Irvin would be turning twenty-nine in 1995. Five offensive linemen were in their thirties. Charles Haley, who retired after the 49er game, then unretired, was thirty-one. That's how it works in professional sports, where phenom turns has-been in the blink of an eye.

In the winters following the two Super Bowl titles, the Cowboys somehow kept their roster largely intact. Now, however, there were mass defections. Defensive end Jim Jeffcoat signed with the Bills and center Mark Stepnoski with Houston. Redskins coach Norv Turner added three of his former players in safety James Washington and linebackers Darrick Brownlow and Matt Vanderbeek. The most shocking blow came via the Tampa Bay Buccaneers, who wooed Kenny Gant, the Cowboys' special teams ace, as well as wide receiver Alvin Harper.

Yes, Freaky Harp.

To Cowboy fans, the defection of Harper was tough to bear. Though he caught only 124 passes in his four seasons in Dallas, 18 of those had resulted in touchdowns. The image of Harper gliding toward pay dirt, football triumphantly raised in the air, was a vivid and familiar one. In a city that craved big things, Harper was a big-play guy. Yet he was also an emperor without clothes. Harper's speed was only slightly above average and his route-running ability atrocious. "He was long-legged and he could stride over the top," says Gerald Alphin, a former Cowboys receiver. "But other than that, Harp had very little to offer." Though he did, indeed, wind up on many a highlight film, his glory was often the result of opposing teams focusing on Irvin. With Deion Sanders covering him one-on-one in the '94 NFC title game, Harper managed a single reception.

What irked teammates most was that Harper's excessive cockiness came packaged with a mediocre work ethic. While Irvin begged for extra reps and weight room time, Harper was the last to arrive and the first to leave. He loved the perks that came with fame—the mounds of naked women, the mounds of marijuana, the mounds of naked women smoking marijuana—but not the effort required to achieve it. "He had a lot of bad habits," says Gant. "You'd see him smiling and think, 'What's Harp up to?'" During a practice midway through the '94 season, Washington spotted Harper crossing the middle of the field and decked him with an illegal blow to the head that nearly knocked the receiver cold. "He deserved it," says Washington. "Alvin Harper was more talented than Mike, but he went about his business differently.

He burned the candle at both ends harder than anyone else, and it showed. There's a reason Michael Irvin is in the Hall of Fame and Alvin Harper is just another guy."

When the Buccaneers made Harper the league's fifth-highest-paid receiver with a four-year, $10.6 million deal, Jones shrugged and moved on. The Cowboys, he assumed, would easily find someone to replace him, just as they had replaced other defectors in the past. But with Jimmy Johnson a distant memory, Dallas was now relying on its owner to guide personnel decisions. It was a joke.

"The Cowboys are Jerry's team and he can do what he wants," says Larry Brown, the veteran cornerback. "But if you want to chart where things began to go wrong, look at the point when he started making the moves."

In April 1994, Jones kicked off his debut draft without Johnson by using the team's first-round pick on a 6-foot-5, 253-pound defensive end from Arizona State named Shante Carver. Neither overwhelmingly fast, quick, strong, nor driven, Carver arrived at training camp and, within a week, established himself as a waste of space. "If you had drafted Shante Carver in the fourth, fifth, sixth rounds people would have said, 'Hey, that's not a terrible pick,'" says Nate Newton. "But you can't take a guy like that in the first round. When you draft guys in the first round you're saying, 'In a year this guy is going to be something.' When did anybody say that with Shante?"

"You could see Shante was far from first-round material," says Alfie Burch, an undrafted free agent safety from Michigan. "[Linebacker] Darrin Smith and I were roommates, and we'd watch Shante and be like, 'Uh, that's weird.'"

Though Jones's first draft yielded Larry Allen, an offensive guard out of Sonoma State who would go on to a Hall of Fame–worthy career, none of the six other players selected in 1994 lasted more than four seasons in Dallas.

The following year was even more disastrous. With the Cowboys in dire need of up-and-coming studs to replace the fleeing veterans, Jones studied the boards, listened to his scouts, swung powerfully—and whiffed. "Jimmy and his guys made the draft look easy," says Dick Mansperger, the team's director of college scouting from 1989 to 1992. "Jerry thought, 'Well, that's not hard.' What he failed to understand was the importance of what happened the three hundred sixty-four days and nights before the draft."

Jones's first pick, University of Alabama running back Sherman Williams, played four undistinguished years with Dallas, smoked enormous amounts of pot, and, following his conviction in 2000 on charges of conspiracy to distribute marijuana, is now inmate No. 07520–003 in the United States Penitentiary in Atlanta. "Sherman didn't have the work ethic you needed to excel at that level," says Gregory Samms, his former agent. "I was constantly telling him, 'Look at Emmitt, look at Michael. See how hard they work.' He didn't listen."

Jones's second pick, tight end Kendell Watkins of Mississippi State, caught a single pass in 1995 and was never heard from again. His third pick, offensive guard Shane Hannah of Michigan State, signed a $1.1 million contract, injured his right knee in training camp, and quit one year later. Jones wasted a fourth-round selection on a defensive back, Alundis Brice, who had been shot in the chest shortly before the draft, and a fifth-round pick on Edward Hervey, a lightning-fast receiver with brick hands. The best of the bunch was tight end Eric Bjornson, a steady performer who caught 48 passes in 1996. "Man, the drafts under Jerry were terrible, just terrible," says Darren Woodson. "Jerry would draft a player and he would come out to minicamp and I just couldn't believe it. I'd say, 'This is our first-round pick?'"

Making the matter worse was Switzer's inability to squeeze water from a rock. Though Johnson was hardly an Xs and Os wizard, he was masterful at pressing the right buttons and placing his players in winnable situations. Under Johnson, Jay Novacek went from a misfit tight end/receiver hybrid to Pro Bowler; Nate Newton went from overweight outcast to Pro Bowler; Emmitt Smith went from undersized question mark to Pro Bowler. "Jimmy was magical," says Woodson. "A great example is Shante Carver. I love Shante as a person, but he was not especially driven. Jimmy would have said, 'You either get your shit together or I'm going to cut you. So figure it out.' But under Barry we lacked that. There were times Shante was late for meetings, and you just didn't see players do that during Jimmy's time. Everyone understood the rules under Jimmy, and we got sloppy after he left."

Indeed, while Switzer's laissez-faire approach was initially lauded by Cowboy players, it was increasingly apparent that America's Team required some semblance of structure. On April 13, 1995, Erik Williams—already on two-year probation for DUI—was arrested in Dallas for allegedly sexually assaulting Angela Russell, a seventeen-year-old topless dancer, ("Actually," says Charles Caperton, Russell's attorney, "she was sixteen.")

"I met [Russell] in a strip bar," said Williams. "We were doing drugs one night. We were doing alcohol . . . There was a setup in the making, but I couldn't see it because I was out there partying. That's what I think happened, because nothing wrong was done to her. She was paid. Nobody was rough. Nothing like [rape] happened."

Two months later a handful of Cowboys reported to the team's annual quarterback school woefully out of shape. The worst transgressor was Newton. Once an obscure USFL journeyman, Newton signed with the Cowboys in 1986 and developed into an above-average offensive lineman and one of the team's most beloved figures. Yet Newton was no innocent. An Olympic imbiber, he was pulled over on multiple occasions for drunken driving, and in 1991 was one of eighteen people arrested at a dogfight near Liberty City in East Texas. Long before the Michael Vick saga, Newton owned a fleet of fourteen pit bulls, going so far as to brag about "raising American Pit Bull Terriers" in the 1992 edition of the *Dallas Cowboys Wives' Cookbook*.

Of all his difficulties, the one that brought Newton the most fame—and grief—was weight. Upon arriving at an offseason session, Newton tipped the scales at 368 pounds—more than 40 pounds overweight. Not that it came as a surprise. Early in Newton's career Tex Schramm loaded his contract with a tasty incentive: Report under 310 pounds and earn an extra $80,000. Newton failed. "I know, I'm a fool," he says. "But if someone offers you eighty thousand dollars to be unhappy, you shouldn't take it. So fuck eighty thousand dollars. I'd rather eat." (Says former Cowboys lineman John Gesek: "Quite frankly, the reason I think Nate went to six Pro Bowls was because his weight was such a joke it got him attention.") Once, during a game, Newton was blocking an opposing pass rusher when a Snickers bar popped out of his uniform. "I was like, 'Did a damn candy bar just fly from Nate's body or am I imagining things?'" says Larry Brown. Two or three nights per week during training camp Newton would make a rookie walk down the street and return with a sixty-piece box of Popeyes fried chicken, biscuits, french fries, and a case of Budweiser. "Whoever was hungry would take some pieces," recalls Stepnoski of the ritual. "Then Nate would eat the last fifteen or twenty pieces himself."

In a moment dismissed as laughable by most players, Switzer opened the 1995 quarterback school by delivering a thirteen-minute, profanity-laced speech. "I told you a year ago at this time that it was your team!" he barked. "What I'm telling you today is now it's my team!"

The general reaction: *Whatever, Coach. Whatever.*

Truth be told, the Cowboys were Jerry Jones's team, and Jerry Jones had a vision for how Dallas could immediately return to glory.

Though he'd pondered it well before the 1994 NFC Championship Game, watching Deion Sanders shut down Alvin Harper sealed the idea in Jones's mind—"We've *got* to have this guy." Sanders wasn't merely another cornerback. He was *the* cornerback—the best ever to play the position. Sanders spent the first five years of his career with the Atlanta Falcons, and when, in 1994, the 49ers restructured the contracts of linebackers Ken Norton, Jr., and Gary Plummer and safety Tim McDonald in order to afford Sanders, Jones teed off. "They're just pushing some pretty significant [financial] obligation to future years," he said. "That may work for them, but there is a wall there. They will be paying a lot of money in the future for players who probably won't be participating."

Of course, Jones's opinion came four months before Sanders

helped the 49ers win a Super Bowl. Now he was a free agent once again, and the Cowboys wanted in. Jones spent much of the winter thinking of ways to afford Sanders, letting veterans depart to free up salary space and maintaining constant contact with Eugene Parker, Sanders's agent. As the two sides negotiated, Sanders was in San Francisco, playing outfield for the Giants alongside Barry Bonds in what—as with Bo Jackson before him—amounted to his "hobby." Sanders was significantly less comfortable (and adept) on the diamond, but baseball peers considered him to be the ultimate teammate. "The guy had no big headedness about him," says Tom Lampkin, a Giants catcher. "When you asked him to sign a football, he'd do it with a smile. He was universally beloved."

Once Sanders stepped inside an NFL locker room, however, something snapped. He was no longer Deion Luwynn Sanders—quiet, relaxed, one of the guys. No, he was "Neon Deion" and "Prime Time," an arrogant, trash-talking blowhard who signed autographs "D$." "Deion's thing was saying, 'I've got this receiver, I'll shut him down, y'all worry about the rest of the field,'" says Antonio Goss, the former 49er linebacker. "And you know what? He did it." That said, many of the 49ers resented Sanders's bravado. San Francisco was the franchise of Steve Young and Jerry Rice, professionals who largely shunned pizzazz for class. When it looked like the 49ers would let Sanders walk instead of meeting his salary demands, few of his teammates shed tears.

In Dallas and Austin, however, Deion Mania swept the landscape. Throughout a preseason that saw the Cowboys go 2–3, all anyone could speak of was Sanders's potential signing. In the August 25, 1995, edition of the *Dallas Morning News*, Chili's Grill & Bar ran a full-page advertisement that read DEION, SIGN WITH THE COWBOYS AND EAT FREE AT CHILI'S. "Chili's had always been known as an irreverent restaurant, and we thought it was funny," says Harry Day, Chili's former director of marketing. "But Deion's agent was screaming on the phone, accusing me of tampering with the negotiations. He threatened to sue us if we didn't pull the ads." Chili's does flame-grilled rib eye, not litigation. The ads ceased.

On the night of Monday, September 4, 1995, the Cowboys opened their season by walloping the Giants at the Meadowlands, 35–0. "That was awesome, man!" Emmitt Smith raved after rushing for 163 yards. "What a way to start a season. You should have seen the hole I ran through. It wouldn't have taken a genius for someone to find it."

Smith's triumphant performance was obscured, however, when Jones used halftime to announce that he and Nike chairman Phil Knight had reached a one-of-a-kind, screw-the-rest-of-the-league partnership. Thanks to the new marriage, Jones would deck his team out in Nike apparel, play preseason games in Nike's hometown of Portland, Oregon, and build a new, Nike-themed, state-of-the-art amusement park outside Texas Stadium. As had an agreement he'd reached one month earlier to make Pepsi the official soft drink of Texas Stadium, the partnership directly challenged NFL Properties, which did *not* deal with Nike. Of the many outraged executives, the one who spoke loudest was Carmen Policy, the 49ers' team president. "The man's gone too far," he said of Jones. "He's out of control."

Left unsaid was that Deion Sanders was a Nike spokesperson being wooed by a Nike team.

The 49ers were toast.

On the Thursday afternoon before he planned on officially signing Sanders, Jerry Jones summoned twelve Cowboy players into his Valley Ranch office. "I just wanna know what you guys think about this," he said. "It's my opinion that we can be a better team with Deion than we are without him. From everyone I speak with he's a good locker room guy, he works hard—"

Jones was cut off by Dale Hellestrae, the veteran long snapper.

"Jerry," he said, "if you can get Deion Sanders, you've gotta do it."

The others in the room—Aikman, Irvin, and Emmitt Smith

among them—nodded. But the Cowboys were far from a united front. "All a lot of people saw was the whole Prime Time image," says Scott Case, a Cowboys cornerback who had played with Sanders for five years in Atlanta. "But Deion and I used to fish all the time together, and he was wonderful. He used to fish with this cheap Cane Fishing Pole. I'd say, 'Deion, you're making two million and you fish with a Cane!?' He'd get a laugh out of that." Yet those only aware of the bright lights and gaudy jewelry were concerned. The peacefulness of an NFL locker room depends on disparate personalities somehow living in harmony. "I was cautious of his prima donna attitude," says Chad Hennings, the defensive lineman. "That can etch away at a team as quickly as any off-the-field problem."

On Monday, September 11, a day after they improved to 2–0 with a 31–21 triumph over Denver, the franchise held a press conference at Texas Stadium to introduce Sanders and announce that the newest Cowboy had agreed to a seven-year, $35 million deal that would include a league-record $12,999,999.99 signing bonus (the Cowboys consider the number 13 unlucky). The relatively low base salary was a creative way of adding Sanders while staying $300,000 below the cap.

The twenty-eight-year-old four-time Pro Bowler stepped before the microphone wearing a snazzy navy blue pinstriped suit, black leather shoes, diamond earrings, and, to quote Ed Werder of the *Morning News*, "a rich cocktail ring the approximate size of a manhole cover." Accompanied by his wife, Carolyn, their two children, and his mother, Sanders was equal parts charming, thoughtful, and arrogant. "I have an ego when I hit the field," he said. "My ego is that I'm the best at my position to play that game. Off the field, my friends and my loved ones know who I really am. I don't care about hype. I care about Super Bowl rings.

"There were other teams where—believe it or not—the financial situation could have been better. I truly wanted to be a Dallas Cowboy because of the players on this team. I definitely plan to have a three-, four-, or five-year run at Super Bowls."

Naturally, Sanders refused to name the teams with whom the financial situation could have been better—because, ahem, they didn't exist. The 49ers, Broncos, and Dolphins had offered significantly less money. Also missing was a definitive date for the beginning of his Cowboy career. Not only was Sanders committed to the San Francisco Giants, with whom he was under contract, but he was also suffering from chronic soreness in his left ankle. He intended to undergo arthroscopic surgery and join the Cowboys "at some point in November."

Yet while Sanders was far removed from the football field, his signing called into question the direction of a franchise. When Jones and Jimmy Johnson had taken over operations six years earlier, the idea was to build through roster flexibility and youthful player development—turning one draft pick into three, three draft picks into eight. No Cowboy fan needed reminding that the two most recent Super Bowl triumphs could never have taken place had the franchise not sent Herschel Walker to Minnesota for a bushel of players and draft choices. Now, in an effort to reclaim the glory, weren't the Cowboys taking the exact opposite approach? As of early September the team had only thirty-five players under contract for the 1996 season, at a cost of $39.9 million. With the salary cap expected to be set at $40 million by the NFL, the Cowboys were—for lack of a better word—screwed. "You've got to reward your Indians at some point, but in football you have to be careful how far you extend yourself," says Kevin Smith, the veteran cornerback. "By the mid-nineties Jerry just gave out money. That's great if you're a player looking to get rich, but it doesn't keep a team hungry. Jerry was right when he said anyone could have coached our team. But not just anyone could sustain it."

Although most media outlets praised Jones for spending to win, some remained skeptical. In the *Pittsburgh Post-Gazette*, columnist Bob Smizik wrote that future historians would "pinpoint the precise beginning of the decline and fall of the Dallas Cowboys' empire as a day early in the 1995 season when owner Jerry Jones became so overwhelmed with the need to stroke his enormous ego to highs not even he had thought possible that he signed a part-time player who was facing surgery to a $35 million contract. The signing certainly garnered Jones all the attention he craved and unquestionably made him the undisputed high roller of the National Football League. But did Jones really get what he wanted?"

The league would have to wait to find out.

In the seven weeks that passed between Sanders's signing and his on-field debut, the Dallas Cowboys played their best football of the Switzer Era, posting a 6–1 record to take an early lead in the NFC East. Away from the field, though, Switzer had his hands full trying to keep his club from falling apart. To start with, he needed Charles Haley to calm the heck down.

Now in his fourth season with Dallas, Haley had disappointed many teammates when, after announcing his retirement following the NFC Championship Game loss, he changed his mind and reported to training camp. In the beginning the Cowboys tolerated and, occasionally, laughed at his penis-waving, insult-slinging ways. But after prolonged exposure, the act had grown old. "Everything with Haley depended on whether he was on his medication or off of it," says Switzer. "On it, he was great. Off it, he was crazy." Kevin O'Neill, the Cowboys trainer, still laughs when he recalls the day in 1993 when the Dallas Mavericks brought their new marquee player, rookie forward Jamal Mashburn, to Valley Ranch for a tour. "Charles had never met the guy before," says O'Neill. "Yet the first time he sees him, he spots the big gap between Jamal's two front teeth and screams, 'Hey, Jamal, you should spend some money and get your teeth fixed!'" One of Haley's favorite bull's-eyes used to be Chad Hennings, the Air Force pilot-turned-defensive lineman whose 6-foot-6, 291-pound frame belied a gentle, Bible-fearing man. "What dumb-ass let you fly a plane?" Haley would crack. "You have enough trouble tackling a fucking running back." During training camp, Haley mocked Hennings incessantly until—*SNAP!* "Charles," warned Hennings, "if you say one more thing I'm gonna kick the shit out of you."

The meeting room went quiet.

Had Chad Hennings just cursed?

"Hennings, you're so fucking stupid," Haley barked, pointing toward a tape of a recent practice. "Look how dumb you are out there doing—"

Hennings spun around, grabbed Haley's neck, and rammed his head through the window. He cocked back his fist and prepared to fire when John Blake, an assistant coach, pulled him away. "I would have tried to kill him," Hennings says. "I've always believed in turning the other cheek. But with Charles, you either took it forever, or you stood up to him. I completely embarrassed him, and it felt great. He never really messed with me again."

With Hennings off the mock market, Haley looked for new victims. He initially took aim at Scott Case, the veteran cornerback who arrived in Dallas in 1995 after eleven seasons with the Falcons. During one meeting, Case was quietly paying attention to a coach's speech when he heard Haley whisper from behind.

"Hey, Scott . . ."

Case ignored him.

"Scott, turn around. I gotta show you something."

Case ignored him again.

"Scott, dammit, turn around. You need to see this!"

Case finally looked back, where he saw Haley's erect penis stretched across the desk.

Haley was unpredictable and unbalanced. Linebacker Jim Schwantz still recalls the day Haley hosted a class of special-needs schoolchildren at Valley Ranch. Before the kids left, Haley insisted on signing autographed cards for each one. "Those are the Charles Haley stories you never hear," says Schwantz. Because they were obscured by the bizarreness. Haley inevitably turned his radar toward Shante Carver, the flop first-round draft pick. Not a day would pass without Haley reminding

Carver that he was useless; dog shit; a punk-ass. "You are the biggest fucking bust I've ever seen," Haley said repeatedly. "You have no business being here."

"Charles was so brutal and belittling toward Shante that after enough abuse you got the feeling Shante wanted to quit," says Hennings. "You don't do that to a young player. You don't do that to any player. But such was Charles."

Switzer did his best to ignore Haley; to treat him in the manner Chicago Bulls coach Phil Jackson would deftly handle his new cosmonaut forward, Dennis Rodman. Yet like Jimmy Johnson before him, Switzer tired of Haley's routine. When he was a peak performer, piling up sacks by the dozen, Haley received some leeway. But now crippled by chronic back pain, he was more hype than substance. In one of the first defensive film sessions of 1995, Haley entered the conference room with a blanket, sat down on the floor, and said, "Now y'all wake me up when No. 94 comes on the screen."

"Charles became pathetic," says a teammate. "In his prime I never saw a guy who could drink an entire case of beer at night and have three sacks over Erik Williams in practice the next morning. But late in his Dallas days he wasn't the same player." In an October 1 loss at Washington, Switzer delivered the ultimate insult, replacing Haley in the starting lineup with—of all people—Carver. The veteran was smoldering, and grew even angrier when Switzer criticized his play to the media after the game. Haley went off to teammates, ripping his coach as a backstabbing SOB. Haley's followers, including younger defensive linemen like Lett and Tolbert, joined their mentor in turning on Switzer. Even when the coach apologized, Haley remained incensed. "Charles was the crazy guy in your neighborhood who was drunk on Monday, functional on Tuesday, and in church on Sunday," says Freddie Coger, a free agent linebacker cut in camp. "You try and figure him out, but it's not possible."

On the weekend following Haley's benching, the Cowboys hosted Green Bay. When the Packers began to rally back from a 24–3 deficit late in the second quarter, Aikman walked up to Haley—who was sitting out with the back injury—and said, "I hope you're fucking happy."

"I was just standing there, eating sunflower seeds, trying to ignore it," Haley wrote in his autobiography. "Eventually I said, 'OK, I'll play. Just leave me the fuck alone.'" He entered the contest and hounded Packers quarterback Brett Favre into repeated rushed throws. The Cowboys ended up beating the Packers 34–24 to improve to 5–1. Afterward the media horde was all over Haley, who tore into Switzer. "It's bullshit what's going on," he said. "I'm getting blamed for everybody's play. They can do this stuff to my mind this year, but they'll never get me back."

Watching from across the locker room, Aikman chuckled. "Sideshows, circuses, controversies," he said. "Just another week in the life of the Cowboys."

Chapter 23

THE
WHITE HOUSE

*We've got a little place over here where we're
running some whores in and out, trying to be responsible,
and we're criticized for that, too.*

**—Nate Newton, Cowboys offensive lineman,
on the "White House"**

HE OFFICIALLY ARRIVED on September 28, 1995, a hobbled man
with a healthy contract and the hope of a city resting upon his shoulders. Deion Sanders was not merely the football phenom who would
save the Cowboys' porous pass defense (and, as he demanded, play a
little receiver, too). No, he was the football phenom who would save
the Cowboys.

Need to shut down Jerry Rice one-on-one? Deion Sanders.

Need a punt or kickoff returned for a touchdown? Deion Sanders.

Need an offensive threat to draw attention from Michael Irvin?
Deion Sanders.

Though Sanders moved to Texas in late September, going so far
as to purchase a $2.95 million home in the suburb of Plano, he came
holding a black cane, his left ankle cocooned in a soft cast. In the
month before his scheduled October 29 debut against the Atlanta

Falcons, Sanders planned on adjusting his family to a new location, rehabbing his injury, and—most important—getting to know his teammates.

If there was any apprehension caused by the arrival of the team's newest superstar on that first day, it evaporated quickly. As Sanders entered the locker room, offensive lineman Nate Newton, the Cowboys' resident jokester, pressed PLAY on the CD player and blasted the volume. A catchy beat filled the air. Players started dancing. And pointing. And laughing. It was a rap tune. But not just any rap tune.

Now playing: "Must Be the Money"

Album: *Prime Time*

Year of Release: 1994

Label: Bust-It Records

Artist: Deion Sanders

Genre: Ear Melting

From a pair of 100-watt speakers on a table in the center of the room, Sanders began to sing/speak/croak:

Well all right
Yeah
You know ever since I turned pro in 1989
When I signed the dotted line
It was strange!
'Cause things change
For the better and for the worse
So I called my mama and she said "Baby,"
Must be the money . . .

Sanders could not stop chuckling. The Cowboy locker room felt like home.

"That was so funny," says Cory Fleming, the Cowboy wide receiver. "It was important Deion could laugh at himself, because Nate played that song every friggin' day for a month." Plastered throughout Sanders's new locker were forty color Xerox copies of him interfering with Irvin in the '94 NFC Championship Game—the play that, had a flag been thrown, could have changed the outcome. "In big red letters

Mike wrote INTERFERENCE on each one," says Jim Schwantz, the linebacker. "Just hilarious."

On one of his early days with the team, Sanders ran into Alundis Brice, who just so happened to wear uniform No. 21, Sanders's digits of choice, at a Dallas-based BMW dealer. The rookie defensive back had long wanted to own a BMW 325i, and he was here to make it a reality. "Brice, what are you doing?" asked Sanders.

"I'm gonna buy this car tomorrow," he said. "But I first have to call my agent and set it up."

"It's your first sports car?" asked Sanders.

"Yup."

"Are you gonna pay cash for it?" Sanders asked.

"Yup."

Sanders nodded and drove off.

The next morning, Brice reported to Valley Ranch and was dismayed to spot his dream car—a brand-new metallic blue 325i with all the trimmings—parked in the players' lot. "I can't believe this," he thought. "Somebody bought *my* car."

When he approached his locker, Brice noticed the keys on his stool alongside a note from Sanders. It read: NOW GIVE ME MY DAMN JERSEY!

"I wore numbers 22 and 38 in college [at the University of Mississippi], but they gave me 21 with the Cowboys," Brice says. "I had no emotional attachment to it. So when I read that note, I took my jersey down, hung it in his locker, and got a new number. I'll never forget him doing that."

With such acts of grace and kindness, it took Sanders little time to develop a following in the Cowboys clubhouse. Like any American office space, Dallas had its cliques, usually divided along lines of race and age. White veterans like Aikman, Daryl Johnston, and Jay Novacek could be found in one pocket. The black defensive linemen, headed by Haley, were in another. Now Sanders was fronting a new group—the younger defensive players who envied both his game and his lifestyle.

This is where the problems began.

For all his Jim Thorpe-esque skills, Sanders was sleeping-dog lazy. In practices, he went all out every third or fourth play and refused to wear shoulder pads because, he would say, "I'm not gonna tackle anyone anyway." In meeting rooms, he was known to doodle and doze off. Told early on that Cowboys who refused to participate in the team's weight training regimen would be fined, Sanders dramatically whipped out his checkbook and jotted down a five-digit figure.

When Mike Woicik, the team's gruff strength and conditioning coach, complained about Sanders's indifference, Switzer sided with his new star. "We're talking about Deion Sanders here," Switzer told Woicik. "If he doesn't want to do something, he doesn't have to."

Woicik was speechless. Credited by many players as a key to the back-to-back Super Bowls, Woicik was a no-nonsense taskmaster who demanded maximum effort. "For Mike, anything short of a funeral was an unacceptable excuse to miss a session," says Kevin Smith. "Mike had the personality of a lamp, but if you had to bench-press he knew exactly how many you were supposed to do. When you came in and you didn't do it, he'd say, 'You were out fuckin' around last night. You must've been drinking last night. You must've been drinking two nights ago.' He'd be pissed. He wouldn't speak to you for a week. If you tested on the bench and you didn't make it, he wouldn't say a word to you for a whole week until you came in and did it. That's how he was. Your goals were his goals."

Throughout the locker room, Woicik was as respected as any Cowboy coach or official. And Deion Sanders had the nerve to treat him . . . *like this?*

Who were the Dallas Cowboys becoming?

"I still remember Deion's first team meeting," says Clayton Holmes, the veteran cornerback. "We were so fundamental about film. The way we studied it was critical. Well, Deion comes in, puts his feet up on a table, and doesn't even watch." When Dave Campo, the Cowboys' new defensive coordinator, asked the $35 million man to break down a play, Sanders let out a sly laugh. "Hey, Coach," he said, pointing toward the screen, "I got that dude right there. Wherever he goes I go. All that Cover Two stuff you're talking about—y'all work that out."

Seeing that the Cowboys' defensive back meetings lasted significantly longer than they had in Atlanta or San Francisco, Sanders took a page out of the Barry Bonds Playbook by investing in a black leather executive's chair and rolling it into the conference room. As his peers sat in standard metal folding chairs, Sanders lounged in comfort. "Guys thought that was kind of funny," says Schwantz. "Maybe not right—but funny."

Although most veterans accepted Sanders's ego and indifference in exchange for the promise of otherworldly play, Aikman—who had offered to defer part of his salary to help Dallas afford the defensive back—was disgusted. It was bad enough Switzer approached discipline as if he were the proprietor of the Moonlite Bunny Ranch. Now here was "Neon Deion," teaching via example that image is everything and practice is overrated. From across the locker room, the quarterback would watch Sanders's postgame dressing ritual and cringe. As Jeff Rude of the *Dallas Morning News* described it: "Most people slip on a shirt when they get dressed. Deion puts on a jewelry store." Around his neck, Sanders placed two thick gold chains with dangling diamond-studded 21s. He wore a diamond-studded Rolex watch, two gold diamond bracelets, and matching diamond horseshoe earrings.

"There was a division between Deion and Troy that began to bubble over," says Kevin Smith. "We called it 'Double Doors' at Valley Ranch. Once we walked through those double doors it was football. We could laugh and joke, but it was all about football. To Aikman, that was sacred.

"When Deion came in, something changed for the worse. Guys who should have been studying football on a Wednesday at twelve o'clock were focused on other things. Deion was such a freaky athlete that he could shake one leg and be ready to cover anyone. But the guys following his lead weren't nearly as talented. You know what they say about dogs that chase cars—they don't live long."

One of Sanders's most devoted disciples was Sherman Williams, the rookie running back with noteworthy talent but zero work ethic. "Deion had Sherman's ear a hundred percent," says Kevin Smith. "He would show up around ten o'clock, eleven o'clock in the morning, smelling like weed and rolling with a posse. Guys like Sherman needed to be reminded of the importance of hard work. That did *not* come from Deion."

"You led by example," adds Dale Hellestrae, the offensive lineman. "And Deion's example wasn't very good."

Sanders made his debut on October 29, when the Cowboys thumped the Falcons, 28–13, in Atlanta. The stars of the game were (ho-hum) Emmitt Smith (26 carries, 167 yards), Irvin (10 receptions, 135 yards), and Aikman (19 of 25, 198 yards, 2 touchdowns), yet the spotlight belonged to Prime Time. It was his moment in the sun. *His day.* In forty-four defensive sets, Falcons quarterback Jeff George threw his way twice. The first time, receiver Bert Emanuel beat Sanders for an 11-yard gain. The second, Sanders batted down the ball.

Though he talked as if he were the Muhammad Ali of the gridiron, Sanders's play in 1995 was merely OK. In nine games as a defensive back, Sanders intercepted 2 passes and contributed a paltry 22 tackles (that's a robust $318,182 per tackle). "Personally," says one Cowboy, "I thought Kevin Smith was a better player." Whereas the other primary cornerbacks—Smith, Larry Brown, and Clayton Holmes —embraced contact, Sanders was a feather duster. When he tackled, it was with the gusto of a ninety-year-old woman. "One time a running back ran a sweep toward him, and Deion dove halfhearted into the turf," says Case. "We're watching film the next day, razzing him pretty good. As serious as could be, he said, 'I saw that dude coming and I had to make a business decision.'"

Amid one of the most drama-packed seasons in team history, it was easy to forget that Dallas was the class of the NFL. Switzer's team improved to 7–1 with the Atlanta victory, prompting some columnists to predict a seamless return to the Super Bowl. Through eight games

Emmitt Smith led the NFL in rushing with 979 yards, Irvin had caught 58 passes, and, with 9 touchdown passes and only 2 interceptions, Aikman was as potent as ever.

Then, on Monday, October 30, the *Dallas Morning News* broke yet another Cowboy-related bombshell: Leon Lett and Clayton Holmes had violated the league's substance-abuse policy and would be suspended for four games. For both men it was the second failed test.

"That was the point where people started to see that the Cowboys had a drug problem," says Jean-Jacques Taylor, the *Morning News* football writer. "There were a lot of guys using, but it's not always easy to tell. I had an uncle who used to smoke crack on weekends, no problem. But he had a really nice-looking girlfriend who was a beautician. He turned her on to it one weekend and she was working the corner a month later.

"The Cowboys were sort of like that. Some guys could do drugs and handle it. But guys like Clayton and Leon couldn't. Leon's problem was he was stupid. Leon would go to a party, have a good time, the joint would come around the circle, and he'd take a hit. He knew a drug test was coming up, but he didn't think he'd test positive. Just plain stupid."

In past decades, Cowboys who wanted to smoke pot or snort cocaine would begin their nights at Holmes's home, then head out to the Cowboys Sports Café or a strip club. During the Switzer Era, however, a handful of players came up with a new, easier-than-ever way to do what they desired without running the risk of being caught by spouses or the media. In the beginning, it was merely known as "The House"—a handsome two-story brick home with a faux Georgian façade on a suburban cul-de-sac next to the Valley Ranch facility. As word of the Cowboys Sports Café had gotten out, players had grown tired of wading through an ocean of celebrity seekers. "So to keep the BS down, a couple of guys got together and got a house," says Newton. "The White House."

Located at 115 Dorsett Drive, the abode was initially rented in 1994 under the name of one Alvin Craig Harper. Any hope of keeping things hush-hush was obliterated when residents of the exclusively white, low-key community noticed their new 6-foot-4, 300-pound African-American neighbors escorting an endless conveyor belt of large-breasted, blond-haired women in Pez-sized miniskirts. Newton insists the White House was a haven for neither prostitution ("What did we need prostitutes for? Women laid down for us") nor drugs ("Never saw 'em"), yet his take is disputed by many. "I'm not going to lie—I went there several times," says Brice, the rookie cornerback. "But I was afraid to try any of the drugs. Because I knew myself, and I liked to have fun. Anything potentially addictive scared me."

"It was a frat house," says Mike Fisher, the team's beat writer for the *Fort Worth Star-Telegram*. "But most frat houses don't specialize in hookers and cocaine."

To visualize the White House, picture a relatively nice suburban home with a swimming pool in the back and a driveway packed with Jaguars, Bentleys, BMWs, and Ferraris. Then walk through the front door (no need to knock—it was always unlocked) and check out the enormous televisions, the pool table, the wet bar, and the prostitutes (often wearing nothing but the gold chains supplied by the residents). Oh, don't forget the handful of video cameras hidden throughout the various bedrooms, allegedly installed by Dennis Pedini, one of Irvin's close friends. "Everything that happened in the White House I'm assuming Pedini had on camera," says Kevin Smith. "He didn't tell the guys they were being filmed at the time, but—surprise!—they were."

To players like Newton, Harper, Irvin, Fleming, Haley, and Lett (among others), the White House was an oasis. To the White House cleaning ladies, it was the worst gig in the neighborhood. For $75 a week, the two women hired to straighten up were subjected to a cornucopia of used condoms, discarded bras, sex toys, and crusty carpet stains. "They used to find all kinds of crazy, crazy shit," says a friend of one of the women. "You can't even imagine . . ."

If Newton, Harper, and Irvin were the mayors, the governor was Haley, who considered the White House a home away from home. Players would escort women through the front door, direct them toward the rear bedroom, then—wham, bam—enjoy and discard them with a sort of automated efficiency. Supposedly happily married to Karen, whom he met while both were undergrads at James Madison University, Haley regularly brought his various flings to the House and fired away. "Charles was banging this girl who lived in the apartment under me," says Joe Fishback, a defensive back in 1993 and '94. "You could literally hear them doing it."

The first member of the media to write of the White House was the *Miami Herald*'s Dan Le Batard, who merely mentioned it in passing in a larger piece about partying in the NFL. "The reality is that many teams throughout the league had places like the White House," says Le Batard. "But the Cowboys were the biggest, baddest, best, and anything they did was vastly more magnetized." Upon reading Le Batard's story, the Dallas media went to work. In truth, many were well aware of the White House and its going-ons, but chose to ignore the story in the name of player-press relations. "Everyone knew about it, but what are you going to do, run a story about the guys cheating on their wives with hookers?" says Rob Geiger, a reporter for KRLD radio in Dallas. "The writers understood not to write about it, the radio and TV guys understood not to talk about it, because we'd be vilified by the fans and locked out by the team."

It was a gargantuan lapse in news judgment. The White House had everything one craves in a story—sex, drugs, fame, football.

When word of the White House finally broke, Jones and Switzer confessed to being shocked (shocked!) that a place of such ill repute existed. The Cowboys, after all, were a wholesome operation, made up of loyal, family-oriented men like, um, Jones and, uh, Switzer who would, eh, never, ah, dream of . . . cheating, uh, on, eh, a female. "Jerry Jones was chasing and fucking the same women Michael Irvin was," says Anthony Montoya, the gofer for Cowboy players. "He was out there just as bad as anyone else. I have no beef with that, because if you can get the pussy at that age, more power to you; I'm happy for you. But Jerry saying he didn't know about the White House is a fucking lie. A big fucking lie. I'd get calls from the team saying, 'Can you get X player. We hear he's out at the White House.'

"And usually," says Montoya, "they were right."

More than ever, the Cowboys missed Jimmy Johnson. Perhaps not his on-field coaching abilities so much as his discipline. His knowledge. His common sense. His authoritativeness.

Had the Cowboys partied under their former coach? Sure. Had they drank and drugged and chased women? Sure. "But you always knew you had to answer to Jimmy," says Darren Woodson. "Under Barry it was pretty much do whatever the hell felt good."

In the aftermath of the Lett-Holmes bombshell, the Cowboys began to show cracks. Though they defeated the Eagles 34–12 on November 6 to improve to 8–1, they followed the victory by getting demolished by the 49ers, 38–20, at Texas Stadium. Leading up to the game, Sanders devoted his time to incessant locker room yapping, claiming he was wronged by the 49ers and would seek revenge. In a team meeting he stood up and said, "Just line me up on Jerry Rice and y'all play zone or whatever you wanna do."

Oops. Despite being 13½-point favorites at home, the Cowboys were embarrassed. San Francisco scored 17 points in the first five minutes. Two plays into the game, the 49ers led 7–0 on an 81-yard catch-and-run by Jerry Rice (Rice finished with 5 catches for 161 yards, laughing at Sanders all the way). A couple of plays later San Francisco was up 14–0 after a fumble recovery and 38-yard touchdown return by defensive back Merton Hanks. On the Dallas sideline, eyes stared downward. On the 49ers sideline, chins were held high. Irvin was limited to a season-low 4 catches for 37 yards. Aikman was forced from the game with a bruised knee following a brutal sack by Dana Stubblefield. Switzer looked, as always, confused. "San Francisco beat us like we stole something," says safety Greg Briggs. "I mean, it was ugly."

At 8–2, the Cowboys were the *worst best* team in football. They won in spite of themselves; in spite of the off-the-field distractions that mounted like a LEGO tower. "We weren't very good," says Woodson, "but we somehow kept winning." Following the 49ers debacle, Dallas defeated Oakland and Kansas City, then lost to the lowly Redskins, 24–17, at Texas Stadium on December 3 to fall to 10–3.

Yet within the intricacies of a relatively meaningless setback (at 3–9, Washington was no longer a threat to capture the NFC East) came a defining, disturbing moment. During the game's third quarter, in what spectators viewed as an otherwise insignificant sequence of events, wide receiver Kevin Williams sprinted 8 yards, turned left, and caught . . . *nothing*. For what had to have been the twentieth time that season, Williams ran the wrong route. Aikman—usually cool, calm, reserved—was tired of it. He was having an erratic day (29 of 48, 285 yards, one late touchdown), and Williams's absentmindedness wasn't helping. "Kevin, get this fucking right!" the quarterback barked. "It's not *that* hard!"

For 99 percent of the Cowboys, the exchange was no big deal. Quarterbacks yell at receivers—it's part of the job description. "Signal callers are supposed to have balls," says Newton. "Troy had big ones." Yet for one Cowboy assistant coach, the incident reeked of wrongheadedness. Of arrogance. Of . . . *racism*.

Not that John "Boo" Blake should have had much say on Aikman's relations with African-Americans or, for that matter, anything. The team's thirty-four-year-old defensive line coach, Blake, who is black, was known to be neither wise nor particularly useful. He did, however, have the ear of Switzer, who had recruited Blake to Oklahoma as a nose tackle out of Tulsa's Charles Page High School, then brought him back as a graduate assistant. While working under Switzer at OU, Blake was mockingly nicknamed "Back 'Em Up Boo," in that his primary task seemed to be scooting players off the sideline during games. Blake was actually hired by the Cowboys in 1993, when Johnson was in need of an assistant, but he gained true power under Switzer. "John wanted to be one of the guys more than he wanted to be a coach," says Tony Casillas, who knew Blake dating back to his collegiate days at Oklahoma. "He talked out of both sides of his mouth, and you can't do that and expect to have players trust you. Instead of just doing his job, he had an agenda."

As the other coaches would congregate among themselves, Blake sat with the black athletes, talking shop and taking mental notes to relay to his boss. Like several of the team's veterans, Blake had his own small crew—Sanders and Kevin Williams chief among them. Though Williams took Aikman's tongue-lashing during the Redskins game in stride, Sanders did not. "Why is it that Troy only screams at the brothers?" Sanders asked Blake. "I never see him yell at a white guy."

Following the game Blake told Switzer that the Cowboys' African-Americans were tired of Aikman's redneck ways. It was a charge Blake had made before, but never so vociferously. So what if Aikman had blown his top at Mark Stepnoski, Kevin Gogan, Dale Hellestrae—*white* offensive linemen—in the past? So what if Aikman considered Irvin to be a brother? ("I am as black as anybody you could ever see," Irvin had said. "I am a black man with a black scarf on and I'm wearing black shades. I am as black as they come. And I know [Aikman] loves me.")

"You have to remember that ninety percent of the team is black," Haley said. "If he's going to yell at someone for making a mistake, it's probably going to be a black guy who made the mistake."

Two days after the game Switzer summoned Aikman to his office for a meeting. By this point, the coach-quarterback dialogue had reached a new low. In Aikman's mind, Switzer was an unadulterated, overmatched buffoon. From Erik Williams's car accident to Lett and Holmes to the White House to undisciplined practices to sloppy game plans, what was going right? In Switzer's mind, Aikman was an arrogant player doing his all to undermine the team.

"Troy," Switzer said, "it's been brought to my attention that some of the black players don't think you're being fair. They think you're taking a lot out on them, but that you never yell at the white guys."

Aikman was dumbfounded.

"I just think you might be wise to apologize to Kevin for yelling at him," Switzer said. "Why not go do it? It'll help your cause a good deal."

His cause? Aikman's cause was winning football games, not resolving inane conflicts with inept wide receivers and do-nothing, big-mouthed assistant coaches.

When word spread through the locker room of what had transpired, most players—black and white—were appalled. "That was just stupid," says Woodson, the African-American safety. "Troy was not racist. He didn't care if you were black, purple, yellow, orange, or green. He wanted to win football games, and he would yell at you whether you were Nate Newton [black] or Mark Stepnoski [white]. There were certain players who confided in John Blake and listened to what he had to say. I was not one of them."

"It was bullshit," says Kevin Smith, another African-American defensive back. "When you hear that Troy was disliked, that comes straight from Blake and Deion."

Though Aikman begrudgingly spoke privately to Kevin Williams, the damage was done. He stormed out of the facility and called Dale Hansen, the Cowboy announcer. "Boy, was he furious," says Hansen. "Beyond furious." Thanks to Sanders, Blake, and Switzer, a once-harmonious locker room was coming undone. A black-white divide had formed among certain players. From this point on, Aikman's relationship with Switzer was over. Throughout the year, he had been convinced that Switzer was bad-mouthing him to Blake and Skip Bayless, the local columnist who, after the season, would publish *Hell-Bent,* a scathing Cowboy biography.

"Troy was able to overlook a lot of things," says Hansen. "But when the Kevin Williams incident took place, Troy pulled me aside and said, 'I'll never trust that sonofabitch Switzer again.'"

Surely, the season could turn no stranger. By early December, Dallas was the drunk-driving, drug-using, hooker-seeking, White House–

frequenting, racism-accusing leader of the NFC East; a 10–3 Super Bowl favorite with a magnetism for turmoil reminiscent of the '77 New York Yankees.

On December 10, they traveled to Philadelphia to play the 8–5 Eagles, a mediocre team that had just lost to the lowly Seattle Seahawks. This was a game the Cowboys should have won.

This was a game the Cowboys blew.

Well, not the Cowboys, per se, but Switzer. The contest encapsulated not merely Dallas's season, but—in the eyes of many—Switzer's NFL career. "Boneheaded coaching," says Hansen, "by a boneheaded coach."

Dallas jumped out to a commanding 17–6 lead, but the league's twelfth-ranked defense allowed Philadelphia to battle back. Behind quarterback Rodney Peete, Aikman's former backup, the Eagles cut the deficit to 17–14. With eleven minutes, fourteen seconds remaining and Dallas on the Eagles' 2-yard line, Emmitt Smith took the handoff from Aikman and charged toward the game-sealing score. Instead of playing hero yet again, however, Smith had the ball knocked from his left arm by linebacker Kurt Gouveia—Smith's seventh fumble in fourteen games. Philadelphia recovered, and a couple of possessions later Gary Anderson's field goal tied the contest. "I still thought we were going to win," says Woodson. "It was the confidence that came with being a Cowboy."

On their next drive, Dallas faced a fourth-and-short from its own 29-yard line, the teams still deadlocked at 17. In the world of PlayStation, it's a no-brainer: You ram the ball down the Eagles' throats. In the NFL, however, you punt. You don't think about punting. You don't debate punting. "You punt the ball," says Randy Galloway, the famed columnist. "Every single time."

Switzer did not punt. With a stiff wind blowing in the Eagles' favor, offensive coordinator Ernie Zampese called "Load Left." As 66,198 fans screamed through the frigid wind, Smith took the handoff, stepped left, and—*BAM!* He was stopped for no gain by Gouveia. The stadium erupted. The Cowboys offense began to move off the field. The Eagles pumped their fists. The . . .

Wait.

Upon further review the referees determined that the two-minute time-out had been reached before the snap. The play didn't count. Dallas would have another chance to punt. Surely, John Jett could at least knock the Eagles out of field goal range with, say, a solid 30-yard boot. "Once you don't make it that first time," says Galloway, "you change tactics."

Undeterred, Switzer not only again went for the first down, but called for another Smith run. "You're just hoping Troy is gonna say, 'This isn't right,'" said Daryl Johnston, the fullback. "Call a time-out. Explain your point. 'Hey, we'll do this but give us a different play.'" But Aikman and Switzer did not have a relationship. Smith again grabbed the ball from Aikman's right hand, headed toward the line, and—BAM! BAM!—was met by linebacker Bill Romanowski and lineman Daniel Stubbs, who stopped him for no gain.

Four plays later, Anderson kicked a 42-yard field goal.

Eagles: 20

Cowboys: 17

Switzer: Humiliated.

"If it was fourth-and-one I would have punted," Switzer maintains to this day. "But it was fourth-and-three inches. I believed in my guys—period."

In Fox's New York studio, Jimmy Johnson was stunned. "I don't care if it's high school football, college football, or what have you," he said. "In a tie game, you punt the football." Switzer defended himself by saying, "If we punt they're going to get a shot at a field goal anyway," which only exacerbated Johnson. "Obviously, people will say the decision to go for it on fourth down was dumb," he said. "But his explanation for not punting the football was dumber."

Former Chicago Bears coach Mike Ditka, now working for NBC, called the sequence "the sequel to *Dumb and Dumber*." Galloway penned a *Morning News* piece titled GET BARRY OUT OF HERE IMMEDIATELY. In the *Kansas City Star*, Jason Whitlock fired away:

"It may go down as the dumbest decision in recent American history—dumber than Chris Darden's glove demonstration, more stupid than Clarence Thomas' Coke-can pickup line, more ignorant than Nixon's cover-up of Watergate and more foolish than major-league baseball's work stoppage. Only the Bootlegger's Boy could blow the easiest yes-no question in football—twice in less than a minute." ("Who are my critics?" counters Switzer. "The guys who sat out of PE class and never dressed in the eighth grade because they didn't want to play.")

On the Wednesday following the loss, Sanders ranted against anyone who dared rip his coach. "We just had fourth down and a pinky to go," he told the press. "We should have gone for it. We're still cool on this team. We're upset by the loss, but there is no great concern, no great panic in motion. But you [the media] have got to be fair . . . we're human beings also. There are no problems on this team even though we've had a few stumbles. Go ask thirty other teams if they would like to be 10–4.

"Around here, if you win it's not good enough and if you lose you are damned. I guess if you win the Super Bowl they [the media] would say you should have won by forty."

Though Sanders's on-field impact had been minimal (Dallas was 4–3 in games he played), his words lit a fire. The players were tired—damn tired—of a press corps that wouldn't rest until the Cowboys were portrayed as fools and losers and hapless morons. "Everyone loves a success story," says Newton. "And once you succeed, everyone loves tearing you down."

Against all odds, a club that had just experienced one of the most humiliating defeats of the decade bounced back. On December 17 it squeaked past the Giants 21–20 on a last-second field goal, then the following Sunday flew to Arizona for a final week of *Monday Night Football*. Two hours into the trip a stewardess announced that the Falcons had shocked San Francisco, 28–27. With a win against the Cardinals, Dallas would clinch home-field advantage throughout the playoffs. "It was like a switch had gone off and all of a sudden the whole plane was excited," said Aikman. "Now we were going to Arizona for a reason."

Newly inspired, the Cowboys crushed the Cardinals, 37–13, as Emmitt Smith scored his NFL-record twenty-fifth touchdown of the season.

Yet in the ups and downs of a trying year, everything returned to Aikman and Switzer, two men who, in the end, did not like, respect, or appreciate one another. Shortly before the Cowboys would open the playoffs, Aikman carefully, cautiously revealed his feelings toward Switzer in a scathing interview with the *Fort Worth Star-Telegram*. Having spent the entire year seething, the quarterback could no longer keep it all inside. He needed to vent. "What I've always believed is that we all need to be committed to reaching our potential," Aikman said, "and if we're ever doing less than that, I don't want to be a part of it." It wasn't difficult to figure to whom Aikman was referring. "For sixty minutes," he continued, "I get to do what I enjoy. But this has not been an enjoyable year for me, in regard to things outside the football field. I know it's totally a business. I do still get the spirit of competition, the camaraderie with the guys, the emotions. But beyond that, everything that's happened has taken a lot out of me. At some point, there will be a physical reason to retire. Or there will be the fact that it's just no fun."

Switzer responded by noting that Aikman was a bright man listening to the wrong people—namely Brad Sham and Dale Hansen, the team's radio announcers. "Troy gets squeezed all the time by people who have their opinions of me," he said. "People who pretend to be his friend are trying to create a separation."

Upon hearing Switzer's response, Aikman lost it. *Create a separation?* All the quarterback desired was a coach who understood what it took to win in the NFL; who worked hard, required some semblance of discipline, and didn't skip meetings to watch his son play small-time college football. "Troy is a low-maintenance guy," says Rob Awalt, his former teammate. "He just wants loyalty. From pals, from teammates, from coaches. He wants to know you've got his back."

Switzer didn't have his back. But at least there was *some* good news. On December 31, the University of Oklahoma concluded an arduous search by naming its new head coach—a thirty-four-year-old alumnus with a passion for all things Sooners and the football IQ of a Girl Scout.

John Blake would go 12–22 in three seasons with the Sooners before being fired. He is regarded as the worst head coach in school history. But for Aikman, his hiring was a blessing.

Blake was leaving Dallas.

As the Cowboys spent their bye week waiting to learn whom they would face in the playoffs, Philadelphia was busy thrashing the Detroit Lions, 58–37. It was one of the most dominant performances in Eagles history, and turned what should have been a modest, hoping-for-the-upset football team into a swaggering, trash-talking, bravado machine.

Instead of returning to Philadelphia to prepare for the Cowboys, whom they would face on January 7, 1996, Eagles coach Ray Rhodes led his team to Vero Beach, Florida, where it would train in seclusion at Dodgertown, the Los Angeles Dodgers' spring training facility. Rhodes compared the Eagles to a military battalion. "We didn't get to the playoffs just to be there," Rhodes said. "We're fighting to get a win. I want to turn this into an army-camp atmosphere."

Quarterback Rodney Peete followed his coach's lead, telling the media that Dallas was overrated and beatable.

Then the Eagles got thumped. Or, more accurately, *Neoned*.

With the game tied 3–3 five minutes into the second quarter, Cowboys offensive coordinator Ernie Zampese called Fake Tailback Jab Right Z Reverse Left. As soon as he heard the play leave Aikman's lips, Sanders looked around the huddle, smiled, and said, "Touchdown, baby!"

Aikman took the snap, faked a handoff to Emmitt Smith, and gave the ball to Sanders, who came dashing by from behind . . .

Whoooooooooooooooooooooooooooooooooooooooosh!

Sanders's 21-yard score wasn't a run, per se. It was a rocket launch.

He took the ball, headed left, then—bottled by defenders—spun and turned right. Sanders exploded toward the end zone, past flailing defenders and through the crisp 26-degree air. "He's got no moves," said an awestruck Emmitt Smith, "but he's as fast as I don't know what."

At long last, a Sunday afternoon in Dallas belonged to Sanders. Upon reaching pay dirt, Sanders did his first jig of the season, a semistylish, New Kids on the Block–meets–the San Diego Chicken number that reminded teammates that football can still be, well, fun. "Deion's my boy," said Irvin. "I ride with him to the airport and all I ever hear is, 'Man, I've got to get into the end zone.' I'm glad he finally got there so I could see the dance."

The game was all Prime Time. He intercepted a pass, returned two punts for 21 yards, caught a pass for 13 yards, and nearly snagged a sideline bomb from Aikman. The Cowboys won handily, 30–11.

"We kicked their ass today," said a visibly relieved Switzer. "If we'd played like that last time, it wouldn't have come down to fourth-and-a-foot."

As soon as the Cowboys and Packers were confirmed to meet in the NFC title game, a predictable local and national media felt compelled to evoke the 1967 NFL Championship clash, which featured Dallas traveling to Green Bay for the now-historic "Ice Bowl."

(Cue Sam Spence music.)

On that day, two evenly matched teams battled through temperatures that plummeted to –13 degrees (coupled with a windchill of –48 degrees) before Packers quarterback Bart Starr dove into the Lambeau Field end zone with thirteen seconds remaining for a 21–17 win. The game was an instant classic.

Yet any comparisons between the teams of the Ice Bowl and the modern-day Cowboys and Packers were forced. Vince Lombardi's 1967 Packers of Bart Starr, Willie Davis, and Forrest Gregg were far superior to the modern, up-and-coming Pack of Brett Favre, Reggie White, and LeRoy Butler. The current version of Green Bay's gridiron heroes won the NFC Central Division with an 11–5 mark, but were merely a good team. The Cowboys of '95, on the other hand, were significantly more talented than the '67 edition.

The opportunity to return to the Super Bowl had Dallas in a renewed state of euphoria. Not only had Cowboy Fever returned to the city, but so had Packer Disgust. In the days leading up to the game, the Kroger supermarket chain pulled all Wisconsin-made cheese products from its Dallas shelves. Minyard's Grocery Store went one step further, firing Sam Young, a twenty-six-year-old bagger, when he arrived at work wearing a Packers T-shirt. "Write me up, send me home, dock my pay," Young said. "But don't fire me."

Though the Cowboys knew they were the better team, there was concern over Favre, a cocky, tobacco-chewing quarterback who turned ordinary receivers into great ones. Dallas's defensive philosophy was simple—badger Favre into committing mistakes—and ineffective. On the second play of the second quarter, Favre hit tight end Keith Jackson with a 24-yard touchdown pass and the Packers took a shocking 17–14 lead. Texas Stadium, earlier swaying with emotion, turned into a ghost pavilion.

Back and forth the teams went, with Favre playing some of the gutsiest football of his life and Emmitt Smith running straight, left, and right without a breather. By halftime Smith had carried 22 times, and he would go on to gain 150 yards and 3 touchdowns on 35 carries. The Packers were emotionally ready for the Cowboys, and Favre willfully picked on the Dallas secondary. But Smith wore the opposition down. Dallas called one run play after another until Green Bay's defenders were hunched over in the huddle, hands on hips, breathing heavily. "They said, 'We're going to run the ball. Try and stop us,'" Green Bay linebacker George Koonce said. "And they still shoved it down our throats."

The Packers led 27–24 entering the fourth quarter, but their defense was spent. Smith's 5-yard touchdown run gave Dallas a 31–27 lead, and on the ensuing series Favre threw a costly interception to Larry Brown. When Emmitt Smith scored his third touchdown, he put the game out of reach. Dallas won, 38–27.

At long last, Barry Switzer felt a sense of NFL-worthiness. The stumbles of his first two NFL seasons were in the past. He had guided the Cowboys to the brink of a championship. Surely, the acclaim would follow. Surely, critics would finally eat some humble pie. Surely . . .

"Let's be realistic," says Randy Galloway, the columnist. "With all that talent, anybody in the world could have coached those Cowboys to the Super Bowl. I know I sure could have. Only I would have been drinking Miller Lite and eating cheeseburgers on the sidelines."

Chapter 24

SUPER BOWL XXX (AKA: ATTACK OF THE SKANKS)

---

*After the Super Bowl ended, nobody wanted to leave
the locker room. It was like being a marine at sea for
seven months. You come to land and think everyone wants to
run off the ship. But no one wanted to leave. They knew
it was the end and they wanted it to last.*

—Robert Bailey, Cowboys cornerback

WHEN THE DALLAS COWBOYS prepared to leave Texas for Tempe,
Arizona, the site of Super Bowl XXX, they made certain every necessary item was packed and loaded for the 1,056-mile journey.

Helmets—*check!*

Pads—*check!*

Athletic tape—*check!*

Shoes—*check!*

Playbooks—*check!*

Skanks—*check!*

Skanks?

Yes, you read that correctly. *Skanks.* Lots of skanks.

Being a veteran team with a wealth of Super Bowl experience,
members of the Cowboys had learned what they needed to survive—and,

indeed, thrive—in the week before the big game. Leading up to the first two Super Bowls, Cowboys players combed the streets, clubs, and bars of Los Angeles and, to a lesser extent, Atlanta. Yet such an approach comes with risk. The women, for example, could be stalkers. Killers. They might have STDs. Or husbands with quick fingers and loaded XM8 lightweight assault rifles.

Hence, the skanks. Knowing that the wives and family members would not arrive in Tempe until the Thursday or Friday before the big game, several Cowboys—ranging from Emmitt Smith and Charles Haley to Erik Williams and Nate Newton—paid for a fleet of eleven white stretches from a local limousine service to drive sixteen hours and a thousand miles from Dallas to Tempe, several with their special skank, *uh*, female friends along for the ride. The price: $1,000 per night per limo (far from objecting, Jerry Jones brought along his own party vehicle, the six-bed tour bus that had once belonged to Whitney Houston). By the time the Cowboys arrived for check-in at The Buttes, the team's first-class, $285-per-night hotel, on the Sunday before the game, the lobby was filled with tacky high heels and legs that stretched from Minneapolis to Mahopac.

"The limo thing was as blatant as anything the Cowboys had ever been a part of," says one team employee. "We had this huge caravan arrive from Dallas, and some guys had a bunch of their dancer girl-friends ride out and party with them. They brought the White House to Arizona."

Irvin enthusiastically endorsed the Port a Skank concept and, in fact, rented his own ten-passenger, thirty-foot monstrosity customized with a black leather-and-brushed-crome interior (and equipped with a bounty of Absolut vodka and hip-hop CDs). What baffled some about Irvin's ways was that his wife, Sandy, was intelligent, loving, an excellent mother to the couple's two daughters—and drop-dead gorgeous. "She's the most beautiful black woman I've ever seen with my eyes," says Kenny Gant, the Cowboy defensive back. "I've loved her to death since the first time I met her." Yet Irvin—who sported a large gold cross around his neck—never thought twice about professing his devotion toward his family one minute, then jumping into the hot tub with two strippers the next. Why, on the evening before the Cowboys departed for Tempe, Irvin had partied with a pair of prostitutes at the Irving Residence Inn.

"This stuff happened more and more under Barry, because the rules were just completely relaxed," says a team employee. "Now here comes Deion Sanders, the most flamboyant guy going. The combination of Sanders's flamboyant ways, Irvin's lifestyle, and the fact that Barry Switzer said, 'Hell, I don't care what you do; I'll see you Sunday afternoon'—it led to bad things.'"

Awaiting the Cowboys and their high-heeled entourage in Tempe were the AFC champion Pittsburgh Steelers, a gritty 11–5 football team that had upended the Indianapolis Colts in the AFC Championship Game to reach its first Super Bowl in sixteen years. If there was ever a textbook example of overlooking an opponent, here it was. The Steelers featured the league's No. 2–ranked run defense and a powerful tailback in 244-pound Bam Morris, but nobody—the Cowboys, the media, the fans—believed Pittsburgh could challenge Big D.

When the Cowboys prepared for Super Bowl XXVII three years earlier, they practiced with an intensity that Jimmy Johnson and his crew demanded. This time around members of the team came and went as they pleased, working out with halfhearted determination. In what was undoubtedly a Super Bowl first, Newton, Williams, Lett, and Irvin took a stretch Lincoln to and from practices. The players stayed out early into mornings and arrived to work hungover following wild sojourns to clubs like Empire and Jetz & Stixx. "The police came in and gave us a list of places not to go," Newton said. "I wrote 'em all down and went there."

The Cowboy who partied the hardest, the longest, the latest was not Irvin or Sanders or Newton or Lett but Barry Switzer, fifty-eight-year-old night owl. The Cowboy coach transformed his two-bedroom suite into a twenty-four-hour rave, with an endless stream of family members, friends, confidants, and strangers. "You have to understand the scene," says Michael Silver, the former *Sports Illustrated* scribe who spent much of the week alongside Switzer. "Barry basically decided, 'OK, this is the only time I'll ever be at a Super Bowl and I'm going to live it up.' So he called everyone he knew and said, 'C'mon, we're all going to the Super Bowl!'" Along for the ride were—among others—Switzer's three children; his girlfriend, Becky Buwick; his ex-wife, Kay (the two women shared a room); and a never-ending conga line of former Oklahoma players, coaches, and boosters. The end-of-the-week liquor bill exceeded $100,000.

On the night following the team's arrival in Tempe, Switzer and a slew of assistant coaches and players attended a Super Bowl party beneath an enormous outdoor tent. Switzer and Larry Lacewell, the Cowboys' director of pro and college scouting (and the man whose wife Switzer once slept with), downed shots until both were stumbling around like kangaroos atop surfboards. Silver was minding his own business when he turned and spotted Switzer furiously kicking with his right foot. "What the fuck are you doing?" Silver asked. Upon stepping closer, Silver saw that Switzer was actually booting Lacewell, who was trying to urinate beneath a wood deck. "Barry was getting Larry to piss all over himself," says Silver. "Urine everywhere." Done harassing his friend, Switzer stumbled to the dance floor and began hyperactively shaking his body—à la Pee Wee Herman. Nearby Emmitt Smith was grooving the night away, showing off the moves that, a decade later, would make him a champion on *Dancing with the Stars*, when he caught a glimpse of Switzer. "Emmitt can't believe what he's seeing," says Silver. "He just stops and stares at Switzer, and his jaw drops. He just gets this look on his face that I can only describe as 'Oh my God, my coach is fucking crazy!'"

Switzer's week was one uproarious blur—a little bit of football (Steelers? What Steelers?) mixed in with a whole lot of debauchery. On the night of Friday, January 26, less than forty-eight hours before kickoff, Switzer hosted his dream party in Suite 4000 at The Buttes—*his* suite. With his son Greg, a trained classical pianist, jamming away on the room's black Steinway, Switzer led an obnoxious, infectious, inebriated sing-along of Ray Charles's "What'd I Say." Instead of repeating Charles's lyrics, however, Switzer and Co. filled in their own words—praising Jerry Jones, mocking Jimmy Johnson.

> *Tell your mama, tell your pa*
> *I'm gonna send Jimmy back to Arkansas*
> *Oh yes, ma'am, Jimmy don't do right, don't do right*
> *Aw, play it, boy*
> *When you see him in misery*
> *Cause Jimmy fuckin' sucks on TV*
> *Now yeah, all right, all right, aw, play it, boy*

"I didn't know if we'd win or lose the Super Bowl," says Switzer. "But I knew I was gonna have one helluva week. You don't reach the heights and then play it down. You make the moments memorable."

Although the Cowboys expended a great deal of time, money, and energy partying it up in Tempe, not every player thought it appropriate to turn Super Bowl week into *Animal House II: Attack of the 300-Pound Texans.* Defensive lineman Russell Maryland, for example, spent much of his free time reading, watching TV, and quietly touring the area. Upon graduating from Chicago's Whitney Young High School in 1986, Maryland—a former usher at St. John Church—made a promise to the congregation that he would live righteously. "My mom and dad would tell me all the time not to embarrass the Maryland name," he said. "And I took that seriously."

Linebacker Robert Jones, about to play his final game with Dallas, avoided the limelight and temptations by sticking with his wife, Maneesha, and their two sons. "I didn't come to party," he says. "I came to win."

And then there was the man deemed Cowboy Most Likely to Blow the Super Bowl. Raised in Southern California, Larry Brown attended Los Angeles High, spending four years as a moderately successful All-City selection. With few available postgraduation options,

Brown enrolled at Los Angeles Southwest College, where he played tailback as a freshman and defensive back as a sophomore. Asked to assess Brown's collegiate legacy, Henry Washington, his former Southwest coach, noted, "Larry wasn't what you'd call a great player. But he always got the job done."

Brown believed his two years of junior college ball would result in attention from UCLA or USC or at least Cal or Stanford. Instead, the only offer came from Texas Christian University, home to the mighty purple-and-white Horned Frogs.

Though Fort Worth was a far cry from L.A., Brown took advantage of the opportunity. He started both seasons for TCU and was named one of the Most Valuable Players of the 1990 Blue-Gray game. "I was sure I'd be drafted in the first four rounds," says Brown. "I'd played on the same stage with the guys from Miami and Florida State and Notre Dame and I more than measured up."

On the afternoon of April 21, 1991, Brown sat before his television and waited to be drafted. On April 22, he waited some more. Finally, with the 320th pick of the twelfth round, the Cowboys nabbed Brown. He was the 57th defensive back selected, following such immortals as Jacksonville State's David Gulledge and James Smith of mighty Ripon College. In the minutes preceding the pick, those in the Dallas draft room debated Brown's merits. "The kid's OK," said one scout. "Not great, not terrible."

"That may well be," said another, "but he's already in Texas. He won't cost us an airplane ticket."

Larry Brown it was.

By Super Bowl XXX, Brown was enjoying his fifth straight season as a Cowboy regular—and nobody could quite figure out why. Neither especially fast, strong, nor tough, Brown worked moderately hard and studied film with average acumen. When Dallas signed Deion Sanders, it was assumed Brown would finally land on the bench. Then Kevin Smith got hurt and the crabgrass of cornerbacks remained. "Larry's hands were awful—just awful," says Clayton Holmes, his fellow cornerback. "He was knowledgeable on defense and he would bust his ass on the field. But he couldn't catch and he played scared. On the sideline, it was always pretty clear he just wanted the game to be over with."

Brown may have had his drawbacks but he was liked. He cracked corny yet well-received jokes, rarely complained, attended church weekly, and never ripped teammates or coaches to the media. "He was a really good guy with a great outlook on life," says Greg Briggs, a Cowboys defensive back. "He appreciated what he had going."

Brown's unyielding positivism was put to the test in August 1995, when his son, Kristopher, was born ten weeks premature, weighing 1 pound, 9 ounces. Immediately following his delivery, the baby was brought to the ICU and placed on a ventilator. With each passing hour, Larry and his wife, Cheryl, gained hope. Their 1½-year-old daughter Kristen had been three months premature, and she'd turned out to be perfectly fine. "Then I was holding him one day and I noticed that the back of his head was kind of soft," says Cheryl. "They took him in to do an X-ray and found that part of his brain had dissolved."

Kristopher Brown was brain-dead.

"The hardest day was when we had to decide to take him off the respirator," says Brown. "We talked and prayed, but when you're not going to have a brain, there's no hope. I'm still in disbelief. Every day, I'm in disbelief."

Kristopher died on Thursday, November 16, the worst day in Larry's and Cheryl's lives. Brown had been away from the team for several days, and Switzer insisted he not return for that Sunday's game against the Raiders in Oakland. "Take whatever you need," Switzer said. "Give yourself time to heal."

Despite his wife's objections, Brown decided the best way to recover would be to do what he loved most. On the day before the game Brown flew to Oakland on Jerry Jones's private jet. He was mentally drained and physically weak—and shocked by the reaction of his teammates. The Cowboys had decided to dedicate the rest of the season to Kristopher. Every helmet was adorned with a small KB sticker. "The whole thing moved me to tears," he says. "Before the game I told myself, 'Play this for Kristopher,' and I did. My conditioning was so poor that they took me out to give me oxygen, but I felt like I was in the right place."

Dallas won 34–21, momentarily lifting their cornerback's blighted spirits. For the remainder of the regular season and into the playoffs, Brown was a mixed bag of emotions. He could focus on football, but thoughts of his son always crept in. There were good days and bad days, smiles and tears. Against Green Bay in the NFC title game, his fourth-quarter interception of a Brett Favre pass sealed Dallas's trip to Tempe. "Larry had a very, very hard season," says Darren Woodson. "He deserved something really great happening to him."

The Pittsburgh Steelers were pissed off. Who could blame them?

In the two weeks leading up to Super Bowl Sunday, members of the AFC champions were asked hundreds of questions—nearly all of them having to do with Dallas's irrefutable advantages in skill, experience, and legacy. It was as if the Steelers were lambs being led to slaughter, the questions from the media their last rites prior to the butcher's knife. "The whole thing was really annoying and disrespectful," says Levon Kirkland, Pittsburgh's standout linebacker. "You got tired of hearing how great Dallas was. Everyone thought Dallas would run us over. We believed we were going to shock those guys."

Throughout the week, members of the slighted Steelers griped incessantly. Why, they wondered, had each of them been permitted to purchase only twenty Super Bowl tickets, while the Cowboys were granted thirty apiece? (This was an understandable complaint. Recalls Greg Schorp, a member of Dallas's practice squad: "Everyone on the team was selling their tickets for two, three thousand dollars a pop. It was a great chance to make a lot of money.") The Steelers also caught wind of Dallas's snazzy digs at The Buttes, which was like the Four Seasons compared with their quarters at the $180-per-night Double-tree Paradise Valley Resort. During a team meeting, linebacker Greg Lloyd was fuming aloud about the "cheap-ass accommodations" when head coach Bill Cowher interrupted him to say, "Greg, I'd like to introduce you to Peter Ottone, the hotel's general manager, who's standing next to you."

As the Cowboys loafed, the 13½-point underdog Steelers felt they had something to prove. Under the thirty-eight-year-old Cowher, Pittsburgh had implemented a 3–4 defense that evoked comparisons to the old Steel Curtain of the 1970s. Like Dallas, Pittsburgh's unit—led by Lloyd, Kirkland, and veteran linebacker Kevin Greene— was built on merging speed, reaction time, and power. "We were the best in the league, and there was no way Dallas was going to take advantage of us," says Kirkland. "Whether they knew so or not."

With lines clearly drawn between the "good" Steelers and the "bad" Cowboys, Dallas nestled comfortably into its black hat. The Cowboys were callous and cocky, perfectly represented by the string of expletives Irvin fired at the assembled TV cameras three days after the victory over Green Bay. "The media can't control my mouth," he said. "I'm not living on the plantation. Get the hell out of my face with that." One week *before* kickoff a PR firm announced that, come February 2, the Cowboy cheerleaders would release a video titled *1996 Dallas Cowboy Superbowl Shuffle.* During Dallas's Media Day session, Sanders said that Arizona was "too white" for his tastes. "I just bought a 747 and I'm telling them to stop in all the other cities and bring some black people in here," he said. "Someone asked me if I'd like to live here. That's like asking Rodney King to take a stroll through the LAPD."

Wrote Dan Shaughnessy in the *Boston Globe:*

The Cowboys are going to Super Bowl XXX, which means two long weeks of bad hair, big egos, big hair, bad egos, arrogance, corporate gluttony, cheap shots and cut blocks.

Ugh. Dallas in the Super Bowl means Nike "swoosh" stickers on every cactus in Arizona. It means 77 Farrah Fawcett look-alikes prancing on the sideline. It means the insufferable Neon Deion as Grand Marshal . . .

Really, how can anyone root for Dallas? If you back the Cowboys, you've got to be an insatiable front-runner, a cabbage or, worse, a Texan.

On the morning of Super Bowl XXX, Larry Brown woke up, brushed his teeth, took a shower, ate some breakfast, and before leaving the hotel for Sun Devil Stadium, heard his wife ask, "Larry, are you nervous?"

It was a fair question, in that Larry Brown was almost always nervous. Whether he was playing for Texas Christian or the Dallas Cowboys, rare were the pregame rituals that didn't include heaping spoonfuls of anxiety. For some reason, this day was different.

"Nah," he said. "With Deion on the other side they're going to be throwing at me all day. I plan on picking off two or three balls by the time it's over."

Although Cheryl would later boast of her husband's Nostradamuslike moment, it didn't take a starting NFL defensive back to know that, in the battle of quarterbacks, Dallas possessed a tremendous advantage. While Pittsburgh's secondary had to contend with the strong-armed Troy Aikman and his two favorite targets, Irvin and tight end Jay Novacek, Dallas's defense would be facing Neil O'Donnell, one of the league's most *ordinary* signal callers.

A fifth-year veteran out of the University of Maryland, O'Donnell possessed above-average accuracy, slightly below-average arm strength, and an introverted personality that hardly inspired teammates. "Neil was very self-critical," says Mike Tomczak, Pittsburgh's backup quarterback. "He was a tough kid from New Jersey who strived for perfection." O'Donnell's stats were always more impressive than the actual, in-the-flesh player. Over twelve games during the '95 season, he threw for 2,970 yards and 17 touchdowns, with a mere 7 interceptions. "Was Neil a good quarterback?" asks Andre Hastings, a Steeler wide receiver. "Well, he was pretty OK, I guess. But I would never say he was a Hall of Fame or Pro Bowl type of guy. He did his job."

"I look at it this way," says Ernie Mills, another Steeler receiver.

"We ran a lot of four- and five-receiver sets, so somebody was going to be open."

After the requisite two weeks of hype, Sunday evening finally arrived. The weather was mild—70 degrees, little breeze, a blue, cloudless sky. As America's Team, the Cowboys were used to charging onto the field and hearing substantially more cheers than boos. Such was certainly the case in the previous two Super Bowls, when the Cowboys were the Rolling Stones playing Madison Square Garden and the Buffalo Bills were Bad Ronald at the Stormville Flea Market. This time was different. The Steelers represented every blue-collar American fatigued by the whole flash-and-dash Dallas mojo. It didn't hurt that Pittsburgh had won four Super Bowls, a past that made them one of the league's more popular franchises. "Usually when we came to Arizona, if there were 75,000 fans at the game, 50,000 or so were Cowboy fans," says Dale Hellestrae, Dallas's long snapper. "Well, this time we go running onto the field for pregame warm-ups and we're getting booed. Cowboy fans were outnumbered by Steeler fans and those Terrible Towels were *everywhere*. I remember us looking around and going, 'What the hell is going on here?'"

Dallas took the opening kickoff and casually marched down the field behind a 20-yard pass from Aikman to Irvin followed by a 23-yard Emmitt Smith run. Though they settled for a 42-yard field goal from a shaken Chris Boniol ("I couldn't make a kick from twenty-five to forty-five yards in pregame," Boniol says. "I mean, not one"), the Cowboys had set a tone.

After limiting Pittsburgh to three plays, Dallas dominated again, this time starting at its own 25-yard line and confidently attacking the vaunted Steeler defense. The key play—the sort of play that becomes a game's signature—came on a first down and 10, when Aikman dropped back and launched a 47-yard spiral to Sanders, who dashed past cornerback Willie Williams to make an artistic, over-the-left-shoulder haul. Four plays later Aikman hit Novacek, and the tight end tiptoed into the end zone from three yards out. When Boniol kicked another field goal on the following series, the score was 13–0.

Across the nation, 94.8 million TV viewers began to wonder whether Diana Ross's halftime extravaganza would feature songs from her Supremes days or the solo years.

"Those Cowboys sure didn't lack for confidence," says Kendall Gammon, the Steelers' long snapper. "But neither did we. We were new to the Super Bowl, so maybe there were some nerves. But we were too good to lie down and get our butts kicked."

Following an exchange of punts, Pittsburgh attacked. Facing a third-and-20 from his own 36-yard line, O'Donnell rifled a 19-yard bullet to Hastings. "That was awful," says Switzer. "[Linebacker] Darrin Smith was supposed to play zone and just stay in the middle. Instead he followed a receiver and [Hastings] was wide open. If the players just followed my damn instructions we would have won easily."

On fourth-and-1, Cowher's directive was a simple one: Make a first down and steal momentum; come up empty again, and the night belongs to Dallas. Into the game came rookie receiver/running back/quarterback Kordell Stewart, who gained the needed acreage with a 3-yard dash. As Stewart popped to his feet, thousands of Terrible Towels twirled in the air, transforming Sun Devil Stadium into a swaying black-and-gold ocean. With thirteen seconds remaining in the first half, O'Donnell hit receiver Yancey Thigpen with a 6-yard touchdown strike. A potential blowout had turned into a legitimate battle. Halftime score: 13–7. "We were rejuvenated," says Hastings. "The rest of the game was going to belong to us."

In the Steelers' locker room, Cowher was at his fiery best. Known for shoving his ironworker's jaw in a Steeler's face and screaming or crying or laughing, he was all rage. "Those sons of bitches thought you were nothing!" he screamed. "They thought they were going to run all over you! They thought you were a joke. Well, they're not laughing anymore! We took their best shots! Now it's our turn! Let's go take what's ours . . ."

As Cowher spoke, not a peep was uttered from his players. Pittsburgh had endured two weeks of ridicule, and it stung. The players stormed back onto the field with a fire Dallas lacked. This was about disrespect; about payback; about overcoming the odds and doubters. "You hear enough trash, you snap," says Hastings. "We snapped."

After unsuccessful drives by both teams to start the third quarter, Pittsburgh began to grind its way down the field, rolling over a sagging Cowboy defense to its own 48-yard line. Facing third down and 9, O'Donnell received the snap, took five steps backward, and was pressured by Chad Hennings, who charged through the middle of the Pittsburgh line. On the verge of being sacked, O'Donnell tossed the ball to the outside, where he expected to find an uncovered Mills. Instead, it floated into the arms of Brown, who returned it 44 yards to the Steelers' 18. On the Dallas sideline, players leapt with excitement. "I can't lie," says Brown. "That one was a gift." With 6:42 left in the third quarter, Emmitt Smith ran in from a yard away, handing Dallas a 20–7 advantage.

"That was Neil's fault," says Mills. "He played great for us that season, but on the one play he made a really bad read."

The Steelers and Cowboys traded aborted drives, and when Pittsburgh got the ball again, it used nine plays to advance from its own 20-yard line to the Cowboys' 19. But on third-and-8, O'Donnell was hammered by Dallas defensive end Tony Tolbert, who slammed the quarterback down for a devastating 9-yard loss. A 46-yard field goal by Norm Johnson cut the Dallas lead to 20–10 with 11:20 left in the game.

Then Cowher—a calculated gambler—took a major chance. With the Cowboys lined up for a run-of-the-mill kickoff, Norm Johnson squibbed the ball off the tee toward the right sideline, where Pittsburgh defensive back Deon Figures scooped it up. First-and-10, Steelers, on their own 48-yard line. "At that moment I was thinking, 'We're gonna lose this thing; I can't believe it,'" says Dallas linebacker Jim Schwantz. "Because I thought it was gonna be an easy game. I thought we'd throw our helmets out there and win."

Nine plays later, Pittsburgh running back Bam Morris rammed through on a 1-yard touchdown run, cutting the deficit to 20–17. "Once we got the jitters out," said Steelers cornerback Carnell Lake, "we outplayed them."

It was going to happen. It was really going to happen. The Pittsburgh Steelers were about to beat the Dallas Cowboys. Impossible. Unimaginable. With 4:15 left in the game, the Steelers got the ball back on their own 32-yard line, momentum on their side, the fans in a frenzy, one of the greatest upsets in Super Bowl history within reach.

And their quarterback was nervous.

Extremely nervous.

O'Donnell's eyes were wide and his breaths were deep. "I talked to some offensive guys later and they said Neil wasn't looking so good in huddle," says Jerry Olsavsky, a Steelers linebacker. "I didn't understand that—we weren't scared on defense. We were never scared on defense."

On first down and 10, O'Donnell scrambled left and threw toward Hastings, who dropped the ball.

On second down and 10, two men sealed their eternal NFL statuses:

One turned into Mookie Wilson.

The other—Bill Buckner.

O'Donnell and the Steelers bounded out of the huddle convinced they had a play certain to work. O'Donnell would take a four-step drop and fire a pass to Hastings, who planned on using his speed to run a slant route across the field and in front of the sagging Dallas secondary. Worst-case scenario, Hastings scoots for a first down. Best-case scenario, he outruns the Cowboys and scores the game-winning touchdown.

"We were going to pull it out," says Olsavsky. "I felt it."

Aware of O'Donnell's reputation for being spineless, Cowboys defensive coordinator Dave Campo spent the game urging his linemen to thump the Steelers quarterback whenever possible. "We caught Pittsburgh by surprise by running zone blitzes," Campo says. "We wanted to confuse their quarterback." When the two teams had met to open the 1994 season, the Cowboys sacked O'Donnell nine times. The memory was in his head. Had to have been. Now, with a Super Bowl in the balance, Campo wisely called out "Zero!"—code for a nine-man blitz. Darren Woodson looked toward Brown and shouted, "Larry, be aggressive here! Be aggressive! They're coming your way!" As O'Donnell dropped back, he was harassed by a collapsing wall of defenders. He did what a good quarterback does—threw to the spot, knowing exactly where Hastings was supposed to be and trusting the route-running abilities of Pittsburgh's second-leading receiver.

Yet instead of slanting one way, Hastings went the other. For the second time that evening, Brown was in the exact right location at the exact right time—all alone with a football fluttering his way. It was Christmas and Easter and Kwanzaa and Purim rolled into one, and Brown eagerly caught the ball and dashed 33 yards to the lip of the end zone.

"It was like a cartoon—*noooooooooooooooooooo!* Poof!" says Hastings. "It was a pretty bad feeling—like, 'This cannot be happening.' It's one thing to get blown out and say, 'OK, it wasn't our Sunday.' But to be that close, it's pretty heartbreaking."

Emmitt Smith scored shortly thereafter, and the game was done. The Steelers had held Smith to 49 yards rushing, limited Irvin to 5 catches for 76 yards, contained Aikman to a single touchdown pass . . . and still lost.

Cowboys: 27.

Steelers: 17.

"We gave away the Super Bowl," said running back Erric Pegram. "We gave the darn thing away."

What few Steelers could know in the immediate aftermath was that while O'Donnell was responsible for interception number one, it was the inexperienced Hastings who, in the final minutes, cost his team the victory with the errant route. Hastings later publicly blamed O'Donnell, kicking off a mini–war of words among ex-Steelers. "That definitely wasn't Neil's fault," says Tomczak. "He made a read and it was right. Mistakes were committed by other people. But the quarterback always gets blamed."

Though O'Donnell turned into Pittsburgh's No. 1 goat, Brown found gridiron salvation. Upon entering the locker room, he was greeted by an unruly serenade of "L. B.! L. B.! L. B.!" The twelfth-round pick was now Super Bowl XXX's unlikely MVP. He would get the car and—as a pending free agent—a $12 million contract to join the Oakland Raiders.

Wrote Shaughnessy in the *Boston Globe:* "[Brown] was like a backup catcher who wins a World Series game by getting hit by a pitch with the bases loaded. He did almost nothing to earn the trophy. Twice Brown was standing in the open field, minding his own business, when an O'Donnell pass came his way. Both of his catches could easily have been made by Mike Greenwell, Jose Canseco, Charlie Brown or Downtown Julie Brown."

Few could argue.

"Man, Larry knows he's lucky," says Briggs, the Cowboy defensive back. "If I'm standing there like he was, minding my own business, I'm the Super Bowl MVP. Shoot, that would have been sweet."

Briggs pauses, taking a minute to reconsider.

"But you wanna know something?" he says. "Larry was a great dude. And guys like that deserve to have their moments too. So God bless Larry Brown. God bless him."

Chapter 25

THE FALL

Whether it was because they were chasing hos or because they had radio shows or because they were getting drunk or doing drugs or having sex parties—whatever it was, after Super Bowl XXX guys on the Cowboys couldn't possibly be as focused on football as they were before they tasted all that.

—Jean-Jacques Taylor, Cowboys beat writer

TWO WEEKS AFTER the Super Bowl, the Cowboys met with President Bill Clinton at the (real) White House. This being the team's third championship in four years, a trip to the nation's capital no longer had the same cachet. It was old hat—the reason a mere eighteen players attended.

As is standard ritual, the president held an East Room ceremony, during which he said some kind words, then was presented with Cowboy memorabilia. Afterward the players formed a line in the Blue Room, and Clinton gradually worked his way down, shaking hands and engaging in a bit of chitchat.

Near the end of the line stood seldom-used running back David Lang, rookie tight end Eric Bjornson, and Charles Haley, who had just won his league-record fifth Super Bowl ring. As Clinton approached, Lang nudged Bjornson and, with a sly grin, said, "Watch this." When the president stuck out his hand, Lang softly grabbed his bicep and said, "Hey, man, you're sorta big!" Clinton was flattered. "Thanks," he said. "Not too bad for an older guy, right?"

With that, Haley leaned over and whispered softly to the leader of the free world, "Don't listen to him, Mr. President. He's bisexual."

What?

"Clinton has this awkward look on his face," says Bjornson. "And I feel like the biggest horse's ass, standing between these two clowns. It was typical crazy, from-the-seat-of-his-pants Charles."

It was also one of the final moments of innocent mischief for a football team that had long ago lost its moral compass, its personnel judgment, and, in many respects, its way. As the Cowboys shuffled off from 1600 Pennsylvania Avenue and back out into the real world, a bitter truth awaited. Throughout football history, few dynasties stretched beyond a decade. Oh, Vince Lombardi's Green Bay Packers had dominated the NFL during much of the '60s, and the Steelers of the '70s and 49ers of the '80s certainly boasted impressive runs. But every successful franchise inevitably encountered a tipping point, be it influenced by age, player turnover, or a mounting lack of discipline.

For the Dallas Cowboys, a team that somehow managed to overcome one drama after another in 1995, all three would apply.

Many believe the downfall officially commenced five weeks after Super Bowl XXX when, at 11:45 P.M. on March 3, 1996, Mike Bailey, a manager of the Residence Inn in Irving, Texas, picked up the phone and dialed 273-2450, the number of the local police department:

OPERATOR: "Irving Police Department. This is Laura . . ."
BAILEY: "We have two individuals that keep checking into our hotel and . . . the better word is, they're prostitutes. They've been running the rooms and when we have to clean up after them we have been finding cocaine and crack and marijuana. Well, they're back . . ."

At 11:55 P.M., four policemen arrived at the hotel. When Officer Matt Drumm knocked on the door of Room 624, he heard shuffling, but nobody answered. "When we did get the door [partially] open, they had the security bar on it," said Drumm. "A big cloud of marijuana smoke came out."

The door was finally opened by Angela Renee Beck, a twenty-two-year-old "model" and former dancer at the Men's Club of Dallas. She was wearing a black miniskirt and halter top. Standing inside the room was another "model" and former Men's Club dancer, Jasmine Jennifer Nabwangu, twenty-one, and two football players. One, former Dallas tight end Alfredo Roberts, remained silent. The other did not.

"Hey," said Michael Irvin, "can I tell you who I am?"

"I know who you are," replied Drumm.

With that Irvin, wearing baggy blue jeans but no shirt, hung his head.

The officers confiscated 10.3 grams of cocaine and more than an ounce of marijuana, as well as rolling papers, a six-inch tube used for snorting cocaine, and two vibrators. Because Beck claimed the drugs were hers, Irvin, Roberts, and Nabwangu were not arrested. But for the brightest of the Dallas Cowboys' stars, the succeeding attention was far worse than a night in the clink. A local television station broke the story, and rival networks quickly followed with their own reports of Irvin's soiree.

"I don't understand how you can be so stupid to get yourself in that position," says Chris Boniol, the Cowboys kicker. "What the hell are you thinking?"

Sandy Irvin, the woman Michael still loved, learned of the drug incident from watching TV. She was hurt, scared, enraged, and—mostly—humiliated. Her marriage had been one embarrassment after another, but this was, hands down, the worst. "I'm on my way home," Michael Irvin later recalled. "I'm thinking, 'What am I going to say? What will I say?' It's one thing to have a thought that your husband is doing something. It's a whole other thing to turn on Channels 4, 7, 10, 11 and he's right there. So . . . I walked in the house—I was getting ready to say, 'I'm sorry, I'm sorry, I'm sorry'—and all she said was,

'Baby, don't apologize to me. You need to go in the room and make your peace with God.'"

Was the five-time Pro Bowler truly addicted to cocaine? Few who know him—friend or enemy—believe the question can be answered with a black-and-white reply. (Anthony Montoya, Irvin's gofer, says, "Mike didn't have a drug problem. He had a pussy problem.") Irvin could spend three days gobbling up drugs as if they were Pez, then devote a month to nothing but football. Repeatedly Irvin told people that winning was the ultimate euphoria, but he also relished the feeling of a quick high, and *really* enjoyed the feeling of a quick high in bed with two or three women.

The Irving police initially seemed willing to back off of Irvin and only pursue charges against Beck. Yet the receiver's arrogance was just too much. Irvin skipped one scheduled grand jury appearance and arrived for another sporting $500 sunglasses and distributing donuts to nearby reporters. The behavior would have been egregious enough had Irvin not been wearing a black floor-length mink coat. "I remember saying to Mike, 'You just can't wear that sort of outfit to court,'" says Jay Ethington, one of Irvin's attorneys. "He turned to me and said, 'Jay, I've got a different audience than you.' That's when it dawned on me—it was all theater to him."

In the month following the incident at the hotel, a Dallas grand jury indicted Irvin and the "models" on two counts of drug possession (the grand jury took no action against Roberts). Irvin pleaded no contest to second-degree felony cocaine possession and was fined $10,000 and placed on four years' probation. He was suspended for the first five games of the 1996 season. "It was around that time when I really felt Mike wasn't in control of himself anymore," says Kevin Smith, the Cowboys cornerback. "He just didn't care. His attitude was, 'To hell with it and to hell with this city. I don't want to play football anymore.'" Indeed, Irvin would spend night after night with different women ingesting different drugs, often going long stretches without contacting his wife. Was Michael high? Was he dead? Sandy Irvin had no idea. "I would call his cell phone, and what I would do is leave a message telling him that we love him," she said. "I knew that Satan had him out there in deep, deep dark hell."

In the Cowboy offices, Irvin's downfall was striking. Yes, he had issues. But he was also a team leader. He was bighearted and open-minded, and would do anything to help a teammate. Why else would Aikman—with nothing to gain from the publicity—attend Irvin's trial for all the public to see?

Why? Because Irvin would have done the same. "Everything that happened in Mike's life was self-inflicted," says Larry Brown. "He wasn't someone who tried to damage others. He's like an alcoholic, in that the problem was something he wanted to handle, but couldn't. His demon was with women and sex. I couldn't be mad at him for that, because it wasn't his choice. It just . . . *was.*"

The Cowboys had planned on marketing themselves as the reigning Super Bowl champs and the dynasty of the decade, but the good vibes were dwarfed by all the bad. Nobody in the media cared about players holding charity bowling tournaments or traveling to unique vacation spots or posing for pictures with poor little Butchie Smith at the Boys & Girls Club (the requisite offseason story lines that fill the three-month dead zone between the Super Bowl and the NFL Draft). Whereas Irvin was once hyped from within as the name and face of the Dallas Cowboys, now he was raw meat for the news media—yet another clichéd-but-irresistible tale of the great athlete gone bad.

The Cowboys hardly helped themselves as an organization. As the Irvin case began to unfold, Jerry Jones decided it wise to sign free-agent linebacker Broderick Thomas, who had recently been arrested for trying to bring a semi-automatic pistol through the metal detector at Houston Intercontinental Airport. Such was the swagger of the Dallas owner, who seemed to take pride in confronting criticism with bold (read: inane) moves that spit in the face of the general public. *You think we're bad off with Irvin. Well, wait'll you get a load of the next guy we sign!* At his best, Thomas was a marginal player whom most NFL teams avoided with a 100-foot goalpost. Not Jones—he was in the business of making statements. *We're the Dallas Cowboys, and we'll do whatever we damn well please.* Noted William Bennett, the former U.S. secretary of education: "If this is America's Team, then woe is America."

By the beginning of the '96 season, the media had made sure the country was fully aware of the Cowboys' thousand-page résumé of misdeeds. There was the White House. There was Erik Williams's drunk-driving accident, as well as charges of sexual assault by the sixteen-year-old topless dancer. There were the drug-related suspensions of Leon Lett and Clayton Holmes. There was defensive end Shante Carver, who during the '94 season wrecked his truck in an accident, but reported it stolen to the police. (Carver would also be suspended six games in '96 for violating the league's substance-abuse policy.) There was wide receiver Cory Fleming, who failed the drug-and-alcohol test administered to him immediately before Super Bowl XXX and was subsequently released. There was, of course, Irvin, who arrived at a south Dallas drug treatment center for his first day of community service accompanied by an entourage of seven hangers-on. "We should have policed ourselves," says Chad Hennings. "When I was in the military, anyone who messed up would be pulled aside and told, 'You're screwing up, and it can cost lives.' In Dallas, it wasn't costing lives. But it was costing livelihoods."

The Cowboys were crumbling. Fans still filed into Texas Stadium in 1996, but the connection between Average Joe and Football Star had disintegrated. Whereas Cowboy die-hards once pulled earnestly for men like Irvin and Lett, now they felt fewer and fewer emotional connections. Drug users? Strip club patrons? Criminals? These were the Cowboys? *Our Cowboys?* Fans love players they can relate to. But who could relate *to this*?

Without their game-breaking receiver and emotional spark plug, the Cowboys were lost. They went 2–3 to start the '96 season, then celebrated Irvin's return by struggling against the woeful Arizona Cardinals in a lackluster 17–3 victory. "We're not close to being a championship team," Darren Woodson said afterward. "If we think getting Michael back fixes everything, we're kidding ourselves."

By now, it was painfully clear that Jones's decision to run Jimmy

Johnson out of Dallas had been a gargantuan mistake. Perhaps Jones was correct that any moron with a clipboard could have coached the '92 and '93 Cowboys to Super Bowls. But Johnson was more than a coach. He was a guru. When Switzer arrived in 1994, so did the first NFL salary cap, which limited teams to $34.6 million in player salaries. Jones was successful in many fields—salary cap management *not* being one of them. "Jimmy understood franchise construction better than Jerry or Barry," says Larry Lacewell, the director of college and pro scouting. "He would have been on top of free agency, would have found a way to figure it out."

With Jones serving as the primary decision-maker, the Cowboys blew a third straight draft, using their first pick in 1996 to select defensive end Kavika Pittman out of McNeese State (ouch), then following with linebacker Randall Godfrey (solid), center Clay Shiver (ouch), wide receiver Stepfret Williams (ouch), defensive lineman Mike Ulufale (ouch), offensive lineman Kenneth McDaniel (ouch), linebacker Alan Campos (ouch), defensive back Wendell Davis (ouch), and running back Ryan Wood (ouch). Save for Godfrey, who enjoyed a productive four-team, eleven-year NFL career, all were busts. "Jerry has done a phenomenal job promoting the franchise," says Hennings. "But is he a football guy? Does he know the Xs and Os? Does he know personnel? It's like the Ronald Reagan principle—you have the best people around, delegate, and stay the hell out of the way. That's where the downfall of the Cowboys organization starts. Sometimes Jerry needs to stay out of the way."

Under Johnson's reign, every Cowboy knew whom he had to answer to. Now, if Switzer called for a meeting and Sanders had a problem with the time, he'd take matters into his own hands. On multiple occasions, Sanders was told he needed to arrive at Valley Ranch for, say, a 7:30 A.M. training session. "And Deion would say, 'Well, that ain't gonna work for my schedule,'" says Jean-Jacques Taylor, the *Morning News* beat writer. "'Let's call 952 [Jones's extension] and see about that.'" Sanders would connect with Jones, ask for the training to be pushed back an hour, and without fail hear the owner say, "Sure. No problem. I'll tell Barry."

In the best of times, Johnson would never, ever, *ever* allow such behavior. Yes, he had his favorite players. Yes, he gave leeway to the stars. But nobody—not even Jones—walked all over the coach. If a meeting was scheduled for 7:30, you damn well better have arrived at 7:15.

"When you look at the best leaders in history, whether we're talking militarily or professional sports, there's usually one voice," says Dave Campo, the Dallas defensive coordinator. "Jerry never tried to coach the football team, but he felt it important to be involved in everything. That doesn't work."

Less than a year after winning the Super Bowl, Switzer had been all but officially reduced to a token. On multiple occasions he would arrive at team meetings still smelling of liquor from the previous night. "To see him in front of a squad in that condition just killed me," says Tony Casillas, the defensive lineman who had played for Switzer at Oklahoma and rejoined the Cowboys in 1996 after two seasons with the Jets. "It was time for him to move on."

Switzer relied on assistants to design the game plan, relied on Jones to judge, acquire, and maintain the players, relied on Rich Dalrymple, the media relations head, to keep the reporters informed. "I don't think he cared to be the head coach anymore," says Dale Hellestrae, the veteran lineman. "When it's ten o'clock in the morning and it's raining in Dallas and you've got to figure out where you're going to practice and your head coach isn't even in yet—that says something, doesn't it?"

Through all the drama, the biggest bombshell of 1996 came with the release of a book, *Hell-Bent,* written by local scribe Skip Bayless. Billed as a biography that would spill the "crazy truth" of the '95 Cowboys, the prime rib of Bayless's text emerged out of a six-page span in which the author suggested Aikman was gay.

Wrote Bayless: "I had heard the rumor since 1991. An off-duty Dallas police officer who traveled with the Cowboys and worked security at their hotels first told me that 'the word on the street' was that Troy Aikman is gay. Over the next four years, I heard the rumor from two more police officers who worked around the team (and I know they mentioned it to team officials). One officer told me Aikman 'was supposed to be' having a relationship with a male member of a country-western band."

While Bayless attempted to ward off critics by noting that *Hell-Bent* featured 284 pages *not* dealing with Aikman's sexual orientation, he had broken two written-in-blood journalistic tenets:

A. Don't out people for the sake of book sales.
B. If you decide to ignore Rule A, know what the hell you're talking about.

Aikman had dated his first girlfriend for seven years, and arrived in Dallas in 1989 in the midst of another serious relationship. "I know for a fact that Troy was having sex with women who, quite frankly, he knew he would never call," says Dale Hansen, the veteran announcer. "Skip thought it was suspicious that Troy had spoken of taking an AIDS test. Well, knowing some of the women Troy slept with, I'd have gotten an AIDS test too."

In short, if he was gay, Aikman was putting on one hell of an act.

Such details mattered not to the attention-obsessed Bayless. *Hell-Bent* was neither righteous nor journalistic, and neither was its author. "While he was working on the book Skip would call me all excited and tell me that he got information about Troy being in the back of a car in a gay area of Melrose," says Dean Blevins, the veteran Dallas radio host. "My reaction was, 'Why are you telling me this? And why are you so happy about it?'" As a former muckraking columnist for Dallas's *Morning News* and *Times Herald*, Bayless was one of the first scribes to hire an agent; one of the first scribes to be featured on billboards; one of the first scribes to negotiate for perks like a company car and stock options. It was often said the best way to torture Bayless was to remove the I key from his laptop. Frank Luksa, a local columnist who refused to speak with Bayless, nicknamed him "Baby Jesus." The tag stuck.

"Skip Bayless could have been one of the really great columnists," says Dave Smith, the legendary *Morning News* sports editor. "But as a columnist, if you're going to beat up on someone, it better be from your heart. You better feel that way. Skip attacked people just for the sake of doing it. His gay take on Aikman was the most unfair thing in my forty-five years in journalism."

When Aikman learned of *Hell-Bent*'s contents, he confided in an attorney, asking what the fallout would be were he to sue and/or slug the writer. "If I've learned one thing covering sports, it's that if you're young, successful, and single, the gay thing will inevitably come up," says Randy Galloway, the veteran columnist. "Skip should have been ashamed."

Aikman found himself in a thankless jam. He could respond to Bayless's book and give it credibility or ignore Bayless's book and allow the rumors to fly. "It's just like politics," says Hennings. "The feces sticks to the walls." As word spread across the country that he might be gay . . . could be gay . . . was probably gay . . . was definitely gay . . . had a boyfriend named Serge . . . was dating another Cowboy . . . loved *Terms of Endearment* and shopping for linens . . . the quarterback remained silent and fumed. Meanwhile, Bayless laughed all the way to the bank.

Hell-Bent became one of the year's best-selling sports books.

Dallas rebounded from the poor start, the unyielding distractions, and a subpar year from Aikman (who compiled 12 touchdown passes and 13 interceptions) to win five of its final seven regular-season games in 1996. The Cowboys earned a wild-card slot in the NFC playoffs. But on December 31, three days after Dallas thrashed the Vikings 40–15 to advance to a divisional playoff clash with the Carolina Panthers, yet another atomic bomb landed atop Valley Ranch.

According to the Dallas police, an unidentified twenty-three-year-old woman complained that, on the prior Sunday night, Irvin had held a gun to her head as Erik Williams and an unidentified man raped her. Well versed in the sordid tales of Irvin and the Cowboys, the media attacked. Dave Anderson, the normally mild-mannered *New York Times* columnist, even penned a piece titled THE COWBOYS SHOULD BAN IRVIN NOW. "If [Jerry] Jones needs a reason, Irvin has provided several," Anderson wrote. "Stupidity. Arrogance. Or, simply, having embarrassed the Cowboys and the NFL again."

That Irvin and Williams were later proven to be innocent was of no consequence. That the twenty-three-year-old woman, a former topless dancer named Nina "Rio" Shahravan, had concocted the entire tale was of no consequence. That the media had fumbled badly was of no consequence. The franchise was battered—in the executive offices, in the community, inside the locker room. The Cowboys traveled to Carolina, played nearly the entire game without Irvin (who was injured on Dallas's second offensive play), and saw their Super Bowl aspirations blow up with a 26–17 defeat.

"Troy wouldn't want to hear this, but he lost his security blanket when Mike got hurt in that game, and his whole demeanor in the huddle changed," says Ray Donaldson, the Cowboys center. "He was chewing out the receivers, cursing and yelling when they dropped a pass or made the wrong turn on a route, acting real nervous. And if your quarterback is like that, you're dead." In the visiting locker room after the game, an unambiguous tension lingered between jocks and journalists. When asked to explain the setback, Newton snapped at Mike Freeman of the *New York Times*, "You guys are the reason we lost this game."

It was, to be kind, a simplistic viewpoint.

And that was that. The Dynasty of the 1990s was over.

Oh, there were flashes here and there. Following Switzer's humiliating arrest for storing a loaded revolver in his carry-on bag at Dallas–Fort Worth International Airport in August, Dallas opened the 1997 season by winning three of its first four games, and talk was of a team refreshed and rejuvenated. But with talent diminished by age and free agency, Switzer's club slumped badly, finishing with a 6–10 mark and missing the postseason for the first time since 1990.

"In previous years it wasn't enough to just win," says Taylor, the *Morning News* writer. "You had to win in a certain way. In the late nineties it started coming off as, 'Well, we won. How many teams would love to be in our situation?' Once you start thinking like that your downfall has begun, because the drive for perfection has stopped."

Especially damaging was the impact of the Cowboys' $35 million cornerback. Following the '96 season, Sanders—who later confessed that, beneath the flash, he was terribly depressed—intentionally steered his car off a cliff in an attempted suicide. Upon surviving, he denounced his past and devoted his life to serving Jesus Christ. To his credit, Sanders woke up to the idea that flashy jewelry and fast cars do not guarantee happiness. To his discredit, he needed to express this new enlightenment to absolutely everyone. Sanders turned into a walking JESUS SAVES billboard, urging all to see the light and attend the ever-increasing number of Bible study sessions held at Valley Ranch.

For the devoutly Christian Cowboys who were called to Jesus the way men like Irvin, Haley, and Newton were called to fishnet stockings, Sanders was the perfect teammate. For the rest of the players, though, he was an annoying distraction. Where was the Sanders who talked trash? Who took his greatest pride in shutting down receivers? In sports, it's no secret that while zealously religious teams might be bound for the pearly gates, they rarely win. "When Deion found God, football study time turned into Bible study time, and a lot of us didn't like that," says Kevin Smith, the veteran cornerback. "Guys should be studying football on a Wednesday at twelve o'clock instead of going to a forty-five-minute Bible study. So what happens is Deion gets all the bottom feeders to follow his lead because he's Deion Sanders. And before long the emphasis on football is woefully reduced."

An especially contentious locker room issue centered on the team's official chaplain. For fifteen years, the position had been held by John Weber, a former collegiate wrestler at Dakota Wesleyan University who approached Christianity in a soft, genteel manner. Sanders felt Weber's mannerisms weren't bombastic enough for a football team, and did his all to have the Cowboys replace him with Terry Hornbuckle, the high-octane founder of Arlington's Victory Temple Bible Church. The ensuing debate among Cowboy players turned racial. The whites supported Weber, who was also white, while most African-Americans leaned toward Hornbuckle, an African-American. "So even though the Cowboys never admitted it, we brought in Hornbuckle because Deion demanded it," says Kevin Smith. "He was there every Wednesday during Bible study, talking up God and all. Personally, I didn't back that change. It didn't seem fair and it led to a whole lot of negativity."

Hornbuckle failed to last long with the Cowboys, which was probably a good thing. Nine years later he would be convicted by a Tarrant County jury on rape charges involving three young women, including two members of his church.

If there was one thing Jerry Jones was certain of entering the 1998 season, it was that his franchise was about to rediscover its greatness. Sometimes, the Cowboy owner believed, dramatic change—no matter how risky or unpopular—could result in wondrous things. "It's not always pleasant," Jones says. "But leadership means making tough decisions."

Hence, after two frustrating, mediocre seasons, Jones urged his head coach to resign. He still respected Switzer; hell, he loved Switzer like a brother. But even Jones, too often blinded by loyalty to his inept friend, could see the reality: Switzer was not capable of leading a Dallas renaissance. That January, a heavy-hearted Switzer stepped aside. "I knew what I had to do," Switzer says. "I was sad, but I knew."

As a replacement, Jones went outside of his personal circle, announcing on February 12, 1998, that he was hiring a well-respected Pittsburgh Steelers offensive coordinator named Chan Gailey.

Ironically, with Gailey's arrival Jones had come full circle—the man who had famously fired Tom Landry had now hired Tom Landry *minus the hat* (and, apparently, the ability and know-how). Gailey was a no-nonsense disciplinarian; a devout Christian; a soft speaker who rarely wore his emotions on his sleeve. Yet the new leader of the Cowboys had no idea what he was walking into. Namely, a cornucopia of arrogance and laziness and indifference and zealotry. Namely, a nightmare.

If the Cowboys maintained any hope of recapturing what they had lost in discipline and preparedness after the Jimmy Johnson years, they needed a throwback—a take-no-crap drill sergeant who would pound men into the ground, then bring them back up with stirring, Lombardi-esque spewings. They needed a coach who would confront Sanders and say, more or less, "I love Jesus too—now get him the hell out of my locker room!" They needed a coach who would gather the impressionable younger players into a room, point to a picture of Aikman or safety Darren Woodson, the team's two hardest workers and most unselfish members, and say, "Follow them." They needed a coach who knew Xs and Os, but who more important knew how to delegate to his assistants. They needed a coach who could stand up to Jerry Jones and say, "If you draft Kavika Pittman, I will bust you up." They needed a coach who knew what it meant to be a Dallas Cowboy; who respected the history and believed in the future.

Really, they needed Jimmy Johnson. Or at least somebody like him.

Alas, the new coach was no Jimmy Johnson.

Gailey was only five months into his new job on that fateful afternoon of July 29, 1998, when Michael Irvin, heart of the Cowboys, took his barber's scissors and thrust them into the neck of Everett McIver, the gargantuan offensive lineman. Gailey was horrified—by the act, of course. But surely also by the aftermath. As the eighteen-stitch gash on

McIver's neck gradually healed, Jones did everything in his power to make certain the incident disappeared. Really, to make certain Irvin—already on probation for cocaine possession—would not be shipped off to jail.

Once upon a time, when Jones first bought the Cowboys and installed Johnson as his head coach, the organization had preached accountability. You miss a block, you admit it. You skip a meeting, you face the consequences. When Jones was hammered by the Dallas media for the cutthroat manner in which he fired Landry, he stepped up and admitted wrongdoing.

But now, nearly a decade later, the Cowboys were engaged in a full-scale cover-up. McIver was offered a high-six-figure payoff to keep the story under wraps. (He accepted.) Gailey publicly dismissed the brawl as "horseplay." When those involved in what came to be known as "Scissorsgate" met with the judge overseeing Irvin's probation, they laughed it off as a simple case of McIver's having engulfed Irvin in a bear hug that led to some playful wrestling and an accidental cut. No big deal. *Ha, ha, ha, hee, hee, hee.*

Of course, the incident *was* a big deal. A *huge* deal. Though the Cowboys under Jimmy Johnson and Barry Switzer often lacked discipline, their talent always compensated. Now, discipline was at an all-time low, and the talent was fading fast. Gailey would guide the Cowboys to a 10–6 record and first-round playoff loss, then last just one more season before being fired after an 8–8 debacle. "Chan tried his best," says Denne Freeman, who covered the Cowboys for the Associated Press. "But he probably didn't realize the mess he was getting into."

In the end, Gailey could do only so much with so little. With his skills in decline and his brain scrambled by repeated concussions, Aikman was never again a marquee player. In 2000 he threw for 7 touchdowns and 14 interceptions, then retired. Though Emmitt Smith lasted with Dallas through 2002, he, too, was gradually slipping. The drive and determination that had been a hallmark of his early years was replaced by selfishness and a single-minded personal goal—to become the league's all-time leading rusher. Smith exceeded 1,200 yards in each of the 1998, '99, and '00 seasons, but in the words of one teammate, "didn't give a shit about us anymore. He was all about Emmitt, Emmitt, Emmitt." Like far too many faded stars, Smith saw his career end ingloriously: Left for dead by the Cowboys, he played the 2003 and '04 seasons with the lowly Arizona Cardinals, running tentatively behind a porous offensive line and bringing to mind Willie Mays's sad final days with the Mets. He retired with an unparalleled 18,355 career rushing yards, but with his dignity tarnished.

Irvin, meanwhile, suffered the harshest blow. In a game at Philadelphia during the 1999 season, Eagles defensive back Tim Hauck tackled him head-first into the turf. As Irvin lay motionless on the Veterans Stadium field, suffering from temporary paralysis, Philadelphia's fans stood and cheered. Finally, they had found a way to stop The Playmaker. "That was as big a victory as we'd had in Philly since the 1980 World Series," says Brian Hickey, former managing editor of the *Philadelphia City Paper* and one of the loudest hecklers that day. "That guy killed us for years, and finally we took him out."

Irvin's malady—a cervical spinal cord injury—was more serious than anyone imagined. Doctors told the receiver he was born with such a fragile spinal cord that, should he continue with his NFL career, a future injury of grave consequence was likely.

He would never play football again.

"That was huge," says Woodson. "It cut out the heart of our team."

To some, Irvin's downfall was an isolated tragedy, the sad decline of a once-great wide receiver. To others, it was the natural continuation of an event that had occurred fifteen months earlier, when Irvin took a scissors to the neck of Everett McIver.

The blood covering the floor that day did not drain merely from a man, but from a franchise.

Chapter 26

REBIRTH

I ran the fast life and I never stopped and thought,
How is this affecting my family? How is this affecting
my kids? How does this affect the public perception of me?
When you're walking with a clouded mind like I did, you can't
see the things you're doing wrong. But when that cloud is
lifted you see the errors of your ways. Do I regret it? Yes.
Would I change it? No way in hell.

—Nate Newton, Cowboys offensive lineman

ON THE AFTERNOON of August 3, 2007, Michael Irvin wandered into the McKinley Grand hotel in downtown Canton, Ohio, and paced the hallways. He paced left. He paced right. He wiggled his fingers and twitched his toes and took one nervous breath after another. When someone asked for a photograph, Irvin smiled widely. When a group of kids requested his autograph, Irvin signed away.

But behind the façade was a genuinely un-Irvin reaction—The Playmaker was nervous.

In roughly twenty-four hours, Irvin would be called upon to make a speech at his Pro Football Hall of Fame induction ceremony, and the man who was never, ever, *ever* at a loss for words was coming up blank. "I have no idea what I'm gonna say," he muttered, shrugging his shoulders. "I mean, I have a lot of things in my head that I want to get out. I'm thinking of just going up there and speaking from the heart."

Standing several feet away, former Bills running back and fellow inductee Thurman Thomas possessed the carefree look of a retiree on a hammock—he had written his speech long ago. The same went for the other inductees: Charlie Sanders, Bruce Matthews, and Roger Wehrli. (Gene Hickerson was ill, so his son, Bob, would speak on his behalf.) They were all relaxed, all prepared, all enjoying the moment. "I'm sure I'll be OK," Irvin said. "Well, I think I might be probably OK."

The following evening the Dallas Cowboys' all-time leading receiver, who had retired with 750 receptions, 11,904 yards, 65 touchdowns, and three Super Bowl championships, strode to a podium inside Fawcett Stadium. He took several deep breaths, looked out among the thousands of faces, and just . . . spoke.

He spoke about his boyhood in Fort Lauderdale, Florida, where seventeen brothers and sisters shared two bedrooms. He spoke about his collegiate career at the University of Miami, where he learned that a merging of hard work and swagger conquers all.

Mostly, he spoke about a man who had once believed the only way to live was lavishly and the only speed to travel was 5 million mph. He looked at Sandy, his wife of seventeen years, and apologized for violating her trust, and looked toward his mother, Pearl, and thanked her for creating a man.

Then he asked his sons, Michael, ten, and Elijah, eight, to rise. The tears streamed from Irvin's eyes and onto his cheeks, where they nestled like tiny ponds.

"That's my heart right there," he said, pointing to his offspring. "That's my heart. When I am on that threshing floor, I pray. I say, 'God, I have my struggles and I made some bad decisions, but whatever you do, whatever you do, don't let me mess this up.'

"I say, 'Please, help me raise them for some young lady so that they can be a better husband than I. Help me raise them for their kids so that they could be a better father than I.' And I tell you guys to always do the right thing so you can be a better role model than Dad. I sat right here where you are last year and I watched the Class of 2006: Troy Aikman, Warren Moon, Harry Carson, Rayfield Wright, John Madden, and the late, great Reggie White represented by his wife, Sara White. And I said, 'Wow. That's what a Hall of Famer is.'"

Irvin's voice cracked. His tears streamed rapidly. Here was a broken man. Here was a saved man.

"Certainly, I am not that," he continued. "I doubted I would ever have the chance to stand before you today. So when I returned home I spoke with Michael and Elijah. I said, 'That's how you do it, son. You do it like they did it.' Michael asked, he said, 'Dad, do you ever think we will be there?' And I didn't know how to answer that. And it returned me to that threshing floor. This time I was voiceless, but my heart cried out . . .

"I wanted to stand in front of my boys and say, 'Do it like your dad'—like any proud dad would want to. Why must I go through so much? At that moment a voice came over me and said, 'Look up, get up, and don't ever give up. You tell everyone or anyone that has ever doubted, thought they did not measure up, or wanted to quit, you tell them to look up, get up, and don't ever give up.'

"Thank you, and may God bless you."

For a moment, the 12,787 spectators made nary a sound. Then the applause began—tepid at first, but building rapidly. By the time Irvin took a step back, he was overwhelmed by the roar of human thunder. An explosion that lasted and lasted *and lasted*.

Among those in attendance were two dozen former Cowboy teammates, including Aikman, Emmitt Smith, Jay Novacek, Nate Newton, Steve Walsh, James Washington, and Darren Woodson. They were present to support their friend, but also to bear witness to his rebirth. Many of the old Cowboys had changed their ways with the passing of years. They looked back at the strip clubs and hookers and Cowboys Café with both joy and humiliation—joy over the excitement and camaraderie of it all, humiliation over having treated women not as people, but objects; over having naïvely believed fame and fortune were God-given rights, not temporary luxuries; over discarding wives and children for short-lived excesses; over trading in humility for ego.

Just a few years earlier, Newton had paid a visit to Robert Jones, the former Cowboys linebacker, to set things straight. Through his years in Dallas Jones had been faithful to his wife and children, and countless teammates had mocked him for it. "I'm so sorry how I treated you when we were in Dallas," Newton said to Jones. "You were one of the guys who lived his life the way it's supposed to be lived, and now look at you. You're still with your wife. I'm divorced, and she was a good woman. You did things the right way and we made fun of you for it. We were wrong."

It was eerily similar to an encounter that took place on October 15, 2001, when Jones was in his final NFL season, with the Redskins. Before a game against the Cowboys, Jones was told by a teammate that Irvin was outside the locker room asking for him. During their time together in Dallas, the two players had loathed each other. In Jones's mind, Irvin was a bully who felt compelled to harass anyone refusing to live the fast life. And now Irvin wanted *him*? No way. "Man, you're full of shit," said Jones. "No way Mike's out there." Yet when Jones stuck his head through door, there was Irvin. He hugged Jones and kissed him on the cheek. "What's that for?" Jones asked.

"Man, I'm so proud of you," Irvin said. "And I apologize for everything I ever did to you. You were righteous. I wasn't."

Now, in Canton, with the jersey-wearing and face-painted fans having departed and darkness settling in, Irvin was hosting a party in a large tent on the Hall grounds. There were mounds of food. White leather couches and cascading floral arrangements. The Pointer Sisters singing their hits. Jerry Jones dancing away as his wife, Gene, sat in the rear and laughed over a handful of plain M&M's. Early on, Irvin called for all his former teammates to climb atop the stage for a group photograph. Among those present were Erik Williams, once responsible for a near-fatal DUI accident; Washington, who had chased after women with an unquenchable thirst; Newton, the man arrested in 2001 for smuggling a mere 213 pounds of marijuana.

More than a decade after their Super Bowl XXX triumph, these Cowboys were different men. Fat had replaced muscle. Gray hairs had started to take up turf. Some possessed run-of-the-mill, 9-to-5 jobs. Others had undergone religious transformations. Washington, once a trash-talking safety, was now a smooth-talking Los Angeles radio host. Even Newton, the largest of the large livers, was primarily focused on helping his son Tré, a star running back at Southlake Carroll High School, attain a college scholarship. (He went on to sign with the University of Texas.)

By 1:30 A.M., the stars who had once reigned over the Dallas nightlife were all gone, back to their hotels and snuggled beneath the covers. In fact, only one member of the Cowboys remained. His tie loosened, the top button of his white dress shirt undone, the man led his wife onto the dance floor and gently kissed her cheek. As the couple began a slow groove, Michael Irvin smiled widely.

It was a facial expression millions of Cowboys fans had come to know. Once upon a time, Michael Irvin smiled when he scored touchdowns. He smiled when he won Super Bowls. He smiled as he strolled into court, a mink coat draped over his shoulders. He even smiled in police mug shots.

Now Michael Irvin was smiling for the purest of reasons.

At long last, he knew what it was to be on top of the world.

He was whole.

★

ACKNOWLEDGMENTS

---

*What you have to understand is that you can't kill
the Cowboys. You can do this book and write all the things
you want, but you can't kill the Cowboys.*

—Nate Newton (to me), January 18, 2007

I am sitting in the café at the Borders in Eastchester, New York—the spot where I have written, oh, 60 percent of this book. Behind the counter is LaToya David, a twenty-four-year-old woman who, two days ago, was mugged while waiting for the bus to take her back home.

On the six days per week that she works, LaToya makes the fifty-minute commute from the Bronx to Eastchester. She spends seven hours here at Borders, slinging defrosted cinnamon scones and over-priced café au lait bullshit to schlubs like me, then drags herself across Post Road for another five hours behind the cash register at Ann Taylor. When LaToya's not working, she cares for her ill grandfather.

Last week LaToya asked her manager at Ann Taylor whether she could slightly alter her schedule to find more time for Grandpa. "Maybe," she was told, "you need to go someplace else."

Every day I take a few minutes and watch LaToya gracefully go about her tasks—make the coffee, heat the bagels, clean the tables, make more coffee. She is a bright young woman stuck in a horrid situation—a person worthy of attending college, not attending to the crazy lady who sits here twelve hours per day sipping from a large cup of hot chocolate while babbling on about Bob Barker's lovely white hair.

Yet mixed in with my feelings of empathy for LaToya is a huge dose of fulfillment. Really, of *appreciation*. Here I am, thirty-six years old, married to a wife I don't deserve, gifted with two healthy children, getting paid to complete my third book. I am, in every sense of the word, blessed.

Hence, this is the last time I will ever include the sentence "Writing a book is a nightmare" in my acknowledgments. Because while it can, indeed, seem nightmarish (*Dammit! Why hasn't Tom Myslinski called me back?*), the experience is literally a dream come true.

As a boy growing up in Mahopac, New York, I would scan the shelves of the public library, burning through biographies of men like Bo Jackson and Rod Carew and Terry Bradshaw and Joe Charboneau (yes, Super Joe). Now I'm the one doing the writing.

Mind-blowing.

Though the praise and scorn heaped upon a book goes directly to the author, it is—like football—a team effort. To that end, I have been gifted with a pair of editors who are not mere coworkers, but friends. David Hirshey—thanks for the chance to continue to write for HarperCollins. The support and guidance have been invaluable. And to Kate Hamill, the baddest MC this side of Slick Rick, big props on the gangsta tip for keeping it old school and poppin'. Word.

My agent, David Black, continues to thrash the notion that his is a profession for rodents and gnats. David, you are a great man, a great sounding board, a great evaluator, and the best agent in the biz. One thousand thanks.

Finding a reporter who doesn't merely go through the motions can be challenging, but fortunately, I've teamed with the Troy Aikman of the profession. Casey Angle, thank you so much for taking this project personally. *Boys Will Be Boys* is your book as much as it is mine (just don't ask for royalties). Furthermore, Tom Cherwin is the best copyeditor I have ever had the pleasure of writing for. The meticulousness is priceless.

My top proofreaders happen to be two of my closest friends, and their dedication over the years can't be overstated. The ultra-talented Michael J. Lewis of the *Daytona Beach News-Journal* is not only one of the finest scribes I know, but a man finally wise enough to ditch the denim jacket and J-E-T-S necklace. (Moment of silence for Adrian Murrell. Thank you.) And while Paul Duer, the onetime Edna's Edibles co-captain, is not a journalist by trade, he possesses a keen eye for what belongs (and doesn't belong) in a sports biography. Now if only he'd trust me on Josh Hamilton . . .

I spoke to 146 Cowboy players, coaches, and administrators for this book, and from Jimmy Johnson and Jerry Jones to Nate Newton and Tommy Hodson, I want to thank them all for the honest recollections of some crazy days. In particular, I'd like to cite the contributions of Kenny Gant, James Washington, Eric Bjornson, Jeff Rohrer, Kevin Gogan, Jay Novacek, Cory Fleming, Hugh Millen, Bill Bates, Michael Irvin, Ray Horton, Kevin Smith, Cliff Stoudt, Mark Stepnoski, Dennis McKinnon, Crawford Ker, Rob Awalt, Dave Harper, Joe Fishback, Rob Higbee, John Gesek, Jim Jeffcoat, Russell Maryland, Chad Hennings, Alexander (Ace) Wright, and Larry Brown. An extra shout-out goes to three remarkable men—Robert Jones, Darren Woodson, and Clayton Holmes—whose lives serve as both lessons and inspirations. And a big thank-you to Barry Switzer, who opened his wide swath of memories to my pen.

This book could not have been completed without the assistance of a cornucopia of characters: Mike Murphy, the sage attorney who initially said, "How about the '90s Cowboys?" when I was thinking my next project might be: *I Sing, Too!: The John Oates Story*; Denne Freeman, a wonderful writer who took the time to add his Dallas-based knowledge; Jeff Donaldson of the Irvine Spectrum Center Apple Store, who rescued my battered MacBook and whose Flux Capacitor tattoo will never escape my mind; Kaitlin Ingram of the *Dallas Observer*; Ileana Pena of Fox Sports; Rich Dalrymple of the Dallas Cowboys; Gary Miller of Raleigh Canine Rescue, Inc.; Kyran Cassidy; Joy Birdsong and Natasha Simon of the *Sports Illustrated* library; David

Schoenfield and Thomas Newman of ESPN.com; Bev Oden of the Oden Family Jug Band; Stanley Herz, author of the amazing *Conquering the Corporate Career*; Arthur Haviland, publicist to the stars; David Kolberg, who doesn't exist; the always smooth Nick Trautwein; Brian (Deep Throat) Johnson; Professor Bill Fleischman; Laurel Turnbull; Mike Freeman of *CBS Sportsline*; Mike Silver of Yahoo Sports; Jarrett Bell; Dean Blevins; Rick Cantu; Larry Charlton; Jody Dean; Jim Dent; Mike Doocy; Bruce Feldman; Kenn Finkel; Mike Fisher; Randy Galloway; Rob Geiger; Mark Godich; Rick Gosselin; Dale Hansen; Norm Hitzges; Barry Horn; Mark Kegans; Joe Layden; Richie Whitt; Frank Luksa; Ivan Maisel; Mike McAlister; Gary Myers; Burl Osborne; Jeff Prugh; Brad Sham; Dave Smith; Mickey Spagnolia; Anne Stockwell; Carson Stowers; Jean-Jacques Taylor; Dave Tepps; Chris Worthington; Larry, Diane, Phoebe, James, and Mookie Luftig (aka The Bad Ronald Fan Club); Kim and Colleen O'Neill; Anthony (Paco) Montoya; Steve Cannella and Jon Wertheim—two excellent friends/sounding boards; David (Doovie) Pearlman; Daniel, Naya, and Abraham Pearlman; Dr. Martin Pearlman; Patsy Clay; Leah Guggenheimer, Jordan and Isaiah Williams; Laura and Rodney Cole; Meghan Scott; Richard, Susan, and Dr. Jessica Guggenheimer; Norma "What's a House Without a Proper Dresser?" Shapiro; Dan, Patrice, and Kyle Monaghan; Reginald Anderson; Lance Lionetti (the biggest Cowboy fan I've ever seen); Gary Galvao (the second-biggest Cowboy fan I've ever seen); Richard Howell—a fair and honest man in an otherwise sketchy industry; Gil Pagovich; Gloria Chebomui of the Mirage Diner (the refills were always appreciated); Bill Oram, Paula Arrojo; the staff of the Regency Hotel in North Dallas, where the smiles are toothy and the shower liners laced with mysterious hairs.

My parents, Joan and Stan Pearlman, continue to serve as my greatest role models and friends. *(Mom, Dad—the Cowboys are a football team. Football . . . that game with the weird ball. They have that Super Bowl thing. Yeah, on a Sunday . . . with all the food . . . eh, never mind.)*

I've seen many marriages, and none match the kinship I have

formed with my incomparable wife, Catherine. In the course of writing this book I had the opportunity to sleep with hundreds of Dallas Cowboys cheerleaders. Because of the unconditional love I possess for my wife, I only took up offers from twelve of them (but I rarely enjoyed it).

Earlie, I write for you.

I am also blessed with two children who have reminded me every day that, when push comes to shove, there are more important things than the intricacies of Leon Lett's sprained knee. Casey, you are everything I've ever dreamed about in a daughter. Emmett, my beautiful (and appropriately named) boy—*fish*!

Lastly, I'd like to dedicate this book to the memory of four people: Henry Capro, who never left home without his pocketknife; Heather Fleischman, whose bylines would have sparkled; J. P. O'Neill, who deserved ninety years of Cowboy fandom; and Ann Goldstein, my great-aunt, who died far too young to know the euphoria that is life.

ENDNOTES

Chapter 1: Scissors to the Neck

2   **When Gene Upshaw visited Dallas minicamp** Randy Galloway, "Personality of Irvin Has a Catch," *Dallas Morning News*,
May 29, 1993.

4   **When Morquisha reached three** Jamie Aron, "A Memory
Drives a Cowboys' Lineman," Associated Press, September
20, 1999.

5   **"He's an example of how if you have skill"** Ibid.

6   **"I just lost it," said Irvin. "I mean, my head, I lost it."** Julie Lyons, "Think Mike," *Dallas Observer*, September 5, 2002.

7   **The tip of the scissors ripped into McIver's skin** Kevin O'Keeffe,
"Smooth move, Jerry: Make Irvin pay up," *San Antonio
Express-News*, August 10, 1998.

Chapter 2: Save Your Gas

9   **"As far back as I can remember,"** Kent Demaret, "Tom Landry is
a Believer: In Himself, His Printouts, His Cowboys and His
Lord," *People* magazine, December 18, 1977.

9   **He crashed but once, following a bombing run over Czecho-**

slovakia. Edwin Shrake, "QB or Not QB: That Is the Question," *Sports Illustrated*, December 10, 1973.

10   **Clint Williams Murchinson, Jr., was willing to take the risk** William Oscar Johnson, "There Are No Holes at the Top," *Sports Illustrated*, September 1, 1982.

10   **"People want to know what makes Tom tick** Shrake, "QB or Not QB: That Is the Question."

10   **Schramm offered Landry a five-year contract paying $35,000** Johnson, "There Are No Holes at the Top."

11   **"LeBaron used to raise his hand for a fair catch** David Moore, "Building America's Team," www.dallasnews.com, no date.

11   **The Cowboys practiced in Burnett Field** Tom Landry with Greg Lewis, *Tom Landry: An Autobiography*, p. 135

12   **"The America's Team concept had swept the country," said Henderson** Skip Bayless, *God's Coach*, p. 148.

14   **Bright had first met Landry in 1957** Peter Golenbock, *Cowboys Have Always Been My Heroes*, p. 693.

14   **Fast forward to 1988, when Bright's holdings** Ibid., p. 710.

15   **"Bum would like to see the Cowboys** Paul Duke, Jr., "Like Many Other Texas Institutions, the Cowboys Haven't Found a Buyer," *Wall Street Journal*, September 8, 1988.

15   **An obscure Arkansas oil driller with a cache** Ibid.

17   **"Jonesie had this unique way of verbalizing** Jim Dent, *King of the Cowboys*, p. 54.

17   **"Nobody," *Sports Illustrated*'s Ed Hinton once wrote,** Ed Hinton, "Deep into His Job," *Sports Illustrated*, September 7, 1992.

18   **Hence, in 1988 Jones managed to spend** Ron Borges, "Dallas Maverick," *Boston Globe*, January 31, 1993.

19   **Located on Lemmon Avenue in Dallas's Uptown area** Joe Simnacher, "Rites Are Wednesday for Mia's Co-Founder," *Dallas Morning News*, January 9, 2001.

20   **People literally drove across the state to indulge** Patricia Sharpe, John Morthland, June Naylor, William Albright, and Eric Gerber, "The Greatest Tacos Ever Sold," *Texas Monthly*, December 2006.

21   **On the morning of February 25, 1989** Bernie Miklasz, "Cowboys Sale Near; Landry Likely Out," *Dallas Morning News*, February 25, 1989.

23   **Bright later presented Jones with a quarter** Matt Mosley, "Jones:

'I Just Remember It Being Overwhelming,'" *Dallas Web*, February 25, 2004.

23 **As if the big news of the day were a 4H bake sale** Jim Dent, *King of the Cowboys*, pp. 96–99.

24 **Normally cool under pressure** Ibid., p 98.

26 *This will be our last . . . meeting* Golenbock, p. 716.

Chapter 3: The Right Man

29 "**We haven't done half a dozen things** Ed Hinton, "Deep into His Job," *Sports Illustrated*, September 7, 1992.

29 "**Jimmy never thought there was any difference** Ibid.

29 **With rare exception, Johnson was** Ibid.

30 **He was nicknamed "Scar Head" by a childhood buddy** Steve Hubbard, *Shark Among Dolphins*, p. 67.

30 **As a senior against Nebraska.** Jimmy Johnson, *Turning the Thing Around*, pp. 70–76.

31 **As an assistant coach at Picayune** Ibid., p. 78.

32 **Lacking gear for so many "players,"** Ibid., p. 99.

33 **Midway through a convention of college coaches** Ed Hinton, "Deep into His Job."

33 **Several weeks later Jankovich offered Johnson the job** Johnson, pp. 104–9.

35 **When safety Bennie Blades intercepted** Bruce Feldman, *'Cane Mutiny*, pp. 60–61.

35 **From his seat in the CBS booth, broadcaster Ara** Johnson, pp. 124–25.

35 **Switzer's Sooners were led by linebacker Brian Bosworth** Feldman, pp. 76–83.

Chapter 4: The Asthma Field

43 **Early in camp kicker Shaun Burdick** Ron Borges, "Jones and Johnson Are Riding Herd on Cowboys," *Boston Globe*, September 19, 1989.

44 **Fifth-round draft choice Keith Jennings** "Draftee Jennings Walks Out," *Dallas Cowboys Official Weekly*, August 5, 1989.

44 "**Ray," Johnson coolly informed the media** Ron Borges, "Jones and Johnson Are Riding Herd on Cowboys."

46 **Though Johnson was open to the idea of bringing Pelluer back**

David Barron, "Cowboys QB White Retires," United Press International, July 12, 1989.

47 **"This is not a formality," he told Sports Illustrated.** Austin Murphy, "A Duel in the Sun," *Sports Illustrated,* August 21, 1989.

Chapter 5: Henryetta Troy

50 **Troy Aikman officially joined the Dallas Cowboys** Gene Wojciechowski, "A Very Good Year—To Forget," *Los Angeles Times,* June 22, 1990.

51 **"It takes a while for someone to gain my trust," he said.** Pat Jordan, "Troy's Triumph; Troy Aikman, Quarterback for the Dallas Cowboys," *Playboy,* October 1993.

51 **Raised in the Southern California town of Cerritos** Troy Aikman, *Things Change,* pp. 2–4.

52 **Though he overcame the condition to become one of the town's best** Pat Jordan, "Troy's Triumph; Troy Aikman, Quarterback for the Dallas Cowboys."

52 **"We ended up seven miles out of town** John Ed Bradley, "Troy Aikman," *Sports Illustrated Presents: Troy Aikman: A Salute to an NFL Legend,* July 26, 2006.

52 **Like countless boys growing up outside of Los Angeles** Aikman, pp. 2–4.

53 **"He was a tough old country boy who loved football,"** Pat Jordan, "Troy's Triumph; Troy Aikman, Quarterback for the Dallas Cowboys."

53 **Hence, Troy Aikman began his junior high gridiron** Aikman, p. 10.

54 **Years later, Troy still recalls** Jill Lieber, "True Grit at Quarterback," *USA Today,* January 5, 1996.

54 **One could throw five hundred jobs into a hat** Jeff Weinstock, "Troy Aikman Interview," *Sport Magazine,* July 1993.

54 **"None of us matured as soon as Troy did,"** Alison Colburn, "Ex-Teammates Say Aikman Era Exciting," *Tulsa World,* January 29, 1996.

55 **"Barry wanted to run the wishbone.** Barry Tramel, "Decision to Leave OU Set Aikman's Career in Motion," *Daily Oklahoman,* August 30, 1992.

Chapter 6: Would the Mother Who Left Her 11 Kids at Texas Stadium Please Come and Get Them!

61   **"Our rivalry is certainly as big as it ever was,"** Mike Rabun, "Cowboys, Redskins Both 0–2 Entering Sunday Showdown," United Press International, September 23, 1989.

61   **To kick off the afternoon, Jones escorted actress Elizabeth Taylor** Tom Friend, "Redskins Envelop Underdeveloped Cowboys, 30–7," *Washington Post*, September 25, 1989.

61   **Receiver Art Monk, a Redskin since 1980** Mike Rabun, "Redskins 30, Cowboys 7," United Press International, September 24, 1989.

64   **While most boys were busy chasing girls** Jeff Prugh, *The Herschel Walker Story*, p. 45.

64   **"Herschel Walker!" wrote Jim Minter** Ibid.

66   **Walker studied dance in college** Howard G. Chua-Eoan, "People," *Time*, April 18, 1988.

66   **"My problem is I have never let people** Jill Lieber, *Sports Illustrated*, "Please, Let Me Run," June 29, 1992.

66   **When the back complained** Robert Kirley, "A Packed Stadium Will Greet Walker," *Times* (London), September 15, 1989.

67   **"We might have an interest," Lynn said, playing coy.** Bob Ackles with Ian Mulgrew, *The Water Boy: From the Sidelines to the Owner's Box*, p. 155.

68   **Wrote Mike Rabun of United Press International: "Let's go over this one more time** Mike Rabun, "Why Did the Cowboys Trade Herschel Walker?" United Press International, October 16, 1989.

70   **The Cowboys had paid him a $1.25 million "exit bonus"** Ron St. Angelo and Norm Hitzges, *Greatest Team Ever*, p. 26.

70   **In his debut with the Vikings, Walker** Peter King, "Sudden Impact," *Sports Illustrated*, October 18, 1989.

71   **Wrote Michael Wilbon of the *Washington Post*:** Michael Wilbon, "Walker's 148 Yards Make Vikings Look Super," *Washington Post*, October 15, 1989.

71   **A hot T-shirt in town read THE H-BOMB HAS LANDED ON MINNESOTA.** Jill Lieber, "Please, Let Me Run."

71   **"When we brought him here, there went our Super Bowl hopes," said Vikings safety Joey Browner.** ESPN; interview with Joey Browner, "The Top 5 Reasons You Can't Blame the

Minnesota Vikings for Trading Herschel Walker on October of 1989."

71 **Months after the deal was completed, Jones and Lynn met in a conference room** Jim Dent, *King of the Cowboys*, p. 120.

72 **"We are making progress," Johnson said afterward.** Tim Cowlishaw, "Alone at the Bottom," *Dallas Morning News*, October 16, 1989.

72 **By now, life at Valley Ranch was unbearable** Eugene Signorini, "Fans in Dallas Losing Interest in 0–8 Cowboys," *Oregonian*, October 31, 1989.

72 **Ed Werder of the *Fort Worth Star-Telegram* summed up the bleakness** Ed Werder, "Report Card Won't Make Cowboys Proud," *Fort Worth Star-Telegram*, November 2, 1989.

74 **The Eagles not only won, 27–0, but left the Cowboys looking foolish.** "Johnson Claims Bounty Was Set," *Washington Post*, November 14, 1989.

74 **"Sunday's futile finish for the Cowboys was an appropriate** Randy Galloway, "Not Everyone Thought Cowbows Franchise Would Revive," *Orange County Register*, January 1, 1993.

74 **Some fifteen hundred miles away Tom Landry** Dave Anderson, "America's Ex-Coach Assesses the Cowboys," *New York Times*, December 17, 1989.

Chapter 7: Welcome to the Emmitt Zone

77 **As he walked toward the podium in a Valley Ranch** Emmitt Smith, *The Emmitt Zone*, p. 106.

79 **His first two cravings, USC linebacker Junior Seau and** Ron St. Angelo and Norm Hitzges, *Greatest Team Ever*, p. 31.

80 **When Howell dismissed the offer as insulting** Ken Brazzel, "Holdout Jones Agrees to Cowboys' Terms," *Arkansas Democrat-Gazette*, August 4, 1990.

80 **In Gainesville, Smith was strolling to and from classes** John Romano, "Emmitt's in Motion: He Makes the Catch," *St. Petersburg Times*, August 28, 1990.

80 **Not only was Timmy Smith heading the depth chart** "Cowboys Trade for Alonzo Highsmith," United Press International, September 3, 1990.

82 **Afterward, a distraught Henning took exaggerated pulls** Don

Patterson, "Chargers Fake Themselves Out of It," *Los Angeles Times*, September 10, 1990.

83 **"In two years Aikman will be the best quarterback in the NFL,"** Jeff Hardie, "Foe's Are Counting on Aikman's Arrival," *Washington Times*, September 18, 1990.

86 **The following year Shula was enrolled in the University of Baltimore Law School when Wally English** Gerald Eskenazi, "Shula Son Works His Own Way," *New York Times*, January 14, 1985.

88 **Any hope of a Shula-Smith bond died in the aftermath** Smith, p. 118.

88 **Finally, after the Week 10 loss to San Francisco dropped** Ibid., p. 120.

89 **During the game, many in the press box noticed a striking sight** Mike Rabun, "Cowboys Coach and Quarterback Try Talking," United Press International, November 19, 1990.

90 **"Everybody in this league knows the road to toughness runs right** John Hawkins, "Eagles KO Aikman, Cowboys," *Washington Times*, December 24, 1990.

91 **In the locker room after the game, Johnson was in a foul mood.** Rick Gosselin, "Losing Cowboys Are Left in Limbo," *Dallas Morning News*, December 31, 1990.

Chapter 8: Making a Run at This Thing

94 **While attending Primitive Baptist Church in Fort Lauderdale** Julie Lyons, "Back in Bounds," *Dallas Observer*, September 5, 2001.

95 **Growing up in a modest three-bedroom** Sally Jenkins, "The Mouth That Roars," *Sports Illustrated*, October 25, 1991.

95 **From Monday through Saturday Walter woke up at 4:30 A.M.** Ian Thomsen, "Irvin: It's Not Child's Play," *Boston Globe*, December 30, 1987.

96 **As a young teenager Irvin spent his summer days alongside his father** Sally Jenkins, "The Mouth That Roars."

96 **"Toward the end I'd take my father to the doctor for visits," Irvin said.** Richard Rosenblatt, *Michael Irvin*, p. 19.

96 **On a fall afternoon during his senior year** Sally Jenkins, "The Mouth That Roars."

97 **To many, what stood out most was his brashness.** Rosenblatt, pp. 30–31.

97 **On the day of the 1988 draft,** Peter King, "A Mouthful," *Sports Illustrated*, November 18, 1991.

97 **In one of his first training camp scrimmages, Irvin wrestled** Bernie Miklasz, "Dallas Gets Wake-Up Call," *Sporting News*, September 26, 1988.

98 **To visiting scouts, he would halfheartedly brag** Randy Galloway, "Proving His Critics Wrong," *Boston Globe*, December 27, 1991.

98 **"Even I was scared," said Irvin.** Gary Shelton, "Irvin's Ego a Motivating Source for Cowboys," *Ottawa Citizen*, December 27, 1991.

99 **His entire system was based on speed** Harry Lister, "Turner Brings Offense of '90s to Cowboys," *Arkansas Democrat-Gazette*, April 27, 1991.

100 **Dallas, in the words of *Morning News* writer Rick Gosselin** Rick Gosselin, "Cowboys Rock Around Clock, 26–14," *Dallas Morning News*, September 2, 1991.

101 **"Mismatch alert!" warned the *Washington Times*.** Dave the Predictor, "Redskins Look Like a Lock," *Washington Times*, September 6, 1991.

102 **"I'm disappointed," said Johnson.** Mike Rabun, "Johnson Likes Cowboys, if Not Results," United Press International, September 10, 1991.

103 **In their first twenty games together, Aikman and Irvin** Richie Whitt, "Aikman and Irvin Ignite Cowboys," *Washington Times*, November 21, 1991.

103 **"We're like Paula Abdul's song 'Opposites Attract,'" said Irvin.** Peter King, "A Mouthful."

106 **Oh, how the mighty have fallen** Steve Wulf, "A Poem About the Cowboys Brings Down the House," *Sports Illustrated*, December 9, 1991.

107 **"I'll live to avenge that game," said Bears quarterback Jim Harbaugh.** Fred Mitchell, "Bears Lick Wounds—and Vow Revenge," *Chicago Tribune*, December 24, 1991.

108 **Two days earlier Smith had donned a Santa Claus** Bob Oates, "Get Call of Wild," *Los Angeles Times*, December 26, 1991.

110 **Afterward, Johnson gave what many consider to be the best post-game speech of his career.** Bob Ackles with Ian Mulgrew, *The Water Boy: From the Sidelines to the Owner's Box*, p. 166.

Chapter 9: The Last Naked Warrior

112 **Twice, his racial barbs resulted in fights with former 49er team-mate Jim Burt,** Skip Bayless, *The Boys*, p. 91.

113 **"We were," said Harris, "two roosters in a henhouse."** Brian Hewitt, "Haley's Move to Dallas Delights 49ers' Harris," *Chicago Sun-Times*, October 4, 1992.

115 **"We can't speak for the 49ers as to why he's available** "Haley Shores Up Cowboys' Defense," *Houston Chronicle*, August 27, 1992.

115 **"I guess the drive back was for about 40 minutes," Jones said.** Thomas George, "Cowboy with Angry Score to Settle," *New York Times*, January 13, 1993.

Chapter 10: Return to Greatness

125 **"There was a lot of I, I, I, me, me, me," Sandy said.** Julie Lyons, "Back in Bounds," *Dallas Observer*, September 5, 2002.

127 **That confidence soared on Thursday, September 3** "Irvin, Cowboys Agree on 3-Year Deal," *Houston Chronicle*; September 4, 1992.

127 **Having been burned repeatedly in his last matchup against Irvin** Denne H. Freeman, Associated Press, September 7, 1992.

130 **When Bob Oates of the *Los Angeles Times* wrote** Bob Oates, "Hands-on Success Story," *Los Angeles Times*, December 21, 1991.

130 **Instead, Jones had treated the most recent draft** Skip Bayless, *The Boys*, pp. 26–27.

133 **Afterward, Tony Wise, the offensive line coach, put the afternoon in perspective** Ibid., p. 115.

133 **Throughout history there have been millions of sightings** Gina Boubion, "Ghost Lets Playful Side Show in Pranks at Haunted Toy Store," *Houston Chronicle*, April 23, 1993.

133 **"He's a con artist," one NFC personnel director told *Sports Illustrated*.** Jill Lieber, "Please, Let Me Run," *Sports Illustrated*, June 29, 1992.

134 **In anticipation of the Cowboy game** Paul Zimmerman, "The Eagles Looked Super," *Sports Illustrated*, October 12, 1992.

135 **The Cowboys defense sacked McGwire four times** Ed Werder, "Cowboys Defense Picks Up Pace, Puts Down Seahawks, McGwire," *Dallas Morning News*, October 12, 1992.

135 On a wall in Wannstedt's office hung a chart featuring the record of the **1976 Pittsburgh Steelers** Paul Zimmerman, "No Names for Now," *Sports Illustrated*, November 16, 1992.

Chapter 11: Turbulence

138 **Bennie Jones was a man with violence running through his veins.** Jason Cole, "Sins of the Father," *Sun-Sentinel*, November 23, 1998.

141 **"We were like movie stars," said Erik Williams, the offensive tackle.** "One for the Boys," *Maxim*, December 2006.

142 **After drafting Jones, Bob Slowik** Denne H. Freeman, Associated Press, April 26, 1992.

143 **"I'm going after the arm," Michael Irvin responded** Richard Justice, "Cowboy Says He'll Target Redskin's Arm," *Washington Post*, December 11, 1992.

143 **After controlling the first three quarters of the game** Leonard Shapiro, "Even After Loss, Players Believe They Did Well Enough to Win," *Washington Post*, December 14, 1992.

144 **"That," said Richie Petitbon, the Washington defensive coordinator, "was the biggest play of the game."** Leonard Shapiro, "Even After Loss, Players Believe they Did Well Enough to Win."

148 **Shortly after the game, CPC/Environment** Kim Durk, "CPC/Environment to Mint Commemorative Medallion Honoring Cowboys NFC Eastern Division Championship," *Business Wire*, December 22, 1992.

148 **Growing up in the Trinidadian town of Laventille Village** Tom Leo, "Richards Discovers Running," *Syracuse Post-Standard*, December 1, 1988.

149 **"He's a great, great tailback," said Syracuse coach Dick MacPherson.** Ibid.

151 **"This is crazy," Tony Wise, the offensive line coach, said.** Skip Bayless, *The Boys*, p. 232.

151 **After addressing (and undressing) the team,** Ibid., p. 233.

Chapter 12: How 'Bout Them Cowboys!

153 **During offseasons he lived in a brick cabin on 3,500** Bill Plaschke, "Genuine Article," *Los Angeles Times*, January 30, 1993.

153   He wore a hat that read, simply, REDNECK "Novacek Proud
      to Be Redneck," *Omaha World Herald*, November 13, 1994.

156   As if this point needed to be reinforced, Philadelphia safety
      Andre Waters Ed Werder, "Waters Puts Smith No. 1 on Hit
      List," *Dallas Morning News*, January 5, 1993.

156   Instead of shuddering, the Cowboys clipped the safety's words
      and added them to a locker room bulletin board. George Wil-
      lis, "Eagles Giving Cowboys an Earful," *Newsday*, January 9,
      1993.

157   "There was a lot of talking before this game," Thomas George,
      "A Dominant Dallas Rings Philadelphia's Bell," *New York Times*,
      January 11, 1993.

158   "[The field] was abominable," wrote Brian Hewitt Brian He-
      witt, "NFL Asks an Expert: Mend Field," *Chicago Sun-Times*,
      January 12, 1993.

158   He and twenty-six coworkers replaced the grass in the middle of
      the field Ron St. Angelo and Norm Hitzges, *Greatest Team Ever*, p.
      67.

161   Wrote Paul Zimmerman in *Sports Illustrated*: "The momen-
      tum had switched, all right," Paul Zimmerman, "Hot Wheels,"
      Sports Illustrated, January 25, 1993.

162   On first down from the Cowboys' 21-yard line, Turner called
      for Ace Right 896 F Flat Ron St. Angelo and Norm Hitzges,
      Greatest Team Ever, p. 73.

Chapter 13: Super Bowl XXVII

165   Before allowing his troops to hit L.A. for a Sunday night of
      all-out debauchery Mike Fisher, *Stars & Strife*, p. 302.

165   Headquartered in the luxurious Loews Santa Monica Beach
      Hotel. Skip Bayless, *The Boys*, p. 275.

165   Such potential conquests were why, in the days after the San
      Francisco triumph Fisher, p. 303.

167   In what may well be an NFL record, Michael Irvin escorted
      Ibid., pp. 250–80.

170   A few days before the game, he drove along Mike Fisher and
      Richie Whitt, *The Boys Are Back*, p. 147.

170   "I know that your thoughts are that you'd like to do this for certain
      individuals," Jimmy Johnson, *Turning the Thing Around*, p. 253.

172 **One evening Johnson and his coaches would be gorging on nachos** Fisher, p. 313.

172 **As they prepared for Buffalo, coaches speculated** Bayless, p. 266.

177 **Had the game been tight, Lett surely would have found himself** Austin Murphy, "Together Again," *Sports Illustrated*, May 17, 1993.

Chapter 14: Nut-Huggers

181 **Tom Vanderveer, mayor of Troy, Texas** Doris Quan, "Aikman Fans Cast Vote in Troy, *Dallas Morning News*, August 4, 1993.

181 **In what surely goes down as one of the most questionable decisions** "Cowboys Become Just the Boys and Sing," *Oregonian*, July 7, 1993.

183 **In 1988, a basketball-loving rookie named Michael Irvin led a Hoopsters revolt** Richie Whitt, "Busted; Off-field Indiscretions Be Damned, Michael Irvin Deserves Football Immortality," *Dallas Observer*, January 18, 2007.

184 **On May 10, 1993, the Hoopsters were scheduled** Ed Werder, "Cowboys Hoopsters Pull Plug on Game," *Dallas Morning News*, May 12, 1993.

184 **That's why, in a May 1991 game against the staff of a Dallas radio station** Associated Press, June 25, 1991.

188 **On March 27, 1993, Ed Werder of the *Dallas Morning News*** Ed Werder, "Smith May Meet with Dolphins," *Dallas Morning News*, March 27, 1993.

189 **The difference between the offer and what Smith desired** Peter Golenbock, *Cowboys Have Always Been My Heroes*, p. 779.

189 **Did Jones really want to get in a battle over greed?** Paul Domowitch, "Owners Derail Jones' Attempt to Pull Fast One," *Daily Oklahoman*, April 10, 1993.

189 **In a game against Florida as a senior** Tim Cowlishaw, "Things Falling into Place for Lassic," *Dallas Morning News*, May 3, 1993.

190 **At Alabama, Lassic was on the fast track to a noteworthy collegiate career** Austin Murphy, "The End of the Run," *Sports Illustrated*, January 11, 1993.

191 **"I had never lost anyone close to me," said Lassic** Paul Newberry, Associated Press, January 2, 1993.

192 **Certainly not after the *Washington Times* set up a Cowboys**

"**hateline**" John Hawkins, "The Object of Our Wrath," *Washington Times*, September 6, 1993.

193   **"The problem was that I fell into the same trap** Tim Cowlishaw, "Second Time Around Special in Many Ways," *Dallas Morning News*, February 6, 1994.

194   **A bawling Haley proceeded to approach Jones** Ed Werder, "Charles Haley Tests Limits, Fills Holes," *Dallas Morning News*, October 17, 1993.

194   **"The fans showed no class," he said of the merciless booing.** Paul Zimmerman, "A Few Feet Short," *Sports Illustrated*, September 20, 1993.

195   **The day after the Bills debacle, the PLO** Golenbock, p. 780.

Chapter 15: Good Time? Let's Meet @ 12

199   **"I heard what he said," responded Ken Norton, Jr.**, Ed Werder, "Cowboys Update," *Dallas Morning News*, October 16, 1993.

203   **While most professional sports franchises recognize** Sam Blair, "Ex-Coach Landry Takes His Place in Cowboys' Ring of Honor Today," *Dallas Morning News*, November 7, 1993.

205   **"We're treating it with ice," Robert** "Aikman Is Injured as Cowboys Win," *Los Angeles Times*, November 8, 1993.

206   **"They talk around here about how they don't have the money," snapped an agitated Emmitt Smith** Will McDonough, "Bernie a Burning Issue," *Boston Globe*, November 14, 1993.

207   **"We're hoping Troy will be back with us,"** Tim Cowlishaw, "Kosar Leads Cowboys Past Cardinals, 20–15," *Dallas Morning News*, November 15, 1993.

207   **To start with, he was the star quarterback of the Cowboys** Pat Jordan, "Troy's Triumph," *Playboy*, October 1993.

207   **Not that Aikman went out of his way to endorse the image.** Jay Mariotti, "Time to Stamp Aikman as Quarterback of the '90s," *Chicago Sun-Times*, January 15, 1993.

208   **He once returned to his house to find** John Ed Bradley, "Troy Aikman," *Sports Illustrated Presents: Troy Aikman: A Salute to an NFL Legend*, July 26, 2006.

208   **In August, Morgan even wrote a guest review** Lorrie Morgan, "Everybody Wants to Be a Cowboy," *Dallas Morning News*, August 3, 1993.

210 **"Sunshine is nice," said Miami fullback Keith Byars** Thomas George, "Slipshod Play," *New York Times*, November 26, 1993.

211 **(Explained Joe Avezzano, the special teams coach:** Ron St. Angelo and Norm Hitzges, *Greatest Team Ever*, p. 77.

211 **"If you're a professional, [the rule] is something you're supposed to know,"** Jason Cole, "Cowboys Lett 'Em Have It," *Sun-Sentinel*, November 26, 1993.

Chapter 16: Courage

214 **"Arguably, Troy Aikman is considered** Jamie Aron, Associated Press, December 24, 1993.

216 **As he fell Smith protected the ball with the left side** Emmitt Smith, *The Emmitt Zone*, p. 5.

216 **Throughout the period Smith calmed himself by repeatedly** Ibid., p. 7.

217 **Following the game John Madden, the CBS announcer** Ibid., p. 9.

217 **Smith spent the next fifteen hours at Baylor University Medical Center** Ed Werder, "Cowboys Take Needed Rest," *Dallas Morning News*, January 4, 1993.

217 **Later, when pressed by Ed Werder of the *Dallas Morning News*** Ed Werder, "Johnson Intrigued by Jaguars," *Dallas Morning News*, December 31, 1993.

218 **He'd heard reports that, with the regular season winding down** Jim Dent, *King of the Cowboys*, p. 161.

218 **"I bought the team and took all the risks," Jones said.** Ibid., p. 160.

220 **Three days before the Cowboys and 49ers were to meet** "No Question About It—Dallas Will Win, Insists Johnson," United Press International, January 20, 1994.

221 **"I majored in physical education, not psychology,"** Ron Borges, "Reaction to Johnson Isn't Too Promising," *Boston Globe*, January 22, 1994.

222 **"We have not often been this humiliated," 49er coach George Seifert said** Bernie Linicome, "ABCs of Cowboys' Success: Arrogant, Boastful, Callous," *Chicago Tribune*, January 24, 1994.

Chapter 17: Super Bowl XXVIII

224 **On the following day Dallas scout Bob Ford** Bill Bates, *Shoot for the Star*, pp. 105–6.

224 **When he arrived at camp in Thousand Oaks** Ibid., p. 110.

225 **As soon as all his healthy teammates left the locker room** Ibid., p. 215.

225 **"Three weeks ago I would have given you ten-to-one odds** Ibid., p. 236.

227 **Such prognostications infuriated the Bills** Vic Carucci, "Bennett Bites Back at Bills Bashers," *Buffalo News*, January 26, 1994.

228 **"It was scary," said Leigh Steinberg, Aikman's agent** Paul Zimmerman, "Superman! Emmitt Smith Powers Dallas Past Buffalo Again," *Sports Illustrated*, February 7, 1994.

229 **One day earlier, Davis and a handful of players had been watching** Ron St. Angelo and Norm Hitzges, *Greatest Team Ever*, p. 97.

230 **The Cowboys took over and commenced upon a 64-yard touchdown drive** Zimmerman, "Superman! Emmitt Smith Powers Dallas Past Buffalo Again."

Chapter 18: Divorce

233 **The article ran on page 2B of the February 18, 1994, *Dallas Morning News*** Frank Luksa, "Johnson, Back at Work, Makes No Waves About Jones," *Dallas Morning News*, February 18, 1994.

233 **"For the first time in about six or seven years I didn't read a newspaper," he said.** Rick Gosselin, "Refreshed Johnson Surfaces at Combine," *Dallas Morning News*, February 23, 1994.

234 **"I knew as early as 1991 that I might want to make a change with Jimmy,"** Jim Dent, *King of the Cowboys*, p. 154.

235 **Johnson still regularly thought back to the 1991 postseason** Dent, p. 157.

235 **To Johnson, the deterioration of a once-cordial relationship** Peter King, "Bad Blood," *Sports Illustrated*, April 11, 1994.

236 **"You okay?" he was asked by Bob Ackles** Bob Ackles with Ian Mulgrew, *The Water Boy: From the Sidelines to the Owner's Box*, pp. 168–69.

236 **In the follow-up to two-straight Super Bowl victories** Doug Bedell, "Cowboys' Club Seating Plans Anger Some Fans," *Dallas Morning News*, October 14, 1993.

238 **The problem seems to be who gets the credit for Restoring the Dynasty.** Staff editorial, "J.R. and Bobby, Part II," *New York Times*, February 2, 1994.

239 **Basking in the glow of another Super Bowl title** Dent, p. 142.

239 **"Here's to the Dallas Cowboys," cackled Jones** Ibid., p. 142.

240 **Jones slammed down his glass and snarled.** Ibid., p. 143.

240 **Without skipping a beat, Jones grabbed Werder** Ibid., pp. 146–49.

241 **"I think it's time that I let you know I'm thinking.** Ibid., p. 147.

242 **As Johnson wandered the hallways of the hotel** Ibid., p. 150.

242 **Moments later Johnson found Gosselin** Ed Werder and Rick Gosselin, "Post-Season Scrimmage," *Dallas Morning News*, March 23, 1994.

243 **Later that day, Jones held a thirty-minute press conference** Gordon Forbes, "Latest Jones-Johnson Spat Begins Over 'Toast' to Cowboys," *USA Today*, March 24, 1994.

Chapter 19: Anal Probe

245 **Jerry Jones would *not* hand over the reins of America's Team** Robert McG. Thomas, Jr., "The New Hire: Glorious Record, Outrageous Past," *New York Times*, March 31, 1994.

247 **Troy Aikman and Emmitt Smith spoke out against Jones** Ed Werder, "Making Up Is Getting Harder to Do," *Dallas Morning News*, March 27, 1994.

247 **On the morning of Monday, March 28,** Tim Cowlishaw, "Fence-Mending at the Ranch," *Dallas Morning News*, March 28, 1994.

248 **"You will never witness anything more fraudulent** NPR Morning Edition, reported by Glen Mitchell, March 30, 1994.

249 **"Barry Switzer, head coach of the Dallas Cowboys?"** C. W. Nevius, "Snake-Oil Barry Back in Saddle," *San Francisco Chronicle*, March 31, 1994.

250 **He was raised in a "shotgun house,"** Ray Kennedy, "Boomingest Sooner of 'Em All," *Sports Illustrated*, August 9, 1976.

251 **To take baths, Barry and his younger brother Donnie** Barry Switzer with Bud Shrake, *Bootlegger's Boy*, p. 26.

251 **Wrote Switzer in his 1990 autobiography** Ibid., p. 29.

252 **During Barry's senior year, the Alcoholic Beverage Control Commission** Ibid., p. 31.

252 **"[At college] I learned to express myself well in public,"** Ibid., p. 38.

254 **In his 1988 autobiography, "The Boz,"** Thomas, "The New Hire: Glorious Record, Outrageous Past."

255 **On March 31, 1994, the Cowboys released tight end Alfredo Roberts** Tim Cowlishaw, "Switzer Gets an Education on First Day," *Dallas Morning News*, April 1, 1994.

Chapter 20: Walking into a Buzz Saw

257 **Switzer could have handled the uncomfortable incident in any number of ways.** Tim Cowlishaw, "Irvin Not Letting Switzer in Easy," *Dallas Morning News*, April 5, 1994.

260 **"Curfews," he once said, "are rat-turd things made to be broken."** Skip Bayless, *Hell-Bent*, p. 104.

Chapter 21: Anarchy on (and off) the Gridiron

268 **"[O'Donnell] was holding the ball because he didn't have anybody to throw to,"** Ed Bouchette, "Now the Steelers Know How the Buffalo Bills Felt," *Pittsburgh Post-Gazette*, September 5, 1994.

269 **"We dismissed a lot of the potential naysayers** Gerry Dulac, "Switzer's First Triumph Vindicates Jones," *Pittsburgh Post-Gazette*, September 5, 1994.

269 **In a far corner of the locker room, Irvin was quietly complaining** Bill Nichols, "Despite the Victory, Touchdowns Missed," *Dallas Morning News*, September 5, 1994.

271 **He maintained a well-known affair with Susan Skaggs** Todd Cawthorn, *Jerry Jones and the "New Regime,"* p. 93.

271 **When, in 1991, his son Stephen was engaged to be married** Ibid., pp. 78–79.

272 **At an Austin bar named the Copper Tank** Jim Dent, *King of the Cowboys*, pp. 218–23.

279 **He'd suffered a broken rib, multiple cuts** Tim Cowlishaw and Dan Barber, "Williams Could Be Out for Rest of Regular Season," *Dallas Morning News*, October 25, 1994.

280 **On November 7 the New York Giants** Mike Freeman, "Big, Bad

Cowboys Knock Giants into Next Season," *New York Times*, November 8, 1994.

282 **From Jerry Jones's standpoint, the lowest of blows** Rudy Martzke, "Cowboys Driven to Distraction," *USA Today*, November 11, 1994.

282 **In the days leading up to the matchup** Clark Judge, "Over the Hump," *San Jose Mercury News*, November 14, 1994.

284 **As was the case two years earlier, California had been hammered** Rick Telander, "Beaten Deep," *Sports Illustrated*, January 23, 1995.

284 **"The second I let it go," said Aikman, "I knew I was in trouble."** Skip Bayless, *The Boys*, p. 129.

285 **"Guys, you know what's great about** Ron St. Angelo and Norm Hitzges, *Greatest Team Ever*, p. 116.

286 **A fitting capper to a rotten afternoon** Mike Freeman, "Switzer Sees Red and the Cowboys Get the Blues," *New York Times*, January 16, 1995.

287 **"I don't even know how to tell you how disappointed I am,"** Dan LeBatard, "Dethroned Cowboys Go with a Tear," *Miami Herald*, January 16, 1995.

287 **"All people had ever really seen** St. Angelo and Hitzges, p. 117.

Chapter 22: Prime Time

292 **"I met [Russell] in a strip bar," said Williams.** "One for the Boys," *Maxim*, December 2006.

293 **In a moment dismissed as laughable by most players** Michael Silver, "Now It's My Team," *Sports Illustrated*, June 19, 1995.

294 **No, he was "Neon Deion" and "Prime Time,"** Charean Williams, "49ers, Cowboys Battle for Supremacy—and Sanders," *Orlando Sentinel*, August 25, 1995.

295 **On the night of Monday, September 4, 1995** Rick Cantu, "Cowboys Open with Giant Jolt," *Austin American-Statesman*, September 5, 1995.

296 **On Monday, September 11** Ed Werder, "Newest Cowboy Visits, but Return Date Unclear," *Dallas Morning News*, September 12, 1995.

297 **As of early September the team had only thirty-five players**

under contract Ed Werder, "Team's '96 Payroll Near Expected Cap," *Dallas Morning News*, September 13, 1995.

297 **In the *Pittsburgh Post-Gazette*, columnist Bob Smizik wrote** Bob Smizik, "The Decline of the Cowboys Started When Deion Signed," *Pittsburgh Post-Gazette*, September 12, 1995.

300 **When the Packers began to rally back from a 24–3** Charles Haley with Joe Layden, *All the Rage*, pp. 10–11.

Chapter 23: The White House

302 **Though Sanders moved to Texas in late September** Ed Werder, "Sanders Arrives Hoping Title Comes with Him," *Dallas Morning News*, September 29, 1995.

306 **As Jeff Rude of the *Dallas Morning News* described** Mal Florence, "Was That Sanders or Liberace in the Cowboy Locker Room?" *Los Angeles Times*, October 25, 1996.

307 **Sanders made his debut on October 29** Ed Werder, "Right on the Money," *Dallas Morning News*, October 30, 1995.

308 **Then, on Monday, October 30, the *Dallas Morning News* broke yet another** Ed Werder and Jean-Jacques Taylor, "Lett, Holmes May Be Suspended for Substance Abuse," *Dallas Morning News*, October 30, 1995.

313 **("I am as black as anybody you could ever see," said Irvin.** Gary Picknell, "Aikman 'Racism' Rebuffed," *Toronto Sun*, January 26, 1996.

316 **"You're just hoping Troy is gonna say, 'This isn't right,'"** Ron St. Angelo and Norm Hitzges, *Greatest Team Ever*, p. 129.

316 **In the *Kansas City Star*, Jason Whitlock fired away** Jason Whitlock, "Jones to Blame for Blunder," *Kansas City Star*, December 11, 1995.

317 **On the Wednesday following the loss, Sanders ranted against anyone** Denne Freeman, "Prime Time Tees Off on Media, Defends Switzer," Associated Press, December 14, 1995.

317 **Two hours into the trip a stewardess announced** St. Angelo and Hitzges, p. 141.

318 **Shortly before the Cowboys would open** "Fort Worth Star-Telegram Reports: Aikman Not Happy with Switzer," *Omaha World Herald*, December 22, 1995.

319 **Instead of returning to Philadelphia to prepare** Terry Larimer,

"Eagles Going to 'Boot Camp' for Cowboys," *Allentown Morning Call*, January 1, 1996.

319 **With the game tied 3–3** St. Angelo and Hitzges, p. 147.

320 **"He's got no moves," said an awestruck Emmitt Smith** Michael Wilbon, "There Goes Deion, Here Comes Dallas," *Washington Post*, January 8, 1996.

320 **"Deion's my boy," said Irvin.** Ibid.

320 **"We kicked their ass today,"** Bill Haisten, "Dallas Back in Prime-Time Form," *Tulsa World*, January 8, 1996.

321 **Not only had Cowboy Fever returned to the city** Aline McKenzie, "Sacked over a Shirt, Now a Celebrity," *Dallas Morning News*, January 16, 1996.

Chapter 24: Super Bowl XXX

324 **The price: $1,000 per night per limo** Skip Bayless, *Hell-Bent*, p. 267.

324 **(far from objecting, Jerry Jones brought along** Thomas Korosec, "Cowboys Living Up to Champagne and Limousine Image," *Fort Worth Star-Telegram*, January 26, 1996.

324 **Irvin enthusiastically endorsed the Port a Skank concept** Korosec, "Cowboys Living Up to Champagne and Limousine Image."

325 **"The police came in and gave us a list of places** Bayless, p. 268.

327 **And then there was the man deemed Cowboy Most Likely to Blow the Super Bowl** Lonnie White, "Brown Doesn't Mind Anonymity in Hometown," *Los Angeles Times*, January 28, 1993.

328 **Asked to assess Brown's collegiate legacy** Irene Garcia, "Former Players Made It a Super Sunday for Coach," *Los Angeles Times*, February 5, 1993.

330 **Throughout the week,** Michael Silver, "Special . . . Delivery," *Sports Illustrated*, February 5, 1996.

331 **"The media can't control my mouth," he said.** Ed Werder, "Switzer, Irvin Shoot from Lip," *Dallas Morning News*, January 18, 1996.

331 **The Cowboys are going to Super Bowl XXX** Dan Shaughnessy, "Cowboys Don't Act Like True Champions," *Boston Globe*, January 17, 1996.

335 **"Once we got the jitters out,"** Mike Preston, "Steelers' Defeat a Team Effort," *Baltimore Sun*, January 29, 1996.

337 **"We gave away the Super Bowl," said running back Erric Pegram.** Austin Murphy, "A Serious Case of the Yips," *Sports Illustrated*, February 5, 1996.

338 **Wrote Shaughnessy in the Boston Globe:** Dan Shaughnessy, "For Brown, Taking MVP Was Nothing," *Boston Globe*, January 29, 1996.

Chapter 25: The Fall

340 **At 11:55 P.M., four policemen arrived at the hotel.** Michael Bamberger and Don Yeager, "Dropping the Ball," *Sports Illustrated*, April 1, 1996.

341 **Sandy Irvin, the woman Michael still loved** Julie Lyons, "Back in Bounds," *Dallas Observer*, September 5, 2001.

342 **Was Michael high?** Ibid.

344 **Noted William Bennett** Peter King, "If This Is America's Team, Woe Is America," *Sports Illustrated*, April 8, 1996.

344 **There was, of course, Irvin** Michael Silver, "Out of Step," *Sports Illustrated*, October 21, 1996.

346 **Wrote Bayless: "I had heard the rumor since 1991.** Skip Bayless, *Hell-Bent*, p. 186.

349 **Dave Anderson, the normally mild-mannered *New York Times* columnist** Dave Anderson, "The Cowboys Should Ban Irvin Now," *New York Times*, January 1, 1997.

350 **When asked to explain the setback, Newton snapped at Mike Freeman** Mike Freeman, "Cowboys Exit Less Than Gracefully," *New York Times*, January 6, 1997.

351 **Hornbuckle failed to last long with the Cowboys** "Terry Hornbuckle Found Guilty," www.religionnewsblog.com, August 22, 2006.

BIBLIOGRAPHY

Ackles, Bob, and Ian Mulgrew. *The Water Boy: From the Sidelines to the Owner's Box.* Montreal: Wiley, 2007.

Aikman, Troy, and Greg Brown. *Things Change.* Dallas: Taylor Publishing, 1995.

Aikman, Troy, and Elise Krige Glading. *Aikman: Mind, Body & Soul.* Chicago: Benchmark Press, 1997.

Bates, Bill, and Bill Butterworth. *Shoot for the Star.* Brentwood, Tenn.: Word Publishing, 1994.

Bayless, Skip. *God's Coach.* New York: Simon & Schuster, 1990.

———. *The Boys.* New York: Simon & Schuster, 1993.

———. *Hell-Bent.* New York: HarperCollins, 1996.

Bosworth, Brian, and Rick Reilly. *The Boz.* New York: Doubleday, 1988.

Buchanan, William, and Stephen Stainkamp. *Glory Days.* New York: Taylor Trade, 2006.

Cawthorn, Todd. *Jerry Jones and the "New Regime."* Irving, Tex.: Sagamore Publishing, 1995.

Coffey, Frank, Ernie Wood, and Tony Seidl. *How 'Bout Them Cowboys!* Dallas: Taylor Publishing, 1993.

Dallas Cowboys Wives. *Dallas Cowboys Wives' Family Cookbook and Photo Album.* Fort Worth, Tex.: Branch-Smith, 1992.

————. *Dallas Cowboys Wives' Family Cookbook and Photo Album.* Fort Worth, Tex.: Branch-Smith, 1993.

————. *Dallas Cowboys Wives' Family Cookbook and Photo Album.* Fort Worth, Tex.: Branch-Smith, 1995.

Dent, Jim. *King of the Cowboys.* Holbrook, Mass.: Adams Publishing, 1995.

Donovan, Jim, Ken Sins, and Frank Coffey. *The Dallas Cowboys Encyclopedia.* Secaucus, N.J.: Citadel Press, 1996.

Feldman, Bruce. *'Cane Mutiny.* New York: New American Library, 2004.

Fisher, Mike. *Stars & Strife.* Fort Worth, Tex.: The Summit Group, 1993.

Fisher, Mike, and Richie Whitt. *The 'Boys Are Back.* Fort Worth, Tex.: The Summit Group, 1993.

Freeman, Denne H., and Jaime Aron. *I Remember Tom Landry.* Champaign, Ill.: Sports Publishing L.L.C., 2001.

Golenbock, Peter. *Cowboys Have Always Been My Heroes.* New York: Warner Books, 1997.

Haley, Charles, and Joe Layden. *All the Rage: The Life of an NFL Renegade.* Kansas City Mo. J: Andrews McMeel Publishing, 1997.

Harris, Cliff, and Charlie Waters. *Tales From the Dallas Cowboys.* Champaign, Ill.: Sports Publishing L.L.C., 2003.

Hennings, Chad. *It Takes Commitment.* Sisters, Ore.: Multnomah Books, 1996.

Herz, Stanley. *Conquering the Corporate Career.* New York: Kimberly Press, 1986.

Hollander, Zander. *The Complete Handbook of Pro Football.* New York: Signet, 1989.

Hubbard, Steve. *Shark Among Dolphins.* New York: Ballantine Books, 1997.

Italia, Bob. *Football Champions 1993.* Edina, Minn.: Abdo & Daughters, 1993.

Jensen, Brian. *Where Have All Our Cowboys Gone?* New York: Cooper Square Press, 2001.

Johnson, Jimmy. *Turning the Thing Around.* New York: Hyperion, 1993.

Johnston, Daryl, and Jim Gigliotti. *Watching Football*. Guilford, Conn.: The Globe Pequot Press, 2005.

Landry, Tom, and Gregg Lewis. *Tom Landry: An Autobiography*. Grand Rapids, Mich.: Zondervan Books, 1990.

Levy, Marv. *Where Else Would You Rather Be?* Champaign, Ill.: Sports Publishing L.L.C., 2004.

Maiorana, Sal. *Game of My Life: Memorable Stories of Buffalo Bills Football*. Champaign, Ill.: Sports Publishing L.L.C., 2005.

Morris, Willie. *The Courting of Marcus Dupree*. Garden City, N.Y.: Doubleday, 1983.

Prugh, Jeff. *Herschel Walker: From the Georgia Backwoods and the Heisman Trophy to the Pros*. New York: Random House, 1983.

————. *The Herschel Walker Story*. New York: Ballantine Books, 1983.

Rentzel, Lance. *When All the Laughter Died in Sorrow*. New York: Bantam, 1972.

Rosenblatt, Richard. *Michael Irvin*. Philadelphia: Chelsea House, 1997.

Rumbley, Rose-Mary. *The Unauthorized History of Dallas, Texas*. Austin, Tex.: Eakin Press, 1991.

Sanders, Deion. *Power, Money, & Sex: How Success Almost Ruined My Life*. Nashville: Word, 1999.

Scholz, Suzette, Stephanie Scholz, and Sheri Scholz. *Deep in the Heart of Texas: Reflections of Former Dallas Cowboys Cheerleaders*. New York: St. Martin's Press, 1991.

Sham, Brad. *Stadium Stories: Dallas Cowboys*. Guilford, Conn.: The Globe Pequot Press, 2003.

Shropshire, Mike. *When the Tuna Went Down to Texas*. New York: HarperCollins, 2004.

Smith, Emmitt, and Steve Delsohn. *The Emmitt Zone*. Dallas: Taylor Publishing, 1994.

St. Angelo, Ron, and Norm Hitzges. *Greatest Team Ever*. Nashville: Thomas Nelson, 2007.

Sugar, Bert. *I Hate The Dallas Cowboys*. New York: St. Martin's, 1997.

Switzer, Barry, and Bud Shrake. *Bootlegger's Boy*. New York: Jove Books, 1990.

Taylor, Jean-Jacques. *Game of My Life: Memorable Stories of Dallas Cowboys Football.* Champaign, Ill.: Sports Publishing LLC, 2006.

Walker, Herschel. *Breaking Free: My Life with Dissociative Identity Disorder.* New York: Simon & Schuster, 2008.

White, Reggie, and Jim Denney. *In the Trenches.* Nashville: Thomas Nelson, 1996.

Whittingham, Richard. *For the Glory of Their Game.* Chicago: Triumph Books, 2005.

Wolffe, Jane. *The Murchinsons: The Rise and Fall of a Texas Dynasty.* New York: St. Martin's Press, 1989.

INDEX

Nadler, Susan, 209
Nelson, Darrin, 68–70
Nevius, C. W., 249
news media. *See* press relations
Newsome, Timmy, 65
Newton, Nate
  on Cowboys, 170, 178, 195, 221,
    287, 290, 303, 312, 317
  draft of, 117
  nickname of, 123–24
  press relations and, 280, 349
  repentance of, 357–59
  sexual issues and, 166–67, 185,
    355
  weight of, 292–93
New York Giants, 82–83, 131–33,
  213–17, 280–81, 295
NFC championships, 11, 13, 148,
  157–63, 220–22, 283–87, 320–22
NFL Drafts. *See* draft choices
Nichols, Bill, 269
nicknames, 30, 122–23, 224
Nike partnership, 295
Norton, Ken, Jr.
  on Cowboys, 157, 199
  defection of, 263, 283, 293
  nickname of, 123
  performance of, 85, 161, 173, 176
Novacek, Jay
  Troy Aikman and, 153–57, 171
  on Cowboys, 199, 257
  draft of, 81, 117, 291
  performance of, 107, 175,
    219–20, 283, 291, 333

Oates, Bob, 130
Olivadotti, Tom, 33–34
O'Neill, J. P., 266–67
O'Neill, Kevin, 260, 262, 265, 298

Palmer, Paul, 72–73
Payton, Michael, 201
Pearson, Drew, 183
Peete, Rodney, 109, 278, 283, 286,
  319
Pelluer, Steve, 46
Pepsi partnership, 295
Perriman, Brett, 35
Philadelphia Eagles, 74–75, 90–91,
  133–34, 156–57, 319–20
Pittsburgh Steelers, 268–69, 325,
  330–38
player relations
  Troy Aikman's, 73, 106–7
  Jimmy Johnson's, 39–45, 73–74,
    119–21, 138–52, 200–203,
    211–12, 220–21, 233, 276
  Jerry Jones's, 60, 124, 178–79
  nicknames and, 122–24
  Tom Landry's, 27
  Deion Sanders's, 294–96, 302–8
  Emmitt Smith's, 127–28, 214–5
  Barry Switzer's, 256–58, 265–67,
    300
playoff games, 107–10, 156–57,
  219–20, 282–83, 319–20
preseason games, 45–46, 82
press relations
  Troy Aikman and, 50, 314, 346–48

press relations (*cont.*)
  Cowboys' downfall and, 344
  hiring of Jimmy Johnson and,
    28–29
  hiring of Barry Switzer and,
    240–44, 247–49
  Jimmy Johnson and, 43
  sale of Cowboys to Jerry Jones
    and, 19–26
  Emmitt Smith and, 76–77
  Barry Switzer and, 258–65
Price, Jim, 180
Prime Time (album), 303
Pro Bowls, 1, 107, 200, 293
prostitution, 309–10. *See also* sexual
  issues

quarterback controversy, 46–49,
  83–85

Rabun, Mike, 59, 68–69
racial issues
  Troy Aikman and, 312–14
  Charles Haley and, 112–13, 116,
    193, 304, 313
  Jimmy Johnson and, 29, 33, 35–38
  player cliques, 304
  Deion Sanders and, 351–52
  Barry Switzer and, 246, 251,
    312–14
Rafferty, Tom, 12, 43, 59
Reeves, Dan, 45, 220
Reilly, Rick, 37
religion. *See* Christianity

Rhome, Jerry, 48, 57
Rice, Jerry, 159–62, 199–200,
  221–22, 286, 311
Richards, Curvin, 148–52
Ring of Honor, 72, 203–4
Roberts, Alfredo, 2, 173, 189, 255,
  341
Rohrer, Jeff, 27, 44
rookies, 4, 124–25
Rookmaaker, Rhonda, 220, 239
Roper, John, 201–3
Rude, Jeff, 306
Rudisill, Fletcher, 235
Ruzek, Roger, 59
Ryan, Bob, 12

salary cap, 345
Sanders, Deion
  Christianity of, 350–52
  draft of, 288, 293–98
  performance of, 284, 286,
    319–20, 333
  player relations of, 302–8, 317
  racial issues and, 313–14, 331
  Barry Switzer and, 345
San Francisco 49ers, 13, 18, 111–
  15, 157–63, 199–200, 220–22,
  282–87, 311
Saxon, Mike, 59, 174
Schorp, Greg, 330
Schramm, Tex, 8–12, 23–26,
  203–4, 292
Schwantz, Jim, 286, 299, 303–4,
  306, 335

Williams, Erik (*cont.*)
  Everett McIver stabbing and, 1, 6
  performance of, 193
  sexual issues, 141–42, 292, 344,
    348–49
Williams, Kevin, 210, 285,
  312–14
Williams, Robert, 131
Williams, Sherman, 291, 307
Williams, Tyrone, 123
Wise, Tony, 89, 132–33, 151,
  194–95
wishbone offense, 55–57
wives
  Cowboys' lifestyle and, 141–42,
    165–67, 273
  Karen Haley, 310
  Jamise Harper, 167, 185
  Lisa Holmes, 165–66, 273, 276
  Sandy Irvin, 125–26, 167, 324,
    341–43, 356
  Linda Kay Johnson, 30, 45

Gene Jones, 18, 20, 271, 358
Criss Lacewell, 270–71
Kay Switzer, 326
Woicik, Mike, 225, 305
women. *See* sexual issues; wives
Woodson, Darren
  on Cowboys, 150, 159, 164,
    178–79, 210–11, 269–70, 282,
    284, 287, 291–92, 311–14, 330,
    344, 354
  draft of, 70, 118
  performance of, 225–26, 337
work ethic
  Alvin Harper's, 289–90
  Michael Irvin's, 2–3, 126–27
  Jimmy Johnson's, 29
  Deion Sanders's, 305–6
  Emmitt Smith's, 195–96
Wright, Alexander "Ace," 101

Zampese, Ernie, 258, 315, 319
Zimmerman, Paul, 161, 227